Who Are We?

Who Are We?

Theories of Human Nature

LOUIS P. POJMAN

New York — Oxford
OXFORD UNIVERSITY PRESS
2006

Oxford University Press, Inc., publishes works that further Oxford University's
objective of excellence in research, scholarship, and education.

Oxford   New York
Auckland   Cape Town   Dar es Salaam   Hong Kong   Karachi
Kuala Lumpur   Madrid   Melbourne   Mexico City   Nairobi
New Delhi   Shanghai   Taipei   Toronto

With offices in
Argentina   Austria   Brazil   Chile   Czech Republic   France   Greece
Guatemala   Hungary   Italy   Japan   Poland   Portugal   Singapore
South Korea   Switzerland   Thailand   Turkey   Ukraine   Vietnam

Published by Oxford University Press, Inc.
198 Madison Avenue, New York, New York 10016
http://www.oup.com

Library of Congress Cataloging-in-Publication Data

Pojman, Louis P.
    Who are we? : theories of human nature / by Louis P. Pojman.
        p. cm.
    Includes bibliographical references and index.
    ISBN-10: 0-19-517927-7 (pbk.)
    ISBN-13: 978-0-19-517927-9 (pbk.)
    1. Philosophical anthropology—History. 2. Man (Theology)—History of doctrines. I.
Title.
    BD450.P5764   2005
    128—dc22

                                                                2005005412

Printing number: 9 8 7 6 5 4 3 2 1

Printed in the United States of America
on acid-free paper

Dedicated to my wife
Trudy

Contents

Preface

Know then thyself, presume not God to scan;
The proper study of mankind is Man.
Placed on this isthmus of a middle state,
A being darkly wise, and rudely great:
With too much knowledge for the skeptic side
With too much weakness for the Stoic's pride,
He hangs between; in doubt to act, or rest.
In doubt to deem himself a god, or beast;
In doubt his mind or body to prefer,
Born but to die, and reasoning but to err;
Alike in ignorance, his reason such,
Whether he thinks too little, or too much:
Chaos of thought and passion, all confused;
Still by himself abused, or disabused;
Created half to rise, and half to fall;
Great lord of all things, yet a prey to all;
Sole judge of truth, in endless error hurled:
The glory, jest, and riddle of the world!

(Alexander Pope, "An Essay on Man")

What more important subject is there but the study of human nature? "The proper study of humankind is humanity," to rephrase Pope's classic poem in gender-neutral language. We want to know *what* we are, *where* we came from, and *where* we are going: our origins, nature, and destiny. An understanding of our nature and destiny should help us live our lives to the fullest or at least give us guidance. Religious thinkers and philosophers have pondered these questions for centuries.

The 17th-century French philosopher Blaise Pascal wrote the following:

What is man in nature? A Nothing in comparison with the Infinite, an All in comparison with the Nothing, a mean between nothing and everything. Since he is infinitely removed from comprehending the extremes, the end of things and their

xiii

beginning are hopelessly hidden from him in an impenetrable secret; he is equally incapable of seeing the Nothing from which he was made, and the Infinite in which he is swallowed up.

—What will he do then, but perceive the appearance of the middle of things, in an eternal despair of knowing either their beginning or their end. All things proceed from the Nothing, and are borne towards the Infinite. Who will follow these marvelous processes? (Pascal, *Pensees*, section 72)

Since the dawn of human history, humans have exhibited contrary qualities: good and evil, love and hate, strength and weakness, kindness and cruelty, aggressivity and passivity, generosity and greed, courage and cowardice. We seem part angel, part demon, part rational, and part animal, capable of great glory and great tragedy, yet "incapable of seeing the Nothing from which [we were] made, and the Infinite in which [we are] swallowed up." Having a sense of eternity in our hearts, but confined by temporal and spatial constraints, we seek to understand ourselves both individually and as a species. What is our nature? What is this enigma called "human"? Who are we?

In this book we seek answers to these questions. We examine some of the main theories in Western philosophy and religion and, to a lesser degree, in Eastern thought. The goal is to use the theories of great religions and philosophers to shed light on question of our nature and identity. Ultimately, all of us must decide for ourselves who and what we are and, based on that answer, how we shall live.

I have set forth more than a dozen classical theories of human nature that grew out of my own research and experience while teaching a course on theories of human nature for several years. I have tried to apply the principle of charity, which enjoins that we give a theory the best interpretation possible.

This book begins with the biblical views of human nature and moves on to the Greek theories of the Sophists, Socrates, Plato, and Aristotle. The Jewish/Christian biblical and Greek theories are the two most important historical sources for our self-understanding in the Western tradition and are vital to an understanding of who we are. The biblical view is deeply religious, defining humanity as a creation of God with magnificent inherent value—made in the image of God, "a little less than god"; our inherent dignity is rooted in having a divine element within us. The Greeks were relatively secular, basing their understanding of human nature on rational self-interest without appeal to religion. The Sophists were ethical relativists; Socrates had a mystical faith in an inner moral voice and the overarching reality of goodness; Plato believed in a transcendental world of Forms under the rule of the form of the Good; Aristotle, more empirical and experimental, held that reason was the defining feature of human nature and sufficient to lead us to happiness. For Aristotle, religion was an unnecessary hypothesis, though his ruminations on the Unmoved Mover provided the basis for the cosmological argument for the existence of God. A synthesis of the biblical and Greek views is provided by Augustine (see chapter 5), culminating in the idea of the **Great Chain of Being,** stretching from God (the fullness of being) to creatures with minimal being, with evil defined as the absence of being, as a nothing.

Chapter 6, on Hindu/Buddhist views of human nature, provides a snapshot into a profoundly different approach to our subject. Suffering, rather than sin, is the great nemesis from which humans need to be saved and meditation, the primary means of that salvation.

Chapter 7 contrasts classically opposing views on human nature: the liberal and conservative approaches, epitomized in Hobbes and Rousseau but extending far beyond them. By "liberal" and "conservative" I mean, not so much political views, though that is part of the approach, but views of who we are. Cautious conservatives honor our tradition and historical loyalties, while liberals are more optimistic, urging us to change and to transform our institutions and, perhaps, our very nature. Chapter 8 examines Kant's Copernican theory of human nature as an expression of rational liberalism, while chapter 9 examines Schopenhauer's profoundly pessimistic theory.

Chapters 10 and 11 analyze two theories that have influenced modern intellectual thought: Marx's **dialectical materialism** and Freud's pansexuality. In chapter 12 we study the existential theories of Kierkegaard, Nietzsche, Sartre, and Camus. In chapter 13 we investigate Darwin's theory of evolution, perhaps the greatest challenge to our self-understanding in the last millennium.

In order to comprehend human nature, one needs to examine the mind/body problem. In chapter 14 we study the three most prominent contemporary positions on the relationship of the mind to the brain: **dualistic interactionism,** materialist **monism,** and **functionalism.** This leads directly to the question of free will. Are we really free agents, or are we entirely determined by antecedent causes? Can the ideas of free will and **determinism** be reconciled? We take up this issue in chapter 15.

We end with a comprehensive overview of our study, bringing the entire project in understanding human nature to a finale. A summary and study questions at the end of each chapter are meant to help the student focus his or her thoughts, while a selective bibliography for each chapter serves as a guide to further study. A glossary of key concepts and specialized words is included at the end of the book.

I am grateful to Stephen Kershnar, Max Hocutt, John Jagger, Michael Levin, and Sterling Harwood for their helpful comments on earlier drafts of this work. Several reviewers offered excellent corrections and suggestions on the original manuscript, which enabled me to improve this book: Rhiannon Allen of Long Island University, George Graham of Wake Forest University, Tyler Hower of the University of San Diego, Jeff Jordan of the University of Delaware, Don Mitchell of Purdue University, and three anonymous reviewers.

I am especially grateful to my editors, Emily Voigt and Robert Miller of Oxford University Press, for suggesting this project and providing strong support all along the way. They provided me with the best support for which an author can hope. Celeste Alexander did an excellent job bringing this work into production. Sterling Harwood prepared the index.

My wife, Trudy, read over the several versions of the entire manuscript and made several improvements. To her, my beloved companion of over 40 years, this book is dedicated. I can identify with Brutus when he said, regarding his Portia, "O ye gods, Render me worthy of this noble wife!" (Shakespeare's *Julius Caesar*). Without her love and support I would not have been able to accomplish whatever good that I have done. She is living proof that human nature can be good and that it can be greatly enhanced by a happy marriage.

Louis P. Pojman
Clare Hall
Cambridge University
January 20, 2005

Who Are We?

Introduction

Know thyself. *(Oracle of Delphi)*

What a piece of work is a man! how noble in reason!
how infinite in faculty! in form and moving how
express and admirable! in action how like an angel!
in apprehension how like a god! the beauty of the
world! the paragon of animals! And yet, to me,
what is this quintessence of dust? Man delights not
me: no, nor woman neither, though by your smiling
you seem to say so *(Shakespeare,* Hamlet *Act II, Scene II)*

Man is but a reed, the weakest in nature, but he is a thinking
reed. *(Pascal,* Pensees, *chapter II.10)*

Who am I? What are we? Why do we want to know who and what we are? What
is the explanation of human existence? Where did we come from? Where are we
going? In between our origins and destiny, why do we want to know how we
should live? What are our resources for life? Do we have free will or are we wholly
determined by antecedent causes? What are our obligations? How can we find
happiness here and now as well as in the future?

These are the central questions we shall be addressing in this book as we examine over a dozen theories of human nature. The theories offer radically different
answers to these questions, ranging from the Platonic and religious (both Western
and Eastern religious traditions), which see human beings as something spiritual
or semidivine, to the materialist, such as those of Hobbes, Marx, Darwin, and
modern neurophysiologists, with several theories somewhere in between, including those of Aristotle, Rousseau, Kant, Schopenhauer, and the existentialists.
Sartre and the deconstructionists hold that there is no overall human nature but
that it is an individual or social construct.

There is no useful template to impose on the plurality of theories to yield exact
answers to our central questions, for each theory has an integrity of its own, with

its own paradigm and internal cohesion. Human nature is a vast, variegated, vital subject wherein many themes and subthemes appear in different contexts. So it is unwise to lay the theories out on a procrustean bed of categories. We want to let each theory manifest itself in its own terms and with its own criteria. However, certain assumptions underlie our study, which are held by virtually all the theories examined.[1] These assumptions are simply that there is an objective truth which the theories claim to have reached or at which they are aiming and that this truth has profound implications for our lives so that it is important that we embark on a quest for the truth by examining the theory. Since many of the theories contradict each other, they cannot all be true; but many could contain parts of the truth, and some may be closer to the truth than others.

Let us briefly list the central perennial questions relevant to our study.

1. What is the truth about human nature? Of what are we made? Is our nature monistic (totally mental or totally material) or dualistic (both mental and material)? Are we spiritual beings, made in the image of God, as the Bible states,[2] or divine sparks as the Eastern religions and Plato believe? Are we wholly material beings as Hobbes, Marx, and contemporary neuroscientists hold? Are we dualistic beings, made up of two substances, mind and matter, as Augustine, Descartes, Kant, and Kierkegaard believe? What our essential nature is has implications for the following questions that we will examine. Plato, Aristotle, and Kant hold that reason is our essence and Schopenhauer, Kierkegaard, and Nietzsche, that it is our will. Freud holds that it is our sexuality, especially our unconscious libido; and Darwinians hold that it is our animal nature.

2. Do we have free will, or are we wholly determined by antecedent causes? Can we transcend the chain of event causation and act as free agents? If we are simply determined by our heredity, neurological brain states, and the way we interact with our environment, then how can we be held responsible for our actions? Our theories differ radically on this question: existentialists like Sartre and Kierkegaard holding to radical free will on one end of the spectrum and philosophers like Hobbes, Schopenhauer, and Paul and Patricia Churchland holding to strong determinism on the other end, with others in between.

3. What is our destiny? Where are we heading? Is there life after death, or do we just rot and disintegrate? Is our destiny to love God and enjoy him forever as the Judeo–Christian tradition holds, or must we simply make the best of this life as Schopenhauer, Nietzsche, Sartre, Freud, and the modern materialists believe?[3] Others like Kant argue that while we cannot know there is an afterlife, we can hope for it. Hinduism holds to reincarnation and the absorption into Brahma in nirvana.

4. What can we know? Can we have metaphysical knowledge, as Plato and Aristotle believed, or is the best we can have faith in eternal verities, as Kant and Kierkegaard claim? Is our knowledge of the world only appearances as Plato and the Eastern religions hold; if so, then how can we be liberated from appearances to behold reality? If we do have grounds for believing that humans can know the truth, how do we establish this? What are the criteria for separating the wheat from the chaff and discriminating between truth and falsity? These are vital epistemological questions which are relevant to our study.

For example, Freud, Adler, and Jung said that we need to undergo psycho-analysis to discover our true self; but how do we know this is true? If it is, how do we know which version of psychoanalysis (Freud's, Adler's, Jung's, or one of the many others) is the correct one?

5. How shall we live? What is the best or right way to carry on our daily activities? How can we find happiness and fulfilment? What are our obligations to others, and how far do our ethical obligations extend: only to our family and friends, to our class, to all humanity, or to all sentient animals? What kind of life is worth living? Socrates said the unexamined life is not worth living, but what is so great about an examined life? Freud said that we must undergo psychoanalysis to find fulfilment, and religions say we must have faith in God in order to be saved and find happiness. Dostoevsky thought that without God no morality existed: "If there is no God, all things are permissible," claims Ivan in *The Brothers Karamazov*.[4] Can we find happiness and live a moral life simply by reason alone, as Kant and Mill held, or do we need something more?

An auxiliary question is how we should organize society so that our nature can flourish. What kind of economic–political policy would we instantiate in order to provide the best context for human flourishing? Plato and Aristotle advocated an aristocracy, with philosophers as kings. Marx described a communist state as the only answer to human misery. Hobbes developed a strong form of contractual authoritarianism and Rousseau, a form of participatory democracy.

6. How are the two sexes related? Are men and women essentially the same, except for reproductive organs, or do their natures differ fundamentally? Plato was the first gender egalitarian, offering equal opportunity to women. This is today's liberal position, developed by Mary Wollstonecraft and John Stuart Mill in the late 18th and 19th centuries.[5] Women should have equal opportunity but not be guaranteed equal results. On the other hand, conservatives, led by Aristotle and contemporary sociobiologists, hold that there are fundamental differences between males and females. Men are by nature (on average) more aggressive and women, more nurturing and suited to childrearing. A third group, Marxist feminists, hold that only when bourgeois society is replaced by a communist classless society can women and men be truly free. A fourth group, androgynous feminists, agree with Plato that the two sexes are basically equal in ability and should be expected to compete equally in every dimension of life. Some feminists hold that gender differences (as opposed to physiological differences) are cultural constructs. A fifth group, radical feminists, believe that all Western societies are oppressive to women and need to be radically changed.[6] A sixth group, "difference feminists," like Carol Gilligan and Nel Nodding, agree with conservatives that women develop differently from men.[7] Our differences should be recognized and respected.

7. What is the relation of the individual to the group? Are we fundamentally social beings, so that it is the group that is primary and the individual secondary, or is the individual primary? As we will see, the classical theories differ on this issue, dividing between *holism* and *individualism*. *Holism* holds that we are inextricably parts of groups which form our being and thus are primary. In the Old Tes-

tament it is Israel that is primary over the individual, and in the New Testament the Church is the center of authority. In ancient Greece it was the city-state, Athens or Sparta, that mattered most and was thus worth dying for. For Marx it is the proletarian class that is the center of history's dialectical unfolding. On the other side, *individualism* holds that the individual matters most. Kant set forth the ideal of autonomy, that every human being was an end in him- or herself, possessing inherent dignity which ought not to be sacrificed even for the good of the group. Existentialists go further and insist that the individual is supreme and freedom, the only relevant value in a value-free world. Where does the truth lie?

8. What are our obligations to future people, to posterity? This question may be related to the last one. Do we have obligations that encompass all humans, including those not yet born, or are our duties confined to the present generation and our friends and acquaintances?

These are the kinds of questions we shall be addressing in our study of theories of human nature. If, as Socrates said and I believe, "The unexamined life is not worth living," it is imperative that we come to a greater understanding of the available options of self-understanding. Let us start our journey by examining the biblical views of human nature.

Notes

1. The sophists studied in chapter 2 and some postmodernists examined in chapter 12 may be exceptions.
2. "What is man that thou art mindful of him, and the son of man that thou dost care for him? Yet thou hast made him little less than God, and dost crown him with glory and honor" (Psalm 8).
3. Although Hobbes was a materialist, he believed in a physical God, as Mormons do. He seems to believe in a physical resurrection, which is found in St. Paul's description of life after death in 1 Corinthians 15.
4. Dostoevsky was pessimistic about the future of society without religious faith. He wrote "The first half of the history of man is the ascent from the gorilla to the man-god; the second half of the history of man is the descent from the man-god to the gorilla" (*The Possessed*).
5. See Mary Wollstonecraft's *Vindication of the Rights of Women* (1792) and John Stuart Mill's *On the Subjection of Women* (1869).
6. See Denise Thompson, *Radical Feminism Today* (Sage Publications, 2001).
7. See Carol Gilligan, *In a Different Voice* (Harvard University Press, 1982).

CHAPTER 1

The Biblical Views of Human Nature: Judaism and Christianity

What is man that thou art mindful of him, and the son of man
that thou dost care for him?
Yet thou hast made him little less than God, and dost crown him
with glory and honor. *(Psalm 8)*

The primary source of the Jewish–Christian view of human nature is the Bible: for
the Jews, the Hebrew Bible, consisting of 39 books written over a 1,000-year period
between 1200 and 200 B.C.E. and, for the Christians, that same set of books, called
the "Old Testament," along with 27 additional books making up the "New Testament," written probably between 60 and 85 C.E. (though possibly, as in the case of
the Gospel of John and Revelations, as late as 150 C.E.). The Hebrew Bible is recognized by both religions as the revelation of God to humankind, the word of God
(Hebrew *Dabar Elohim*), setting forth his will for humankind, as well as the record
of the relationship between God and his people, Israel. Its history is "his story,"
the unfolding of his plan for humanity, especially his chosen people, Israel, and
the record of Israel's failure, downfall, and restoration under Ezra and Nehemiah.
Finally, for Christians, the New Testament is authoritative as it records the coming
of the Messiah, Jesus of Nazareth; his life, death, and resurrection; and the establishment of his church as the new Israel.

In what follows I will divide my discussion of the biblical view of human nature
into two sections, the Hebrew Bible and the New Testament, focusing primarily
on the moral dimension of these works. However, first, let me say a few general
things about the biblical view of human nature, ideas accepted by both mainline
Jews and Christians. Humans are made from the dust of the earth but have the
breath of life (*ruach*) infused by God. They are created with high dignity, responsibility, and authority over the rest of creation. The idea of a separate soul does not
appear in the Bible, though one might read the idea into some passages. The
body/soul dualism appears to be a Greek idea, prominent in Pythagoras, Plato,

and Orphism (see chapter 3). Nor does the idea of immortality or life after death feature prominently in the Hebrew Bible, though life after death does play a prominent role in the New Testament, where believers in Christ are promised eternal life (Jn. 3:16). However, it is not the eternal life of a soul but of a glorified, resurrected body (1 Cor. 15:35 f). With these preliminary remarks as a background, let us turn to the concept of human nature in the Hebrew Bible.

The Hebrew Bible (Old Testament)

The Concept of Human Nature

The first book of the Bible, Genesis, begins with the words "In the beginning God (Elohim) created the heavens and the earth." In 6 days he completed his work and pronounced it "good."

The Bible depicts God as the maker of heaven and earth, a very powerful, just, benevolent being who sees into the hearts of humankind. He is holy (*qadosh*), inscrutable, mysterious, tremendously awe-inspiring, but good.[1] He creates human beings in his own image.

> So God created man in his image, in the image of God he created him, male and female he created them. And God blessed them and God said to them, "Be fruitful and multiply, and fill the earth and subdue it; and have dominion over the fish of the sea and over the birds of the air and over every living thing that moves upon the earth." (Gn. 1:27–29)

Humanity is the pinnacle of creation. Being made in God's image, humanity has intrinsic worth. Human beings alone, among all of God's creation, have the breath of God blown into their nostrils (Gn. 2:7). The contrast with other Near Eastern creation stories is striking. For example, in the Babylonian epic *Enuma Elish*, humanity is fashioned as an afterthought in order to look after the nourishment and physical needs of the gods. In Greek mythology, humanity is fashioned by lesser gods as a whim and is of little or no value. By contrast, in Genesis, humans are themselves creators, told to "be fruitful and multiply" and sovereign, to "have dominion" over the rest of creation. In Psalm 8, humanity is described as "a little less than divine and crowned with glory and honor."

Although human beings have been created in the image of God, God's relationship to humanity is complex and ambivalent. On the one hand, having been created in the image and likeness of God (Gn. 1:27, 9:6), humans possess inviolable worth and dignity. They are free, rational beings, able to decide whether to follow or reject the word of God. On the other hand, God seems almost to be jealous of the fact that humans, whom he created in his image, should become more like him in knowing good and evil. God places his created people, Adam and Eve, in the paradisiacal Garden of Eden, giving them dominion of the area but admonishing them to refrain from eating of the tree of the knowledge of good and evil. The tree is attractive, and the wily serpent tempts the couple so that they succumb, eating the forbidden fruit and discovering their nakedness. God finds them wandering about with fig leaves covering their genitals, curses them for their disobedience, and expels them from paradise (Gn. 3). The message of the third chapter, the grand document of alienation, is that the knowledge of good and evil is powerful stuff and that once people know the possibility of evil they will be tempted to use it to the destruction of others and, inevitably, themselves.

The curse of Adam and Eve extends to their descendants, all humanity now being born in sin, alienated from their maker. The litany of cruelty and corruption manifests itself through this drama. Man and woman are alienated from paradise, doomed to death after a short but unenviable existence. Jealous Cain kills his brother Abel. The sons of God go hustling after human women. The world is soon so corrupt that God decides to destroy it and begin again with righteous Noah. Unfortunately, Noah's family comes along with him; they are not as righteous as he, so the drama plays itself out again. Ham inadvertently sees his father Noah's nakedness, and surreally, his children are cursed into slavery for it. Just when humankind begins to organize in a united group, building the symbol of unity, a great tower, God intervenes to spread confusion in their midst. "Behold, they are one people, and they have all one language; and this is only the beginning of what they will do; and nothing that they purpose to do will be impossible for them. Come, let us go down and confuse their language, that they may not understand one another's speech" (Gn. 11:6).

The history of humanity as sinful begins, as a litany of deceit, self-aggrandizement, greed, violence, fratricide, and lust unfolds before us in the rest of the Bible. Yet, throughout this saga of sin and alienation, God's goodness and mercy are always in the shadow, pursuing humanity, calling them to repentance. He calls the patriarch Abraham to leave his family in Ur of the Chaldees and follow him, thus inaugurating the story of Israel and the Jewish people as the chosen people of God.

The second book of the Bible, Exodus, continues the saga of the fall and grace, depicting God's (now named *Yahweh*) struggle to develop a close relationship with a tribe only recently pulled out of slavery in Egypt. The drama of Moses' birth, upbringing, and leadership in bringing Israel from bondage to freedom in the wilderness is one of the most fascinating and moving stories in Western literature. Plucked from the bull rushes, brought up and educated in Pharaoh's household, identifying with his oppressed people, negotiating with Pharaoh for the release of Israel, then leading his people across the Red Sea on dry land and into the wilderness around Mt. Sinai, where he takes up the duties of a successful governor and judge: Moses must rank as one of the few truly great heroes of history.

Rules for Successful Living

It is while journeying in the wilderness that God gives Moses the Ten Commandments, divided into two parts. The first four are religious commands regarding one's relationship to Yahweh, while the final six concern relationships to others. The second group is similar to primitive lists of rules found throughout history in primitive groups and acknowledged in virtually every civilized society. It is hard to imagine social existence without a rule against manslaughter and stealing or in favor of reciprocal care between parents and children. The one interesting rule is that prohibiting coveting, for that seems to involve more than just actions, but intentions. It calls on us to control our jealousy of others and be satisfied with our own lot.

The commands are as follows:

1. Do not worship other gods
2. Do not make graven images of God
3. Do not take the name of God in vain
4. Observe the Sabbath rest
5. Honor your father and mother
6. Do not kill
7. Do not commit adultery
8. Do not steal
9. Do not bear false witness against your neighbor
10. Do not covet your neighbor's property

These principles cover a comprehensive set of religious and moral duties. Let us focus briefly on each of them. The first commandment finds its significance in the fact that Israel was constantly tempted to worship other gods or mix the worship of Yahweh with that of other religions. In the early parts of the Old Testament, Yahweh is recognized, not as the only god, but as the God of Israel, the leading god. This is sometimes called **henotheism.** There are many gods, but one is better than the rest, the one to whom we are committed. The second commandment signifies the holiness of God. He cannot be seen or represented by human images. Furthermore, images are otiose since he is dwelling in the midst of his people, in the Holy of Holies, in the ark of the tabernacle.

The third commandment signifies the holiness of the very name of Yahweh. That name was not mentioned by the people or priests. Only the high priest was permitted to pronounce it and only on one day each year, the Day of Atonement. For others to pronounce it was to court death.

The fourth commandment is an innovation in Israel: humans need rest even as God does, and not humans only but all of creation. Neither slaves nor animals are to work on the Sabbath. The fourth commandment is even mentioned in Is. 58:13f as perduring even in the kingdom of God.

The fifth commandment is understood to cover all positions of authority—to defy legitimate authority is to court disaster. Respect for parents is a sacred duty. "Whoever strikes his father or mother shall be put to death" (Ex. 21:15). The sixth, which was part of the Noahic code, is found in every known code of ethics. The first rule of civilization is the rule against homicide.

The seventh commandment applies to the family in general. As W. S. Bruce says,

Upon the well-being [of the family] depended the moral welfare of the nation. Were the homes pure, then the nation was strong. Were they honeycombed with vice, then the strength of the nation was gone, and Israel would flee before its enemies. Hence adultery is regarded as a crime of such heinousness that both offenders were put to death. No punishment was too severe to guard the sanctity of the home and the continuity of the family line.[2]

The death penalty was the punishment meted out for disregarding the first seven commandments.

The eighth commandment refers to property, which is the reward of moral labor and a legitimate end of moral effort. Property only becomes sinful when it is exalted to the position of supreme good. Property is, in the biblical light, the externalizing and enlargement of a human's own personality. Accordingly, one has an ethical right to its enjoyment but not to its exclusive enjoyment since the law of love enters in to modify it. The law of love, first put forth by Moses in Leviticus 19:18 and repeated by Jesus in the Gospels, states "You shall love your neighbor as yourself." Hence, I ought to share my surplus property with my neighbor in need.

The ninth commandment refers to lying under oath or perjury, but it was later interpreted to cover truthfulness in general. As the psalmist puts it, "Who shall dwell in Thy holy hill? He that walks uprightly and does what is right, and speaks truth in his heart, who does not slander with his tongue" (Ps. 15:1f).

The tenth commandment is significant in that it refers beyond actual acts to intentions and anticipates Jesus' own interpretation of all of the commandments as intentional. In Exodus 20, women are included as part of a man's property, whereas in the later version of Deuteronomy 5, women are treated as valuable in their own right.

To my mind the most interesting thing about these commands and those that follow is the context in which they are given and which is often omitted in discussions of the commandments. They are part of a loving relationship, a covenant between God and his beloved people, whom he would make into a "holy nation" and a "kingdom of priests" (Ex. 19:4). Although the rhetoric is harsher than in the fifth book of the Bible, Deuteronomy, it is clear that the fundamental basis for obedience of the law is gratitude. Obedience is a child's response of gratitude to a parent who has just redeemed him or her from the degradations of slavery ("I am the Lord your God who brought you out of the land of Egypt, out of the house of bondage" [Ex. 20:2]) and now wants to teach the meaning of freedom.

The covenant idea has a communitarian emphasis. Members of the tribe of Israel must see themselves as part of a holy nation, the chosen of God, so that individual identity and flourishing are intimately related to the fate of Israel. Israel's fate is likewise linked to the behavior of its members. When Achan disobeys the command of Joshua and takes the spoils of war, a beautiful mantle and 200 shekels of silver, he and his family are stoned to death (Jos. 7:16–26). God will punish those who do evil, but he will also punish their children for the sins of their parents. "I am a jealous God, visiting the iniquity of the fathers upon the children to the third and fourth generations of those who hate me, but showing steadfast love to thousands who love me and keep my commandments" (Ex. 20:5–6).

In the appendix to these main commandments are found rules dealing with slavery, incidental manslaughter, miscarriage, striking a parent, kidnapping (for which death is the penalty), punishment in general ("An eye for an eye, a tooth for a tooth and a life for a life" [Ex. 21:23]), the seduction of virgins, bestiality, and finally the treatment of strangers, orphans, and widows (all of whom are to be treated with compassion [Ex. 22:21f]). Interestingly enough, for the contemporary discussion of abortion, the fetus is not treated as a full person but as a valuable bit of property. When a miscarriage is caused by violence but the woman is unharmed, "the one who harmed her shall be fined, according as the woman's husband shall lay upon him" (Ex. 21:22). However, if the woman is harmed, then the *lex talionis* comes into effect: the offender shall be punished in proportion to the harm caused. Bestiality is punishable by death (Ex. 22:19).

The third book of the Bible, Leviticus, begins with an elaboration of ceremonial sacrifices for different sorts of sin offerings. In all but one case, the priest sacrifices an animal. The exception is the sacrifice for Israel's collective sins. In that case, the priest symbolically lays all of the sins onto a goat and drives it out into the wilderness (Lv. 16:20f). Even sins committed unwittingly need atonement. A ram without blemish is killed to rid the ignorant of guilt (Lv. 5:17).

It is important to get the details precisely right, for a mishap could be dangerous—as Aaron's sons, Nadab and Abihu, discovered, to their demise. "Now Nadab and Abihu, the sons of Moses' brother, Aaron, each took his censer and put fire in it, and laid incense on it, and offered unholy fire before the Lord, such as he had not commanded them. And fire came forth from the presence of the Lord and devoured them" (Lv. 10:1). Apparently, Yahweh was not complemented by creative innovations, such as adding incense to the fire.

Most of the book deals with dietary laws, the "kosher laws" (there are over 600 in the Old Testament). The Scriptures prohibit consumption of blood (Lv. 7:26–27, 17:10–14). Of the "beasts of the earth" (which basically refers to land mammals with the exception of swarming rodents), one may eat any animal that has cloven hooves and chews its cud (Lv. 11:3, Dt. 14:6). On three separate occasions, the Jews are told not to "boil a kid in its mother's milk" (Ex. 23:19, 34:26, Dt. 14:21). This passage prohibits eating meat and dairy together. The rabbis extended this prohibition to include not eating milk and poultry together. One is not to eat the blood of any animal, nor the fat of the ox, sheep, or goat, on pain of being "cut off from his people" (Lv. 7:27). The necessary and jointly sufficient conditions for being permitted food among land animals are having parted hooves, cloven feet, and chewing the cud (Lv. 11:1f). By this criterion, camels, badgers, hares, and pigs are excluded from the diet. Fish may be eaten if they have fins and scales, and birds are fair game except for several species, including the eagle, falcon, raven, ostrich, seagull, hawk, owl, pelican, stork, and vulture (Lv. 11:14–19). All winged insects which go on all fours are an abomination unless they have legs above their feet and leap (e.g., grasshoppers, v. 20). These dietary laws were important to the separate identity of the Jews but made it difficult for others to join in fellowship with them or for them to join with non-Jews.

Women are unclean for 7 days after the onset of the menstrual period, for 7 days after giving birth to a boy, and for 14 days after giving birth to a girl. The boy must be circumcised on the eighth day of his life (ch. 12). The emission of semen is unclean, and the man must wash. The emission of fluids in sexual intercourse also makes the couple unclean, and they must wash after sex (Lv. 15:16, 19f). Homo-sexual relations warrant the death penalty (18:22). Capital punishment is also warranted for blasphemy (24:14), bestiality, cursing of one's parent, and adultery (20:9–15). Even one who sees a sibling of the opposite sex naked must be "cut off" (20:17).

The concept of a Just War was unknown in the early world. In the Torah, or first five books, all wars are total wars. The sixth commandment does not apply to neighboring peoples. Yahweh is a God of war as he commands the Israelites to blot out the memory of their neighbors. No negotiations are held, no compro-mise—only utter destruction (Ex. 23:23–33, Dt. 7:1–7). Judged by Just War theory, of course, Moses' actions seem inexcusable, more like the concept of *jihad* exem-plified by modern-day suicide bombers. He seems to engage in preemptive strikes without any attempt to live in peace, carries out his slaughters without regard to distinguishing between combatants and noncombatants, and does not believe in taking prisoners. Even children are to be destroyed. "Happy shall he be who takes your little ones and dashes them against the rocks" (Ps. 137:9). There is no notion of human rights at this stage of Israel's development, in spite of a general adher-ence to the notion that God created all people in his image. No doubt, our notion of a Just War would be inapplicable in their situation, which seems to resemble a Hobbesian state of nature; but one cannot help but feel that Israel used Yahweh's name to excuse senseless slaughter.

In Joshua 6–8, which records Joshua's destruction of the Canaanite city of Jeri-cho, the rhetoric is explicitly that of a jihad, a complete slaughter of men, women, and children without regard for a combat/civilian distinction:

> And at the seventh time, when the priests had blown the trumpets, Joshua said to the people, "Shout; for the LORD has given you the city. And the city and all that is within it shall be devoted to the LORD for destruction; only Rahab the harlot and all who are with her in her house shall live, because she hid the messengers that we sent. But you, keep yourselves from the things devoted to destruction, lest when you have devoted them you take any of the devoted things and make the camp of Israel a thing for destruction, and bring trouble upon it. But all silver and gold, and vessels of bronze and iron, are sacred to the LORD; they shall go into the treasury of the LORD." So the people shouted, and the trumpets were blown. As soon as the people heard the sound of the trumpet, the people raised a great shout, and the wall fell down flat, so that the people went up into the city, every man straight before him, and they took the city. Then they utterly destroyed all in the city, both men and women, young and old, oxen, sheep, and asses, with the edge of the sword. (Josl. 6:15–21)

The Prophets' Message

When we come to the Old Testament prophets, a more individualistic sense of moral responsibility begins to replace the tribal sense of morality of the early books of the Bible. In the ninth century B.C.E., the process begins of separating a prophetic ministry from the priestly one. The priestly function, examined in our discussion of the book of Leviticus, emphasized adherence to the ceremonial laws, ritual, sacrifice, and proper oracular form (the *ephod,* or plated image; the *teraphim,* or lot; and the *Urim* and *Thummim,* two sacred stones that were thrown like dice in order to decide on courses of action). It was paternalistic and intermediary, the priest and ritual process standing as the link between God and the people of Israel. Burnt offering and ritual atonement centered around the ark of the covenant were the focus of the religious life. Only the high priest had access to Yahweh. Now, with the prophets, concepts of social justice replace ceremony and kosher laws as being at the heart of religious worship.

The most famous of these, Amos (760 B.C.E.), the herdsman from Tekoa, set the tone for those who followed. As J. Powis Smith writes, "He [Amos] called Northern Israel to the bar, declared her guilty, and passed sentence of death upon her."[3] The declaration was not based on empirical studies of the comparative military strength of Israel and her enemies. Indeed, there was really no reason to suspect a coming doom, for Israel was enjoying an era of peace and unprecedented prosperity at the time. Instead of being based on empirical observations of international affairs, his prophecies were based on the fact of Israel's moral failure, which is identical with breaking covenant with God and brings forth retributive justice. While the nation awaited a grand and glorious "Day of Yahweh," Amos warned them that that day was a day of "darkness and not light" (Am. 5:18). "Prepare to meet Thy God, O Israel!" (Am. 4:2).

First, Amos declares against the neighboring tribes and nations, Damascus, Philistia, Ammon, and Moab, condemning them for violating basic moral principles (Am. 1:3–2:3). The interesting thing is that it is not simply their actions against Israel that condemn these tribes but their violation of the moral law, what we would call basic human rights.

Israelite hearers of his imprecations must have applauded Amos' insightful condemnation of the Gentile neighbors but been taken aback when he next turned to Israel. "You only of all the nations have I known, therefore I will punish you" (Am. 3:2). To whom much is given, much is expected. Israel's special relationship with God entailed special obligation and responsibility. Therefore, having reneged on her part of the contract, she is all the more culpable. Here for the first time ritual takes second place to the moral law. The priestly mode of life will not save her.

> *Was it sacrifices and offerings that ye brought unto me*
> *Forty years in the wilderness, O house of Israel. (Am. 5:25)*
>
> *I hate, I despise your feasts,*
> *And I take no delight in your solemn assemblies.*
> *Yea, though ye offer me your burnt offerings and cereal offerings,*
> *I will not accept them;*
> *Neither will I regard the peace offerings of your fatted beasts.*
> *Take away from me the noise of your hymns;*
> *For I will not listen to the melody of thy harps.*
> *But let justice roll down as waters,*
> *And righteousness as an everlasting stream. (Am. 5:21–24)*

The prophet Samuel condemns King Saul for sacrificing instead of obeying Yahweh's fiat, but Amos' criticism is principled. It is not the individual command of God but the general principles that are the criteria of right behavior. God expects us to obey the Moral Law.

Amos condemns Israel for selling the innocent into slavery for their inability to pay a small debt (Am. 2:5, 8:6), for "buffeting the heads of the poor" (2:7), for "trampling" them into the dust (5:11), and for keeping the much needed poor man's garment overnight as security for a loan (2:8). The rich sell the needy inferior quality grain (8:6) and cheat them with false weights and measures (8:5). They bribe judges (5:12), setting justice at naught (5:7, 6:3). Wealthy women ("the fatted cows of Bashan") who have become addicted to luxury, in order to enhance their lifestyle, urge their husbands to take actions that oppress the poor (4:1f). The poor are without an advocate (5:10f). Oppression and violence are destroying the people (3:9f, 6:3). Drunkenness and sexual promiscuity are prevalent (2:8, 12; 4:1; 2:7), and there is a general tendency of riotous living (3:12f, 4:1f, 6:1f). The people are impervious to moral decency. "They know not how to do right" (3:10).

Amos calls on Israel to repent. His message is for a moral conversion:

Seek good, and not evil, that ye may live;
And so Yahweh, the God of hosts, may be with you as ye say.
Hate the evil and love the good and establish judgment in the gate.
Let justice roll down as waters,
And righteousness as an everlasting stream. (Am. 5:14f, 24)

In the end there is good news: a restored kingdom:
Behold the days are coming, says the Lord,
When the plowman shall overtake the reaper
And the treader of grapes him who sows the seed;
The mountains shall drip sweet wine
And all the hills shall flow with it.
I will restore the fortunes of my people Israel,
And they shall rebuild the ruined cities and inhabit them.
They shall plant vineyards and drink their wine,
And they shall make gardens and eat their fruit. (Am. 9:13–15)

Note that Amos, unlike other prophets (e.g., Elijah), makes no mention of idolatry, wrong religious commitments, or eclectic religious practices. Amos condemns Israel on purely moral grounds and identifies these with the covenant with God.

Finally, we should note the cosmopolitan contribution of the prophet Isaiah (ca. 740 B.C.E.), who carries on Amos' focus on personal morality, condemning Israel for mistreating the poor (Is. 1:16, 3:14), for bribery (5:23), injustice (1:21), violence (5:7), drunkenness and debauchery (5:11, 22:13), luxurious living (2:16f), and the perversion of moral values in general:

Woe to those who call badness good and goodness bad,
That regard darkness as light, and light as darkness,
That consider bitter sweet, and sweet bitter.

Woe to the wise in their own eyes,
And intelligent in their own sight. (Is. 5:20f)

Who say "Let us eat and drink,
For tomorrow we may die. (Is. 22:13)

Israel's sacrifices are no substitute for morality:

"My soul hates [your rituals].
I am weary of bearing them.
Put away the evil of your doings from before mine eyes.
Cease to do evil;
Learn to do good;
Seek justice,
relieve the oppressed;
Judge the fatherless;
Plead for the widow." (Is. 1:10–17)

Holiness is given a distinctly moral tone, and that moral tone has a universal scope. All nations will eventually be saved and enjoy the benefits of Yahweh's love, mercy, and justice.

In the latter days the mountain of the Lord
Shall be established as the highest of the mountains,
And shall be raised up above the hills;
And people shall flow to it,
And all nations shall come and say:
"Come, let us go up to the mountain of the Lord,
To the house of the God of Jacob;
That he may teach us his ways
And we may walk in his paths."
For out of Zion shall go forth the law,
And the word of the Lord from Jerusalem.
He shall judge between many peoples,
And shall decide for the strong nations afar off;
And they shall beat their swords into plowshares,
And their spears into pruning hooks;
Nation shall not lift up sword against nation,
Neither shall they learn war any more. (Is. 2:2–4)

Later in the book, perhaps written by a different author, the same sentiment is expressed. Yahweh will make a new heaven and a new earth and "all flesh shall come to worship before me, says Yahweh" (Is. 66:22, cf. 60:3). The curse of the Fall shall be removed from humanity, and all violence, even the killing of animals and the eating of meat, shall cease.

The kingdom of God, inaugurated by the Lord's anointed, the Messiah, will be universal, peaceful, and blessed.

They shall not labor in vain, or bear children in calamity, for they shall be the off-spring of the blessed of the Lord, and their children with them. Before they call I will answer, while they are yet speaking I will hear. The wolf and the lamb shall feed together and the lion shall eat straw like the ox; and dust shall be the serpent's food. They shall not destroy life in my holy mountain, says the Lord. (Is. 65:23–25)

We see the continuation with this universalist dimension to God's love in his sending Jonah to call the people of Nineveh to repent and in the book of Malachai (Mal. 2:10). God is recognized as the father of all humanity, not just the Jews, the implication being that we are all brothers and sisters of one another. The prophet Micah puts the universalist message this way:

But in the last days it shall come to pass, [that] the mountain of the house of the LORD shall be established in the top of the mountains, and it shall be exalted above the hills; and people shall flow unto it. And many nations shall come, and say, Come, and let us go up to the mountain of the LORD, and to the house of the God of Jacob; and he will teach us of his ways, and we will walk in his paths: for the law shall go forth of Zion, and the word of the LORD from Jerusalem. And he shall judge among many people, and rebuke strong nations afar off; and they shall beat their swords into plowshares, and their spears into pruninghooks: nation shall not lift up a sword against nation, neither shall they learn war any more. But they shall sit every man under his vine and under his fig tree; and none shall make [them] afraid: for the mouth of the LORD of hosts hath spoken [it]. (Mi. 4:1–4)

Micah's message seems the most universalist of all the prophets. No mention is made of the kosher laws or rituals, but a simple prescription for moral living is offered: "[God] has showed you, O man, what is good; and what does the Lord require of you, but to do justice, to love kindness, and to walk humbly with your God." (Mi. 6:8)

The prophetic movement lasted from 880 (Elijah) until 587 (Jeremiah) B.C.E. After the Babylonian captivity in 586 B.C.E., there is mostly silence. After the Jews reestablish themselves in Palestine in the late fifth century B.C.E., led by Nehemiah and Ezra, the ceremonial law is reintroduced as the dominant mode of serving God. Rabbinic Judaism commences with its commentaries on the Torah and sayings of the rabbis. During this period, the Pharisees (who believed that these extrabiblical writings were authoritative and in a final judgment and life after death) and the Sadducees (who denied the three propositions mentioned in regard to the Pharisees) grew and developed their traditions.

A brief word is in order on the Rabbinical writings in the times between the Old and New Testaments. While the Talmud contains endless legalistic injunctions in casuistic detail, a more universalist and rational motif is also present throughout as a minority or balancing aspect. The major sins are idolatry, adultery, and murder. "Rather than commit any one of these capital sins . . . man (even the Gentile) should give up his life" (Sanhedrin 74a, b). Adherence to these commands secures even heathen love and support ('Ab Zarah 2b, Sanh. 108a, Sifra). A version of the Golden Rule is enunciated by Hillel (ca. 30–10 B.C.E.): "Whatever thou hatest to have done unto thee do not unto thy neighbor; wherefore do not hurt him; do not speak ill of him; do not reveal his secrets to others; let his honor and his property be as dear to thee as thine own" (*Aboth Rabbi Nathan*, xxvi, xxix, xxx, xxxiii). When

Rabbi Hillel was approached by a heathen who insisted that he be told the entire Torah while standing on one foot, the rabbi responded, "Do not unto others that which you would not have them do unto you. That is the entire Torah. The rest is commentary. Now go and study."[4]

A certain self-love is enjoined: enjoyment is seen as a blessing from God, as is marriage. The world is said to rest on three things: justice, truth, and peace. It is not merely the New Testament (Mt. 5:22) but Pharisaic ethics which places insulting, nicknaming, or putting others to shame in the same category as murder and which brands as calumny the spreading of evil reports even when true, listening to slanderous gossip, causing suspicion, or provoking unfavorable remarks about a neighbor (Pes. 118a, B.M. 58b).[5] There is recognition of autonomous ethics throughout the rabbinical writings, which anticipates both the New Testament and later philosophical ethics.

Summary for Hebrew Bible

The Hebrew Bible gives us a long, progressive revelation of God's dealing with humanity, especially one part of humanity, the tribe of Israel. God is a moral agent who draws up a covenant with Israel, to whom he has sworn reciprocal, loving loyalty. Persons are responsible moral agents who must obey their God and his rules. We can sum up the theory of human nature in the Hebrew Bible by identifying five salient features. (1) The Hebrew Bible contains a profound view of the human as a moral being, with free will, responsibility, and authority over the animal world. He is a steward of God's creation. Humans are made in the image of God, each of equal worth with everyone else. (2) Human beings are always an intricate part of the community. God's covenant is not made with an individual but with the community, Israel, so it is the community in which primary value inheres. An individual may justly be sacrificed for the good of the community. The relation of the community to God is one of loyalty and trust. (3) A broad set of rules, the Ten Commandments, penetrates Israel's life, supplemented by the kosher rules. (4) Broad issues of social justice and mercy gradually replace the ritualistic kosher rules as decisive for pleasing God. (5) We see progressive development from tribal particularism, where only members of the tribe of Israel have moral rights, to universalism, encompassing all people everywhere. The kingdom of God is characterized by universal peace, wherein even nature is transformed and "the lion will lie down with the lamb."

The Hebrew Bible contains the symbols and narratives that define the history of Israel, but they may also be seen as the prelude to the Christian New Testament, to which we now turn.

The New Testament

A lawyer asked Jesus a question to test him, "Teacher, which is the greatest commandment in the law?" And he said to him, "You shall love the Lord your God with all your heart, and with all your soul and with all your mind. This is the great and first commandment. And a second is like it, You shall love your neighbor as yourself. On these two commandments depend all the law and the prophets." (Mt. 22:36–40)

The New Testament view of human nature is continuous with that of the Hebrew Bible or Old Testament. It presumes the background history and theories discussed in the preceding section. Human nature, intrinsically good, bearing the image of God, has been corrupted by sin. "All have sinned and come short of the glory of God" (Rom. 3:23). We are like dirty, dented coins that still bear the image of the sovereign and, as such, still have their original value. However, like the damaged coins, we need to be cleaned up and straightened out by grace before we are worthy of appearing in the kingdom of God.

Christ and the Concept of Human Nature

Jesus of Nazareth is both the paradigm of the perfect human being (the exemplar of moral virtue) and the savior of the world. He is the *Logos* (which means both "Word" and "Reason"), God's rationale incarnate in human flesh.

> In the beginning was the logos and the logos was with God and the logos was God. . . . All things were made through him, and without him was not anything made that was made. In him was life, and the life was the light of men. The light shines in the darkness and the darkness has not overcome it. . . . This true light enlightens every man coming into the world. . . . And the logos became flesh and dwelt among us, full of grace and truth. (Jn. 1:1–5, 9, 14)

He is divine, the Son of God and the Son of man, born of a virgin, and sent into the world to fulfill Old Testament prophecies about a promised messiah; he is the savior of all persons who will repent and believe in him. As the logos, he *enlightens* every person who is born. I take this to mean that Christ is the incarnation of reason, that which sets us apart from the other animals and is expressed in language (the word). Humans, as rational and linguistic beings, can become "a little less than divine" (Ps. 8), create their own words, and join in fellowship with God, the ultimate Logos.

The universalism that we witnessed in the writings of the prophets at the end of the Hebrew Bible is taken as the starting assumption in the New Testament. The Gospels affirm that God is the universal father of all humanity, who, as a good father, loves all and wills their salvation (Mt. 6:9, Lk. 15, Jn. 3:16). Paul refers to humans as bearing the "image and glory of God" (1 Cor. 11:7) and affirms the universal fatherhood of God, "we are his offspring" (Acts 17:26ff), so that even the Gentiles have his law written in their hearts, thus enabling them to exercise moral judgment. "The [Gentiles] show that what the law requires is written on their hearts, while their conscience also bears witness and their conflicting thoughts accuse or perhaps excuse them" (Rom. 2:15). However, humankind has fallen and been corrupted by sin. While Adam and Eve were the original cause of this degradation, we have all freely sinned and are deserving of damnation. God has sent his only begotten son to earth to redeem us from sin. "While we were yet helpless, at the right time Christ died for the ungodly . . . God showed his love for us in that while we were yet sinners Christ died for us." (Rom. 5:5–7). By God's grace through faith we may find salvation. Through Christ's death and resurrection we may be reconciled to God and granted eternal life. "In a moment, in the twinkling of an eye, at the last trumpet . . . we shall be changed. For this perishable nature must put on the imperishable and the mortal puts on immortality" (1 Cor. 15:54).

All contingent distinctions, such as race, ethnicity, and gender, are erased in the kingdom of God, the ideal community. "In Christ there is neither Jew nor Greek, there is neither slave nor free; there is neither male nor female; but all are one in Christ" (Gal. 3:28). The kingdom of heaven is a color-blind and gender-blind community ruled by love, not racial or social pedigree.

The Church becomes the new Israel, the bearer of God's sacred oracles, his covenant, word, and mission. The communitarian aspect of the Old Testament is continued in the new epoch of the Church. All Christians are bound together as in a single body. "For just as the body is one and has many members, and all the members of one body, though many, are one body, so it is with Christ. For by one Spirit we were all baptized into one body—Jew or Greek, slaves or free—and all were made to drink of the same Spirit" (1 Cor. 12:12). When one member succeeds, we all succeed. When one member suffers, we all suffer.

While we are saved by grace through faith and not by works, good works (morality) become the evidence and genuine expression of our salvation. This morality is based on gratitude and love. "We love because he first loved us" (1 Jn. 4:19). This love is radical **agapeism,** high **altruism.**

Jesus' Radical Message: Humanity is Made to Love

Beloved, let us love one another; for love is of God, and he who loves is born of God, and knows God. He who does not love, does not know God, for God is love. We love because he first loved us. (1 Jn. 4:7–9, 19)

The radicality of Jesus' ethics is first seen in the Sermon on the Mount. The homily begins with a set of antiworldly blessings, signifying a transvaluation of normal evaluations.

Blessed are the poor in spirit, for theirs is the kingdom of heaven.
Blessed are those who mourn, for they shall be comforted.
Blessed are the meek, for they shall inherit the earth.
Blessed are those who hunger and thirst for righteousness, for they shall be satisfied.
Blessed are the merciful, for they shall obtain mercy.
Blessed are the pure in heart, for they shall see God.
Blessed are those who are persecuted for righteousness' sake, for theirs is the kingdom of heaven.
Blessed are you when men revile you and persecute you and utter all kinds of evil against you falsely on my account. Rejoice and be glad, for your reward is great in heaven, for so men persecuted the prophets who were before you. (Mt. 5:3–11)

Suffering, mourning, humility, hungering for moral goodness, mercy, and purity of heart—these are not the Greek virtues, nor are they identical with those found in the Torah. They are closest to those found in the prophets. Furthermore, "blessedness" (Greek *makarios*) is not to be identified with the Greek notion of happiness (*eudaimonia*), in the sense of pleasure and well-being that includes outward circumstance. Rather, it signifies deep and abiding inner joy independent of external goods, for one can be blessed while poor and persecuted; but one who is not poor and pure in spirit, merciful, or meek cannot be blessed.

The Sermon on the Mount goes on to promote pacifism.

> You have heard that it was said, "An eye for an eye and a tooth for a tooth," but I say unto you, Do not resist one who is evil. But if any one strikes you on the right cheek, turn to him the other cheek also; and if anyone would sue you and take your coat, let him have your cloak as well . . . give to him who begs from you, and do not refuse him who would borrow from you. You have heard that it was said, "You shall love your neighbor and hate your enemy." But I say unto you, Love your enemy and pray for those who persecute you, so that you may be sons of your Father who is in heaven; for he makes his sun rise on the evil and good, and sends rain on the just and on the unjust. (Mt. 5:38–45)

The followers of Jesus are to hunger after moral righteousness and seek the life of the spirit, the virtues that belong to the kingdom of God. As peacemakers, theirs is a kingdom yet to come, a fulfillment of Isaiah's prophecy of the peaceable kingdom (see p. 14).

While the great Jewish rabbi Hillel stated the Golden Rule in its negative form (see p. 16), Jesus gives the first positive version of the rule: "All things therefore which you want people to do unto you, do to them; for this is the law and the prophets" (Mt. 7:12). We are to put ourselves in the shoes of others and treat them as we would want to be treated. This is really what the Old Testament law and the prophets were saying. It is a simple rule, though its ramifications are far-reaching. However, it needs qualification within a context of a set of normative practices. For example, taken literally, the jailer, by putting himself into the shoes of the prisoner, would be enjoined to free the dangerous criminal; but that would be dangerous to the rest of society. Whatever its limitations, the Golden Rule seems a good rule of thumb for ordinary human relations.

Jesus' interpretation of the Golden Rule can be applied to the Parable of the Good Samaritan (Lk. 10). A robbery takes place and the victim, probably a Jew, lies wounded on the side of the road. After a priest and a Levite pass by, a Samaritan, a despised minority, comes upon the victim, stops, and renders aid. The Samaritan takes him to an inn, where he ministers to his wounds and helps restore him to health. The priest and the Levite fulfilled the negative version of the Golden Rule, which requires that they not harm him; but the Samaritan went further than that negative version and treated the victim as he would have liked to be treated were he the victim of a robbery. Jesus not only transforms the Golden Rule to a positive rule but extends it to cover not only people of one's own race or religion but all people everywhere.

If Jesus' disciples are to be fit citizens of the kingdom of God, their righteousness must exceed that of the Jewish scribes and Pharisees. They must be perfect even as their father in heaven is perfect. Rather than abolishing the rigor of the Mosaic and ceremonial laws, Jesus claims to fulfill them by spiritualizing their content. To this end, he extends the scope of the Ten Commandments. Whereas in the Mosaic law only the first and last commandments clearly entailed intentionality (worship of God and coveting one's neighbor's property), now all of the commands are intentionalized. The prohibition against murder is extended to cover unjustified anger and hatred. The prohibition against adultery is extended to cover lust. The prohibition against false witness is extended to cover needing to take an oath at all; rather, let your word be your bond. The legalism that surrounded honoring one's father and mother is cut through so that responsible love replaces casuistry. Likewise, the fourth commandment, keeping the Sabbath, is interpreted as making wise use of a day of rest so that meeting human needs is permitted. "The Sabbath is made for man, not man for the Sabbath" (Mt. 2:23–28). Even the tenth commandment (against coveting a neighbor's goods) is broadened to cover all coveting of possessions (Lk. 12:15). Instead, we are to "seek first the kingdom of God and his righteousness, and all these things will be added unto you" (Mt. 6:33). We are not to worry about the mundane things in life,

> what you shall eat or what you shall drink, nor about your body, what you shall put on. Is not life more than food, and the body more than clothing? Look at the birds of the air: they neither sow nor reap nor gather into barns, and yet your heavenly Father feeds them. Are you not of more value than they? (Mt. 6:25f)

> Don't be anxious about the morrow for the day's problems should be sufficient for us. (Mt. 6:34)

The gospel of love (*agape*; Mt. 22:36–40, Jn. 3:16; 1 Cor. 13; 1 Jn. 4) predominates in the Gospel and Epistles.[6] While the two great commandments are mentioned in the Torah (Dt. 6:4, Lv. 19:18), Jesus brings them together and uses them to sum up the essence of the whole law and the prophets. "You shall love the Lord your God with all your heart, and with all your soul, and with all your mind. This is the great and first commandment. And a second is like it, You shall love your neighbor as yourself. On these two commandments depend all the law and the prophets" (Mt. 22:37–39).

John reports that among Jesus' last words to his disciples the principle of living in mutual love was invoked.

> This is my commandment, that you love one another as I have loved you. Greater love has no man than this, that a man lay down his life for his friends. You are my friends if you do what I command you. No longer do I call you servants, for the servant does not know what his master is doing; but I have called you friends, for all that I have heard from my father I have made known to you. (Jn. 15:12–15)

Love becomes the bond between God and humanity that makes the disciple autonomous, which, of course, really means that he is theonomous.

In this regard, perhaps the most moving words in the New Testament are Christ's words from the cross regarding his enemies: "Father, forgive them; for they know not what they do" (Lk. 23:34).

Christ is seen as the incarnate love of God. God's love through him becomes the motivating force in the lives of the believers (2 Cor. 5:4f). We love God and others because he first loved us and shed forth his love in our hearts (1 Jn. 4). As we will see when examining Paul's ethics, love is even paramount to faith (1 Cor. 13:13).

The quintessence of the command is summed up in Augustine's "Love God and do whatever you please"—a command not permitting libertinism but indicating the source of right action. Only the person who has a proper character, set in the right direction, can hope consistently to do the right acts. Love takes rules of thumb and applies them sensitively to situations such as artificial casuistry. It not only comes up with the right answer, but supplies the requisite motivational force necessary to combat weakness of will and actualize the deed.

Paul's Vision of Human Nature

The apostle Paul continues and develops the ideal of love (*agape*) as the very heart of the Christian character.

If I speak in the tongues of men and of angels, but have not love,
I am a noisy gong or a clanging cymbal.
And if I have prophetic powers, and understand all mysteries and all knowledge,
And if I have all faith, so as to remove mountains,
But have not love,
I am nothing.
If I give away all I have,
And if I deliver my body to be burned,
But have not love, I gain nothing.
Love is patient and kind;
Love is not jealous or boastful; it is not arrogant or rude.
Love does not insist on its own way; it is not irritable or resentful;
It does not rejoice at wrong, but rejoices in the right.
Love bears all things, believes all things, hopes all things, endures all things.
Love never ends;
As for prophecies, they will pass away; as for tongues, they will cease;
As for knowledge, it will pass away.
For our knowledge is imperfect and our prophecy is imperfect;
But when the perfect comes, the imperfect will pass away.
When I was a child, I spoke like a child, I thought like a child, I reasoned like a child;
When I became a man, I gave up childish ways.
For now we see in a mirror dimly, but then face to face.
Now I know in part; then I shall understand fully, even as I have been fully understood.
So faith, hope, love abide, these three; but the greatest of these is love. (1 Cor. 13)

The highest virtue for humanity is not reason but love, followed closely by faith. Love and faith are under the domain of the will, not reason. Indeed, by the canons of reason, Christianity is foolishness. God chose the foolish things of this world to shame the wise (1 Cor. 1:21–27). Because we are sinful, we pervert reason so that our foolish minds are darkened (Rom. 1:21).

Justice and Responsibility (Mt. 25:14–30)

God will judge us with perfect justice. Thus, we are responsible for everything we do or say. "I tell you, on the day of judgement men will render account for every careless word they utter; for by your words you will be justified, and by your words you will be condemned" (Mt. 12:36).

Unlike several versions of secular ethics (see Nagel and Williams[7]), the synoptic Gospels (especially Matthew) exclude moral luck—unless it is the good luck of grace and forgiveness. Otherwise, each person is judged according to his or her actions. God is a perfect judge. This is brought out most vividly in the Parable of the Talents (Mt. 25:14–30). Three men are given various amounts of money (five, two, and one talent, respectively) to invest while their master goes on a long trip. A, who has doubled his investment from five to ten, is rewarded in proportion to his product. Likewise, B has doubled his two talents and is so rewarded. However, C has—in fear—hidden his talent rather than invested it. He is condemned and his talent taken from him and given to the person who has gained ten talents. "For to everyone who has will more be given, and he will have abundance; but from him who has not, even what he has will be taken away." This is a difficult passage and can be taken to mean that rewards are all or nothing—the "haves" get more and the "have-nots" lose even what they deserve. However, this may be too crude an interpretation of this enigmatic passage. Perhaps we should see it as enjoining stewardship. We are stewards who are accountable for what we have been given. There is a divine reckoning, a transcendent calculus, so that he who is "faithful over little" will be amply rewarded. "I will set you over much; enter into the joy of your master" (v. 21). That is, grace adds to our good works, but exact retributivism may apply to those who fail to make a serious effort to be moral.

This sense of accountability is seen in evaluating the deeds of the rich contributors and the widow. Although the rich gave more, the widow gave from the heart her two copper coins. Jesus' verdict is "Truly I tell you, this poor widow has put in more than all of them; for they all contributed out of their abundance, but she out of her poverty put in all the living that she had" (Lk. 21:1–4).

There is one passage that seems to contradict the notion of just reward/punishment. Jesus compares the kingdom of heaven to a householder who goes out early in the morning to hire laborers to work in his vineyards all day for a denarius (a few dollars). A few hours later, he finds some idle men and agrees to pay the same wages to them for working in the vineyards the rest of the day. He repeats this act every three hours with new men until one hour before closing (the eleventh hour), when he employs the last batch of men to work one hour for the same wages as everyone else. That is, everyone, whether they worked twelve, nine, six, three, or one hour, got the same pay! Those who worked all day complained that this was not fair, but the householder replied, "Friend, I am doing you no wrong; did you not agree with me for a denarius? Take what belongs to you, and go; I choose to give to this last as I give to you. Am I not allowed to do what I choose with what belongs to me? Or do you begrudge my generosity? So the last will be first and the first last" (Mt. 20:13–16).

At face value this looks like a violation of the principle of equal pay for equal work. God seems to be a grand capitalist in a market economy. On second glance, it may only signify that all who accept grace, all who work for the kingdom of God, will be rewarded equally. It is reminiscent of David's decision to share the spoils of battle equally with those who guarded the supply post as well as with those who risked their lives in battle (1 Sm. 30:21–31). Grace is a divine equalizer, and those who serve God must do so disinterestedly. It almost sounds like the Kantian good will. In the end, the moral person does what is right simply from the goodness of his or her heart.

In the Gospel of John, the situation seems more ambiguous. On the one hand, it seems that all those who are sincerely seeking the truth will find it. "If any man will do his will, he shall know whether the teaching is from God or whether I am speaking on my own authority" (Jn. 7:17). Whoever will believe will be saved (Jn. 3:16f). On the other hand, grace seems to annul all human effort and calculations. "You did not choose me, but I chose you and appointed you that you should go and bear fruit" (Jn. 13:16). This tension between grace and works will become more pronounced in the letters of Paul, where grace will predominate.

Ultimately, in the kingdom of God, the restored Garden of Eden, people will live in love and cooperation. All needs will be met, and there will be no more suffering or war. The paradigm of all utopias, it is enough to fill a person's soul with everlasting longing and sacrifice (Rv. 21–22).

Meanwhile, we are to live in the spirit of that utopia, making ourselves, with God's help, worthy of citizenship in it. We are to do God's will not simply because of rewards or punishments but because our will has become one with his and there is an inner impulse to do what is pleasing to him, what he desires us to do. We are to forgive, not seven times but seventy times seven, loving even our enemies and doing good to them who persecute us (Mt. 5:44).

Finally, we should point out that much of the actual content of Jesus' ethics is located in the Old Testament and the rabbinical tradition. The Jewish theologian Joseph Klausner writes, "Throughout the Gospels there is not one item of ethical teaching which cannot be paralleled either in the Old Testament, the Apocrypha, or in the Talmudic and Midrashic literature of the period near to the time of Jesus."[8]

However, while there is some truth in Klausner's contention, it goes too far. Jesus' teachings are in line with the Hebrew Bible, but he develops the thought of "the law and the prophets," transforming the negative version of the Golden Rule into a positive principle and extending the notion of love to all people, not only Jews. For example, whereas the Torah did command us to love God (Dt. 6:4) and our neighbor as ourself (Lv. 19:18), Jesus singles these two commandments out as the sum of all the law, thus abrogating the 618 kosher laws, and expands the compass and scope of love to include even one's enemies. Furthermore, he put a fresh emphasis on the importance of intention in carrying out the commandments.

Motive is everything. The poor widow who could only give her mite, gave more than all the rich who gave from their abundance (Mk. 12:42f). Jesus views ethics not simply as a striving to obey God but as an expression of gratitude to God for the blessings of salvation.

Summary for New Testament

The concept of human nature in the New Testament is a consistent development of that found in the Hebrew Bible. Humans are made in the image of God, free, responsible beings with dignity and authority, made for fellowship with God; but humanity has sinned, and people now find themselves alienated from God and in need of salvation. As St. Augustine wrote, "Thou has made us for thyself, and our hearts are restless until they find rest in thee."[9] Answering the promise of redemption, found in the Hebrew Bible, God sends his son, Jesus Christ, to procure our salvation.

There is a new covenant (or testament) with humanity. The scope of God's love is universal, extended from Israel to all people everywhere. We are to do good to all people, as much as we are able, though "especially to those of the household of faith" (Gal. 6:10). God loves people of all races and both genders and offers salvation to every individual. Whoever will believe in Christ will be saved and have eternal life. However, a significant expression of eternal life here and now is how we live our lives, our morality. In Jesus' Sermon on the Mount, in his positive version of the Golden Rule, and in Paul and John's teachings on love, we see the beginning of Christian ethics, most notably an ethic of altruism (*agape*) such as never before existed.[10]

The primary virtues are not reason and courage but faith, love, and hope. Humans are not mere rational animals but beings who need love, trust, and emotional fulfillment in order to flourish. They belong to God, have a "God-shaped heart," and cannot satisfy that heart with substitutes.

Study Questions

1. Describe the concept of human nature in the Hebrew Bible (Old Testament). What are its key features?

2. Should the story of Adam and Eve in the Garden of Eden be taken literally? Why or why not? What is the meaning of this story?

3. Describe the development of human nature from the early books in the Hebrew Bible to those of the prophets. What are the main changes?

4. What are the kosher laws, and how do they define Jewish identity?

5. Describe the view of humankind in the New Testament. What are the central features?

6. How would you compare and contrast the view of human nature in the Old and New Testaments?

7. What is meat by the Logos? How does it apply to human nature?

8. Discuss the negative and positive versions of the Golden Rule. What are the implications of the difference for the moral life?

9. Read over the Sermon on the Mount. How should we interpret Jesus' teachings? Should we love our enemies, turn the other cheek when struck by an assailant, and give our clothes away to those who request them?

10. Examine the doctrine of the Great Chain of Being. How has it influenced Christian culture?

11. Following up on question 8, what is the New Testament law of love (*agapeism*)? What are the strengths and weaknesses of using the law of love as the sole guide to moral living? How does it adjudicate between possible courses of action?

12. The Bible seems to place faith over reason (see 1 Cor. 1). Explore the implications of this doctrine.

Notes

1. See T. C. Vriezen, *An Outline of Old Testament Theology* (Blackwell, 1958), chapter VI, for a good discussion of God's holiness. See also Walter C. Kaiser, *Toward Old Testament Ethics* (Academie Books, 1983), chapters 9–15.
2. W. S. Bruce, *The Ethics of the Old Testament* (Eerdmans, 1979), p. 93.
3. J. Powis Smith, *The Ethics of the Old Testament,* (University of Chicago Press, 1941) p. 73.
4. Quoted in Adin Steinsaltz, *The Essential Talmud* (Basic Books, 1976), p. 26.
5. Quoted in the *Jewish Encyclopedia* ("Ethics"), 1901–1906.
6. See Robert M. Adams, *The Virtue of Faith* (Oxford University Press, 1987).
7. See Thomas Nagel, *Mortal Luck* (Cambridge University Press, 1979), and Bernard Williams, *Moral Luck* (Cambridge University Press, 1981).
8. Joseph Klauser, *Jesus of Nazareth* (Macmillan, 1925), p. 384.
9. St. Augustine, *Confessions,* I.1.
10. J. L. Holden sums up Jesus' ethics this way:

    The first reality is the person of Jesus, the mysterious Son of Man sent from God to battle against the powers of evil and 'give his life as a ransom for many' (x.45). The second reality is the kingdom of God, that immediate and complete sovereignty of God that Jesus embodies and establishes. Moral lessons are taught chiefly as exemplifying and demonstrating these realities. Thus the Sabbath law must give way, not before a set of amended regulations, but before a God who has only one choice when it comes to saving life or destroying it (iii.4), and before the Son of Man who is the Sabbath's lord (ii.28). Divorce may no longer be tolerated, not because of a new divine decree, but because God created man for life-long marriage—it is at the root of his nature (x.2f). (J. L. Holden, *Ethics and the New Testament* [Oxford University Press, 1973], p. 43)

For Further Reading

Adams, Robert M., *The Virtue of Faith* (Oxford University Press, 1987).

Anderson, Bernard, *Understanding the Old Testament* (Prentice Hall, 1957).

Brewer, Julius, *Literature of the Old Testament* (Columbia University Press, 1933).

Bruce, W. S., *The Ethics of the Old Testament* (Eerdmans, 1979).

Drane, John, *Introducing the New Testament* (Harper & Row, 1986).

Forell, George, *History of Christian Ethics* (Augsburg Publishing Co., 1979).

Holden, J. L., *Ethics and the New Testament* (Oxford University Press, 1973).

Interpreter's Bible, 12 volumes (Abingdon Press, 1952).

Kaiser, Walter C., *Toward Old Testament Ethics* (Academie Books, 1983).

Klauser, Joseph, *Jesus of Nazareth* (Macmillan, 1925).

Lovejoy, Arthur, *The Great Chain of Being* (Harper & Row, 1960).

Niebuhr, Reinhold, *An Interpretation of Christian Ethics* (Harper & Row, 1963).

Smith, J. Powis, *The Ethics of the Old Testament* (University of Chicago Press, 1941).

Steinberg, Milton, *Basic Judaism* (Roman & Littlefield, 1987).

Steinsaltz, Adin, *The Essential Talmud* (Basic Books, 1976).

Vriezen, T. C., *An Outline of Old Testament Theology* (Blackwell, 1958).

Wattles, Jeffrey, *The Golden Rule* (Oxford University Press, 1996).

CHAPTER 2

The Greek Tradition on Human Nature:
The Sophists and Socrates

Two great traditions inform the Western view of human nature: the Hebrew–Christian view of the Bible and the ancient Greek philosophers. We examined the Hebrew–Christian view in the last chapter. We now turn to the second great tradition, that of the Greeks, concentrating on Socrates, Plato, and Aristotle but covering minor theorists as well.

The first philosophers (called the *pre-socratics*) were Greeks, living in the 6th century B.C.E. off the coast of Asia Minor (present-day Turkey). Most were materialists (*hylicists*), who sought a naturalistic and unified answer to the cosmological questions: What is reality? What is the explanation of the world? Is there one fundamental substance that underlies reality or are there many? Their theories provoked a reaction from idealists and mystics. The most prominent mystic was Pythagoras, who rejected the materialism of the early hylicists and set forth a theory of number mysticism in which mathematics took on spiritual and cosmic import. The Eleatics, Parmenides, and Zeno argued for an underlying **monism,** that reality was one and that change, including time, was unreal, mere appearance. Heraclitus rejected the notion of there being one or many underlying substances and said all was in process, fire. The pluralist atomists rejected both the Eleatic monism and Heraclitus' process theory for an atomistic materialism. Anaxagoras attempted to synthesize the work of his predecessors, claiming that there was a unity of being in which everything was part of everything else. A godlike Mind (*Nous*) ruled the universe. Others, like Eratosthenes and Aristarchus, calculated the circumference of the earth and put forth a heliocentric theory almost two millennia before Copernicus.

The Rise of the Sophists

In the middle of the 5th century B.C.E. Athens flourished both materially and culturally, partly due to an unexpected and resounding victory over the Persians and partly due to exceptional leadership of the likes of Solon and Pericles who invented democracy. Athens became a prosperous economic force. In the arts, it produced such geniuses as the playwrights Euripides, Sophocles, Aeschylus, and Aristophanes; great literature, such as Homer's *Iliad* and *Odyssey*; and the first history, *Histories* by Herodotus and Thucydides. The Parthenon was built, and sculpture and the plastic arts reached their pinnacle. Geometry was invented. Because the city's prosperity depended on a large number of slaves, citizens enjoyed an unprecedented amount of leisure time to think and converse. The state religion, which was based on the Homeric gods, was scrutinized, tried, and found wanting by the brightest citizens; and secularism increased. Political speech making and the use of rhetoric to persuade citizens grew in importance.

In this world, a new profession arose, one bent on teaching citizens how to win cases in court: the Sophists. The Sophists were secular relativists, skeptical, even cynical, about religious and idealistic pretensions, aiming at material and political success in democratic society by using rhetoric and oratory to persuade people. They rejected the quest of the pre-Socratic philosophers as useless speculation. The big question of the pre-Socratics was, What is the nature of reality? The Sophists' question, however, was more mundane: How can I succeed in the practical affairs of life, or how can I play the game of life and win? These are always appealing questions. Some Sophists made enormous sums of money selling their services to rich young men, teaching them how to win at litigation and to use debating tricks to defeat their opponents.

The Sophists were prominent between 460 and 380 B.C.E. The older generation, Protagoras of Abdera in Thrace (ca. 490–420 B.C.E.), Gorgias of Leontini in Sicily (ca. 485–380 B.C.E.), Prodicus of Ceos (ca. 460–399 B.C.E.), and Hippias of Elis (ca. 460–400 B.C.E.), consisted of urbane, socially responsible, professional teachers, who even held political offices. Protagoras greatly influenced Pericles, the developer of Athenian democracy; and Gorgias was his friend. They took a pragmatic view toward social conventions and religious worship. Although these leaders were skeptical about religion, they advised worship of the gods for socially prudent reasons as laws and religious beliefs and rituals are the "glue" that holds society together. Even though these are probably human inventions, they are useful and should be valued for that reason.

The younger generation, consisting of men like Callicles, Critias (Plato's uncle, ca. 480–403 B.C.E.), Antiphon, and Thrasymachus (the antagonist in the *Republic*), were much more hardened, not merely skeptical but cynical about religion, law, and moral conventions. For them, religion was a fraud, and conventional justice was simply a way of keeping the naturally superior from exercising their ability. Breaking with the older Sophists on attitude, it can be argued that they simply took the ideas of the older generation and developed their logical implications. However, some later philosophers believe that this view is incorrect. The views of the early Sophists, they would argue, do not entail the more cynical ones of the later group. Perhaps the hardening of the position is due to the violence and destructive character of the Peloponnesian War (431–404 B.C.E.), in which Sparta and her Peloponnesian allies defeated Athens. Whatever the cause, there was a change toward radical cynicism to the point where Thrasymachus called immorality a virtue and morality a vice. While recognizing these differences in attitude and the fact that the Sophists sometimes disagreed among themselves, it will, nevertheless, be useful to set forth a rough composite of their main ideas.

1. The Sophists were secularists, skeptical or atheistic on religious belief, often cynical of the use of religion as a mechanism for social control. The gods were invented to function as an invisible, all-seeing police force. The Sophist Critias wrote as follows:

> *There was once a time when human life was chaotic,*
> *Brutal and subservient to force,*
> *When there was neither a reward for being decent*
> *Or any restraint on evil men.*
> *In consequence human beings*
> *Have enacted laws to be avengers*
> *So that justice might be ruler*
> *And keep violence in subjection;*
> *And if anybody did wrong he would be punished.*
> *After this, since the laws prevented people*
> *From doing violent deeds that could be seen,*
> *They committed them in secret, and it was then*
> *I think some man of clever well-compacted intellect*
> *Invented fear of the gods for mortal men so that*
> *It might be a kind of terror for wrongdoers*
> *Even if in secret they did or said or thought*
> *Some wrongful thing:*
> *Further to this he introduced the divine principle*
> *That there exists a spirit flourishing in life that*
> *Is free from decay,*
> *Hearing and seeing with its intelligence with supreme*
> *Power of thought, applying its vast faculties and*
> *Bearing a god-like nature, that will*
> *Hear everything said amongst mankind and see their*
> *Every act.*[1]

Thus, the institution of religion can be explained as an invention by those who would provide incentive for obeying the laws. However, as noted earlier, Sophists like Protagoras, who were not quite as cynical, advocated worship of the gods for social reasons.

2. The Sophists developed the art of *rhetoric*, the process of using language to persuade. Their chief tool was *eristics*, argument used to win debates, not to pursue truth, and aimed at defeat rather than enlightenment. Aristotle called eristics "dirty fighting in argument."[2] What was needed was cleverness and ready speech to sway the passions of the mob and citizens. The Sophists were justly accused of "making the worse argument seem better." Another rhetorical tool was *antilogic*, arguing by means of **contradictory** propositions, leading to an *aporia*, or dead end.

The Sophists taught their disciples to argue both sides of the case and showed that, regarding any act, it could be seen as good, bad, or indifferent.

3. The Sophists made education into a business; they were the first teachers to be paid for their services, charging fees for teaching "wisdom" and "virtue." Their key question was, Can virtue be taught? They answered that it could be taught and they were the ones skilled to teach it. Holding that virtue was relative to the culture, Protagoras taught that teachers and enlightened parents could train children to be good, law-abiding citizens. The laws and sanctions of society could also play a role.

4. The Sophists were pragmatists. They were not speculative, systematic, or concerned with cosmology as the pre-Socratic philosophers were. However, they took the joint, mutually exclusive conclusions of the pre-Socratic philosophers to show that the best minds could know virtually nothing of the nature of ultimate reality. Because knowledge is impossible, they embraced **skepticism** about ultimate reality and concentrated on that which is certain: success in business, politics, and the practical life is very satisfying; use common sense on a social and individual scale.

The Sophist Gorgias exemplifies this pragmatic attitude better than anyone. He said,

1. Nothing exists.
2. But if something does exist, it cannot be known.
3. But even if it can, it cannot be communicated.
4. Therefore: Live by appearances. Practice prudence. Be practical. Avoid idle speculation. Seek practical education—that which has an optimum payoff.

As one might expect, Gorgias taught rhetoric to the wealthy young men so that they might win political offices and court cases (which they could now confidently create; Sue Your Opponent if He Is Rich might have been their motto).

5. The Sophists believed that egoism was proper or natural. One must look out for oneself. Hence, manipulation of others is permitted. Callicles argued that Socrates was being either naive or disingenuous in holding that laws are objectively true. Essentially, nature teaches that the superior should exploit and rule the weaker.

6. The Sophists were moral relativists, even subjectivists, contending that each person is his or her own measure of truth, thus abandoning the notion of an independent reality apart from our consciousness. Truth is whatever we take it to be. Perhaps the greatest Sophist of all was Protagoras of Abdera, an exceptional man who was renowned for arguing either side of a legal case successfully. He gave us the "Hymn to Relativism":

Man is the measure of all things:
Both of things that are,
Man is the measure that they are,
And of the things that are not,
Man is the measure that they are not.

Protagoras was reacting against the distinction between sensation and thought, which was held by the Eleatics as well as Heraclitus. Sensations are private, but thought is public. One person's experience of the color green cannot be had by another, but both can understand the concept (thought) of green and can assent to the proposition that nothing green can be red. According to the Eleatics, the senses are untrustworthy, whereas thought, via reason, leads to truth, which is universal and public. Protagoras denied the objectivity of reason as well as the universality and public nature of truth. He subordinated thought under the same private world as is appropriate to sensation. Each person is his or her own measure or standard of what is true and false. What seems true to me is true. What seems true to you, though it contradicts what I believe, is true relative to you. In the same way, your pain is true for you, and my pain is truly painful for me. *All* opinions are true.

Similarly, in ethics, whatever I deem morally right for me is right for me, and whatever seems right for you is morally right for you. Actually, there are two types of ethical **relativism:** conventional and subjective ethical relativism. Some Sophists held conventionalism, and still others held subjectivism. *Conventionalism* states that the validity of moral principles depends on cultural approval. The conventional relativists were influenced by the diversity of customs in the ancient world. One such example is found in the Greek *Histories*, where Herodotus (ca. 485–430 B.C.E.) tells the story of how Darius, the king of Persia, once brought together some Callatians (Asian tribal people) and some Greeks. He asked the Callatians how they disposed of their deceased parents. They told how they ate the bodies of their dead parents. The Greeks, who cremated their parents, were horrified at such barbarous behavior. No amount of money could tempt them to do such an irreverent thing. Then Darius asked the Callatians, "What should I give you to burn the bodies of your fathers at their decease?" The Callatians were utterly horrified at such barbarous behavior and begged Darius to cease from such irreverent discourse. Herodotus concluded that "custom is the king o'er all."[3]

Sophists like Protagoras and Gorgias seem to have generally held this conventional sense of moral relativism, but sometimes the Sophists seem to be subjectivists, holding that virtue or the moral good is relative to individual perception. Like beauty, virtue is in the eye of the beholder. In this way, the Sophists anticipated contemporary moral relativists and subjectivists like Ernest Hemingway, who once wrote "What is moral is what you feel good after and what is immoral is what you feel bad after."[4]

To challenge the Sophists' reliance on rhetoric, their businesslike pragmatism, cynicism and relativism about values and morality, and egoism, Socrates came forth and declared war against the panoply of their ideas.

Socrates' Simple Moralist View of Human Nature: Knowledge Is Virtue

A dramatic turn occurs in philosophical inquiry under the influence of Socrates (470–399 B.C.E.). Before him, as we have seen, two intellectual groups dominated the Greek world, the cynical and egoistic Sophists and the speculative cosmologists, discussed in the last section. The big question asked by the Hylicists and other early cosmologists was, What is the nature of reality? Thales (585 B.C.E.) had taught that the ultimate stuff of the universe was water; Anaximander (547 B.C.E.), an infinite mixture; Anaximenes (520 B.C.E.), air; and Heraclitus (480 B.C.E.), fire. Parmenides (480 B.C.E.) and Zeno of Elea (460 B.C.E.) taught that the universe was a single, unmoving oneness, that all change was an illusion. Anaxagoras (460 B.C.E.) posited a pluralistic universe with four essential elements (fire, air, water, and earth) under the direction of a great universal Mind (*Nous*). Socrates rejected both the cynicism and crass pragmatism of the Sophists and the ethereal speculation of the cosmologists.

Socrates was born in 470 B.C.E. in Athens. His father was a stonecutter and his mother, a midwife. A stonecutter himself by profession, Socrates also served his city as a soldier. He was captivated by the philosophical quest. He spent his youth studying the philosophy of nature under the tutelage of Archelaus, the disciple of Anaxagoras, but abandoned the pursuit for a more pressing concern, a philosophy of human nature, specifically a concern for how we ought to live. Perhaps he was spurred on to this study by the Sophists, who claimed to make people wise or virtuous through their instruction. Perhaps Socrates saw that the problems that concerned the Sophists were the important issues but that they misunderstood them. They asked the right questions:—How should I live? What is virtue? How can I succeed in life?—but lacked the passionate and disinterested use of reason in the pursuit of truth, which is necessary in order to answer these questions. They seemed to accept an unexamined cynicism about higher truth in settling for shallow, relativist answers to these questions, substituting rhetoric for reason and oratory for logic. Socrates' genius was to transfer the rigorous truth-centered methods of scientific inquiry to questions of human nature and ethics. With him, ethical inquiry originates as a discipline worthy of regard. He is the father of moral philosophy. As Cicero said, "It was Socrates who first called philosophy down from the sky, set it in the cities and even introduced it into homes, and compelled it to consider life and morals, good and evil."[5]

What makes Socrates especially interesting with regard to ethics is that he apparently was an extraordinarily good person, one who was modest, wise, self-controlled, courageous, honest, and truly concerned about the well-being of others. The renowned hero Alcibiades (ca. 450–404 B.C.E.) confessed that Socrates defended his life on the battlefield and deserved the distinguished medal that he, Alcibiades, had won. During the Peloponnesian War, after the disastrous battle of Arginusae in 406 B.C.E., in which Athens paid for a naval victory by losing 25 ships and 4,000 men, the eight naval officers involved in the battle were tried for culpable negligence. Rather than being tried one by one in the presence of their accusers, they were condemned to death in absentia by a bloc vote. Socrates, at that time a member of the senate, risked his life by rendering a lone, courageous protest against this illegal verdict. A few years later (403 B.C.E.), after Athens had lost the Peloponnesian War and surrendered to Sparta, the violently reactionary Commission of Thirty, under the leadership of Critias, came to power in Athens. The commission forced the leading democrats to leave the city, executed some enemies and confiscated their property, and tried to implicate Socrates in their dealings. They sent him with four others to arrest one of the wealthy democrats, Leon of Salamis, whose property they planned to confiscate. While the other men obeyed, Socrates exercised civil disobedience and refused to be a part of these nefarious proceedings. He probably would have been executed as a traitor for this act had not a democratic revolution overthrown the oligarchy.

We learn a great deal about Socrates' character and professional activity in Plato's report of one of the most famous trials of all history (399 B.C.E.). Socrates was accused of religious heresy, that is, of not believing in the Olympian gods and of corrupting the youth. These were trumped-up charges. While Socrates, like most of the educated, did not believe in the Olympian pantheon but was a monotheist, there was no law mandating such orthodoxy. What was important was to observe the religious rituals and festivals of the city, and there is no evidence that Socrates went out of his way to disrupt these. With regard to the charge of corrupting the youth, Socrates was unfairly blamed for the bad behavior of his students, especially the betrayal by Alcibiades, who was responsible for the catastrophic defeat at the battle at Syracuse. It is closer to the truth that many of the leading citizens lost face before the youth of the city due to Socrates' relentless probing into their **value** system.

The opponents of Socrates, especially the moderate democrat Anytus, expected him to flee Athens, thus saving them the trouble of defending their charges; but instead, Socrates chose to stand trial and face the unjust charges. He told the jury of 500 that the real reason for his being brought to trial was his public ministry of trying to persuade his fellow citizens to place the care of their souls before the care of their fortunes. He sought wisdom and worked to get others to seek it too. In the process, he not only incurred poverty but also made powerful enemies.

This eventually led to his being put on trial for his life. His friend Chaerephon went to the sacred shrine of Delphi and asked the god Apollo whether there was anyone wiser than Socrates. The god answered through the priestess that no one was wiser than Socrates. When Chaerephon returned to Athens and reported this story, Socrates thought that there must be some mistake, so he proceeded to attempt to disprove the god's assertion. He went into the marketplace and began to quiz those citizens who had a reputation for wisdom, the civic leaders and politicians. Through a process of intense questioning, in which the answer to one question was followed by questions about the implications of that answer (which he immortalized as the "Socratic method"), he discovered that although these notables made great pretensions to wisdom, they possessed very little of it. Having exposed the ignorance of the leading citizens in front of the youth of the city, Socrates went to the poets and quizzed them on the meaning of their poetry. He discovered that while the poets were very gifted individuals, their own interpretations of their work were banal, not especially superior to the common person's insights. Leaving the poets enraged, he turned to the skilled craftsmen and questioned them on the nature of wisdom, only to discover that they pretended to have but really lacked wisdom. Perturbed by the results of his investigation, he reluctantly concluded that he was indeed wiser than any of these others, for while both he and they lacked wisdom, he had one advantage over them: they knew nothing but did not know that they knew nothing, while he knew nothing and knew that he knew nothing. "Neither of us knows anything of beauty or of goodness, but he thinks he knows something when he knows nothing, and I, if I know nothing, at least never suppose that I do. So it looks as though I really am a little wiser than he, just in so far as I do not imagine myself to know things about which I know nothing at all."[6]

One may detect the renowned "Socratic irony" in the narration of his ignorance, for Socrates certainly did think he knew something of the meaning of virtue—that virtue is knowledge and can be attained. Socrates tells the jury that the real goal of life is to perfect one's soul by becoming wise, so it is the quest for truth and understanding that should preoccupy us, not the quest for success, fame, or fortune. Really, the unexamined life is not worth living, implying that the examined life constitutes a worthwhile life.

Socrates was found guilty by a vote of 280 to 220. He was now expected to offer a penalty for his crime to match the prosecution's proposal of the death penalty. It was normal for the accused, at this point, to grovel before the jury, display his wife and children, and plead for mercy, lest the jury leave his children fatherless. Instead, Socrates refused to admit guilt and proposed as a fitting "penalty" that he be given free, deluxe meals at the Prytaneum, the dining hall of the Olympian and military heroes.

> And so the prosecution proposes death as the penalty. And what shall I propose on my part, O men of Athens? Clearly that which is my due. And what is my due? I who neglected my own affairs in order to persuade every man among you that he must seek virtue and wisdom before he looks to his private interests. What should be done to such a one? Surely some good thing. What would be a suitable reward for a poor man who is your benefactor? There can be no reward so fitting as maintenance in the Prytaneum, O men of Athens, a reward which he deserves far more than the citizen who won the prize at Olympia in the horse or chariot race.

At this display of insolence, the jury became infuriated and voted for the death penalty, 360 to 140. Eighty jurors who had voted that he was innocent now voted to execute him. Upon receiving the sentence, Socrates forgave his accusers; "I am not angry with my condemners, or with my accusers; they have done me no harm, although they did not mean to do me any good; and for this I may gently blame them."

While condemned to death and awaiting his execution, instead of taking a safe opportunity to escape, Socrates engaged in a discussion of civil disobedience and argued that it was proper for him to accept the decision of the court. Before his grieving, agonizing disciples, he dutifully drank the hemlock without a trace of repugnance and, thus, became the first philosophical martyr. Phaedo, a witness, summed up a consensus view of his followers: "Such was the end, Echecrates, of our friend, who was, I think, of all the men of our time, the best, the wisest, and the most just."[7]

Socrates' life was deeply committed to the pursuit of truth and moral goodness. Unlike the Sophists, he refused to take money for his services and carried on his pilgrimage at great personal and material sacrifice. The effect he had on others was phenomenal. Here is what the Greek hero Alcibiades said:

> When I listen to him my heart leaps up much more than in a corybantic dance, his words move me to tears. I see this happening to many others too. When I listened to Pericles and other fine orators, I thought: they speak well. But nothing like this happened to me, my soul was not thrown into turmoil. I was not enraged at myself for living so like a slave. But this Marsyas* has often put me into a state where I felt that the life I lived was not worth living. He is the only man who ever made me feel ashamed.[8]

Socrates' Moral Philosophy: Virtue Is Knowledge

What were the distinguishing features of Socrates' ethics? What exactly did he believe about the good life? We can set forth five theses that he held.

1. Care for the soul is all that matters.
2. Self-knowledge is a prerequisite for the good life.
3. Virtue is knowledge (no such thing as weakness of will; evil is ignorance).
4. The invincibility of goodness. The Good is good for you, and the Bad is bad for you.
5. The autonomy of ethics. To the dilemma set forth in the Euthyphro, is the Good good because God chooses it, or does God choose the Good because it is good? Socrates answers that God chooses it because it is good.

Let us elaborate these theses. We begin by examining the first two.

1/2. Care for the soul (or inner self) is all that matters and Self-knowledge is a prerequisite for the good life. Socrates asks us the same question as Jesus asks in the Gospel of Matthew: "What good would it do to gain the whole world and lose my own soul?" What good is knowledge of the heavens if I am unhappy or spiritually diseased or in despair? What good is it to live in a perfect society if I see no value in life itself or in my life? The one thing necessary is spiritual or psychological health. We need to discover the right sort of regimen to follow in order to promote excellence of soul. However, this entails that we understand what the soul is. We need to scrutinize our values, measuring our lives by the highest possible standards. The unexamined life is not worth living.

How can we know the soul? Such knowledge comes, not necessarily through introspection, but by understanding its function. Just as the function of a knife is to

---

Marsyas: A satyr (a man with horns who was a goat from the waist down) who challenged Apollo to a flute-playing contest, lost, and was punished by being flayed alive.

cut and the function of a ruler is to rule, the function of the soul is to attain virtue, to perfect itself in goodness and truth, or, as Socrates says in Plato's *Phaedo*, to prepare for death. To purify one's soul through the attainment of wisdom so that the soul will enter the next life worthy of blessedness is the function of philosophy.

> [As] a craftsman can only do good work if he is in command of his tools and can guide them as he wishes, an accomplishment which demands knowledge and practice, similarly life can only be lived well if the soul is in command of the body.[9]

This meant purely and simply that in a properly ordered life, intelligence is in complete control of the senses and emotions. Its proper virtues are wisdom, thought, and truth. This identification of the psyche with the self and the self with the reason might be said to have roots both in Ionian scientific thought and in Pythagoreanism, yet there was certainly novelty in Socrates' development of it.

3. Virtue is knowledge. Self-knowledge is a prerequisite for the good life. One cannot tend, care, or improve anything without knowing its nature. Knowing how must be preceded by knowing what. To know the good is tantamount to trying to do the good, for everyone wants to succeed, to flourish, and to be happy, and goodness is good for us. Vice is simply the product of ignorance. Evil people simply do not know what is in their interest and so think that they are harming others when they are mainly harming themselves. No wise person would ever do evil voluntarily.

Socratic ethics are thoroughly intellectualist. To know the good is to do the good. There is no place for weakness of will. Evil is ignorance. "My own opinion is more or less this: no wise man believes that anyone sins willingly or willingly perpetuates any base or evil act; they know very well that every base or evil action is committed involuntarily."[10] Aristotle tells us that Socrates believed that the virtues are sciences, that doing well was analogous to knowing the truth of mathematics.

> Socrates believed that knowledge of virtue was the final aim, and he inquired what justice is, and what courage and every other kind of virtue. This was reasonable in view of his conviction that all the virtues were sciences, so that to know justice was at the same time to be just; for as soon as we have learned geometry and architecture we are architects and geometricians. For this reason he inquired what virtue is, but not how or from what it is acquired.[11]

Aristotle goes on to point out that while this relationship of knowing to being is true of the theoretical sciences, it is not so with the productive sciences, where knowledge is only a means to a further end. For example, knowledge of medicine is necessary but not sufficient for health. Knowledge of the good state is necessary but not sufficient for producing the good state.

Again, Aristotle points out

> The effect of [Socrates'] making the virtues into branches of knowledge was to eliminate the irrational part of the soul, and with it emotion and moral character. So his

treatment of virtue was in this respect mistaken. After him Plato, rightly enough, divided the soul into the rational and irrational parts and explained the appropriate virtues of each.[12]

We are more likely to agree with Euripides' infamous Medea that sometimes people act against what they know to be good ("Evil be thou my good") and with St. Paul, that sometimes people suffer weakness of will and do not do the good that they would but the evil that they would not (Rom. 7:19f).

Furthermore, Aristotle points out there is something deterministic about the Socratic theory of virtue:

> Socrates claimed that it is not in our power to be worthy or worthless men. If, he said, you were to ask anyone whether he would like to be just or unjust, no one would choose injustice, and it is the same with courage and cowardice and the other virtues. Evidently any who are vicious will not be vicious voluntarily. Neither, in consequence, will they be voluntarily virtuous.[13]

So what is the point of exhortation to seek the truth and the good if it is all determined, if we cannot help being virtuous or vicious?

It may well be that Socrates, the consummate rationalist, is harmed here by his own rationality. He apparently really would always choose according to the dictates of reason. He may have lacked a substantial degree of irrationality in his soul, and this may have blinded him to the fact that most people are less fortunate and that weakness of will and evil do exist.

4. The invincibility of goodness. You cannot harm the good person, but in trying to harm the other you harm yourself. The Good is good for you, and the Bad is bad for you. The classic illustrations of this are found in the second book of the *Republic,* the story of Gyges' ring and the thought experiment of the two men, the seemingly bad good man who suffers injustice and the seemingly good bad man who enjoys the fruits of the virtuous. Socrates argues that, in spite of all appearances, the tortured virtuous man is really better off than the apparently happy evil man, for the former has a healthy soul and the latter, a sick soul. Since it is the soul that truly defines our state of being, we can conclude that it always is better to suffer evil than to do evil!

This argument has been criticized, for unless there is an afterlife where a just reckoning takes place, it is hard to see why anyone should choose a state of suffering just because of some theoretical notion of spiritual health—one that has no actual benefit. Since Socrates does not rely on religion to sustain his conclusion, it seems implausible. Nonetheless, he may be right in showing that virtue is a necessary condition for a fully flourishing life. It simply is not sufficient for happiness. Bad things happen to good people and produce tragedy.

5. The autonomy of ethics. To the dilemma set forth in the dialogue *Euthyphro*— is the Good good because God chooses it or does God choose the Good because it is good?—Socrates implies that God chooses it because it is good. Socratic ethics lack a transcendental dimension. If there is an afterlife, well and good, it is icing

on the cake; but it is not necessary for the justification of morality. Goodness has to do with the proper functioning of the soul and can be discovered through reason alone. There is no need for revelation, and if there are gods, they too must obey the moral law and keep their souls pure through virtuous living. There is not even a hint that religion helps to motivate people to virtuous living. Goodness is its own reward, and it is obviously so to anyone who knows what virtue is and how the soul functions. Religion is a fifth wheel, useless in the moral domain. The charge Meletus brought against Socrates at his trial, that he did not worship the gods of the city, was not without some foundation. The gods certainly played no role in his moral theory.

We can sum up Socratic ethics by saying that it is based on a knowledge of human nature and proper functioning; that the self has a **telos,** or purpose, that involves living virtuously (i.e., wisely and justly); that happiness is predicated on proper functioning, hence on living virtuously; that knowing the good necessarily results in doing the good; and that we do not need religion to inform us of the good or to motivate us to be virtuous.

Socrates' theory is programmatic. It is not hard to see how it might be modified in order to meet some telling objections. What's more, it has an existential thrust that is impressive. Here is a man who lived his ethic! Socrates not only sought the true and the good with all his heart but also displayed incredible endurance and self-control in that pursuit and in living within the light that he had.

Summary

The Sophists arose in 5th-century B.C.E. Athens in order to enable the emerging entrepreneurial class to succeed in litigation. They were cynics about truth and religion, relativists, pragmatists, egoists, and very successful at making money. Socrates appeared on the scene disillusioned with the speculations of the early cosmologist philosophers but possessed with their optimism and love of truth. He opposed the Sophists at every point, especially on their notions of moral relativism and egoism, and developed a simple idea of human nature as centered in the idea that virtue is knowledge. We have an innate, intuitive knowledge of moral truth. There is an omission of metaphysical claims in his dialogues, but he seems to hold to the autonomy of ethics; that is, one can discover the morally right thing to do by reason alone, apart from religion. He believed that goodness leads to the highest happiness.

Study Questions

1. Who were the Sophists, and what was their view of human nature?

2. What does Protagoras mean by "Man is the measure of all things"? Analyze this statement. Does it mean that human beings have no essential nature?

3. What was Socrates' view of human nature?

4. Do you agree with Socrates on the invincibility of goodness, that no one can harm a good person?

Notes

1. H. Diels and W. Kranz, *Fragments of the Pre-Socratics*, 88b25. Quoted in J. M. Robinson, *An Introduction to Early Greek Philosophy* (Houghton Mifflin, 1968).
2. Aristotle, *Sophistic Elenchi*, 171b.
3. Herodotus, *Histories*, III. *The Persian Wars*, trans. G. Rawlinson (Modern Library, 1942).
4. Ernest Hemingway, *Death in the Afternoon* (Scribners, 1932), p. 4.
5. Quoted in W. K. C. Guthrie, *Socrates* (Cambridge University Press, 1971), p. 98.
6. Plato, *Apology*, trans. Benjamin Jowett (1889).
7. Ibid.
8. Plato, *Symposium*, trans. W. Hamilton (Penguin Books, 1951), p. 101.
9. Plato, *Phaedo*, trans. Benjamin Jowett (1889).
10. Plato, *Protagoras*, 345d.
11. Aristotle, *Eudemian Ethics*, 1216b.
12. Aristotle, *Magna Moralia*, 1182a.
13. Aristotle, *Magna Moralia*, 1187a.

For Further Reading

Brumbaugh, Robert, *The Philosophers of Greece* (SUNY Press, 1981). An easy-to-read, yet philosophically rich survey of classical Greek philosophy.

Guthrie, W. K. C., *Socrates* (Cambridge University Press, 1971). A clear, accessible, scholarly work of the first order, which has influenced me greatly.

Guthrie, W. K. C., *The Sophists* (Cambridge University Press, 1971). A clear, comprehensive, and scholarly book.

Kerferd, G. B., *The Sophistic Movement* (Cambridge University Press, 1981). A cogently argued contemporary study, challenging many of the standard views about the Sophists.

Plato, *Apology, Euthyphro, Crito, Protagoras, Gorgias, Republic,* and *Phaedo* are especially important for a firsthand account of Socrates.

Stace, W. T., *A Critical History of Greek Philosophy* (St. Martin's Press, 1967). Chapters 9 and 10 are especially relevant for this chapter.

Stone, I. F., *The Trial of Socrates* (Little, Brown, 1988). A provocative investigative probe into the causes of the downfall of Socrates.

Vlastos, Gregory, *Socrates: Ironist and Moral Philosopher* (Cornell University Press, 1991). A brilliant work by the best Plato scholar the U.S.A. has produced.

CHAPTER 3

Plato's Theory of Human Nature

The safest general characterization of the European philosophical tradition is that it consists of a series of footnotes to Plato. *(Alfred North Whitehead,* Process and Reality)[1]

Plato (427–347 B.C.E.) is generally recognized as the father of philosophy, the first systematic metaphysician and epistemologist, the first philosopher to set forth a comprehensive treatment of the entire domain of philosophy from ontology to ethics and aesthetics. He was born into an Athenian aristocratic family during the Periclean Golden Age of Greek democracy. During most of his life, Athens was at war with Sparta, the Greek city-state to the south. He was Socrates' disciple, who systematized and developed his teacher's ideas; he founded the first university and school of philosophy (the Academy in Athens). He was Aristotle's teacher and an advisor to emperors. His goal was to found an ideal state where philosophers ruled with justice. Among his important works are the *Republic, Phaedo, Meno,* and *Phaedrus,* which will be examined in this chapter. Most of his books are dialogues in which Socrates is the key spokesman and interlocutor, who seeks an understanding of difficult concepts. Virtually every issue discussed in the history of philosophy is cogently discussed in Plato's dialogues. In the early dialogues, such as the *Apology* and *Crito,* Plato may be reporting Socrates' own thoughts; but as Plato developed his own philosophy, he continued to use Socrates as his mouthpiece.

The Theory of Forms

What do all triangles or all green objects have in common? Triangles come in different shapes and sizes. It is true that all triangles are closed plain figures with three sides and three angles adding up to 180 degrees, but the sides may be different sizes and the shape of the triangle may be isosceles or scalene. Even before we can articulate the definition of a triangle, we seem to know one when we see it. Regarding green objects, we cannot even define their common property—*green.* We cannot help a blind person understand what it is or even describe it to one who knows what green is. It is an unanalyzable simple property. All green things have this undefinable property in common. To the objection that we can define *green* by its place on the electromagnetic spectrum, a modern-day Platonist would respond that this is knowledge about *green* but not knowledge of *green* since if the construction of our retinas or visual centers in the brain were different, we would have a different phenomenal experience of *greenness*, even as color-blind people do.

Now let us go from perceptual objects (e.g., triangles, colors, chairs, and tables) to abstract ideas (e.g., equality, justice, beauty, goodness, and friendship). What do all exemplars of each of these properties have in common? Plato's Theory of Forms (sometimes referred to as his theory of Ideas) seeks to give us a satisfactory answer to this question. They have an unanalyzable, unperceived, simple, eternal form in common: the Equal, Justice itself, the Beautiful, the Good, and so on.

Aristotle tells us how Plato first came upon this theory:

The Theory of Forms occurred to Plato because he was persuaded of the truth of Heraclitus' doctrine that all things accessible to the senses are always in a state of flux, so that if knowledge or thought is to have an object there must besides things accessible to the senses be certain other entities which persist; for there is no knowledge of things which are in a state of flux. Socrates occupied himself with the moral virtues, and was the first to look for general definitions in this area. There are two things which may fairly be ascribed to Socrates, arguments by analogy and general definitions, both of which are concerned with the starting point of knowledge. But whereas Socrates made neither the universal nor the definition exist separately, others gave them a separate existence and this was the sort of thing to which they gave the name of forms. So for them it followed by almost the same argument that there are forms for everything to which general words apply.[2]

Whereas Socrates sought clear definitions of concepts in order to have a common basis for discussion (how can we even settle on an understanding of what a "just society" will be if we have different definitions of *justice?*), Plato went beyond verbal definitions and posited a comprehensive theory of reality.

According to Plato, every significant word (noun, adjective, and verb) and thing partakes of and derives its identity from a Form, or Forms. The Forms are single, common to all objects and abstract terms, perfect as the particulars or exemplars are not, independent of any particulars but their cause, having objective existence (they are the truly real, while particulars are only apparently so). While independent of the human mind, they are intelligible and can be known by the mind alone and not by sense experience. The Forms are a divine, eternal, simple, indissoluble, unchanging, and self-subsisting reality, existing outside space and time. They are the cause of all that is. Here is a key passage from Plato's *Phaedo*, in which Socrates is instructing two disciples, Cebes and Simmias.

SOCRATES: Well what I mean is this. As I am going to try to explain to you the theory of causation which I have worked out myself, I propose to make a fresh start from those principles of mine which you know so well—that is, I am assuming the existence of absolute Beauty, Goodness, Greatness and all the rest of the Forms. If you grant my assumption and admit that they exist, I hope with their help to explain causation to you, and to find a proof that the soul is immortal.

CEBES: Certainly I grant it. You need not lose any time in drawing your conclusion.

SOCRATES: Then consider the next, and see whether you share my opinion. It seems to me that whatever else beauty is apart from the Beautiful itself, it is beautiful because and only because it partakes in the Beautiful. Do you accept this kind of causality?

CEBES: Yes, I do.

SOCRATES: Well, now, that is as much as I can understand, for I cannot understand these other ingenious theories of causation. If anyone tells me that what makes something beautiful is its having a gorgeous color or shape or any other such property, I dismiss these explanations, for I find them confusing. I simply cling to the explanation that the one thing that makes that object beautiful is the presence in it or association with it, in whatever way the relation comes about, of the Beautiful. All beautiful things become beautiful through the Beautiful. For this seems to me the safest answer to give to myself and to other people, and if I cling to this I cannot fall. Do you agree?

CEBES: I do.

SOCRATES: Then is it also through Largeness that large things are large and larger things larger, and by Smallness that smaller things are smaller?

CEBES: Yes.

SOCRATES: Suppose next that we add one to one. You would surely not say that the cause of our getting two is the addition, or in the case of a divided unit, the division? You would say that you know no other way in which an object can come into existence than by participating in the reality peculiar to its appropriate universal, and that in the cases which I have mentioned you recognize no other cause for the coming into being of two than participation in duality, and that whatever is to become two must participate in this, and whatever is to become one must participate in unity. You would dismiss these divisions and additions and other such niceties, leaving them for persons wiser than yourself to use in their explanations, while you, being nervous of your own shadow, as the saying goes, and of your inexperience, would hold fast to the security of your hypothesis and make your answer accordingly. If anyone should fasten upon the hypothesis itself, you would disregard him and refuse to answer until you could consider whether its consequences were mutually consistent or not.[3]

Plato's theory of the forms is an instance of the idea of the *One* and the *Many*. What do the *many* similar things have in common? The *one* Form. All beautiful things have in common participation in the Form of the Beautiful; all good things have in common participation in the Form of the Good.

Plato's Theory of Recollection and A Priori Knowledge

In the dialogue *Meno*, Plato, through his spokesman Socrates, seeks to prove that we are born with innate ideas of the Forms. The dialogue begins with Meno raising a puzzle about learning: How do you know when you have found the answer to a question you are asking? Either *(1)* you do not know the answer and so will not know when you have found it or *(2)* you already know the answer, in which case why make an inquiry in the first place? Socrates sets about to solve this riddle about the impossibility of learning through the theory of recollection of knowledge. The specific question Meno raises is whether virtue can be taught, but the question goes beyond virtue. How can we know any **metaphysical** truth?

Almost everyone admits that if we know anything at all, we know truths about the world—that is, how it appears to us—as well as some truths about the way the world really is. For example, I know that some objects move and that I am now typing this paragraph; but the question is, Are there also other types of knowledge not dependent on our experience of the world? Do we have innate knowledge or ideas prior to experience? Can we know necessary truths apart from observation? Is it possible to have knowledge of what is beyond empirical reality: God, the soul, free will, moral truths?

The issue was first formulated in Plato's dialogue *Meno.* Meno asks Socrates whether or not virtue can be taught. How do people come to know what virtue is? Socrates replies that he does not even know what virtue is. The following exchange takes place:

> **MENO:** How will you look for it, Socrates, when you do not know at all what it is? How will you aim to search for something you do not know at all? If you should meet with it, how will you know that this is the thing that you did not know?
>
> **SOCRATES:** I know what you want to say, Meno. Do you realize what a debater's argument you are bringing up, that a man cannot search either for what he knows or for what he does not know? He cannot search for what he knows—since he knows it, there is no need to search—nor for what he does not know, for he does not know what to look for.[4]

Socrates then calls Meno's uneducated slave and, drawing a square in the sand, asks the boy to try to double the area of the figure. Through a process of questions and answers in which the boy consults his own unschooled understanding, he eventually performs this feat. He seems to have "brought up knowledge from within."

> **SOCRATES:** Do you observe, Meno, that I am not teaching the boy anything, but only asking him questions; and now he fancies that he knows how long a line is necessary in order to produce a figure of eight square feet; does he not?
>
> **MENO:** Yes.
>
> **SOCRATES:** Do you see what advances he has made in his power of recollection? Were not all these answers given out of his own head? . . .
> Then he who does not know may still have true notions of what he does not know?
>
> **MENO:** He has.
>
> **SOCRATES:** And this spontaneous recovery of knowledge in him is recollection?
>
> **MENO:** True.[5]

The only explanation, argues Plato, of how the boy was able to do geometry is that he already possessed knowledge of geometry in his soul. He must, then, have a soul that existed before his present life and that somehow learned geometry. It follows that the soul must be separate from the body in which it is contained. One has to awaken the soul to knowledge, which is already hidden in the soul, by putting question, making what is implicit explicit. Socrates likens his method to that of a midwife who induces labor in a pregnant woman: he induces intellectual labor in a soul pregnant with knowledge. This is how Socrates answers Meno's question about how it is possible for virtue to be taught: we can teach virtue only by causing our auditors to recollect what they have forgotten about the Good.

According to Plato, the bridge between the World of Being and the World of Becoming is constructed of *innate ideas*. He held, as we have seen, that learning is really a recollecting of what we learned in a previous existence. The soul, which is immortal, has been born many times and has had a single view of the truth:

> The soul having seen all things that exist, whether in this world or in the world below, has knowledge of them all; and it is no wonder that she should be able to remember all that she ever knew about virtue and about everything; for as all nature is akin, and the soul has learned all things, there is no difficulty in her eliciting, or as men say learning, out of a single recollection all the rest.[6]

In coming into existence, the soul has forgotten all the essential truths of reality that she had learned. The educator should be a spiritual midwife who stimulates the labors of the soul, enabling a person to recall what he or she really possesses but has forgotten.

Plato thought that all knowledge was **a priori** (literally "that which is prior or first")—knowledge one has independently of sense experience—as opposed to **a posteriori** ("that which is posterior")—contingent, empirical knowledge, which comes to us from experience through the five senses. Ordinary empirical beliefs, according to Plato, unless they are related to the Forms, are not knowledge since they are related to unstable appearances. An example of a priori knowledge is the mathematical equation $5 + 7 = 12$. One does not have to appeal to experience in order to see that this equation is true. Experience, as in the case of Meno's slave, may be necessary in eliciting such knowledge; but once made active, the soul is able to recall it without aid of the senses.

The doctrine of Innate Ideas was held by a large number of philosophers after Plato, through the Middle Ages down to René Descartes (1596–1650) and Gottfried Leibniz (1646–1716), who gave it a Christian interpretation. For Descartes, the soul is not immortal. It does not have a previous existence, though it is everlasting; it will live on forever once it is created by God. Unlike Plato, Descartes did not believe that the soul is born with knowledge of all essential truths but only certain ones. The "natural light of reason" yields substantive metaphysical truths to those who use their faculties correctly. The Christian existentialist Søren Kierkegaard (1813–1855) held that we have innate knowledge of God's existence, free will, and immortality. Locke and the empiricists deny the doctrine of innate ideas altogether.

So what is Plato's answer to the question set forth in the puzzle mentioned at the beginning of this reading, How is learning possible? It is this: we possess innate knowledge of the Forms. Learning consists in having a suitable guide, a teacher, to bring out the best in us, to question and stimulate us like a midwife inducing labor, until at last we give birth to knowledge. The teacher has no truths of his or her own to impart but helps us to recover knowledge that we must have learned in a previous existence.

Is Plato correct? How good is Socrates' argument in this dialogue? Has he proven his point? Has the slave recollected knowledge that he had learned in a previous existence but forgotten? Whatever the answer, one thing is clear: Plato believed that we were immortal and in a previous existence had knowledge of the Forms, which we forgot in coming into worldly existence. The role of philosophy is to challenge us, stirring up the soul in the right way so that we regain our memory of the truth. Thus, we ascend to the ecstasy of the truth, of knowledge.

The Ascent to Knowledge

The ascent to knowledge of the highest Forms is the theme of Plato's great dialogue, the *Republic*. While this work is about justice in the soul (the microcosm) and the city (the macrocosm), it is the fullest description of Plato's theory of human nature, focusing on the role of reason and the quest for knowledge as our proper purpose in life. In the *Republic,* Plato distinguishes two possible approaches to knowledge: sense perception and reason. We may call these the *empirical* way and the *rational* way. Sense perception has as its object the fleeting world of particular objects, which appear differently at different times. Hence, it is an unstable relationship, yielding only fallible opinion, appearances but not reality, not knowledge, the ultimate Truth. Reason, however, grasps that which is absolute, unchanging, and universal—the Forms (or Ideas, as they are sometimes called). Sense perception causes us to see particular triangles, horses, chairs, and people; but reason gives us understanding of the universal triangle, horse, chair, and person. Sense perception may be the starting point for knowledge, but it can never itself bring us to the realm of reality, the world of being. By itself, sense perception leaves us in the realm of appearances, in the world of becoming.

> As for man who believes in beautiful things, but does not believe in Beauty itself nor is able to follow if one leads him to the understanding of it—do you think his life is real or a dream? Is it not a dream? For whether a man be asleep or awake, is it not dream-like to mistake the image for the real thing?[7]

According to Plato, the role of the philosopher is to use the world of sense perception in order to lead the soul out of the dreamlike state of becoming and into the real world of being.

Justice and Human Nature

Is the choice of a moral way of life a rational or an arbitrary one? In book 2 of the *Republic*, Plato's brother, Glaucon, asks Socrates whether justice, or moral goodness, is something that is only a necessary evil. That is, he wants to know whether it would be better if we could have complete freedom to indulge ourselves as we wish or whether, since others could do the same, it would be better to compromise and limit our acquisitive instincts. Glaucon tells the story of a shepherd named Gyges who comes upon a ring that at his behest makes him invisible. Gyges uses it to escape the external sanctions of society, its laws and censure, and to serve his greed to the fullest. He kills the king, seduces his wife, and becomes king himself. Glaucon asks whether we all would not do likewise.

> Suppose now that there were two such magic rings, and the just put on one of them and the unjust the other, no man can be imagined to be of such an iron nature that he would stand fast in justice. No man would keep his hands off what was not his own when he could safely take what he liked out of the market, or go into houses and lie with any one at his pleasure, or kill or release from prison whom he would, and in all respects be like a God among men. Then the actions of the just would be as the actions of the unjust; they would both come at last to the same point.[8]

Glaucon is not finished with his thought-experiment. If we are to make a case for the absolute superiority of justice over injustice, we need to be able to explain why we should choose justice over injustice even when all appearances lead to the contrary conclusion. Imagine two brothers, one utterly corrupt but seemingly moral so that everyone praises his character and admires him as a paragon of virtue. He thrives in the city, marries a beautiful woman of a wealthy family, and gives his children the best education possible. He has all the right friends, associates, and business contacts one could wish. He is a paragon of wealth and success. He is the successful egotist who appears to be a moral saint. The other brother is unimpeachably honest but has an undeserved reputation for dishonesty. He is despised and suffers as though he were the exact opposite of what he really is. He will be "whipped, stretched on the rack, imprisoned, have his eyes burnt out, and, after suffering every kind of evil, he will be impaled and realize that one should not want to be just but to appear so."[9]

The question put to Socrates is, Why be moral? Isn't it better to be immoral with success than moral with failure? Isn't the true nature of humans **egotism,** the unremitting, selfish striving for happiness and success and isn't this obtained by manipulation and deceit? Since the sanctions involved in getting caught being immoral are so bad and we do not want others to act immorally against us, we have to compromise and act minimally moral as a lesser evil.

Socrates begins his long response to Glaucon's question by suggesting that they discover the nature of justice in the city and then apply it to the individual. Just as a person with weak eyes would rather read a book with large print than one with small print, so we creatures with weak philosophical sight may need to find justice in the city (the large) before we can locate it in the individual (the small).

Plato assumes that there is an organic unity in the state, seeing the state "not as a piece of political machinery, but as a political person with a life and character of its own."[10] That is, there is an isomorphism between the state and the individual soul. The thesis has aesthetic appeal and some explanatory force. It also complies with **Occam's razor,** offering one set of laws as an explanation for two sets of phenomena instead of two sets of laws.

Turning then to the city or state, Socrates hypothesizes that the city comes about because people realize that they are not self-sufficient but lack many necessities.[11] They discover that they can share skills and resources with others and thus come out ahead. This city is wholly economic, being concerned with the procurement of food, housing, and clothing.

Some people are innately gifted in various ways. They should be encouraged to develop those skills. Each person should develop the skills he or she does best, thus promoting specialization. The specialist will be far more efficient at production of goods than the generalist and will be able to create a surplus, which will be exchanged for goods produced by other specialists. So the twin principles of Division of Labor and Specialization of Task will be adhered to in order to meet the needs of the community.

This simple bucolic community is adequate for our basic economic needs, but it lacks beauty and interest. Glaucon calls it "Pig City" because it is fit for pigs, not human beings, purely economic, utterly devoid of culture, education, or anything spiritual. "Man cannot live by bread alone" (to quote Jesus, Mt. 4:4). So Socrates introduces artists, musicians, poets, actors, dancers, barbers, teachers, cooks, hunters (the bucolic society was vegetarian). The community has now grown and needs more land and wealth. So the people will need guardians, an army, to defend their property. Plato compares these guardians to high-spirited pedigree dogs, "who are gentle to their own people but hard on the enemy."[12]

Soon, the guardian class is divided into two: (1) the guardians proper, or the rulers, and (2) the auxiliaries, or the defenders of the people, the army and police. These, in turn, are separate from the economic class, the workers. Further, these guardians must be the best naturally endowed people in the community. They must love wisdom and be unimpeachably honest, hating all falsehood. In order to nurture such leaders, a special type of education is required, implementing folk stories which show that virtue is noble and admirable. Plato advocates censorship of the works of Homer and Hesiod since they contain sections that are unedifying and would set a bad example for the young.

The guardians are to live simple lives, being trained in athletic excellence. Medicine is primarily preventive and restorative and should not be wasted on the elderly or chronically ill. If the sick cannot be restored to full vigor, they should not be treated. In the golden age of old, Socrates says, the ideal physician "did not consider the life of those who were inherently sick and unrestrained to be beneficial either to themselves or anyone else . . . even if they were richer than Midas."[13]

At this point, Plato suddenly introduces into the education of the guardians an element that seems contradictory to his whole program, the "noble lie." In order to socialize the future leaders properly, they are to be taught that they were fashioned and nurtured inside the earth and that the education that they were given was only a dream.

> All of you in the city are brothers . . . but the god who fashioned you mixed some gold in the nature of those capable of ruling because they are to be honored most, in those who are auxiliaries he has put silver, and he has put iron and bronze in those who are farmers and other workers. You will for the most part produce children like yourselves but, as you are all related, a silver child will occasionally be born from a golden parent, and vice versa, and all the others from each other.[14]

Socrates is rightly hesitant to declare this strategy, and one can only wonder what motivated Plato to include such a patently absurd notion. Not only does it violate the integrity of the guardian ideal as lovers of truth and wisdom, but it seems self-defeating. Even if it convinced the kindergarten pupils, how could the educators convince the pupils as they grew into adulthood with philosophical, analytical minds? Only gullible fools, and not philosopher kings, would even entertain such myths.

The ignoble "noble lie," at best, seems an inept way of making an otherwise plausible point. If we apply the principle of charity, which says we ought to give a philosopher the benefit of the most plausible interpretation before we criticize him or her, we must treat this maneuver as a metaphor or myth, a fictional story containing a universal truth, much like Christ's parables.[15] I interpret Plato as saying that although all human beings have a common humanity, being formed out of Mother Earth, they differ in natural endowments (types of metal); but since we cannot see the soul's qualities like we can metals, we must have a program of equal opportunity to bring the gold or silver or bronze or mud to the surface and make what is implicit explicit, what is potential actual. His system of rigorous holistic education is wholly meritocratic and meant to instantiate a program of equal opportunity. Women as well as men are to be given the same life chances so that the golden souls will reveal their true nature regardless of sex. Plato addresses the nature/nurture debate by saying that although we are primarily products of our hereditary endowments, our environment is a relevant factor for bringing our potential to realization. If you plant an acorn in the desert, you will not get an oak tree. Likewise, poor education can corrupt an otherwise noble soul. As we shall see in chapter 6, the Hindu doctrine of reincarnation serves the same purpose as Plato's myth. Our qualities in this life are a result of the rule of karma, of how we have behaved in a past life.

Our city is now established, and Socrates analyzes it in order to discover what justice is in "the large." The analysis shows that each of the three classes embodies one of the classic virtues: the economic class embodies self-control (*sophrosune*), the auxiliary class embodies courage (*andreia*), and the guardian class embodies wisdom (*sophia*). However, where is justice (*dikaiosune*)?

Justice, Socrates argues, is not associated with a single class but exists in the relationship of each class to its peculiar virtue and of the parts to the whole. When any one class is performing its peculiar virtue, "minding its own business," justice is present, and when all of the classes are exemplifying their virtues, justice emerges as the holistic virtue.[16]

Now we are ready to apply our analysis to the soul. There also are three parts to the soul: the intellectual part, the spirited part, and the emotional, or appetitive, part, which humans have in common with animals. The appetitive part (analogous to the working class), which has to do with bodily desires such as food, shelter, and sex, is located in the stomach and genitals. Like its analogue, the working class, its proper virtue is self-control. The proper spirited part, having to do with self-assertion and anger, is the analogue of the auxiliary class and is located in the breast. It seems to be endowed with reason and judgment, for it gives rise to shame and guilt at doing wrong.[17] Finally, the rational aspect of the soul, which corresponds to the guardian class, is located in the head. Just as the guardian class directs the ideal city, the rational mind (located in the head) should direct the individual.

> Justice does not lie in man's external actions, but with regard to that which is within and in the true sense concerns one's self, and the things of one's self. It means that a man must not suffer the principles in his soul to do each the work of some other and interfere and meddle with one another, but that he should dispose well of what in the true sense of the word is properly his own, and having first attained to self-mastery and beautiful order within himself, and having harmonized these three principles, the notes or intervals of three terms quite literally the lowest, the highest, and the mean, and all others there may be between them, and having linked and bound all three together and made of himself a unit, one man instead of many, self-controlled and in unison, he should then and then only turn to practice if he find aught to do either in the getting of wealth or the tendance of the body or it may be in political action or private business—in all such doings believing and naming the just and honorable action to be that which preserves and helps to produce this condition of soul, and wisdom the science that presides over such conduct, and believing and naming the unjust action to be that which ever tends to overthrow this spiritual constitution, and brutish ignorance to be the opinion that in turn presides over this.[18]

Justice, this state of psychic wholeness or spiritual health, is according to our nature. It is the way humans ought to function. Our essence is to be self-controlled, courageous, rational beings. In Book IX, Plato illustrates his theory with the metaphor of the many-headed beast, one head being human, another a lion. Those who believe that injustice is superior to justice are like farmers who feed the lion and neglect the human, while the righteous are like farmers who control the lion and feed the human. They are like those "who should care for the many-headed beast, raising and domesticating its tame heads, and preventing the wild ones from growing, making the lion's nature his partner and ally, and so raise them both to be friends to each other and to him."[19]

Socrates develops his argument to the place where he concludes that the just person reaches the apex of human happiness, whereas the unjust person, exemplified in the tyrant, sinks to the nadir of misery. Using mock arithmetic, he concludes that the just person is 729 times happier than the unjust person.

This is the response to Glaucon's challenging question: why be moral when one can succeed in being immoral? One can never succeed, no more than the wealthy sick person can be healthier than the healthy poor person. (King Midas nearly starved to death when he gained his wish that everything he touched turn to gold, including his food.) To be immoral is to have a sick, chaotic, distorted soul, whereas morality goes to the heart of our nature, a spiritual health. So the seemingly just but really unjust man, mentioned in Glaucon's thought-experiment, is far less happy than the seemingly unjust but really morally good man, even though he is poor and despised and languishes in prison.

Plato's analysis is nonsexist. He was the first philosopher to apply his analysis to women as well as men, calling for equal opportunity for all in order to produce the best rulers, regardless of gender. Both men and women ought to live a rational life, according to their nature. Because rationality was the major value in his system, he advocated the abolition of marriage (which, Plato thought, leaves too much to emotion and chance) and urged selective breeding in order to produce a superior class of leaders. He advocated a communal living arrangement, at least for the guardian class, so that they would not be compromised by considerations of property and wealth.

The Allegory of the Cave and the Meaning of Life

When we bring together Plato's theory of the ascent of the soul through philosophy to ultimate knowledge and wisdom, we see a combination of rationalism and mysticism. This is set forth in his most famous allegory, the Allegory of the Cave.

Imagine a group of prisoners who from infancy have had their necks and legs chained to posts within a dark cave. Behind them is a parapet or raised walkway on which people and animals travel to and fro, bearing diverse objects. Behind the parapet is a large fire that projects the shadows of the people, animals, and objects onto the wall in front of the prisoners. The shadows on the wall grow and diminish, move up and down and around, as the fire behind the objects wafts and wanes. However, the prisoners do not know that the shadows are merely appearances of real objects. They take the shadows for reality, talk about them as though they were real, name them, reidentify them, incorporate their knowledge of the various forms into their social life. Their lives are centered on the shadows.

Now imagine that someone tried to liberate one of the prisoners from the cave. At first, the prisoner kicked and screamed as he was forcibly moved from the only home and social milieu he had ever known. Being dragged through the cave against his will, he was, at last, taken outside, where the dazzling bright sun's light blinded him. Our prisoner cries to be allowed to return to his safe shelter in the cave, but the way is closed. Gradually, his eyes adjust to the sunlight, and he is able to see the beautifully colored flowers and wide spreading branches of oak trees, to hear the songs of birds, and to watch the play of animals. Delighted, his powers of sight increase until, at last, he is able to look at the bright sun itself and not be harmed.

Now his liberator, who has become his friend and teacher, instructs him to return to the cave to teach the other prisoners of the real world and to get them to give up their chains and journey upward to the sunlight. Our hero quakes with fear at such an ordeal, for he wants no part of that dark, dismal existence, preferring to enjoy the light of day to the dark of the abyss.

He is told that it is his duty to go, so he makes his way into the cave again, returns to his mates in chains, tells them that the shadows are merely illusions and that a real world of sunlight and beauty exists above outside the cave. As he is proclaiming this gospel, his former mates grab him, beat him for impugning their belief and value system, and put him to death. However, every now and then, the liberator comes back, drags one or two prisoners out of the cave against their will, teaches them to enjoy the light, and sends them back to instruct the slaves to appearances.

If we connect this allegory with Plato's idea of the ascent of the soul, we get a mystical understanding of the **telos** of human existence.

> But of the heaven which is above the heavens, no poet has ever sung nor ever will sing worthily. It is such as I will describe; for I must dare to speak the truth, when truth is my theme. There abides the very being with which true knowledge is concerned; the colorless, formless, intangible essence, visible only to mind, the pilot of the soul. The divine intelligence, being nurtured upon mind and pure knowledge, and the intelligence of every soul which is capable of receiving the food proper to it, rejoices at beholding reality, and once more gazing upon truth, is replenished and made glad, until the revolution of the worlds brings her round again to the same place. In the revolution she beholds justice, and temperance, and knowledge absolute, not in the form of generation or of relation, which men call existence, but knowledge absolute in existence absolute; and beholding the other true realities in like manner, and feasting upon them, she passes down into the inner heavens and the soul goes home.[20]

Ultimately, the purpose (*telos*) of life is to use philosophical reasoning to work our way back to immortality, to an ineffable knowledge of the Good.

Summary

Let us summarize what we have discussed. Plato's theory of human nature may be outlined into six major theses or ideas.

1. The Forms, most importantly the form of the Good, exist in the Ideal World. In the *Phaedo* and the *Republic*, Plato argues that a world of ideas really exists. For every basic type of thing we experience there is a form, for example, a form of Triangle, Equality, Chairness, Man. These forms exist apart from their object, and the objects participate in the forms. The highest form is that of the Good. This world is the *real* world, which we must ascend to if we are to know the Truth and find salvation from illusions and false values.

2. The body/mind dualism thesis. Our souls are our true essence or self, made for eternity, and separate from the body, which is fraught with change, decay, and

illusion. However, our souls are capable of a higher-order existence in the life of reason. Philosophy is a method of dying to the world and discovering the nature of reality and our true identity.[21]

3. The doctrine of immortality and the recollection of Innate Ideas. Our souls preexisted in a world of forms, but in coming into existence, we lost conscious knowledge of the Forms. The task of the philosopher is to be a midwife of the mind, stimulating labor so that the inquiring soul can recollect knowledge of the Forms and find salvation. In the dialogue *Meno*, Socrates illustrates this thesis by teaching an uneducated slave boy geometry. Similarly, in the *Republic*, Plato shows that we have a deep innate idea of justice. In other dialogues he shows that we have innate ideas of goodness, friendship, and immortality.

4. Reason must be our primary guide in life. We must follow reason wherever it leads. We must discipline ourselves to suppress the passions of emotion and concentrate on the form of the argument, seeking the truth above all. The Socratic method is one of putting questions so that the other person is forced to reason about the problem in question. Through rational discourse we can obtain the truth. The truth discovered in the *Crito* is that Socrates must accept his fate at the hands of Athenian law; in the *Phaedo*, that our souls are immortal; in the *Republic*, that justice consists of a holistic hierarchical arrangement of wisdom, courage, and self-control. After one has ascended via reason to a higher stage, deep intuition or a mystic vision takes place so that one beholds the Forms, the Good, and other truths (see 6 below).

5. Justice as the holistic harmony of the soul (and state). Justice in the soul is the harmony of wisdom, courage, and self-control and, similarly, in the state, the hierarchical arrangement of the guardians (representing the head and wisdom) over the auxiliaries (representing the heart and courage), who in turn are over the economic class (representing the stomach and genitals, whose virtue is obedience to the guardians and self-control). Justice in the soul is synonymous with moral goodness and equivalent to spiritual and psychological health, so it should be sought over material goods and social status. It is in our interest to be moral, as it is in our physical interest to be healthy; just as no rational person wants to be unhealthy, no rational person wants to be spiritually sick. Here, Plato has developed Socrates' insight (see chapter 2) that the good is good for you.

6. The mystical element in Plato's philosophy. As the Allegory of the Cave and the passage from *Phaedrus* show,[22] Plato thought that the rational quest for truth resulted in an ineffable vision of the Good. Reason takes us up the ladder, but the final ascent is a mystical experience in which we see the Good and are transformed by it. The human soul via rational discourse is capable of reaching the heavens, returning to its spiritual home, beholding the Form of the Good in inexpressible, ecstatic blessedness and beauty.

Study Questions

1. Explain Plato's theory of the Forms and its implications for his theory of human nature.

2. Explain Plato's idea of innate ideas.

3. What is the puzzle about learning that Meno describes? Why does it seem impossible to learn anything? What is Socrates' response to the puzzle? How do we learn, and why is learning possible?

4. What is Plato's theory of justice? How does it relate to human nature and political organization?

5. Evaluate Plato's theory of human nature.

6. When Socrates says that the Good is really good for you and that only ignorant people would do evil because it only harms them, is he implicitly appealing to a religious view of the world?

7. Examine the Allegory of the Cave and draw out its lessons.

Notes

1. Alfred North Whitehead, *Process and Reality* (1929; Harper Torchbooks, 1960, reprint), p. 63. Thelma Z. Lavine elaborates on this:

   Plato is the most celebrated, honored and revered of all the philosophers of the Western world. He lived in Athens twenty-four centuries ago, in the fourth century before Christ, and throughout history since then the praise of Plato has been expressed in figures of speech which compare with one another in their eloquence. He is said to be the greatest of the philosophers which Western civilization has produced; he is said to be the father of Western philosophy; the son of the god Apollo; a sublime dramatist and poet with a vision of beauty which enhances all human life; and a mystic who, before Christ or St. Paul, beheld a transcendent realm of goodness, love, and beauty; he is said to be the greatest of the moralists and social philosophers of all time. The British philosopher and mathematician Alfred North Whitehead said of him that the history of Western philosophy is only a series of footnotes to Plato. And the American poet and philosopher Ralph Waldo Emerson said of him, "Plato is Philosophy, and Philosophy is Plato," and also, "Out of Plato comes all things that are still written and debated among men of thought" (T. Z. Lavine, *From Socrates to Sartre* [Bantam Books, 1984], p. 9).

2. Aristotle, *Metaphysics,* 1078.
3. Plato, *Phaedo,* trans. Hugh Tredennick, in *Plato: The Collected Dialogues,* eds. Edith Hamilton and Huntington Cairns (Princeton University Press, 1961), pp. 100–101. I have slightly revised the translation for pedagogical reasons.
4. *Meno,* trans. W. A. Grube (Hackett, 1980).
5. Ibid.
6. Ibid.
7. R. C. Cross and A. D. Woozley, *Plato's Republic* (Macmillan, 1964), p. 76.
8. Ibid., BK2: 360b.
9. Ibid., 362a.
10. Ibid., p. 76.
11. Ibid., 369b.
12. Ibid., 375c.
13. Ibid., 408b.

14. Ibid., 415a.
15. See John H. Hollowell, "Plato and His Critics," *Journal of Politics,* vol. 27.2 (May 1965), p. 277, for this kind of interpretation.
16. R. C. Cross and A. D. Woozley, Plato's *Republic* (Macmillan, 1964), 433b.
17. Ibid., 439e.
18. Ibid., 443d.
19. Ibid., 589a.
20. *Phaedrus,* trans. W. A. Grube, 247c.
21. Note the similarity to St. Paul's teaching in Rom. 8:23: "For if you live according to the flesh you will die, but if by the spirit you put to death the deeds of the body you will live."
22. *Phaedrus,* trans. W. A. Grube, 247c.

For Further Reading

BY PLATO

The Dialogues of Plato, 4th ed., revised by D. J. Allan and H. E. Dale. (Oxford University Press, 1953). Jowett's translation is still among the best—literary and accurate. I have used this translation in the chapter.

Plato: The Collected Dialogues, eds. Edith Hamilton and Huntington Cairns. (Princeton University Press, 1982). This complete set of Plato's dialogues is the best single-volume collection of his works. The translations are typically excellent.

Plato's Republic, trans. G. M. A. Grube. (Hackett, 1980). This is the most accessible accurate translation available.

ABOUT PLATO

Annas, Julia, *An Introduction to Plato's Republic* (Oxford University Press, 1981). An accessible, scholarly commentary.

Cross, R. C. and A. D. Woozley, *Plato's Republic* (Macmillan, 1964). Still the best commentary on Plato's *Republic.*

Grube, G. M. A., *Plato's Thought* (Methuen, 1935). An insightful discussion of Plato's thought, especially of the Forms.

Ross, W. D., *Plato's Theory of Ideas* (Oxford University Press, 1951). This book traces the theory of the Forms from the early dialogues to the laws. A brilliant analysis.

Stace, W. T., *A Critical History of Greek Philosophy* (St. Martin's Press, 1967). Chapters 9 and 10 are especially relevant for this chapter.

Taylor, A. E., *Plato: The Man and His Work* (Methuen, 1950). A splendid exposition of the entire Platonic corpus.

White, Nicholas, *Plato: On Knowledge and Reality* (Hackett Publishing Co., 1976). A clear, cogent analysis.

ABOUT THE PERIOD

Jones, W. T., *The Classical Mind* (Harcourt, Brace, 1952). A helpful overview of the ancient Greeks and their culture.

Plato, *Phaedo*, trans. Hugh Tredennick in *Plato: The Collected Dialogues*, eds. Edith Hamilton and Huntington Cairns (Princeton University Press, 1961).

Plato, *Republic*, trans. Benjamin Jowett (Oxford University Press, 1896). I have edited the dialogue for pedagogical purposes.

Renault, Mary, *The Last of the Wine* (Pantheon Books, 1956). A novel depicting Athens in the days of Socrates.

CHAPTER 4

Aristotle's Theory of Human Nature

Reason is the true self of every person, since it is the supreme and better part. It will be strange, then, if he should choose not his own life, but some other's. . . . What is naturally proper to every creature is the highest and pleasantest for him. And so, to man, this will be the life of Reason, since Reason is, in the highest sense, a man's self. *(Aristotle,* Nicomachean Ethics, I.7)[1]

It is evident that the state is a creation of nature, and that man is by nature a political animal. *(Aristotle,* Politics, I.2)

Introduction

Aristotle (384–322 B.C.E.), Greek physician, biologist, tutor to Alexander the Great, and one of the most important philosophers who ever lived, wrote over 150 important treatises on every major subject in philosophy. He is the founder of formal logic, formalizing the major types of reasoning. Plato was Aristotle's teacher in the Academy, where Aristotle studied and taught for 20 years. When Plato passed him over in choosing his successor as president of the Academy, Aristotle broke from Plato and his school and moved to Macedonia, where he tutored the son of the king, a young man named Alexander, who would later become Alexander the Great. In 335 B.C.E., he returned to Athens to found a second university, the Lyceum. He was known as the peripatetic philosopher, for he taught while walking about. In 323 B.C.E., he was accused of blasphemy and called to trial. Rather than stand before a biased jury, he fled Athens, stating that he was fleeing "lest Athens should sin against philosophy twice," referring of course to the trial and execution of Socrates. He soon contracted an illness and died a year later, leaving behind a widow and two children.

Aristotle wrote brilliantly on virtually every philosophical topic. Unfortunately, most of his works are lost, including his dialogues, which were said to be eloquent. What we have are mostly his very technical works. They are a bit dry, technical, highly qualified, and intricately argued; but a careful reading usually pays high dividends. I will discuss his general orientation in comparison to Plato and examine his views of human nature, especially as they appear in his major work *Nicomachean Ethics* (hereafter abbreviated NE), written to his son Nicomachus. In addition to his ethics, I will consider his ideas on the good life and the ideal human being; but first a brief comparison with his teacher Plato is in order.

Plato and Aristotle

In Raphael's great painting *The School of Athens*, Plato and Aristotle stand together in the center of a group of philosophers, conversing, presumably about philosophy. Plato is pointing upward to the heavens, as if to say "That's where reality is." Aristotle has his hand flattened out before him, as if to counter his teacher, "No, reality is down here." Simply put, Plato was an idealist, who took mathematics as his model and believed in a transcendent reality, the Forms, governed by the form of the Good, whereas Aristotle was a realist, who took biology as his working model for philosophy and produced a functionalist account of human nature and all reality.

The relationship between Plato and Aristotle is complex. Antiochus of Ascalon, president of Plato's Academy three centuries after Plato's death, claimed that Plato and Aristotle held similar positions on ethics.[2]

There are similarities in their positions. Both Plato and Aristotle sought knowledge as a good in its own right. Both were teleologists in that they believed that all things had an ideal goal, which was their "good" or "final cause." In this they differ from modern science (nature knows no purposes), especially Darwinian evolution, where chance or random selection and survival of the fittest replace rational order. Aristotle believed in teleology because of the regularity displayed in generation, astronomy, and physical behavior (nature has unconscious purposes).

Both accepted a functionalist account of ethics as linked with politics, whose purpose is to produce good citizens in a flourishing society. Both saw reason as the essence of human nature (see epigram at the beginning of this chapter), and both held to a transcendent absolute. Plato's Form of the Good plays a roughly similar role as Aristotle's Unmoved Mover, who moves the world but is not Itself moved. Aristotle held that all souls are the form (or essence) of a body with one exception. There must be a pure intellect, which is perfect and able to cause the universe to go through its continuous cycles forever. It causes motion by attracting all things to itself, but it does not move. It is the Unmoved Mover. This is not a personal god but resembles Plato's Form of the Good in being the highest transcendent reality, the ultimate reason for the existence of the universe. Later Christian theologians like Thomas Aquinas (ca. 1224–1274 C.E.) would use Aristotle's doctrine to construct the Cosmological Argument for the existence of God.

Both Plato and Aristotle were rationalists who saw reason at the heart of the human essence. Both held that moral insight is not simply a function of logical reasoning but depends on a proper relationship between reason and deeper aspects of the soul, a type of deep intuitive judgment. Aristotle called this *phronesis*, a moral perception (NE, II.9).

However, the differences between Plato and Aristotle are enormous. Aristotle rejected Plato's notion of the Forms as divine patterns of all the types of things and relationships on earth as well as the ontological dualism that underlies Plato's philosophy.

1. Aristotle's main disagreement with Plato is over the theory of the Forms. Aristotle criticized it from various points of view: as a logician, he offered a different analysis of predication; as an ontologist and epistemologist, he argued that it is the concrete particular, not the universal or form, that is substance in the primary sense and that provides the starting point in our investigation of form.

2. As a proto-physicist, Aristotle pointed out that the separate and transcendent Forms are useless in accounting for change and coming into existence. Plato's Forms belong to the world of unchanging being, but the study of change involves the investigator of forms in the changing objects of the world of becoming. Aristotle shifted the focus from the study of pure, immutable being to physics, the study of nature (and natural change).

3. Whereas Plato viewed matter as evil and the mental as good and believed that humans had a soul that inhabited a material body, which in turn would be liberated from the body at death, Aristotle had no such metaphysical notions. The soul (*psyche*) is not a separate entity but the form of the person whose matter is the body. It is a function of the whole physical person. Reason is not a jewel in a corpse, as Plato held, but a distinguishing feature in a special kind of animal. The soul cannot exist without a material substratum. It follows that, whereas Plato believed in the immortality of the soul, Aristotle held that when the body died, so did the soul.

4. Aristotle also rejected Plato's theory of recollection and innate ideas and seemed uninterested, if not skeptical, about life after death. Whereas for Plato the Good is One, for Aristotle goodness is a functional concept, having to do with satisfying the **telos,** or purpose, of some natural or artificial being. Whereas for the Socratic Plato virtue is knowledge, for Aristotle one can know the good but fail to do it. For Socrates and Plato all evil is ignorance, but Aristotle accepted a notion of weakness of will, much like the theory found in St. Paul's account in Romans chapter 7 ("The evil that I would not, that I do and the good that I would do, that I do not"). Evil can be committed through being in the grip of an emotion even though you know you ought not do what you are about to do.

5. Finally, the two philosophers differed on the nature of the relation of virtue to happiness. Socrates and Plato viewed moral virtue as a necessary and sufficient condition for happiness so that even Socrates on the rack (a medieval torture device) is happy. The good person may be rejected, despised, tortured, ugly, sick, and poor but still be happy. Aristotle rejected such an idea as naive (NE, VII.13). Morality is a necessary but not sufficient condition for happiness. One also needs other external and internal goods for a completely good life. Externally, one needs moderate wealth, leisure, health, friends, a family, a well-managed state, good

looks, and good luck. Internally, one must have a good upbringing, practical wisdom, and self-control. Given Aristotle's emphasis on external goods, Socrates could not be considered happy.

Yet, for all their differences, the similarities remain equally impressive. Both Plato and Aristotle believed that it is the universal Form that is knowable and that the world as a whole (and natural change in particular) exhibits order and purpose. Aristotle demythologized Plato's otherworldly idealist metaphysics, but for both the universe manifests purposefulness (a goal-like structure or *telos*).

The Nature of Ethics

The main work where Aristotle's ethical theory is found is the *Nicomachean Ethics*, written to his son Nicomachus, who was still a small boy when Aristotle died in 322 B.C.E. at the age of 62. It has the format of a series of lectures, intended for the educated male minority of Athens.

As we noted, for Aristotle, humanity has an essence, or function. Just as it is the function of a doctor to cure the sick and restore health, the function of a ruler to govern society well, and the function of a knife to cut well, so it is the function of humans to use reason in pursuit of the good life (**eudaimonia**). The virtues indicate the kind of moral–political characteristics necessary for people to attain happiness.

Ethics for contemporary individuals is mainly a matter of right and wrong actions, of following principles of duty, such as the Ten Commandments discussed in chapter 1. However, for Aristotle, the case is different: ethics refers primarily to character, to virtue (*arête*). He is concerned with producing good citizens who are happy and who feel and act in ways consonant with good character. Whereas we might characterize a moral person as one who follows the right rules, making no mention of happiness, Aristotle would characterize him or her as one who is essentially happy, for the moral person exhibits excellence in the way he or she thinks and feels as well as acts. Whereas most modern ethical systems emphasize abstract principles, Aristotle emphasized character and human excellence, the **virtues,** hence the name **aretaic** (or virtue) **ethics.**

Whereas according to Kant (see chapter 8) and his followers, moral integrity consists in following rules for the correct reasons, for Aristotle the criterion for moral rightness is good character. The good person acts out of a set disposition to do the right act in the right way, at the right time, and for the right reason. If you want to know what the right thing to do is, find the good person and watch what he or she does. If you ask "How will I recognize the good person?" Aristotle would reply "You'll know him when you see him." Judgment lies in perception. Aristotle's reply seems circular, but we must remember that Aristotle was writing to his Athenian contemporaries, who already had a pretty clear idea of what a good person is. He supposed that his readers had been well brought up and had good character, judged by Athenian standards.

A Political Person

Like Plato before him, Aristotle saw ethics as a branch of political science, whose task is to produce good citizens. The virtues are simply those characteristics that enable individuals to live well in communities. In order to live well (i.e., achieve a state of happiness, *eudaimonia*), proper social institutions are necessary. Thus, the moral person is both the end and a necessary means to a flourishing political arrangement. Only the good state can produce good and happy people, and good people along with good laws are necessary for a well-governed state. Furthermore, the state must be actively engaged in moral education. "Legislators make the citizens good by forming habits in them" (NE, II.1). The legislator who fails to accomplish this task has failed in his task as a legislator.

Humans by nature are political animals. They are suited to developing their personalities, ranging from families and friendship to loose confederacies. So citizens must be actively engaged in social legislation. Good institutions and laws are necessary for personal happiness. The apolitical citizen is irresponsible. Exceptions to this degrading designation are philosophers, who, taking advantage of the well-governed state, devote all their time to contemplation (*theoria*); but these are rare beings.

We spoke of responsible citizens, but only a minority of Athenians were free citizens. Both Plato and Aristotle believed in aristocracy (from the Greek, *aristos*, "excellent"), rule of the best. They, like most of the Greeks, were meritocrats, advocating a hierarchical structure. As we saw in the last chapter, Plato believed that everyone should have an equal opportunity (males and females), but early on a caste system would separate children on the basis of ability. The golden-souled children would be separated from the silver-souled, bronze-souled, and iron-souled. Plato rejected democracy as an unjust distribution of offices, treating unequals (the rabble) as though they were equal to the excellent. As we would not allow just anyone to fly a 747 jet filled with people but only a trained, skilled pilot, we should not let the ignorant masses control the state.

Aristotle's inegalitarianism was even more pronounced than Plato's. He thought we could detect a class of inferior beings, large muscular men, who were fit only for manual labor. They are natural slaves. It is morally permissible for the highly rational to enslave the inferior.

> Where then there is such a difference as that between soul and body, or between men and animals (as in the case of those whose business is to use their body, and who can do nothing better), the lower sort are by nature slaves, and it is better for them as for all inferiors that they should be under the rule of a master. For he who can be, and therefore is, another's and he who participates in rational principle enough to apprehend, but not to have, such a principle, is a slave by nature. . . . Indeed the use made of slaves and of tame animals is not very different; for both with their bodies minister to the needs of life. Nature would like to distinguish between the bodies of freemen and slaves, making the one strong for servile labor, the other upright, and although useless for such services, useful for political life in the arts both of war and

peace. . . . It is manifest that there are classes of people of whom some are freemen and others slaves by nature; for these slavery is an institution both expedient and just.[3]

Aristotle thought that one could tell these natural slaves from their appearance and behavior. Rational people will treat them kindly, so it is in their interest to be ruled by superior people.

While all humans have a common form (reason), in most people recalcitrant matter prevents reason from ruling. Women, while being more rational than slaves, and children, being more material and less rational than men, are inferior to males. "Again, the male is by nature superior, and the female inferior; and the one rules, and the other is ruled; this principle, of necessity, extends to all mankind."[4] Their place is in the home, governing slaves and children just as men govern them. This is a law of nature.

Most people are worthless (those lacking deliberative ability), and some of these are natural slaves. Some are all right (they have some ability to engage in deliberation and are able to participate as citizens in the community). Only a few are excellent (the philosophers).

The Functionalist Account of Human Nature

For both Plato and Aristotle, to know what something is, is to know what it is used for, what it is meant to become—that is, what its function is. Like everything else, human beings have a distinct function, and some humans fulfill this function better than others. Since one's value is determined by his or her capacity to fulfill this function, some people are more valuable than others.

Presumably, however, to say that happiness is the chief good seems a platitude, and a clearer account of what it is is still desired. This might perhaps be given, if we could first ascertain the function of man. For just as for a flute-player, a sculptor, or any artist, and, in general, for all things that have a function or activity, the good and the "well" is thought to reside in the function, so would it seem to be for man, if he has a function. Have the carpenter, then, and the tanner certain functions or activities, and has man none? Is he naturally functionless? Or as eye, hand, foot, and in general each of the parts evidently has a function, may one lay it down that man similarly has a function apart from all these? What then can this be? Life seems to be common even to plants, but we are seeking what is peculiar to man. Let us exclude, therefore, the life of nutrition and growth. Next there would be a life of perception, but it also seems to be common even to the horse, the ox, and every animal. There remains, then, an active life of the element that has a rational principle (of this, one part has such a principle in the sense of being obedient to one, the other in the sense of possessing one and exercising thought); and as this too can be taken in two ways, we must state that life in the sense of activity is what we mean; for this seems to be the more proper sense of the term. Now if the function of man is an activity of soul in accordance with, or not without, rational principle, and if we say a so-and-so and a good so-and-so have a function which is the same in kind, e.g. a lyre-player and a good lyre-player, and so without qualification in all cases, eminence in respect of excellence being added to the function (for the function of a lyre-player is to play the lyre, and that of a good lyre-player is to do so well): if this is the case, and we state the function of man to be a certain kind of life, and this to be an activity or actions of the soul implying a rational principle, and the function of a good man to be the good and noble performance of these, and if any action is well performed when it is performed in accordance with the appropriate excellence: if this is the case, human good turns out to be activity of soul in conformity with excellence, and if there are more than one excellence, in conformity with the best and most complete. But we must add "in a complete life." For one swallow does not make a summer, nor does one day; and so too one day, or a short time, does not make a man blessed and happy. (NE, X.7, 1097b–1098a)

As we have noted, for Aristotle, all nature is teleological, purposive. Its function is to reach some definite predesigned *telos*. An acorn's function is to become an oak tree, and a fetus's function is to become an adult member of the species. All of the elements have proper functions: fire is to rise, earth is to settle, water is to rest on earth, and air to hover over earth. The knife's function is to cut, and a good knife is one that does this well. All social roles have functions; the carpenter is to build, the shoemaker is to create shoes, the teacher is to teach, the mother is to bear and raise children.

If we suppose that all humans have a function or essence, we must distinguish what our proper function is. For Aristotle it was via the *differentia* that species distinguished themselves. We need nutrition in order to grow, but that is not what distinguishes us from plants and animals. We have sensory capacity, but that is not our function as lower animals have that also. Only the ability to deliberate, to use reason in a practical and theoretical manner, makes us different from other animals: we are rational animals.

Reason is the true self of every person, since it is the supreme and better part. It will be strange, then, if he should choose not his own life, but some other's. . . . What is naturally proper to every creature is the highest and pleasantest for him. And so, to man, this will be the life of Reason, since Reason is, in the highest sense, a man's self. (NE, X.7)

Reason contributes to the human good on two levels: the practical and the theoretical. Practically, reason informs us as to the correct means to achieve our goals and steers us away from inappropriate means. Practical reason (*phronesis*) includes judicial, legislative, and executive aspects. The judicial (deliberative) aspect enables us to discern our ends and evaluate the necessary means to reach them. The legislative aspect results from the judicial aspect and sets forth rules of action. The executive capacity enables us to carry out our plans and avoid succumbing to emotions or weakness of will. For example, in pursuing a valuable college degree, the judicial first determines the worthiness of the goal (*telos*), the legislative sets about determining the best way to reach that goal, and the executive acts to reach it, rejecting detours and sidetracks.

Theoretically, reason is used to think logically about scientific and philosophical problems and to contemplate the nature of reality. Reason culminates in philosophical contemplation, which is the kind of life engaged in by the gods. The gods have rational form but not bodies (or emotions) and do nothing but contemplate. Humans have both material bodies and rational essences, so they can go in either direction, toward animal life or the life of the gods. When they are engaged in philosophical reflection, they become like gods.

> But such a life [of complete contemplation] would be too high for man; for it is not in so far as he is man that he will live so, but in so far as something divine is present in him; and by so much as this is superior to our composite nature is its activity superior to that which is the exercise of the other kind of virtue. If reason is divine, then, in comparison with man, the life according to it is divine in comparison with human life. But we must not follow those who advise us, being men, to think of human things, and, being mortal, of mortal things, but must, so far as we can, make ourselves immortal, and strain every nerve to live in accordance with the best thing in us; for even if it be small in bulk, much more does it in power and worth surpass everything. This would seem, too, to be each man himself, since it is the authoritative and better part of him. It would be strange, then, if he were to choose not the life of his self but that of something else. And what we said before will apply now; that which is proper to each thing is by nature best and most pleasant for each thing; for man, therefore, the life according to reason is best and pleasantest, since reason more than anything else is man. This life therefore is also the happiest. (NE, X.7)

What Is the Good Life?

Next, we ask, What kind of life is most worth living? Aristotle wrote long ago that what all people seek is happiness.

> There is very general agreement; for both the common person and people of superior refinement say that it is happiness, and identify living well and doing well with being happy; but with regard to what happiness is they differ, and the many do not give the same account as the wise. For the former think it is some plain and obvious thing, like pleasure, wealth or honor. (NE, I.4)

What is happiness? The field divides up among objectivists, subjectivists, and combination theorists. The objectivists, following Plato and Aristotle, distinguish happiness from pleasure and speak of a single ideal form of human nature; if we do not reach that ideal, then we have failed. Happiness (Greek *eudaimonia*, literally "good demon") is not merely a subjective state of pleasure or contentment but the kind of life we would all want to live if we understood our essential nature. Just as knives and forks and wheels have functions, so do species, including the human species. Our function (sometimes called our "essence") is to live according to reason and thereby to become a certain sort of highly rational, disciplined being. When we fulfill the ideal of living the virtuous life, we are truly happy.

The objectivist view fell out of favor with the rise of the evolutionary account of human nature, which undermined the sense of a preordained essence or function. Science cannot discover any innate *telos*, or goal, to which all people must strive. The contemporary bias is in favor of value pluralism, that is, the view that there are many ways of finding happiness: "Let a thousand flowers bloom." This leads to subjectivism.

The subjectivist version states that happiness is in the eyes of the beholder. You are just as happy as you think you are—no more, no less. The concept is not a descriptive one but a first-person evaluation. I am the only one who decides or knows whether I am happy. If I feel happy, I am happy, even though everyone else despises my lifestyle. Logically, happiness has nothing to do with virtue, though—due to our social nature—it usually turns out that we will feel better about ourselves if we are virtuous.

The combination view tries to incorporate aspects of both the objectivist and the subjectivist views. One version is John Rawls' "plan-of-life" conception of happiness: there is a plurality of life plans open to each person, and what is important is that the plan be an integrated whole, freely chosen by the person, and that the person be successful in realizing his or her goals. This view is predominantly subjective in that it recognizes the person as the autonomous chooser of goals and a plan. Even if a person should choose a life plan "whose only pleasure is to count blades of grass in various geometrically shaped areas such as park squares and well-trimmed lawns . . . our definition of the good forces us to admit that the good for this man is indeed counting blades of grass."[5]

However, Rawls recognizes an objective element in an otherwise subjective schema. There are primary goods that are necessary to any worthwhile life plan: "rights and liberties, powers and opportunities, income and wealth . . . self-respect . . . health and vigor, intelligence and imagination."[6]

The primary goods function as the core (or the hub of the wheel), from which may be derived any number of possible life plans (the spokes); but unless these primary goods (or most of them) are present, the life plan is not an authentic manifestation of an individual's autonomous choice of his or her own selfhood. So it is perfectly possible that people believe themselves to be happy when they really are not.

Although subjectivist and plan-of-life views dominate the literature today, there is some movement back to an essentialist, or Aristotelian, view of happiness as a life directed toward worthwhile goals. Some lifestyles are more worthy than others, and some may be worthless. Philosopher Richard Kraut asks us to imagine a man who has as his idea of happiness the state of affairs of being loved, admired, or respected by his friends and who would hate to have his "friends" only pretend to care for him. Suppose his "friends" really do hate him but "orchestrate an elaborate deception, giving him every reason to believe that they love and admire him, though in fact they don't. And he is taken in by the illusion."[7] Can we really call this man happy?

Suppose that a woman centers her entire life around an imaginary Prince Charming. She refuses to date—let alone marry—perfectly eligible young men; she turns down educational travel opportunities lest they distract her from this wonderful future event; for 95 years she bores all her patient friends with tales of the prince's imminent appearance. As death approaches at age 96, after a lifetime of disappointment, she discovers that she has been duped; she suddenly realizes that what appeared to be a happy life was a stupid, self-deceived, miserable existence. Would we say that our heroine was happy up until her deathbed revelation? Do these thought-experiments not indicate that our happiness depends, at least to some extent, on reality and not simply on our own evaluation?

Or, suppose that we invent a happiness machine. This machine is a large tub that is filled with a chemical solution. Electrodes are attached to many parts of your brain. You work with the technician to program all the "happy experiences" that you have ever wanted. Suppose that includes wanting to be a football star, a halfback who breaks tackles like a dog shakes off fleas and who has a penchant for scoring last-minute game-winning touchdowns. Perhaps you have always wanted to be a movie star and to bask in the public's love and admiration. Maybe you have wanted to be the world's richest person, living in the splendor of a magnificent castle, with servants faithfully at your beck and call. In fact, with the happiness machine you can have all of these, plus passionate romance and the love of the most beautiful (or handsome) persons in the world. All of these marvelous adventures would be simulated, and you would truly believe you were experiencing them. Would you enter the happiness machine?

Plato and Aristotle would argue that the happiness machine is an illusion, a modern analogue to his allegory of the cave. For in both the happiness machine and the cave we are living in an illusion, not in reality. We do not know who we are or the nature of reality. We are not free and have no character, for we are not acting but only passive pleasure blobs reacting to sensory stimuli and imagining this is the real world. Also, we are not related to other people in love or friendship, for there are no other people in the machine.

The happiness machine, like Plato's Allegory of the Cave (see chapter 3), is a myth, all appearance and no reality—a bliss bought at too high a price, a deception! If this is so and if reality is a necessary condition for the truly worthwhile life, then we cannot be happy in the happiness machine; but neither can we be happy outside of the happiness machine when the same necessary ingredients are missing: activity, freedom, moral character, loving relationships, and a strong sense of reality.

The Aristotelian objective and the modern subjective views of happiness assess life from different perspectives, with the objectivist assuming that there is some kind of independent standard of assessment and the subjectivist denying it. Even though there seems to be an immense variety of lifestyles that could be considered intrinsically worthwhile or happy and even though some subjective approval or satisfaction seems necessary before we are willing to attribute the adjective *happy* to a life, there do seem to be limiting conditions on what may count as happy. We have a notion of fittingness for the good life, which would normally exclude being severely retarded, a slave, or a drug addict (no matter how satisfied) and would include being a deeply fulfilled, autonomous, healthy person. As John Stuart Mill said in *Utilitarianism*, "It is better to be a human being dissatisfied than a pig satisfied; better to be Socrates dissatisfied than a fool satisfied" (chapter 2). The pig may be satisfied because it has minimal needs, but only Socrates can be truly happy.

Mill gave a definition which is a combination of the Aristotelian and subjective views.

> Happiness is not a life of rapture; but moments of such, in an existence made up of few and transitory pains, many and various pleasures, with a decided predominance of the active over the passive, and having as the foundation of the whole, not to expect more from life than it is capable of bestowing.[8]

This conception of happiness is worth pondering. It includes activity, freedom, and reality components, which exclude being satisfied by the passive experiences in the happiness machine, and it supposes (the context tells us this) that some pleasing experiences are better than others. We might supplement Mill's definition with the ingredients of moral character and loving relations. An approximation might go like this:

> Happiness is a life in which exist free action (including meaningful work), loving relations, and good moral character, and in which the individual is not plagued by guilt and anxiety but is blessed with peace and satisfaction.

For Aristotle happiness, or the good life, is rooted in the virtues. Virtue ethicists often cite Kant's **deontic** theory (see chapter 8) as a paradigm of an anti-virtue, **deontological ethics.** They point out that an examination of Kant's extreme action-centered approach highlights the need for a virtue alternative. For Kant, natural goodness is morally irrelevant. The fact that you actually want to help someone (because you like them or just like doing good deeds) is of no moral importance. In fact, because of the emphasis he puts on the good will (doing duty for duty's sake), it seems that Kant's logic would force the conclusion that you are actually moral in proportion to the amount of temptation that you have to resist in performing your duty: for little temptation you receive little moral credit; if you experience great temptation, you receive great moral credit for overcoming it.

To virtue ethicists this is preposterous. Taken to its logical conclusion, the homicidal maniac who always just barely succeeds in resisting the perpetual temptation to kill is actually the most glorious saint, surpassing the "natural saint" who does good just because of a good character. True goodness is to spontaneously, cheerfully, and enjoyably do what is good. As Aristotle said,

> We may even go so far as to state that the man who does not enjoy performing noble actions is not a good man at all. Nobody would call a man just who does not enjoy acting justly, nor generous who does not enjoy generous actions, and so on. (NE, 1099a)

It is not the hounded neurotic who barely manages to control himself before each passing temptation, but the natural saint—the one who does good out of habit and from the inner resources of good character—who is the morally superior person.

A criticism of rule-governed, deontic ethics, set forth by the Aristotelian scholar Alasdair MacIntyre in *After Virtue* (1981),[9] claims that ordinary rule-governed ethics is a symptom of the European Enlightenment movement of the 17th and 18th centuries, which exaggerated the principle of **autonomy,** that is, the ability of each person to arrive at a moral code by reason alone. In fact, all moral codes are rooted in practices that themselves are rooted in traditions or forms of life. We do not make moral decisions as rational atoms in a vacuum, and it is sheer ideological blindness that allows this distorted perception. MacIntyre does not want to embrace relativism. We can discover better ways of living, but they will probably be founded on an account of what the good life is and what a good community is.

It is in communities that such virtues as loyalty, natural affection, spontaneous sympathy, and shared concerns arise and sustain the group. It is out of this primary loyalty (to family, friends, and community) that the proper dispositions arise and flow out to the rest of humanity. Hence, moral psychology is more important than traditional ethics has usually recognized. Seeing how people actually learn to be moral and how they are inspired to act morally is vital to moral theory itself, and this, it seems, has everything to do with the virtues.

In sum, rule-governed systems are uninspiring, unmotivating, negative, improperly legalistic, neglectful of the spiritual dimension, overly rationalistic, and atomistic. Against this background of dissatisfaction with traditional moral theory, virtue ethics has reasserted itself as offering something that captures the essence of the moral point of view.

As we saw in the last chapter, Plato speaks of happiness as "harmony of the soul." Just as the body is healthy when it is in harmony with itself and the political state is a good state when it is functioning harmoniously, so the soul is happy when all its features are functioning in harmonious accord, with the rational faculty ruling over the spirited (motivational) and emotional elements. Though we no doubt know when we are happy and feel good about ourselves, the subjective feeling does not itself define happiness, for people who fail to attain excellence can also feel happy via self-deception or ignorance.

The Ideal Type of Human

"Man is a political animal," Aristotle wrote in *Politics*. For Aristotle the virtues are those characteristics that enable individuals to live well in communities. In order to achieve a state of human flourishing, proper social institutions are necessary. Thus, the moral person cannot really exist apart from a flourishing political setting that enables him or her to develop the requisite virtues for the good life. For this reason, ethics is considered a branch of politics. The state is not neutral toward the good life but should actively encourage citizens to inculcate the virtues, which in turn are the best guarantee of a flourishing political order.

As we have shown, for Aristotle, humanity has an essence, or function. Just as it is the function of a doctor to cure the sick and restore health, the function of a ruler to govern society well, and the function of a knife to cut well, so it is the function of humans to use reason in pursuit of the good life. The virtues indicate the kind of moral–political characteristics necessary for people to attain happiness.

After locating ethics as a part of politics, Aristotle explains that the moral virtues are different from the intellectual ones. Whereas the intellectual virtues may be taught directly, the moral ones must be lived in order to be learned. By living well we acquire the right habits. These habits are in fact the virtues. The virtues are to be sought as the best guarantee to the happy life. However, again, happiness requires that we be lucky enough to live in a flourishing state. The morally virtuous life consists in living in moderation, according to the "Golden Mean." By the "Golden Mean" Aristotle means that the virtues are a mean between excess and deficiency (e.g., courage is the mean between cowardice and foolhardiness; liberality is the mean between stinginess and unrestrained giving):

> We can experience fear, confidence, desire, anger, pity, and generally any kind of pleasure and pain either too much or too little, and in either case not properly. But to experience all this at the right time, toward the right objects, toward the right people, for the right reason, and in the right manner—that is the mean and the best course, the course that is the mark of virtue. (NE, 1099a)

Aristotle himself was an elitist who believed that people have unequal abilities to be virtuous: some are endowed with great ability, while others lack it altogether; some are worthless, natural slaves. In addition, external circumstances could prevent even those capable of developing moral dispositions from reaching the goal of happiness. The moral virtues are a necessary but not sufficient condition for happiness. One must, in addition to being virtuous, be healthy, wealthy, and wise and have good fortune.

What seems so remarkable to contemporary ethicists is that Aristotle hardly mentions principles. It was not that he thought them unnecessary; they are implied in what he says. For example, his condemnation of adultery may be read as a principle ("Thou shalt not commit adultery"). Aristotle seems to think that such activities are inherently and obviously bad, so it is laboring the point to speak of a rule against adultery or against killing innocent persons. What is emphasized in place of principles is the importance of a good upbringing, good habits, self-control, courage, and character, without which the ethical life is impossible. A person of moral excellence cannot help doing good; it is as natural as the change of seasons or the rotation of the planets.

Let me elaborate on the idea of the Golden Mean. We spoke above about the moral life being a life of virtue. Like becoming healthy or strong, the moral life is lived by avoiding the extremes of excess or deficiency, habitually hitting instead the middle or mean. In maintaining health one must not eat too little or too much but just the right amount, and in building up strength one must avoid too much or too little exercise, getting the right balance. So in becoming virtuous one must avoid the Scylla and Charybdis of opposite vices and hit the intermediate, the golden mean. Greek society already had as one of the famous sayings of the sacred Oracle of Delphi, "Nothing in excess." Aristotle was reaffirming that wise saying in a philosophical manner.

> Moral Virtue: for it is this that is concerned with passions and actions, and in these there is excess, defect, and the intermediate. For instance, both fear and confidence and appetite and anger and pity and in general pleasure and pain may be felt both too much and too little, and in both cases not well; but to feel them at the right times, with reference to the right objects, towards the right people, with the right motive, and in the right way, is what is both intermediate and best, and this is characteristic of virtue. Similarly with regard to actions also there is excess, defect, and the intermediate. Now virtue is concerned with passions and actions, in which excess is a form of failure, and so is defect, while virtue is the intermediate. (NE, II.6)

Some examples may help. The mean between the vices of rashness and cowardice is courage, knowing what to fear and what not to fear and acting accordingly. The mean between irascibility and insensitivity is an even temper, getting appropriately angry for the right reason and in the right amount. The mean between prodigality and stinginess is liberality, giving away the right moderate amount in the right situation. Aristotle warns us that this kind of reasoning does not apply to every kind of act. There is no golden mean between too much and too little adultery or murder or injustice. These kinds of acts are simply wrong (NE, II.6). The following chart, from *Eudemian Ethics,* shows the kinds of intermediate relationship the virtues have to vices:

VICE	VIRTUE	VICE
Irascibility	Even temper	Impassivity
Foolhardiness	Bravery	Cowardice
Shamelessness	Modesty	Over-sensitiveness
Intemperance	Temperance	Insensibility
Envy	Fair-mindedness	[no name]
Unfair advantage	Justice	Disadvantage
Prodigality	Liberality	Meanness
Boastfulness	Truthfulness	False modesty
Flattery	Friendliness	Churlishness

Applying the idea to the moral virtues, concerned with emotions and actions, Aristotle says that finding the mean is an act of discernment. In every life situation the wise person (*phronimos*) discerns the right act from an indefinite number of possible actions, most of which are wrong. Bad people have many ways, good people but one. There are many ways to miss the bull's-eye but only one way to hit it. There is no set of rules telling us exactly how to do the right thing, for each situation is different; but the skilled, moral craftsperson, an expert in human virtue, knows just what the right thing to do is in every situation. "The judgment lies in perception" (NE, II.9).

Summary

The background of Aristotle's philosophy of human nature is his response to the idealism of his teacher, Plato. Rejecting the otherworldly dualism of Plato, Aristotle developed a more naturalist and realist account of human nature and the moral life.

Being a biologist as well as a philosopher, Aristotle's theory of human nature is a functional account of all living beings. Believing that everything in nature has a purpose (*telos*), he held that the *telos* of human beings is to live as worthy, moral–political citizens, using practical reason to solve our problems and resolve our conflicts of interest. The highest form of life for the best humans was that of the philosopher, who engaged in contemplation, the life of the gods.

Aristotle's ethics is connected to his politics and centered on the virtues. Virtues are inculcated by a good upbringing in a good society and lead to happiness (*eudaimonia*).

Happiness is an objective state of affairs, which requires health, friends, family, as well as good character. The wise person (*phronimos*) uses reason to navigate through life, living in moderation, by the golden mean, avoiding excesses.

Study Questions

1. Compare Aristotle's philosophy with that of Plato, noting the similarities and differences.

2. Describe Aristotle's theory of ethics.

3. Describe the ideal human being according to Aristotle.

4. Describe Aristotle's functional account of human nature.

5. According to Aristotle, how is ethics related to politics and politics to the heart of human nature?

6. What is Aristotle's view of happiness? Compare it with the thought-experiment of the happiness machine.

7. What is the Golden Mean?

8. What is Aristotle's view of women and slaves? Why did he hold this view?

Notes

1. All translations from Aristotle's works are by W. D. Ross, though in places I have edited his translation for purposes of readability.
2. Henry Sidgwick, the greatest ethical theorist of the 19th century, agrees. See his *Outlines of the History of Ethics* (Macmillan, 1886), p. 51.
3. Aristotle, *Politics,* I.5, trans. B. Jowett. All my translations of *Politics* are by Benjamin Jowett.
4. Aristotle, *Politics,* I.5.
5. John Rawls, *A Theory of Justice* (Harvard University Press, 1971), p. 432.
6. Ibid., p. 62.
7. Richard Kraut, "Two Concepts of Happiness," *Philosophical Review* (1979).
8. John Stuart Mill, *Utilitarianism* (1863), chapter 2.
9. Alasdair MacIntyre, *After Virtue* (University of Notre Dame Press, 1981).

For Further Reading

Ackrill, J. L., *Aristotle, the Philosopher* (Oxford University Press, 1981).

Aristotle, *The Complete Works,* ed. J. Barnes (Princeton University Press, 1984), 2 vols.

Barnes, J., *Aristotle* (Oxford University Press, 1982).

Hardie, W. F. R., *Aristotle's Ethical Theory* (Oxford University Press, 1968).

Irwin, Terrance, *Aristotle's First Principles* (Oxford University Press, 1988).

Lloyd, G. E. R., *Aristotle, the Growth and Structure of His Thought* (Cambridge University Press, 1968).

MacIntyre, Alasdair, *After Virtue* (University of Notre Dame Press, 1981).

Taylor, A.E., *Aristotle* (Dover Publications, 1955).

Urmson, J. O., *Aristotle's Ethics* (Basil Blackwell, 1988).

CHAPTER 5

‿‿‿‿‿‿‿⊃

St. Augustine's Theory of Human Nature

> Thus has made us for Thyself and our hearts are restless until they find rest in Thee. (*St. Augustine,* Confessions, *henceforth abbreviated* Conf., Bk 1.1)

Like Atlas bestriding two universes, Augustine stands as a bridge between the ancient Greeks and the medieval Christians, the epitome of Christian Neoplatonism. He Christianized Plato and Platonized Christianity, providing the great synthesis of philosophy and theology that would influence Christianity and Western thought from that time forward, through the Middle Ages and the Protestant Reformation (Martin Luther, its driving force, was an Augustinian monk) until our own.

Augustine's Life and Early Thought

Aurelius Augustinus (354–430 C.E.), Bishop of Hippo (now Annaba, Algeria), was born in Thagaste, North Africa (part of Algeria). He grew up in Carthage (at that time, a major city on the Mediterranean; now, an ancient ruin in Tunisia). His father was a pagan and his mother, a Christian. As a rhetoretician, his career took him from his native Carthage to Italy, first to Rome, where he soon came under the spell of *Manichaeism.* The Manichaean philosophy was a dualist system which held to the idea of two divine powers: the God of Light and the God of Darkness. They identified the good god with the sun (an ethereal corporeality) and the equally powerful evil god, with matter. Augustine quickly became dissatisfied with its inability to answer philosophical problems, especially the problems of God's corporeality (how could God be omnipotent and yet have a body?) and the problem of evil.

In 385, Augustine went to Milan, at that time the center of the intellectual world, and met the great Christian philosopher Bishop Ambrose. During this time, he read the Neoplatonists, Plotinus (204–270), and others (Conf., Bk 7). He was impressed by the idea of an invisible reality of being, the idea of the good and the Forms, which could not be seen but could be experienced by the mind. He confesses this attraction to Platonism to God in his *Confessions:*

> By having thus read the books of the Platonists, and having been taught by them to search for the incorporeal Truth, I saw how thy invisible things are understood through the things that are made. And, even when I was thrown back, I still sensed what it was that the dullness of my soul would not allow me to contemplate. I was assured that thou wast, and wast infinite, though not diffused in finite space or infinity; that thou truly art, who art ever the same, varying neither in part nor motion; and that all things are from thee, as is proved by this sure cause alone: that they exist. (Conf., Bk 7.20)

The idea of an infinite, immutable, invisible reality discovered by the mind seemed to be the final piece in the puzzle, enabling Augustine to come to terms with Christianity. He was soon converted to Christianity and identified with a Neoplatonic version of the faith. Neoplatonism, especially the thought of Plotinus, enabled him to make sense of the incorporeality of God and accept that true knowledge was spiritual, grasping ideas via the mind, not the senses. Four years later, he was ordained a priest; and in 395, he became Bishop of Hippo.

His numerous works include his *Confessions*, one of the great spiritual autobiographies of all time, and *On Free Will*, the first treatise on that subject, which has defined the problem ever since. We will also look at some of his ideas in *The City of God*, in which he responds to the charge that Christianity is responsible for the fall of the Roman Empire under Alaric and the Visigoths in 412 and develops a Christian political philosophy. Once converted, Augustine never doubted his faith but took the Christian revelation as the starting point for all further reflection. Taking from Isaiah 7:9, "Unless you believe you shall not understand," Augustine developed the idea of faith seeking understanding (*fides querens intellectum*). Not reason but faith is the way to the truth. One begins with God's revelation and gradually comes to understand it. The task of Christian philosophy was to present a coherent defense of the content of Christian revelation.

In his *Confessions* Augustine exhibits a depth of psychological insight that rivals anything ever written. It is also a display of Platonic–Christian anthropology. Human beings are sinful and live in pride, lust, and greed. They know what is right, but sin in spite of the knowledge.

> I will now call to mind my past wickedness and the carnal corruption of my soul, not for love of them, but that I may love Thee, O my God. I collect my self out of that broken state in which my very being was torn asunder because I was turned away from Thee. (*Conf.,* Bk 2.1)

He ponders his own perverse theft as a teenager:

> Theft is punishable by Thy law, O Lord, and by the law written in man's hearts, which not even ingrained wickedness can erase. For what thief will tolerate another

thief stealing from him? Even a rich thief will not tolerate a poor thief who is driven to theft by want. Yet I had a desire to commit robbery, and did so, compelled to it by neither hunger nor poverty, but through a contempt for well-doing and a strong impulse to iniquity. For I pilfered something which I already had in sufficient measure. . . . I did not desire to enjoy what I stole, but only the theft itself. (*Conf.*, Bk 2.4)

Augustine similarly deplores his greed, lust, and willingness to cheat in order to succeed in sports. This perversity of soul, doing wickedness in spite of the voice of conscience to the contrary, confirms the Christian doctrine of original sin. We know the good but do evil anyway, and, moreover, we take pleasure in doing evil. For Socrates (see chapter 2), immorality was a function of ignorance, for no one would rationally choose evil over good since the good was good for you. Augustine rejects that position in favor of the Pauline idea (see pp. 21–22), making the will, not reason, the essence of human nature. The relationship of will to evil is set forth in Augustine's first major philosophical work, *On Free Will*.

Evil and the Free Will Defense

In the dialogue *On Free Will* (*liberum arbitrium*) between Augustine and his disciple Evodius, Augustine is concerned to understand the problem of evil. What is its definition, source, effect on human nature, and remedy? Implicit in his thinking is Epicurus' classic puzzle: if God is willing to prevent evil and suffering but is unable to, then He is not omnipotent and, hence, not worthy of worship; if God is able to prevent evil and suffering but unwilling, then He is not all good and still unworthy of worship. Augustine defines evil as "the absence of good." Since existence is good (as it is created by God), evil is the negative element of existence, a privation of existence, an absence of good. "If things are deprived of all good they cease to exist. So long as they are, they are good. Whatever is is good. The evil then whose source I sought is not substance, for were it a substance, it would be good" (Conf., Bk 7.12). It is compared to a disease or wound (i.e., absence of health) that ceases to exist when the cure comes, "for the wound or disease is not a substance, but a defect in the fleshly substance."

The source or cause of evil is the will, the falling away from the unchangeable good of a being made good but changeable. First, the angel Satan and all his followers fell from the high ideal and then humanity, led by the first man, Adam, followed after. The angels and Adam were created with a will that permitted a free option between good and evil. They chose the later and thereby limited the choice of all succeeding human beings. When the will ceases to adhere to what is above itself, its source (God), and turns to what is lower (itself or created objects), it becomes evil, not because it is itself evil but because of the improper valuing of things.

As we have noted, this turning from the good represents a clear break from the Socratic idea of virtue as knowledge. For Socrates, no one would purposefully choose evil since it is bad for us. All evil is chosen under the guise of the good, through ignorance. However, Augustine, following St. Paul (Romans ch. 7), makes the will, rather than reason, our dominant feature. We are defined by our choices, so the will sometimes overruns reason.

Originally, we were made for fellowship with God, living happily under God's domain; but our forefather and -mother, Adam and Eve, rebelled, choosing to run their own lives without God's authority. This is the sin of pride. "Pride is the beginning of all sin, and the beginning of man's pride is revolt from God."[1] This is the original sin, that of wanting to be one's own god. The effects of this sin are inherited in every person who is born, who, though still free and responsible for his or her choices, labors under an inexorable tendency to sin. Augustine speaks of two wills within himself, a lower, carnal will, a servant of the flesh, and one touched by God's grace, struggling to choose heaven (Conf. Bk 8.5).

Whereas for Socrates ignorance led to bad choices and evil, for Augustine bad choices and evil lead to ignorance. Evil's power over human beings leads to ignorance of duty and lusting (libido) after what is hurtful, which in turn lead to error and suffering, which lead to fear. Error also leads to a false evaluation of values and virtues, which alone explain human pride or foolish joy in earthly success and goods. From these basic evils flow all other forms of misery. A just God must punish evil.

The answer to Epicurus' puzzle is that free will is a good, necessary for doing good, but, as such, it can be directed to evil (through false valuations, created things over the Creator). So it is not God's fault that humans sinned and that, consequently, moral evil exists; but God does intervene and save an elect, so the Fall turns out to be a good thing for those elected (a felix culpa, or "happy fault"). When we are rescued from sin, we appreciate our relationship with God more fully than we would have had we not sinned, for we know the tremendous contrast between being lost and tossed on the restless sea of life and being brought safe to God's blessed shore, which is our true home.

In this early work, Augustine is at pains to absolve God from any responsibility for humanity's plight of being in sin, lost from God, suffering evil and the punishment for sin. Each of us is free to choose one way or the other. However, in his later works, Augustine adopts a view based on predestination. The occasion for the change was the appearance in Rome of an eloquent British monk, Pelagius. Pelagius was a moralist who preached that human beings, made in the image of God, were basically good. Each person, being in an identical position to Adam before the Fall, must choose either to obey or reject God. He admitted that Adam's Fall set in motion a culture of sin which might incline us to follow his bad example. The coming of Christ was to set a good example, to show us how we could live morally perfect lives according to God's law. Humans can be saved by moral merit. Pelagius probably thought that this was consistent with what Augustine had written in his essay On Free Will, and it does look that way. However, Augustine had developed his position and now believed in **predestination,** the idea that we are foreordained to heaven or to hell. God in his infinite wisdom chose who should be saved and who should be damned, and we must simply accept our fate. Pelagius was offended by this doctrine, believing that it made a mockery of free will. For Augustine, Pelagius' message was heresy, at best naiveness about the profundity of human perversity. The heresy was to be utterly rejected, for it undermined the importance of divine grace. If humans could reach moral perfection without grace, what need was there for the incarnation of God in Christ, for the crucifixion, death, and resurrection of Christ?[2]

Augustine had developed his doctrines of original sin and the necessity of grace even before Pelagius' appearance, but Pelagius provided the occasion for their full articulation. Augustine argues that original sin means that we are in solidarity with Adam so that through his fall, we have fallen. "All sinned in Adam on that occasion, for all were already identical with him in that nature of his which was endowed with the capacity to generate them."[3] Now no possibility exists not to sin. It would seem that true free will has been lost, but Augustine does not want to go that far. We still have the image of God within us. It just has been badly tarnished. We have been corrupted but not completely separated from God's likeness. We have reason and the ability to discover God's law within and to resist temptation, though the resistance will be difficult and we are bound to fail at times. Ultimately, we are slaves to ignorance, concupiscence, and death.[4] Concupiscence, for Augustine, is the inclination in humans to turn from God and find fulfillment in sensual and material things, which are fleeting and unworthy of devotion. Passionate sexual desire, lust, is the most powerful example of this vice. Even chaste people are conscious of this tumultuous temptation, which did not exist in the Garden of Eden but is the result of the Fall. If we had not sinned, we would copulate for the purpose of procreation, without passion but out of duty to procreate.

Furthermore, through the Fall, we have lost our liberty (*libertas*) to avoid sin, which we had in innocence, though we have not lost our free will (*liberum arbitrium*), our ability to choose. That is, we can make better or worse choices within the framework of our slavery to sin. We can choose to resist temptation on a given occasion, to resist eating that extra piece of cake or drinking that shot of whiskey; but only when grace comes to liberate us from sin can *liberum arbitrium* become *libertas*, true freedom from sin and for God.

In the process of attacking Pelagianism, Augustine develops the doctrine of predestination. We cannot save ourselves. It is not possible for someone even to accept God's grace unless God's grace enables him or her to do so. God chose those to be elected, or saved, and those to be lost before the creation of the world. Augustine interprets the biblical passages that "whosoever believeth in [Christ] shall be saved" (Jn. 3:16) and "God wills all men to be saved" (1 Tm. 2:4) as meaning that He wills the salvation of all the elect. From all eternity, some were elected for heaven and some for hell.

This seems problematic, for it takes any choice away from us. It seems to make God responsible for sin and the damnation of those who go to hell. Augustine simply acknowledges that it is a mystery but that we ought to trust that God has a good reason. One might be forgiven for thinking the idea of predestination to damnation inconsistent with the idea of an omnibenevolent deity, one led by love. The early Christian philosopher Origen (ca. 185–253 C.E.) developed the theory of

Regathering (*apocatastasis*), or universal salvation, the idea that in the end there would be a restoration of all souls to heaven.[5] God's love would triumph over human sinfulness and moral weakness and bring his erring children home again. God would reeducate sinners in purgatory until they were ready for his divine presence, the last one to make it back home, being Satan himself. However, this sanguine doctrine was too optimistic for Augustine, and it seems to contradict a number of scriptural passages which indicate that the final judgment is eternal. Nevertheless, many Christian thinkers, such as Gregory of Nyssa (ca. 350–388), Karl Barth (1886–1968), and John Hick (1922–), have found it consistent with the idea of a totally benevolent God.

Augustine's Doctrine of Love as the Essence of Religion and Ethics

Love is my weight.

For Augustine, the highest form of existence was to live in love, love for God and love for one's friends. The two cities of the world, the City of God and the Earthly City, are defined by their love:

> So two loves constitute two cities—the earthly is formed by love of self even to contempt of God; the heavenly by love of God even to contempt of self. For one seeks glories in herself, the other in the Lord. The one seeks glory from man; for the other God, the witness of the conscience, is the greatest glory. The one lifts up her head to her own glory; the other says to her God, "My glory and the lifter up of my head." In one the lust for power prevails, both in her own rulers and in the nations she subdues; in the other all serve each other in charity, governors by taking thought for all and subjects by obeying.[6]

Love is the drive that determines our destiny. Commenting on the passage from Genesis 2, on the Spirit's "moving over the face of the waters," Augustine writes:

> Why, then, is this said of thy Spirit alone? Why is it said of him only—as if he had been in a "place" that is not a place—about whom alone it is written, "He is thy gift"? It is in thy gift that we rest. It is there that we enjoy thee. Our rest is our "place." Love lifts us up toward that place, and thy good Spirit lifts our lowliness from the gates of death. Our peace rests in the goodness of will. The body tends toward its own place by its own gravity. A weight does not tend downward only, but moves to its own place. Fire tends upward; a stone tends downward. They are propelled by their own mass; they seek their own places. Oil poured under the water rises above the water; water poured on oil sinks under the oil. They are moved by their own mass; they seek their own places. If they are out of order, they are restless; when their order is restored, they are at rest. *My weight is my love.* By it I am carried wherever I am carried. By thy gift, we are enkindled and are carried upward. We burn inwardly and move forward. We ascend thy ladder which is in

our heart, and we sing a canticle of degrees; we glow inwardly with thy fire—with thy good fire. (Conf. 13.10)

The model referred to here is that of Aristotle's four elements, each with its proper place: water to settle on earth, earth tending to sink, air to hover over earth, fire to rise to the heavens. The proper place of love is in God. It is the element that wants to rise up to the almighty and find its home there and there alone. Love of material and sensual objects is a perversion of love.

In the *Confessions,* he writes almost mystically about love with God.

Late have I loved thee, O Beauty so ancient and so new, belatedly I loved thee. For see, thou wast within and I was without, and I sought thee out there. Unlovely, I rushed heedlessly among the lovely things thou hast made. Thou wast with me, but I was not with thee. These things kept me far from thee; even though they were not at all unless they were in thee. Thou didst call and cry aloud, and didst force open my deafness. Thou didst gleam and shine, and didst chase away my blindness. Thou didst breathe fragrant odors and I drew in my breath; and now I pant for thee. I tasted, and now I hunger and thirst. Thou didst touch me, and I burned for thy peace.

When I come to be united to thee with all my being, then there will be no more pain and toil for me, and my life shall be a real life, being wholly filled by thee. But since he whom thou fillest is the one thou liftest up, I am still a burden to myself because I am not yet filled by thee. Joys of sorrow contend with sorrows of joy, and on which side the victory lies I do not know. (Conf., Bk 10.27)

Friendship is the highest form of love humans can experience with one another, and Augustine writes eloquently of it. One of the most moving passages in literature is his reflection on the death of his friend:

My heart was utterly darkened by this sorrow and everywhere I looked I saw death. My native place was a torture room to me and my father's house a strange unhappiness. And all the things I had done with him—now that he was gone—became a frightful torment. My eyes sought him everywhere, but they did not see him; and I hated all places because he was not in them, because they could not say to me, "Look, he is coming," as they did when he was alive and absent. I became a hard riddle to myself, and I asked my soul why she was so downcast and why this disquieted me so sorely. But she did not know how to answer me. And if I said, "Hope thou is God," she very properly disobeyed me, because that dearest friend she had lost was as an actual man, both truer and better than the imagined deity she was ordered to put her hope in. Nothing but tears were sweet to me and they took my friend's place in my heart's desire. (Conf., Bk 4.4)

Of ethics, Augustine writes "Love God and do what you want," for if your heart is directed upward to the Good, you will do what is suitable for the Good, only what is good. Morality does not consist in following rigid rules against one's nature but in having a transformed character whereby one does the right thing out of a moral motive, the motive of love. There is a divine moral law written within our hearts which becomes the map by which love steers its course, for "love seeketh not her own" but that of the beloved.

Although Augustine set love at the heart of his theology of human nature, he believed that Christians may use force to defend the Christian state from enemies. Recall Jesus' words in the Sermon on the Mount, "Render no man evil for evil . . . whoever shall smite you on one cheek, turn to him the other cheek. . . . Love your enemy." Augustine interprets this passage as a advocating a disposition of the heart. One must never hate one's enemy, even while destroying him or her. Here, Augustine breaks from the Christian pacifism of early Christianity and sketches *just war theory*. While the state may not lawfully aggress on other people, it may use force to defend itself and its innocent citizens from enemy invasion. A morally legitimate war must only be fought after a country has been attacked and negotiations have failed.[7] It must be declared by a legitimate authority, such as the king, and peace must be the aim. Later, Thomas Aquinas (1224–1274, C.E.) and others developed Augustine's theory into two parts: *jus ad bellum* (justice in going to war) and *jus in bello* (justice in waging the war). Aquinas added the ideas of proportionality and discrimination. That is, the force used must be proportionate to the goal of peace. No more force should be used than necessary to win the peace. The idea of discrimination means that warriors may only attack other warriors and not innocent noncombatants. As soon as an enemy soldier surrenders, he is to be treated as a noncombatant and given immunity from harm. We may use violence to defend our country, but we must not intentionally harm noncombatants, though they may be harmed as an unintended side effect of our attacks. For example, we may intentionally bomb a weapons factory and in the process kill innocent civilians working in or walking by the factory.

The main contribution of just war theory was to limit the violence of war. It represented a break with the practice of total war, which had been practiced from time immemorial and in which noncombatant men, women, and children were killed. The doctrine of just war is practiced by most states today though not by terrorists.

The Doctrine of the Great Chain of Being

Finally, we must mention the doctrine of the Great Chain of Being, which is implicit in the New Testament and early Church but was developed to the full doctrine of the plentitude of being (*pleroma*) by Augustine and other theologians in the Middle Ages. In this theory, the universe is set down in a hierarchical manner, with degrees of being. All reality is continuous, connected to God (identified with Plato's Form of the Good; (see chapter 3). That is, some things have more reality than others. Being, following Plato and the Neoplatonists, is good. Evil is the absence of being, *Nonbeing*. God is Perfect Being and from Him everything is derived as an attenuated form of being. Reality is divided into two parts, the celestial and the terrestrial, with the moon being the cut-off point.

It assumed a geocentric universe, with Earth at its very center—the apple of God's eye. The sphere of the moon divided the universe into an unchanging perfection in the heavens above and a corrupt degeneration on the earth below ("sublunary nature"). Surrounding the moon were the spheres for the inner planets, the sun, the outer planets, and the fixed stars, each cranked by a higher angel. Surrounding them all were the heavens, home to God, Father, Son, and Holy Spirit, in descending order, followed by the Virgin Mary and the higher angels. Contained within the sphere of the moon, and thus a little lower than the angels, were human souls and then, in descending order, human beings, other animals (in order, beasts, birds, fish, and insects), then planets, minerals, inanimate elements, nine layers of devils, and finally, at the center of the Earth, Satan in hell. The theory was a complete hierarchy of the universe with a place for everything. The meaning of life was found in keeping one's place. In 1 Corinthians 11, Paul speaks of the divine teleological order in this manner:

> But I want you to understand that the head of every man is Christ, the head of a woman is her husband, and the head of Christ is God. Any man who prays or prophesies with his head covered dishonors his head, but any woman who prays or prophesies with her head unveiled dishonors her head—it is the same as if her head were shaven. For if a woman will not veil herself, then she should cut off her hair; but if it is disgraceful for a woman to be shorn or shaven, let her wear a veil.
>
> For a man ought not to cover his head, since he is the image and glory of God; but woman is the glory of man. (For man was not made from woman, but woman for man. Neither was man created for woman, but woman for man.) That is why a woman ought to have a veil on her head, because of the angels. (Nevertheless, in the Lord woman is not independent of man nor man of woman, for as woman was made from man, so man is now born of woman. And all things are from God.)

There is a natural, divinely ordained order to the world, with Christ over man and man over woman and woman over children and slaves. The state is part of that divine hierarchy, given by God for the orderly progression of social interaction. We are to obey the government as part of the divine hierarchy (Rom. 13:1–3) and not rebel. This sublime order justifies even remaining a slave:

> Only, let every one lead the life which the Lord has assigned to him, and in which God has called him. . . . Every one should remain in the state in which he was called. Were you a slave when called? Never mind. But if you can gain your freedom, avail yourself of the opportunity.
>
> For he who was called in the Lord as a slave is a freedman of the Lord. Likewise he who was free when called is a slave of Christ. (1 Cor. 7:17, 20–22)

It is this Great Chain of Being that was the underlying paradigm of the Middle Ages through the Renaissance until the Enlightenment and coming of the Age of Science.[8] In this geocentric universe, with the Earth as the center stage, humanity, being made in the image of God, was seen as having semi-divine value. From this value flowed our dignity and moral principles. It was a perfect construction, so one must accept such seemingly unjust doctrines as predestination because God's ways were perfect even if we could not comprehend them. This Great Chain of

Being was undermined by the Copernican, Kantian, and Darwinian revolutions, which we shall examine in succeeding chapters.

Summary

Augustine's theory of human nature synthesizes Greek Platonic idealism with the biblical view of humanity as fallen through sin but redeemable through grace and faith. Through the prideful revolt of our ancestors Adam and Eve, we find ourselves locked in sin and headed for damnation. However, God's grace through the incarnation and atonement of Christ enables us to find our way back home to our heavenly father. We must ground our lives and minds in faith based on God's revelation. Philosophy must seek ways to understand that faith, to make sense of its doctrines. However, Augustine admitted that some doctrines, such as predestination, must be accepted even though we may not be smart enough to understand them. Love is the fire that drives our passions upward toward the heavens and into the arms of God. Love becomes the basis of ethics. Though we may use force to defend the innocent, we must keep our hearts pure and wage a just war with an attitude of love toward our enemy. He advanced the doctrine of the Great Chain of Being, which linked all of reality to God, the ultimate source of all good.

For 800 years, until the work of St. Thomas Aquinas, who synthesized Augustinian theology with the philosophy of Aristotle (see chapter 4), Augustine was without a peer in the Christian theological world. His theology had a renaissance during the Protestant Reformation through the work of Martin Luther, himself an Augustinian monk, as well as in the work of the Protestant reformer John Calvin. The ideas of Augustine continue to live, in contemporary Calvinism, evangelical Protestantism, as well as the Roman Catholic church, where his theology has never been absent. The idea of the Great Chain of Being, the theological doctrine of the era, offered a complete teleological explanation of all reality and, as such, gave people a deep sense of meaning, making sense of the universe as an intelligible, coherent reality.

Study Questions

1. How would you describe Augustine's theory of human nature? Compare it with the biblical views discussed in chapter 1 and with Socrates' view in chapter 2.

2. What is Augustine's doctrine of original sin? How does it function in his total theory? Compare his doctrine of human sinfulness with Socrates' theory of virtue as knowledge.

3. Discuss Augustine's doctrine of free will and evil. Do you see any problems with it? Explain.

4. Discuss Augustine's controversy with Pelagius. Who is closer to the truth? What is the doctrine of predestination?

5. What is Augustine's theory of love? Evaluate it.

6. What is the doctrine of the Great Chain of Being? Why was it important? Do you think it is plausible?

Notes

1. Augustine, *On Free Will*, in *Augustine; Earlier Writings*, ed. and trans. J. H. Burleigh (SCM Press, 1953), chapter XXV, p. 76.
2. For a good account of Pelagius' views and Augustine's reaction to them, see J. N. D. Kelly's *Early Christian Doctrines* (Harper & Row, 1960), pp. 357–368.
3. Ibid., p. 364.
4. See Augustine, *The City of God*, 13.3, 13f.
5. Origen, *First Principles*, I.6, II.10.
6. *The City of God*, 14.28.
7. For a good discussion of Augustine's role in developing just war theory, see Paul Christopher, *The Ethics of War and Peace* (Prentice-Hall, 1994), chapter 3.
8. The classic treatment of this doctrine is Arthur Lovejoy, *The Great Chain of Being* (Harper & Row, 1932).

For Further Reading

Armstrong, A. H., ed., *The Cambridge History of Later Greek and Early Medieval Philosophy* (Cambridge University Press, 1967), chapters 21–27.

Augustine, *Confessions*. There are several good translations. Albert Outler's, 1955, which I have used, can be found on the Web at www.ccel.org/a/augustine/confessions/confessions.html.

Augustine, *City of God*. (Doubleday & Co., 1958).

Augustine, *On Free Will*, in *Augustine; Earlier Writings*, ed. and trans. J. H. Burleigh (SCM Press, 1953).

Brown, Peter, *Augustine of Hippo* (University of California Press, 1967).

Chadwick, Henry, *Augustine* (Oxford University Press, 1986).

Christopher, Paul, *The Ethics of War and Peace* (Prentice-Hall, 1994).

D'Arcy, M. C., ed., *Augustine: A Collection of Critical Essays* (Meridian, 1957).

Gilson, Etienne, *The Christian Philosophy of Saint Augustine*, trans. L. Lynch (Random House, 1960).

Kelly, J. N. D., *Early Christian Doctrines.* (Harper & Row, 1960).

Kirwin, Christopher, *Augustine* (Routledge, 1989).

Lovejoy, Arthur, *The Great Chain of Being* (Harper & Row, 1960).

Meagher, E., *An Introduction to Augustine* (New York University Press, 1978).

Nash, Ronald, *The Light of the Mind: St. Augustine's Theory of Knowledge* (University of Kentucky Press, 1969).

CHAPTER 6

The Hindu and Buddhist Theories of
Human Nature

> The Self is the honey of all beings, and all beings are the honey
> of this Self. Likewise this bright, immortal person in this self,
> and that bright, immortal person who is in that self, they are
> indeed in the same Self, that Immortal, that Brahman, that
> All. *(Brihad Aranyaka Upanishad, II.5.14)*

Hinduism

History and Main Ideas

Hinduism, one of the most ancient religions known to humankind, arose in what
is now India and traces its roots back as far as 3,000–4,000 years. It is a complex,
multifaceted religion. It has many forms, which differ greatly from one another, so
almost anything one says about it must be viewed as limited to certain versions of
the religion, not to the whole.

The sources of Hinduism are the ancient Scriptures, the Vedas (literally "Wisdom"), consisting mostly of hymns of praise and rituals, and the Upanishads, containing myriad myths and discourses on cosmology, the gods, and human existence. While exact dates are not known, the oldest Scriptures, the Vedas, may have
been written as along ago as 2000 B.C.E., while most of the Upanishads were probably written between 1000 and 100 B.C.E.[1] Finally, all Hindus accept the Bhagavad
Gita (henceforth, BG), written between 500 and 200 B.C.E., as authoritative.[2] Both
Buddhism and Jainism, in breaking away from Hinduism in the 6th century B.C.E.,
rejected the authority of these Scriptures and the caste system, while holding on
to many of the central doctrines, such as reincarnation and the Law of Karma.

All Hindus revere the Vedas and hold to certain central doctrines, such as the
Law of Karma and reincarnation, but there are many types of Hinduism. *(1)*
Advaitanism, which is monistic, holds that reality is one and emphasizes the

impersonal nature of God as ultimate reality. *(2)* **Vaisnavism** is centered in the worship of Vishnu and his avatar Krishna. This version is a form of theism, closest to Western ideas of God. It is dualistic, keeping the ideas of God and humanity separate. *(3)* Shivaism is centered in the worship of Shiva, the Destroyer, and his consort, Kali. *(4)* Although there is only one god, Brahma, he takes many forms; so it looks like polytheism, with the masses seeming to worship many gods, but the many gods are really forms of one God. Advaitanism and Vaisnavism are the two most prominent forms of Hinduism. Our discussion will focus on them, Hindu metaphysics, epistemology, and its theory of human nature.

Metaphysics

Classical Hinduism, as described in the Vedas and Upanishads, holds that there are four forms of reality: *(1)* the absolute, *Brahma; (2)* the creative spirit, *Isvara; (3)* the world-soul, *Hiranya-garbha;*[3] and *(4)* the world. These are not always clearly distinguished or defined.

Absolute Brahma seems to emerge from the world-soul. The Scripture Rig Veda (I.10) tells the story of the primordial god Prajapati inseminating the sea, which becomes a golden egg (*Hiranya-garbha*) that, when hatched, develops into the whole universe. In another Veda, reality proceeds from nonbeing, three-quarters of which is taken up into heaven and one-quarter of which makes up the known universe, the finite universe open to human inquiry. The Rig Veda contains this speculative poem about the creation of the universe:

> *There was not then what is nor what is not. There was no sky, and no heaven beyond the sky. What power was there? Where? Who was that power? Was there an abyss of fathomless waters?*
>
> *There was neither death nor immortality then. No signs were there of night or day. The ONE was breathing by its own power, in deep peace. Only the ONE was; there was nothing beyond.*
>
> *Darkness was hidden in darkness. The all was fluid and formless. Therein, in the void by the fire of fervor arose the ONE.*
>
> *And in the ONE arose love. Love the first seed of soul. The truth of this the sages found in their hearts: seeking in their hearts with wisdom, the sages found the bond of union between being and non-being.*
>
> *Who knows the truth? Who can tell us whence and how arose this universe? The gods are later than its beginning: who knows therefore whence comes this creation?*
>
> *Only the God sees in the highest heaven: He only knows whence comes this universe, and whether it was made or uncreated. He only knows, or perhaps he knows not.*[4]

How unlike the Hebrew cosmology, "In the beginning, God created the heavens and the earth" (Gn. 1:1). The Vedic Scriptures are more like pre-Socratic speculations about the origins and nature of the universe rather than authoritative revelations. They raise the questions but leave the answers open. Maybe God knows, but maybe he does not. God, the One, arose gradually from love (or desire); but whence did love arise?

In the ancient Scripture Brihad Aranyaka Upanishad, the female philosopher Gargi asks the great sage Yajnavalka to explain the origins of the world. Since the whole world is woven back and forth on water, on what is the water woven back and forth? Yajnavalka answers, "On air." However, Gargi is not satisfied and asks, "Fine, but on what, then, is air woven back and forth?" Yajnavalka answers, "On the worlds of the sky, O Gargi." Gargi persists, "On what are the worlds of the sky woven back and forth?" Yajnavalka replies, "On the worlds of the sun." Gargi still is not satisfied and asks, "On what is the world of the sun woven back and forth?" Yajnavalka answers that they are woven on the stars. Gargi pursues the sage still further until he finally comes to Brahma. This is as far back as one can go. Brahma, derived from the Sanskrit word meaning "to grow," is the ultimate source of all there is. When Gargi asks what is the source of Brahma, Yajnavalka admonishes her: "If you persist in such endless questioning, your head will fall off."[5]

Sometimes Hinduism is seen as polytheistic as many gods are adoringly mentioned: Indra, thunder and lightning; Agni, fire; Prakriti; Viraj; Varuna; Ganesh; Vishnu the Creator; and Shiva, the Destroyer, along with his consort Kali. In a famous passage, Yajnavalka states that there are 3,003 gods, but when pressed, he lowers the amount to 33, then to six, to three, to two, and finally to one, which he names Brahma.[6] Some verses attempt to unite all the gods in Prajapati, who gradually becomes known as Brahma: "All these gods are in me."[7] There is unity in plurality, many attributes and perspectives but only one Supreme Reality.

Beyond vague generalizations, we can describe the absolute only in negative terms. We can say what he is not, but we cannot say what he is. "It is not gross, not subtle, not short, not long, not glowing, not shadowy, not dark, not attached, flavorless, smell-less, eye-less, ear-less, speech-less, mind-less, breath-less, mouthless, not internal, not external, consuming nothing, and consumed by nothing."[8] He (or it) exists outside time and space and the world of motion. Time and space and motion are **maya,** illusory. Just as we sometimes mistake a rope for a snake, so we mistake time and space for reality; but only one reality exists, Brahma. He is non-dual, *advaita*. This *via negativa* description of God does not mean that God is nonbeing, only that we cannot comprehend his essence. He is beyond our categories, beyond personhood, beyond male and female, yet all-inclusive. Nothing exists outside of him.

The Hindu Scriptures depict God as being in all of the universe. The doctrine is not **pantheism** (God is all things) but **panentheism** (God is *in* all things and all things are in God). However, God is more than the universe. "He sees himself in the heart of all beings and he sees all beings in his heart. . . . And when one sees me in all and he sees all in me, then I never leave him, and he never leaves me" (BG, 6:29–30): *tat tvam asi*—that art thou, you are really God as a vital part of his being. We will return to the relationship of the self to God later.

We turn to the final form of reality, the world. The world is not what it seems. The material world seems real, but it is not. It is an illusion (*maya*), a cosmic one.[9] The empirical world, with its change and decay, its unceasing flow, its loves and hates, its wars and strivings, its pains and joys, is a phantasmagoria, a dream. It is the world of time and space, which have no ultimate reality. We find ourselves in *maya,* ignorance (*avidya*), desire, hate, and suffering, groping for fantasies. "All beings are born in *Maya,* the delusion of division which comes from desire and hate" (BG, 7:27). The real world is not seen but can be discovered through meditation, devotion, and philosophical speculation, through various forms of *yoga.*

One main idea common in all forms of Hinduism is the doctrine of *reincarnation,* or transmigration of the soul. This is the view that after death human beings will live again in other forms. The doctrine was held by Plato as well as by Buddhists. A person's body differs in every reincarnation, but the soul remains the same. "As a man leaves an old garment and puts on the one that is new, the Spirit leaves his mortal body and then puts on one that is new" (BG, 2:47). Hindus typically offer evidence of people remembering experiences from past lives. A story is told of a little boy from a village who is taken by his family to visit a castle museum in Calcutta. While there, the boy begins to describe the rooms in the castle and to relate events from the distant past. The inference is that he experienced these events in his past life.

Reincarnation is linked with the Law of **karma,** an inexorable moral law that rules the universe, determining that whatsoever you sow, that shall you also reap.[10] If you sow seeds of greed, hate, and lust in this life or fail in your caste duties, you will be reincarnated in the next life as the fruit of those vices, as a lower animal, a pig or dog, or as a member of a lower caste, even as an outcast. If you sow seeds of love and justice and fulfill your caste duties, you will advance to the next stage, a warrior (*kashatrya*) becoming a brahmin, a brahmin being absorbed into God (Brahma). Thus, the wheel of karma is broken and the self attains Nirvana.

Nirvana literally means "waning away," as of a flame when its fuel is exhausted. What must wane away is the deluded egocentricity which is involved in sensuality and selfish desires. These deluded desires (*maya*) imprison humans and all sentient beings around the cycle of death, rebirth, and suffering. When the ego is transcended by those who follow the correct path, or yoga (see p. 90) salvation follows, which is Nirvana.

Epistemology

There are two kinds of knowledge: the lower and the higher. Lower knowledge is the knowledge of the senses and intellect. It consists primarily of empirical knowledge, everyday, commonsense knowledge, which enables us to survive in the world, the world of *maya.* It also includes knowledge of the Vedas, as well as the rituals and ceremonies of our culture and religion. Higher knowledge is metaphysical, that which apprehends the divine, changeless reality of Brahma. "None behold him with the eyes, for he is without visible form. Yet in the heart is he revealed through self-control and meditation. Those who know him become immortal."[11] One must learn how to experience the Brahma, practicing the appropriate spiritual exercise, or yoga.

A story is told of a father who instructs his son to take a lump of salt and place it in their garden pool. A few days later, the father asks the son to retrieve the lump of salt. The child goes to the pool but cannot find the lump of salt. He reports back to his father, who accompanies the child back to the pool. Taking a cup of water from the pool, he offers it to his son. "Now can you taste the salt?" he asks. Likewise, we cannot point to the absolute, Brahma, but we can taste and feel him in mystical experience. We can receive him in self-authenticating, ecstatic joy (*ananda*).

Hinduism teaches that there are many ways to the truth, to knowledge of the absolute, to the experience of *ananda*. The religious pluralism of Hinduism calls on us to give up our claims to exclusivity and accept the thesis that many paths lead to God and to salvation or liberation. No religion has all the truth, but each complements the others. If you are a Christian, be a good Christian. If you are a Muslim, be a good Muslim. This ecumenical ideal will be highlighted in the Buddha's parable of the elephant and the six blind men (see p. 99). In the BG, Lord Krishna puts the point this way: "In whatever way men approach me, I am gracious to them; men everywhere follow my path."

Along these lines, Hinduism holds that God has manifested himself in many times and places, most notably in ten incarnations (**avatar**), the last four being Rama, Krishna, the Buddha, and Kalki. In modern times, Jesus Christ is mentioned as an avatar.

Theory of Human Nature

We turn now to the Hindu theory of human nature, the human condition being one of suffering and ignorance, and the way of salvation.

The Human Condition

1. The immediate, existential condition of humanity is alienation. We find ourselves driven by desire, cravings which are never really satisfied, for many desires are never met, leaving us frustrated, or if they are satisfied, the satisfaction is ephemeral. As soon as one desire is met, a new desire takes its place. We soon tire of the object of desire and want a new object. Like persons with an addictive habit, our cravings only increase to the point where more and more satisfies us less and less. This ongoing process of desire and fulfillment followed by new desire leads to frustration and suffering. Our individual suffering is projected onto others and onto the universe as a whole, so we despise those who frustrate our desires and seek to subordinate them under our power. Feeling pain and suffering, we accuse the universe of harming us and infer that the world is evil, meaning that the world does not serve our every whim and caprice. Suffering and ignorance distort our vision, leaving us confused and blind to who and what we are.

In the literary epic the *Mahabharata*, a work three times as long as the King James Bible, the heroic king Yudhistira is approaching a lake where he wishes to parch his thirsty throat when he hears a voice warning him of the poisonous waters. He sees the corpses of his brothers lying on the bank of the lake. The voice then says, "You may drink only on the condition that you answer my questions. If you answer correctly, you and your brothers shall live. If you fail, then you shall die." The voice then presents him with a series of questions, which Yudhistira answers correctly. The final question is, "Of all the amazing things in the world, what is the most amazing?" The king replies, "The most amazing thing is that although everyone sees his parents dying, and everything around him dying, still we live as though we will live forever. This is truly amazing."[12] Thus, Yudhistira recognizes the most fundamental truth about human existence: that we are mortal. You and I will die. What does that mean? How shall we come to terms with the inevitable? The sober person ponders these questions. However, this raises an even more fundamental question.

2. According to Hinduism, the "Identity Problem" is that we all suffer from an identity crisis: "Who am I?" We do not know who we really are. Hindu scholars tell the following story. A lioness, looking for food, attacked a flock of sheep, but as she lurched forward for the kill, she suddenly went into labor, delivered a cub, and died. The cub grew up among the sheep, behaving like a sheep, eating grass and bleating like a sheep. He thought of himself as a sheep. One day another lion encountered this lion–sheep in the forest. He was astonished to see a lion cavorting with the sheep, eating grass, and bleating like a sheep. He approached the lion-sheep and said, "Don't you know that you are a lion, not a sheep?" "No," said the lion–sheep and began to bleat. The stranger lion brought his cousin to a lake and urged him to look into the water in order to behold his own image. The lion–sheep gazed into the pool and beheld a lion looking back at him. Then the stranger began to roar and motioned to the lion–sheep to imitate him. The lion–sheep tried, but at first his voice only uttered loud "baas" but as he tried to imitate the stranger, the voice grew louder. After a time, he was roaring so that the sound shook the forest and he knew he was a lion, not a sheep.[13]

The Upanishads distinguish between our empirical (sheep) self (*jiva*) and our real (lion) self (**atman**). We are acquainted with *jiva*, our everyday individual conscious self, our ego. It exists in time and space, in the Heraclitean world of flux; but this world is an illusion. Time and space and flux do not exist. We are really divine, *atman*.

The term *atman* is derived from the Sanskrit *an*, "to breathe." It is the breath of life. It is the immortal part of us, our true essence, unconditioned by our intellect, mental states, or outward events. The goal of life is to realize this true nature, to experience ourselves as varied expressions of the one universal self, Brahma. The *atman* is the Brahma. We are all part of God as waves are part of the great ocean: *tat tvam asi*, "that art thou." "As all spokes are contained in the axle and in the rim of the wheel, just so, in the self, all beings, all gods, all works, all breathing creatures, all these selves are held together."[14] As the Hindu scholar Radhakrishnan put it in *The Principal Upanishads*, "He whose self is harmonized by yoga sees the Self abiding in all beings and all beings in the Self; everywhere he sees the same." The *atman* is our ultimate self, pure being (*sat*), infinitely great, yet smallest of the smallest, like a point. Self-realization is realization that we are all interconnected in the one, God. Alternately, Brahma, the absolute principle of the universe, is known through the *atman*.[15]

This state of being one with God and every other being is paradoxical and hard for Westerners to comprehend. Hindus use the metaphor of cells in the body to illustrate the unity of all things. Just as all cells are similar, developing from each other, so we are all intimately related in one spiritual body. The metaphor of being members of a spiritual body was used by St. Paul in 1 Corinthians 12 to describe the functional unity of the church, but in Hinduism it takes on cosmic proportions. A second illustration comes from physics. Ions and electrons would seem to be simply energy units in a field of universal energy. Each energy unit seems to be as inexhaustible as the entire storehouse from which it is produced. Likewise, each soul is an inexhaustible spiritual universe, yet only a small part of the whole, infinite God.

The Way of Salvation

Just as the lion–sheep needed a mentor to realize its true nature, so we too must be led by a guide or guru to realize our true nature and be liberated at death from our human condition. We are not simply finite, feeble mortals (*jiva*) but infinite, immortal, *atman,* divine, part and parcel of the great ocean of Brahma. The *atman* is *Brahma.* The realization of this truth is salvation (*moksha*) Since this knowledge is primarily "knowledge-how" (skill knowledge), rather than merely "knowledge-that" (descriptive knowledge), there is no do-it-yourself recipe for liberation. One needs an expert spiritual gymnast to teach one the paths of yoga. According to Hinduism, there are four ways (*yogas*) to salvation: bhakti yoga, karma yoga, raja yoga, and ginana yoga. *(1) Bhakti yoga* is the practice of devotion to God. *(2) Karma yoga* prescribes good works as the way to enlightenment (*samadhi*). *(3) Raja yoga* enjoins meditation and psychic control as the way to salvation. *(4) Ginana yoga* holds that *samadhi* comes through philosophical inquiry and speculation. Each form of yoga seeks to reduce the ego's selfish desires, replacing them with God consciousness. In *samadhi, moksha* occurs in joyous ecstasy (*ananda*), and the soul, released from *maya,* discovers God, not merely in some future existence but here and now, salvation while living. The goal of life is to be reabsorbed into God. This is called reaching Nirvana. Thus, one breaks free from *maya* and the wheel of karma.

The sacred word *om,* sincerely chanted, is an indispensable ingredient of yoga practice. The word contains all language and the divine essence, so by meditatively chanting it, we touch the divine nature. Through realization of our true nature in God, we overcome ignorance, selfishness, suffering, and alienation from the truth. We are taken up into the divine being and become aware of the infinite, universal consciousness in which we really live. According to Advaitan Hinduism, the subject–object distinction* is abrogated and we realize our oneness with all consciousness, our oneness with God. For Advaitans, this means a state of passionless peace, where the self ceases to exist as a separate entity. For Vaisnavans, it means blissful, loving service and fellowship with Lord Krishna. According to Vaiasnavan Hinduism, we remain separate individuals while enjoying personal knowledge and love of God (Vishnu).

---

*The subject–object distinction refers to the distinction between the self and the world, for example, between you and what you are aware of. Advaitans hold that the two are one.

Morality, Dharma, and the Caste System

Morality is at the heart of the universe. The BG opens with the words "On the field of Kuruksheta, the field of the working out of *Dharma*." Roughly, the story is a moral parable about the nature of duty. *Dharma* consists of the basic core morality which is universal, but it also consists of specific caste obligations. One finds a negative version of the Golden Rule, "Let no man do to another that which would be repugnant to himself."[16] The statement *tat tvam asi* ("that art thou") can be interpreted as seeing yourself in all other beings, inspiring a sense of moral identity.

Morality includes obeying the specific rules of one's hereditary caste. There are four castes in Hinduism. *(1) Brahmin,* the priestly aristocrat, should be dedicated to learning and attaining wisdom. He is a religious philosopher whose rules include no meat eating, no drinking of alcoholic beverages, no premarital sex, no gambling, and no violence (*ahimsa*). *(2)* The *kashatrya,* the warrior, must possess valor and integrity. He is not subject to some of the other brahmin principles. He may gamble and indulge in violence against the enemy. *(3) Vaisya,* the business and productive class, is made up of the entrepreneurs and farmers in society. *(4) Sudras,* the servants, are subordinate to the other three cases. Finally, there are the "outcastes," who are excluded from all the benefits of the caste system. Many Hindus believe that the outcastes are either criminals (people who failed to fulfill their caste obligations) or their descendants. They are "untouchables," people who have forfeited their rights. Traditionally, each caste has inflexible rules which govern people's behavior (e.g., whom one may marry) and vocation. The doctrine of karma holds that members of a caste deserve their status, but if they obey their *dharma,* they will rise in status in the next life. The caste system may have originally been an equal-opportunity one, in which a person could attain a certain level of dignity by works, but gradually that was transformed into a rigid system of social rules and regulations which severely limit personal mobility. The British government tried to abolish the caste system, and the Indian government has followed suit, concentrating on abolition of the outcast class, of which there are millions of people. Gandhi tried to abolish this non-class, naming them children of God (*harijans*), even adopting an outcaste child. However, great resistance has met these abolitionist efforts, especially in rural areas, so that remnants of the system remain alive today. Hindus point out that the caste system reflects a deep expression of morality: if justice demands that I suffer in this life as a *harijan* or *sudra,* it would be immoral for me to refuse to pay my debt. In the caste system, biology may be seen as recapitulating morality. One's past moral deeds determine present class–family status.

Another aspect of moral behavior in Hinduism is understanding that the proper life consists of four stages: *(1) bramaharya,* the period of education, being a student; *(2) garhasthya,* the period of being a producer, a married man with family, a productive member of the community; *(3) vanaprasthya,* retirement; and *(4) sannyasa,* the life of renunciation and retreat, leaving family in order to prepare for death and transmigration to the next life. Living according to the four stages of life within one's proper caste constitutes a vital part of *dharma.*

Bhagavad Gita

A central Hindu work on morality is the Bhagavad Gita (literally, "the song of God," written between 500 and 200 B.C.E.), in which the central doctrines are poetically and philosophically set forth. It is the most famous and the most widely read ethical text of ancient India. As an episode in India's great epic, the *Mahabharata*, the BG is one of the principal texts that define and capture the essence of Hinduism. Though this work contains much theology, its kernel is ethical and its teaching is set in the context of an ethical problem. The teaching of the BG is summed up in the maxim "you must do your duty without regard for the result." When Arjuna, the third son of King Pandu (dynasty name: Pandavas), is about to begin a war that became inevitable once his 100 cousins belonging to the Kaurava dynasty refused to return even a few villages to the five Pandava brothers after their return from enforced exile, he looks at his cousins, uncles, and friends standing on the other side of the battlefield and wonders whether he is morally prepared and justified in killing his blood relations even though it was he, along with his brother Bhima, who had courageously prepared for this war. Arjuna is certain that he would be victorious in this war since he has Lord Krishna (one of the ten avatars of Vishnu) on his side. He is able to visualize the scene at the end of the battle, the dead bodies of his beloved teacher and cousins lying on the battlefield, motionless and incapable of vengeance. It is then that he loses his nerve to fight.

> Life goes from my limbs and they sink, and my mouth is sear and dry; a trembling overcomes my body, and my hair shudders in horror. . . . The destruction of a family destroys its rituals of righteousness, and when the righteous rituals are no more, unrighteousness overcomes the whole family. . . . O day of darkness! What evil spirit moved our minds when for the sake of an earthly kingdom we came to this field of battle ready to kill our own people. (BG, 1:29,40,43)

Arjuna would rather die than lift his sword against his kin.

Lord Krishna comforts the unenlightened warrior Arjuna, who trembles before this war against his cousins, by telling him that there is no reason to grieve over the death of someone we love, for the "Eternal in man cannot die. . . . We have all been for all time: I, thou, and those kings of men. And we shall be for all time, we all for ever and ever. . . . If any man thinks he slays, and if another thinks he is slain, neither knows the way of truth. The Eternal in man cannot kill; the Eternal in man cannot die" (BG, 2:12,19). Krishna is telling Arjuna that he ought not take himself so seriously but do his duty for its own sake, leaving the results to God. "Set thy heart upon the work, but never on its reward. . . . Do thy work in the peace of yoga and, free from selfish desires, be not moved in success or failure" (BG, 2:47f).

Then comes the message of reincarnation. "As a man leaves an old garment and puts on the one that is new, the Spirit leaves his mortal body and then puts on one that is new" (BG, 2:22).

The wise person, through knowledge of this metaphysical truth about the eternal in human beings, will find peace within so long as he or she does his or her duty. "Even as all waters flow into the ocean, but the ocean never overflows, even so the sage feels desires, but he is ever one in his infinite peace. For the man who forsakes all desires and abandons all pride of possessions and of self reaches the goal of peace supreme" (BG, 2:70). One must make a complete renunciation of all possessions, even family. "Freedom from the chains of attachment; even from a selfish attachment to one's children, wife, or home; an ever-present evenness of mind in pleasant or unpleasant events" (BG, 13:9). The message is that of hyper-Stoicism, divine **ataraxia** through resignation to duty. "Let the Yogi practice harmony of the soul; in a secret place, in deep solitude, master of his mind, hoping for nothing, desiring nothing" (BG, 6:10).

The rest of the BG is an elaboration of the various yogas or methods of renunciation, of disciplined, ascetic devotion, intended to squelch desire, egotism, and hate and to develop the soul in knowledge of the truth. One is to utter the sacred word *om*, which reflects in sound the all-encompassing nature of God. Sincerely uttering *om* leads to truth and salvation. "I will teach thee the truth of pure work, and this truth shall make thee free" (BG, 4:16). The goal is Nirvana. "The Yogi attains the Nirvana of Brahman: he is one with God and goes unto God. Holy men reach the Nirvana of Brahman; their sins are no more, their doubts are gone, their soul is in harmony, the joy is in the good of all" (BG, 5:25–26).

The BG exalts Krishna as God. "I am the Father of the universe, and even the source of the Father. I am the mother of the universe, and the Creator of all. I am the highest to be known, the path of purification, the holy OM, the three Vedas" (BG, 9:17).

The *dharma* of the kashatrya, or warrior, in the BG seems a long way off from the ideal of *ahimsa* of the Brahmin caste, which Gandhi made the hallmark of his non-violent liberation movement. However, this may show how plastic and diverse Hinduism really is.

Conclusion to Hinduism

1. It is impossible to speak definitively about Hinduism. It comes in monist (Advaitan) and dualist (Vaisnavan) forms, and scholars from both traditions interpret the same texts in vastly different ways. All forms hold to the central doctrines of the Law of Karma, reincarnation, *maya*, salvation through yoga, and the goal of attaining Nirvana, though they interpret these doctrines somewhat differently, depending on their background assumptions.

2. We can say that Hinduism is inclusive, holding that there are many ways to the Truth and that God manifests himself in many ways and incarnations, including the Buddha and Jesus Christ.

3. There is a deep moral core in Hinduism, one of seeking stoic resignation and tranquility (*ataraxia*), of living in humble love and respect for all living things, for *tat tvam asi* ("that art thou")—we are somehow one with all living beings. The ultimate experience seems mystical, an ecstatic joy (*ananda*) characterizing the supreme relationship with God and leading to Nirvana.

4. For Westerners, Hinduism, with its emphasis on the illusoriness of the world, alienation, and suffering, seems pessimistic. We would prefer to focus on the glass half full rather than half empty. The caste system and Law of Karma seem to outsiders to give people, especially the outcastes, a false sense of their role in life, causing them to be resigned to their station rather than to work to improve their lot in life. Compared with the Jewish–Christian world view, the basic human condition is ignorance and suffering, not sin; and salvation is ecstatic liberation from suffering through yoga rather than redemption through divine grace. Its inclusivity and pluralism are at odds with traditional Christianity and Judaism.

Millions of people continue to find these doctrines and this way of life deeply meaningful. It is a view of human nature worth taking seriously.

Buddhism

> To do no evil;
> To cultivate good;
> To purify one's mind:
> This is the teaching of the Buddhas (The Dhammapada)

Life of Buddha

The Buddha was born Siddhartha Gautama, a prince of the Sakya tribe of Nepal, in approximately 563 B.C.E. He married the beautiful princess Yasodara and fathered a son by her. His father kept him confined in an idyllic palace, where he lived in luxury; he was not allowed to behold sickness, suffering, old age, or death. One day, when he was 29, he asked his chariot driver to take him outside the palace compound to see life in the outside world. They entered a village and there beheld an old man, weak and decrepit. Gautama was horrified at the sight. "Will I become old, weak and decrepit too?" he asked. "Yes, all men grow old and weak." Gautama was depressed at this knowledge and pondered it for a long time. However, his curiosity got the best of him, and he asked to go outside the temple once more. He and his chariot driver rode into the nearby village again and this time saw a sick man, feverish and suffering greatly. "Will I become sick and suffer?" he asked. "Yes," responded the chariot rider. "All men become sick some time and suffering is the way of life." Gautama was thrown into paroxysms of revulsion, but he was determined to learn the truth, so a few days later he went into the village once more. There they beheld a man bearing a corpse. It was his first encounter with death. He again asked his chariot driver, "Will I too die?" "Yes," answered the guide. "All men must die. That is the truth about existence. It must end." He was filled with profound, unremitting sorrow. Nothing consoled him. A few nights later, while his wife and son were sleeping, Gautama left the luxurious palace compound to seek the meaning of the suffering (dukkha) he saw around him. He renounced the world and all its pleasures. He sought for the meaning of life, to understand and overcome suffering. First, he sought out teachers to help him gain wisdom. Then, when that failed, he wandered about as an ascetic for 4 years, living, so it is reported, on one grain of rice a day and gathering companions to himself. However, this ascetic existence was too harsh for him, and one day he fainted and was at death's door. Realizing the futility of self-mortification, he renounced his renunciation and began to eat normally, developing the idea of the middle way, a life of moderation between asceticism and **hedonism.**

On the full moon of May, with the rising of the morning star, while sitting under the Bo (wisdom) tree, Gautama became the Buddha, the enlightened one. When someone asked him who he was, he replied "Awakened," as though the mass of humankind was still asleep. The Buddha wandered the plains of northeastern India for 45 years more, teaching the path, or *dharma*, he had realized in that moment. Around him developed a community, or *sangha*, of monks and, later, nuns, drawn from every tribe and caste, devoted to practicing this path. His message was for everyone regardless of caste, social status, gender, or race. In approximately 483 B.C.E., at the age of 80, the Buddha died. His last words are said to be "Impermanent are all created things; strive on with awareness."

Buddha's Teachings

Buddhism began as a reform movement within Hinduism, accepting the minimal core of Hindu doctrine: the basic moral teachings (*dharma*), the idea of karma, reincarnation, and nirvana. However, the Buddha modified them. He accepted the Hindu idea of nonviolence (*ahimsa*) but took it further. Whereas Hindus made exceptions for war and punishment, Buddha renounced violence totally. One may not use violence even to defend oneself. He rejected the formalistic rituals, the Vedas, the caste system, the pantheon of gods, and of course, the asceticism. Along with rejecting the idea of Brahma, he also rejected the idea of *atman,* the self, and in its place put the *an-atman*, the not-self. The idea is that we must identify with all life as linked together by karmic laws. The self and its desires are part of the problem, and they must be renounced in order to escape suffering (*dukkha*).

Buddha did not make reference to gods, nor was he worshipped as one during his lifetime. Centuries later, a form of Buddhism arose that taught that there are other Buddhas besides Guatama. These Buddhas are celestial ones who can be worshiped and can help Buddhists in following the path to Buddhahood, becoming a *Bodhisattva* (an enlightened one). Buddhism is an agnostic, spiritual movement. It is not intellectual or metaphysical but practical. One does not find a theology or set of metaphysical theses in Buddhism.

After Buddha was enlightened, he wondered whether there was any point in sharing his enlightenment. "I have realized this Truth which is deep, difficult to see, difficult to understand, comprehensible only by the wise. . . . Men who are overpowered by passions and surrounded by a mass of darkness cannot see this Truth, which is against the current, which is lofty, deep, subtle, and hard to comprehend." So he hesitated whether to share his experience with others. Then the metaphor of the lotus appeared to him. In a lotus pond, some lotuses are still under the water and others have barely risen to water level, but a few lotuses have risen above the water's surface. Similarly, there are people at different levels of spiritual progression. While most will not profit from his teachings, some will. So he began to share his ideas with others.[17]

One day a young disciple, eagerly seeking the answer to metaphysical questions, asked Buddha several of them: Was the universe eternal, or did it have a beginning? Was it infinite or finite? Is the soul really the same as the body, or are they separate? Is there life after death? The disciple asked why Buddha did not answer these questions.

Buddha responded by means of an analogy. Suppose a man is wounded by a poisoned arrow and taken to a doctor to have the arrow removed. Suppose the injured man should protest,

> I will not let this arrow be taken out until I know who shot me. Whether he was of the kashatrya, brahman, vaisya or sudra caste; what his name and family may be; whether he is short, tall, or, of medium height; whether his complexion is black, brown, or golden; from which city, town, or city he comes. I will not let this arrow be taken out until I know the kind of bow with which I was shot; the kind of bow-string used; the type of arrow; what sort of feather was used on the arrow and with what kind of material the point of the arrow was made.[18]

If the injured man insisted on receiving answers before allowing the poisoned arrow to be removed, he would die without knowing the answers. Similarly, if someone will not follow a holy life before receiving answers to these metaphysical questions, he would die with these questions unanswered. Buddha is a spiritual pragmatist, who is concerned that we remove the arrow (*dukkha*) and live a holy life. Instead of being preoccupied with metaphysical questions, one must pull out the spiritual arrow of *dukkha* and begin the healing process. That process involves understanding and living by the Four Noble Truths. These, including the Eightfold Path to those truths, are all the philosophy we need to know in life in order to find salvation. The rest is *maya*.

The Four Noble Truths

What are the Four Noble Truths? Here is the list:

1. *The Noble Truth of Suffering:* Birth, decay, illness, death, presence of hated objects, separation from loved objects, failure to obtain one's desires = suffering (*dukkha*).
2. *The Noble Truth of the Cause of Suffering:* Desire ("thirst") that leads to rebirth is the cause of suffering.
3. *The Noble Truth of the Cessation of Suffering:* Suffering ceases with the complete cessation of desire.
4. *The Noble Truth of the Path that Leads to Cessation of Suffering:* The Eightfold Path (middle way).

Let us briefly elaborate these truths.

1. The Noble Truth of Suffering (*Dukkha*). *Dukkha* includes birth, decay, illness, death, presence of hated objects, separation from loved objects, failure to obtain one's desires, and all discontentment and dissatisfaction. It includes sadness and sorrow. Suffering is everywhere, ubiquitous. Even in the most ecstatic moment the opposite is present, for one cannot remain ecstatic permanently but will experience the loss of ecstasy in a little while. For every joy there is sorrow, though for every sorrow there may not be a joy. The conception of *dukkha* may be divided into three modes: *(1)* ordinary sufferings such as pain, sickness, distress, and death, which are common to all people; *(2)* suffering produced by change, such as when a joyful state of mind passes and one experiences depression, longing, or boredom; and *(3)* suffering produced by conditioned states or consciousness (i.e., for every stage of existence there is a corresponding karmic effect). This is the deepest form of suffering. It has to do with the idea of *atman* or self. As long as fire has flammable material, whether wood or straw, it continues to burn; but take away the material or let it burn to extinction and there is nothing to burn. So with suffering. It is the idea of the self which is the source of suffering. Take the self away and suffering evaporates. Here, Buddhism distinguishes itself from Hinduism and Western philosophy and religion: it denies the existence of the self. Hinduism has the idea of *atman*, which is connected to *Brahma*, but Buddha denied such an entity and postulated the *an-atman* ("not-self"). There are continuous experiences and states of consciousness (an empirical self), but these do not require an essential soul or self to exist. The stream of consciousness goes on but not a self, so once we can eliminate the myth of *atman*, we are on the way to liberation. We will return to this point below.

2. The Noble Truth of the Cause of Suffering. Desire ("thirst") that leads to rebirth is the cause of suffering. The thirst for desire is threefold: *(1)* desire for pleasure, *(2)* desire for existence, *(3)* desire for prosperity. Seeking pleasure is counterproductive because it inevitably disappoints or turns into displeasure. Seeking to continue to exist leads to frustration and desperate clinging to life. Seeking prosperity leads to eventual frustration, for one's appetite is insatiable. The unenlightened always desires more pleasure, more wealth, and more status. A law of karma operates here that is different from the Hindu version, which has to do with moral justice and reincarnation (what you sow you will also reap). For Buddhists, the law has nothing to do with justice but is simply one of cause and effect. Every action has an effect: bad actions have bad effects and good actions have good effects. This continues into future life, but there is no self that will be reborn, no reincarnation. Nirvana consists in becoming enlightened in this life, here and now.

As noted earlier, Buddha does not deny that we have empirical selves, those connected with our bodies, but he denies that there is an essential substance called the self (as we found in Plato [see chapter 3] and will find in Kant's noumenal self [see chapter 8]). The cosmic energy of which you are a part will manifest itself in new empirical selves after your death. The cosmic life force continues to manifest itself through infinity.

To understand the *an-atman*, we need to understand Buddha's idea of the *Five Aggregates* that make up the empirical self. These are *(1)* the material form or the body, *(2)* sensation, *(3)* perception (e.g., seeing and hearing particular sights and sounds), *(4)* mental formations (e.g., hate and love), and *(5)* consciousness (mental awareness, thoughts, and discrimination). The self is only the compilation of these aggregates.[19] Since it is obvious that none of these aggregates is permanent, the self cannot be permanent. The empirical self is a shifting continual flux; but if this is so, what is an enlightened self?

3. The Third Noble Truth of the Cessation of Suffering. Suffering ceases with the complete cessation of desire. Destroy desire and suffering ends. This is the way to Nirvana. When we understand that suffering is caused by desire and the selfish quest for individual success and prosperity, that no substantial self really exists, we can take steps to give up desiring. We do not have to become ascetics to annihilate the self, as Hindu saints do, for there is no self to annihilate. It is the annihilation of the illusion of the self. It is the annihilation of craving, lust, and selfish desire.

4. The Fourth Noble Truth of the Path that Leads to Cessation of Suffering: The Eightfold Path. This is sometimes referred to as the "middle way" because it rejects the extremes of sensuous living of the carnal person as well as the ascetic living of Hinduism. It says that the way to enlightenment is through a certain path of spiritual, moral, and mental exercise. The eight aspects of the path are as follows:

1. Right Views (Understanding)
2. Right Aspirations (Thoughts)
3. Right Speech
4. Right Conduct or Action
5. Right Livelihood
6. Right Endeavor or Effort
7. Right Mindfulness
8. Right Meditation or Concentration

We can classify these eight aspects of the Eightfold Path under three headings: *ethical conduct, mental discipline,* and *wisdom.*

1. Ethical conduct (*sila*): universal love and compassion, tolerance. The Buddha gave his teaching for "the good of the many, for the happiness of the many, out of compassion for the world." This involves aspects 3, 4, and 5. Right speech includes truth telling and refraining from gossip, malicious words, impoliteness, and backbiting. Right conduct refers to honesty, peacemaking, and refraining from violence, cheating, and illicit sexual liaisons. Right livelihood refers to earning one's living through honorable employment. Negatively, it prohibits manufacturing or selling weapons, producing or serving intoxicating drinks or drugs (which are camouflaged poisons), and killing animals.

2. Mental discipline (*samadhi*, for Hindus "holy vision"): One must be disciplined, exercise self-control, and concentrate one's mind on the noble truths (aspects 6, 7, and 8). Recommended ways to accomplish this include practicing

concentration breathing and other modes of yoga or meditation. In the first stage of spiritual exercise, one learns to overcome or reject sensuous lust, ill will, worry, boredom, and doubt. In the second stage, all intellectual activities are suppressed. In the third stage, all feelings of joy disappear so that only the disposition of happiness remains. In the fourth stage, even dispositions of happiness and unhappiness disappear so that only equanimity and awareness remain. One is perfectly imperturbable.

3. Wisdom: By living in universal love and discipline, one attains wisdom and, at the highest point, enlightenment, Nirvana (aspects 1 and 2). One becomes enlightened, realizing that the self does not exist but only the cosmic energy which unites all living beings. As such, one now understands the puzzle of existence and becomes patient, tolerant, and accepting of what might otherwise seem repugnant.[20] One has attained Nirvana, and one has attained it here and now, not in a future existence.

Buddha's practical, commonsense, but deeply spiritual (though not religious in the usual meaning of the word) philosophy has inspired many people to live peaceful, fulfilled lives. Here is one instance of that wisdom.

The following story illustrates both the Buddhist ideal of tolerance and the inclusivity of Hinduism. This story is said to have been told by the Buddha, though it may have come down through Mahvira, the founder of Jainism.[21] It is known as "The Six Blind Men and The Elephant." Once upon a time, a group of religious seekers from different traditions came together and began to discuss the nature of God. Offering quite different answers, they began quarreling among themselves as to who was right and who wrong. Finally, when no hope for a reconciliation was in sight, they called in the Buddha and asked him to tell them who was right. The Buddha proceeded to tell the following story. There was once a king who asked his servants to bring him all the blind people in a town and an elephant. Six blind men and an elephant were soon set before him. The king instructed the blind men to feel the animal and describe the elephant. "An elephant is like a large waterpot," said the first, who touched the elephant's head. "Your Majesty, he's wrong," said the second, as he touched an ear. "An elephant is like a fan." "No," insisted a third, "an elephant is like a thick snake," as he held the trunk. "On the contrary, you're all mistaken," said a fourth, as he held the tusks. "An elephant is like two prongs of a plow." The fifth man demurred and said, "It is quite clear that an elephant is like a pillar," as he grasped the animal's rear leg. "You're all mistaken," insisted the sixth. "An elephant is a long rope," and he held up the tail. Then they all began to shout at each other concerning their convictions regarding the nature of an elephant.

The Buddha commented, "How can you be so sure of what you cannot see? We are all like blind people in this world. We cannot see God. Each of you may be partly right, yet none completely so."

Conclusion to Buddhism

1. As with Hinduism, it is hard to give an authoritative definition of Buddhism, but we can provide a broad outline of its central teachings. Buddhism arose out of

Hinduism, rejected the caste system and the metaphysical speculations of Hinduism, but accepted its theses of *ahimsa* and karma.

2. Buddhism centers around the Four Noble Truths via the Eightfold Path, which involve escape from suffering and attainment of Nirvana. However, in Buddhism, Nirvana is attained in this life, not in a future existence. If we live by the Four Noble Truths via the Eightfold Path, we will escape the wheel of karma and enter Nirvana. Unlike Hinduism, which insists that this can happen only after death, Buddha taught "nirvana now!"—an existentialist version of Hinduism.

3. There is no essential self (*atman*), as Hinduism and most Western religions and philosophies maintain. There is simply a cosmic force that links all life together. The idea of the *an-atman* is a difficult concept for many to grasp, but it is the key to enlightenment. Nevertheless, there is a problem with it. If there is no permanent self, what is the significance of enlightenment? Is enlightenment also an illusion?

4. Among its modes of living are the dispositions of compassion and tolerance (as illustrated by the story of the six blind men and the elephant).

5. Buddhists have no creed. They do recite this simple formula:

I take refuge in the Buddha.
I take refuge in the dharma (his teachings).
I take refuge in the sangha (the Buddhist community).

Although at first glance this seems a simple formula, it involves continual practice and rigorous discipline to internalize the Four Noble Truths and reach enlightenment. Buddhists practice meditation and good deeds, renouncing violence, lust, greed, and other practices fed by desire. Aiming at moderation rather than extreme asceticism may be an arduous endeavor requiring the fullest commitment of the person or the not-person.[22]

6. There is a widespread tendency in Hinduism and Buddhism to assume universal justice. As John Koller has written, "The world is seen as a great moral stage directed by justice. Everything good, bad and indifferent is earned and deserved. The impact of this attitude is to place the responsibility for the human condition squarely upon human beings themselves. We are responsible for what we are and what we have become."[23] We have determined what we now are by what we have done in the past and what we now do will determine what we will become, even our future existence. This is the law of karma, a law common to both Hinduism and Buddhism.

Study Questions

1. Describe the Hindu metaphysical doctrines: the creation, the nature of God, and *maya*.

2. Explain the meaning of *atman*.

3. What is the Law of Karma?

4. Explain the meaning of *dharma* and the caste system. Can you imagine a reformed version of the system, or is it a violation of the Western idea of equal opportunity? Compare the caste system with Plato's noble lie.

5. What is the message of the Bhagavad Gita?

6. What, according to Yudhistira, is the most amazing thing in the world? What does this mean?

7. Compare the Hindu idea of creation with the Hebrew biblical story of creation.

8. Some scholars think that Hinduism, with its emphasis on *maya* and unconditional renunciation, is a pessimistic religion. Do you think this is accurate?

9. Compare the Hindu doctrine of alienation as suffering and ignorance with the Judeo–Christian doctrine of alienation through sin. What are the implications of this difference in perspective?

10. Compare the Hindu idea of *ahimsa* with the Sermon on the Mount by Jesus. What is the difference between the Hindu and Buddhist versions of *ahimsa?*

11. Discuss the teachings of Buddha. What are the Four Noble Truths?

12. Explain the Eightfold Path. Why is it called "the middle way"?

13. How does Buddhism differ from other religions like Hinduism and Christianity?

14. Examine Buddhism's notion of the not-self (*an-atman*). Compare it with the Hindu idea of the *atman.* Compare it also with David Hume's denial of personal identity (in the following passage):

> From what impression could [the idea of the self] be derived? . . . It must be some one impression, that gives rise to every real idea. But self or person is not any one impression, but that to which our several impressions and ideas are supposed to have a reference. If any impression gives rise to the idea of self, that impression must continue invariably the same, through the whole course of our lives; since self is supposed to exist after that manner. But there is no impression constant and invariable. . . . For my part, when I enter most intimately into what I call *myself,* I always stumble on some particular perception or other, of heat or cold, light or shade, love or hatred, pain or pleasure. I never can catch *myself* at any time without a perception, and never can observe any thing but the perception. . . . If any one upon serious and unprejudiced reflection, thinks he has a different notion of *himself,* I must confess I can reason no longer with him. All I can allow him is, that he may be in the right as well as I, and that we are essentially different in this particular. . . . But setting aside some metaphysicians of this kind, I may venture to affirm of the rest of mankind, that they are nothing but a bundle or collection of different perceptions, which succeed each other with an inconceivable rapidity, and are in a perpetual flux and movement.[24]

15. What is the meaning of the parable of the six blind men and the elephant?

16. What does *Nirvana* mean? Compare the Hindu and Buddhist views on nirvana.

17. If, as Buddha claims, there is no real self (*atman*), who is it that becomes enlightened? Is the awakening or enlightenment also simply an illusion?

Notes

1. See S. Radhakrishnan, *The Principal Upanishads* (Harper & Brothers, 1953), pp. 15–27, for a good discussion of the sources of Hinduism.
2. There are many good translations of the *Bhagavad Gita*. I have used the Penguin edition translation of Juan Mascaro (1962).
3. *Isvara,* the creative force, and *Hiranya-garbha,* the world-soul, are not clearly distinguished in the Upanishads.
4. Rig Veda, X. 129 (quoted in Juan Mascaro's introduction to the Bhagavad Gita, p. xiii).
5. Brihad Aranyaka Upanishad, III.6.1.
6. Ibid., III.9.1.
7. *Jaiiniya Brahmana,* VII.4.
8. Brihad Aranyaka Upanishad, II.8.8.
9. Westerners will be reminded of Bishop George Berkeley's idealism, wherein matter is viewed as an illusion and only spirits, God and souls, exist.
10. This idea is similar to St. Paul's statement in Gal. 6:7, "Whatsoever a man sows, that shall he also reap."
11. Upanishads: Mundaka, I.1.4–6.
12. I am indebted to Prasannatma Das for bringing this story from the *Mahabharata* to my attention.
13. Swami Vivekananda, *The Complete Works of Vivekananda,* vol. I, p. 324 (Advaita Ahrama, 1950), p. 324
14. Brihad Aranyaka Upanishad, II.5.15.
15. Brihad Aranyaka Upanishad, I.4.
16. *Mahabharata,* 5.49.57.
17. This incident is related in Walpola Rahula, *What Buddha Taught* (Weidenfeld, 1974), p. 52. I am indebted to this book and to Don Mitchell, *Buddhism: Introduction to the Buddhist Experience* (Oxford University Press, 2002), for my exposition of Buddhism.
18. See Rahula, op. cit., pp. 13–14.
19. For an excellent discussion of the Five Aggregates and their relation to the self, see Don Mitchell, *Buddhism: Introduction to the Buddhist Experience,* pp. 36–40.
20. See Rahula, op. cit., chapter V.
21. Mahvira (599–527 B.C.E.) was a contemporary of Buddha who founded Jainism. He rejected much of the theology and rituals of Hinduism and attained enlightenment through renunciation and meditation.
22. Edward Conze, writing from a Buddhist perspective, sees the continuous thread as such:

> Three avenues of approach to the spiritual are, I think, handed down by the almost universal tradition of the sages: [1] to regard sensory experience as relatively unimportant; [2] to try to renounce what one is attached to; [3] to try to treat all people alike—whatever their looks, intelligence, color, smell, education, etc. (Edward Conze, *Buddhism: Its Essence and Development* [Philosophical Library, 1951], p. 11)

23. John Koller, *Oriental Philosophies* (Scribners, 1985), p. 12.
24. Hume, *Treatise of Human Nature* (Oxford University Press, 1978), p. 252.

For Further Reading

Bhagavad Gita, trans. Juan Mascaro (Penguin, 1962).

Braden, Charles, *The World's Great Religions* (Abingdon, 1949).

Deussen, Paul, *The Philosophy of the Upanishads* (Dover, 1966).

Dhammapala, Bhikkhu, *Basic Buddhism* (Associated Press of Ceylon, 1956).

Eck, Diane, *Seeing the Divine Image in India* (Columbia University Press, 1996).

Eliot, C., *Hinduism and Buddhism* (Longman's, Green, & Co., 1921).

Hiriyanna, M., *Outlines of Indian Philosophy* (George Allen & Unwin, 1973).

Koller, John M., *Oriental Philosophies* (Scribners, 1985).

Mitchell, Don, *Buddhism* (Oxford University Press, 1999).

Prabhvandanda, Swami, *The Spiritual Heritage of India* (Sri Ramakrishna Math Printing Press, 1981).

Radhakrishnan, S., *Eastern Religions and Western Thought* (Oxford University Press, 1939).

———, *The Principal Upanishads* (Harper & Brothers, 1953).

Rahula, Walpoli, *What the Buddha Taught* (Grove Press, 1959).

Schweitzer, Albert, *Indian Thought and Its Development* (Beacon Press, 1936).

Sen, K. M., *Hinduism* (Penguin, 1961).

Suzuki, D. T., *Zen Buddhism: Selected Writings* (Doubleday, 1956).

———, *The Thirteen Principal Upanishads*, trans. Robert E. Hume (Oxford University Press, 1971).

Vivekananda, Swami, *The Complete Works of Vivekananda* (Advaita Ahrama, 1950).

Zaehner, R. C., *Hinduism* (Oxford University Press, 1962).

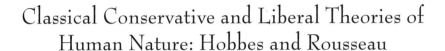

CHAPTER 7

Classical Conservative and Liberal Theories of Human Nature: Hobbes and Rousseau

> I often think it's comical
> How nature always does contrive
> That every boy and every gal,
> That's born into the world alive,
> Is either a little Liberal,
> Or else a little Conservative! *(Gilbert and Sullivan's comic opera Iolanthe)*

In this chapter we examine and contrast the views of two philosophers, Thomas Hobbes and Jean-Jacques Rousseau, the former a representative of conservatism and the latter, of liberalism.

Thomas Hobbes: A Conservative Theory of Human Nature

Introduction

Thomas Hobbes (1588–1679), the greatest English political philosopher, gave classic expression to the idea that human beings are pleasure-seeking machines who invent government as a social contract. The son of a poor clergyman, he was born in Malmesbury, Wiltshire, during the approach of the Spanish Armada. Upon hearing of the approach, his mother panicked and prematurely gave birth to little Thomas. He would later write in autobiographical verse "Fear and I were born twins." Indeed, he was a fearful child, who lived through fearful times, developing a political philosophy predicated on fear of death and insecurity. He was educated at Oxford University and lived through an era of political revolutions and civil war. He was a scholar, and tutor to Prince Charles II of England. Hobbes was widely traveled; in communication with most of the intellectual luminaries of his day, both on the Continent (Galileo, Gassendi, and Descartes) and in England (Francis Bacon, Ben Jonson, and William Harvey); and regarded as a brilliant but somewhat unorthodox and controversial intellectual.

Hobbes is known today primarily for his masterpiece on political theory, *Leviathan* (1651, hereafter abbreviated as L),[1] a book he wrote during the English Civil Wars (1642–1652), sometimes referred to as "The Great Rebellion," which pitted the forces of monarchy (the royalists) under Charles I against those of Parliament under Oliver Cromwell. Hobbes' work was intended to support the royalists as he believed that the monarchy was the best guarantee for an orderly and stable government. Yet, the royalists misconstrued his interpretation as supporting the rebels. For this reason and because the book conveyed a materialist view of human nature thought to be dangerous to religion, it was suppressed or violently attacked throughout Hobbes' lifetime.

Hobbes' doctrines were repugnant to his generation as well as succeeding generations, until modern times. He extinguished the notion of a soul and reduced human beings to machines. He denied spiritual forces, viewing human beings as egoists who always did what they saw to be in their self-interests. No philosophical system attracted more venom and hatred than that of Hobbes.

Hobbes' Account of Human Nature: Humans as Machines

Hobbes' theory of human nature derives from his comprehensive materialist theory of nature, which holds that nature simply consists of bodies in motion. There is nothing in the universe except bodies in motion. Even God is a physical body in motion. The universe is one interconnected "macroclock" and everything in it, a part of that clock. Humans and other animals are "microclocks." Psychology is reduced to physiology. Humans and other animals are sentient, but their sentience is reducible to inner motions in the body.

> THERE be in animals two sorts of motions peculiar to them: One called vital, begun in generation, and continued without interruption through their whole life; such as are the course of the blood, the pulse, the breathing, the concoction, nutrition, excretion, etc.; to which motions there needs no help of imagination: the other is animal motion, otherwise called voluntary motion; as to go, to speak, to move any of our limbs, in such manner as is first fancied in our minds. That sense is motion in the organs and interior parts of man's body, caused by the action of the things we see, hear, etc., and that fancy is but the relics of the same motion, remaining after sense. . . . And because going, speaking, and the like voluntary motions depend always upon a precedent thought of whither, which way, and what, it is evident that the imagination is the first internal beginning of all voluntary motion. And although unstudied men do not conceive any motion at all to be there, where the thing moved is invisible, or the space it is moved in is, for the shortness of it, insensible; yet that doth not hinder but that such motions are. For let a space be ever so little, that which is moved over a greater space, whereof that little one is part, must first be moved over that. These small beginnings of motion within the body of man, before they appear in walking, speaking, striking, and other visible actions, are commonly called endeavor. (L, chapter 6)

Our consciousness and feelings are fancy, impressions produced by motions in the machine. Hobbes today would be considered a central state materialist (see chapter 14), for he reduces mental states to brain states, physical states. Hobbes was a theist materialist, who believed that all reality except God is material. God alone is spirit. We are entirely material beings.

> The world (the universe, that is the whole mass of all things that are) is corporeal, that is to say, body; and hath the dimensions of magnitude, namely, length, breadth, and depth; also every part of body, is likewise body, and hath the like dimensions; and consequently every part of the universe is body; and that which is not body, is no part of the universe. And because the universe is all, that which is no part of it, is nothing; and consequently no where. Nor does it follow from this that spirits are nothing; for they have dimensions, and are therefore really bodies; though that name in common speech is only given to visible bodies. Spirit, that which is incorporeal, is a term that rightly belongs to God himself, in whom we consider not what attribute expresses best his nature, which is incomprehensible, but that which best expresses our desire to honor him. (L, chapter 46)

Hobbes is a determinist. Since there is only matter in motion, the notion of free will is incoherent. Freedom simply means motion without obstruction. Just as a stream flows downhill when nothing obstructs its motion, human acts are free when no external obstacles hinder them. What people call free will is merely the "last appetite in deliberation."

> The whole sum of desires, aversions, hopes and fears, continued till the thing be either done, or thought impossible, is that we call deliberation. . . . And it is called deliberation; because it is a putting an end to the liberty we had of doing, or omitting, according to our own appetite, or aversion. . . . In deliberation, the last appetite, or aversion, immediately adhering to the action, or to the omission thereof, is what we call the will; the act, not the faculty, of willing. And beasts that have deliberation must necessarily also have will. (L, chapter 6)

Hobbes was a **psychological egoist,** who held that it was in our nature to be selfish. A friend saw him giving alms to a beggar and asked whether this really was an act of selfishness. Hobbes replied that the beggar's distress caused him such distress that by relieving it, he relieved his own.[2] For Hobbes, humans are all equal in the sense that each is able to kill another, but this "equality" is not so much a description of human worth as it is of human insecurity. Each of us has a lethal first-strike capacity. Human worth is one's market value, how much one would pay for another's services. It is because of our insecurity that we need morality and government.

Hobbes' Account of Morality: The State of Nature

Why do we need morality? What is its nature and purpose? What does it do for us that no other social arrangement does? Hobbes and Rousseau give radically different answers to this question. Hobbes, as we noted, believed that human beings always act out of perceived self-interest; that is, they invariably seek gratification and avoid harm. His argument goes like this: nature has made us basically equal in physical and mental abilities so that, even though one person may be somewhat stronger or smarter than another, each has the ability to harm, even kill, the other, if not alone, then in confederacy with others. Furthermore, we all want to attain our goals, such as having sufficient food, shelter, security, power, wealth, glory, and other scarce resources. These two facts, equality of ability to harm and desire to satisfy goals, lead to an unstable state.

> From this equality of ability arises equality of hope in the attaining of our ends. And therefore if any two people desire the same thing, which nevertheless they cannot both enjoy, they become enemies; and in the way to their end, which is principally their own preservation and sometimes their enjoyment only, endeavor to destroy, or subdue one another. And from hence it comes to pass, that where an invader hath no more to fear, than another man's single power; if one plant, sow, build, or possess a convenient seat, others may probably be expected to come prepared with forces united, to dispossess, and deprive him, not only of the fruit of his labor, but also of his life or liberty. And the invader again is in the like danger of another. (L, chapter 13)

Given this state of insecurity, people have reason to fear one another. Hobbes calls this a "state of nature," in which there are no common ways of life, no enforced laws or moral rules, and no justice or injustice, for these concepts do not apply. There are no reliable expectations about other people's behavior—except that they will follow their own inclinations and perceived interests, tending to be arbitrary, violent, and capricious.

> Hereby it is manifest, that during the time men live without a common power to keep them all in awe, they are in that condition which is called war; and such a war, as is for *every man, against every man.* For war consists not in battle only or in the act of fighting; but in a tract of time, wherein the will to contend in battle is sufficiently known: and therefore the notion of *time,* is to be considered in the nature of war; as it is in the nature of weather. For as the nature of foul weather lies not in the shower or two of rain, but in an inclination thereto of many days together; so the nature of war consists not in actual fighting, but in the known disposition thereto, during all the time there is no disposition to the contrary. (L, chapter 13)

Hobbes described the consequence of the state of nature, this war of all against all, as follows:

> In such a condition, there is no place for industry; because the fruit thereof is uncertain: and consequently no cultivating of the earth; no navigation, nor use of the comfortable buildings; no instruments of moving, and removing, such things as require much force; no knowledge of the face of the earth; no account of time; no arts; no literature; no society; and which is worst of all, continual fear, and danger of violent death; and the life of man *solitary, poor, nasty, brutish and short.* (L, chapter 13)

However, this state of nature, or more exactly, state of anarchy and chaos, is in no one's interest. We can all do better if we compromise, give up some of our natural liberty—to do as we please—so that we will all be more likely to get what we want: security, happiness, power, prosperity, and peace.

In this state of nature, nothing is unjust or immoral.

> To this war of every man, against every man, this also is a result; that nothing can be unjust. The notions of right and wrong, justice and injustice have there no place. Where there is no common power, there is no law: where no law no injustice. Force, and fraud, are in war the two cardinal virtues. Justice, and injustice are none of the faculties either of the body, nor mind. If they were, they might be in a man that were alone in the world, as well as his senses, and passions. They are qualities, that relate to men in society, not in solitude. It is consequent also to the same condition, that there be no property, no ownership, no *mine* and *thine* distinct; but only that to be every man's, that he can get; and for so long, as he can keep it. And thus much for the ill condition, which man by mere nature is actually placed in; though with a possibility to come out of it, consisting partly in the passions, partly in his reason. (L, chapter 13)

Thus, being rational egoists, we give up some of our liberty and agree to a social contract or covenant.[3] The rules which we are to obey are set and enforced by a mighty ruler, the state, the "leviathan." Only within this contract does morality arise and do justice and injustice come into being. Where there is no enforceable law, there is neither right nor wrong, justice nor injustice.

Hobbes meets the objection that his description of an original state of nature is fictitious. This is probably true, Hobbes admits, though primitive situations described by explorers come close to it. One contemporary account is Colin Turnbull's description of the displaced Ik society in northern Uganda (see For Further Reading), but Hobbes does not claim that such a state actually exists. What he describes is what life would be like if people did not have government. Perhaps we can get a feel for this state by reading about civil wars, whether they be the English Civil Wars (1642–1652), which Hobbes witnessed; the American Civil War (1860–1865); the Serbo–Croatian–Bosnian War, which decimated the former Yugoslavia in the 1990s; or the Rwandan Civil War of the mid-1990s. The Sunni and Shiite violence in Fallujah and Najaf, Iraq, in the Second Gulf War in 2004, is supporting evidence for Hobbes' thesis.

Morality, then, is a form of social control. We all opt for an enforceable set of rules such that if almost all of us obey them almost all the time, almost all of us will be better off almost all the time. A select few people, conceivably, may actually be better off in the state of nature, but the vast majority will be better off in a situation of security and mutual cooperation. Some people may cheat and thus renege on the social contract, but so long as the majority honors the contract most of the time, we will all flourish.

Hobbes does not claim that a pure state of nature ever existed or that humanity ever really formally entered into such a contract, though he notes that such a state actually exists among nations so that a "cold war" keeps us all in fear. Rather, Hobbes offers an explanation of the function of morality and political organizations by answering the question, Why do we need morality? We need morality because without it existence would be an unbearable hell in which life is "solitary, poor, nasty, brutish and short."

Lord of the Flies

William Golding's classic novel *Lord of the Flies* brilliantly portrays the Hobbesian account of morality. In the story, a group of boys aged 6–12 from an English private school, cast adrift on an uninhabited Pacific island, create their own social system. For a while, the constraints of civilized society prevent total chaos. All the older boys recognize the necessity of substantive and procedural rules. Only he who has the white conch, the symbol of authority, may speak during an assembly. They choose the leader democratically and invest him with limited powers.

After some initial euphoria in being liberated from the adult world of constraints and entering an exciting world of fun in the sun, the children come up against the usual banes of social existence: competition for power and status, neglect of social responsibility, failure of public policy, and escalating violence. Two boys, Ralph and Jack, vie for leadership, and a bitter rivalry emerges between them. As a compromise, a division of labor ensues in which Jack's choirboy hunters refuse to help the others in constructing shelters. Freeloading soon becomes common as most of the children leave their tasks to play on the beach. Neglect of duty results in failure to be rescued by a passing airplane. The unbridled lust for excitement leads to the great orgiastic pig kills and finally, at its nadir, to the thirst for human blood.

Civilization's power is weak and vulnerable to atavistic, volcanic passions. The sensitive Simon, the symbol of religious consciousness (like Simon Peter, the first disciple of Jesus) who prophesies that Ralph will be saved and is the first to discover and fight against the "ancient, inescapable recognition" of the beast in us, is slaughtered by the group in a wild frenzy. Only Piggy and Ralph, mere observers of the orgiastic homicide, feel vicarious pangs of guilt at this atrocity.

The title *Lord of the Flies* comes from a translation of the Greek Beelzebub, which is a name for the devil. Golding shows that we need no external devil to bring about evil but that we have found the devil and, in the words of Pogo, "he is us." Ubiquitous, ever waiting for a moment to strike, the devil emerges from the depths of the subconscious whenever there is a conflict of interest or a moment of moral lassitude. As E. L. Epstein says, "The tenets of civilization, the moral and social codes, the Ego, the intelligence itself, form only a veneer over this white-hot power, this uncontrollable force, 'the fury and the mire of human veins.'"[4]

Beelzebub's ascendancy proceeds through fear, hysteria, violence, and death. A delegation starts out hunting pigs for meat. Then, they find themselves enjoying the kill. To drown the incipient shame over bloodthirstiness and to take on a persona more compatible with their deed, the children paint themselves with colored mud. Their lust for the kill takes on all the powerful overtones of an orgiastic sexual ritual so that, being liberated from their social selves, they kill without remorse whomever gets in their way. The deaths of Simon and Piggy (the symbols of the religious and the philosophical, the two great fences blocking the descent to hell) and the final orgiastic hunt with the "spear sharpened at both ends" signal for Ralph the depths of evil in the human heart.

The fundamental ambiguity of human existence is visible in every section of the book, poignantly mirroring the human condition. Even Piggy's spectacles, the sole example of modern technology on the island, become a bane for the island as Jack uses them to ignite a forest fire that will smoke out their prey, Ralph, and burn down the entire forest and destroy the island's animal life. It is a symbol both of our penchant for misusing technology to vitiate the environment and of our ability to create weapons that will lead to global suicide.

Golding gives literary expression to Hobbes' idea of the state of nature where human beings become vicious and bloodthirsty, showing that an external force must be introduced to keep the peace. From an evolutionary perspective, the Hobbesian would say, we have descended from countless generations of aggressive, violent ancestors, the fittest who survived in an ongoing state of nature, so is it any wonder that we, especially males, act aggressively?

Some feminist critics have argued that the society depicted in Golding's Hobbesian novel *Lord of the Flies* is a male anomaly, showing at most what uprooted little boys are made of. If girls were introduced into the story, they argue, it would make it different. Similarly, they contend, a group of girls would behave less violently. However, Marianne Wiggins' novel *John Dollar* portrays a group of girls stranded on an island who also engage in some vicious behavior, including cannibalism.[5]

Conclusion to Hobbes

Philosophers have criticized Hobbes' theory as too crude. Though we would agree that the state of nature is an unacceptable situation in which to live, too much is given away in Hobbes' absolute state. We want to retain human rights, including the right to oppose and reform abuses of state power. Indeed, it is doubtful that rational beings, the kind Hobbes describes, would agree to the absolutist, authoritarian rule of the leviathan when they could settle for something more accountable to rational appeal. That is, Hobbes paints a picture of extreme options: either anarchy (and chaos) or **absolutism** (and order). However, much middle ground lies between those extremes, from which we may make our choices. Still, there may be considerable truth in Hobbes' theory of human nature. It seems to be a classic expression of a conservative view of human nature.

Although most conservatives would balk at Hobbes' materialism, three themes stand out in his theory of human nature: *(1)* humans are selfish egoists, *(2)* life is tragic, and *(3)* morality and strong government are necessary to constrain humans and provide a deterrent against mischief. Let us briefly examine each of these points:

1. Humans are egoists. We saw in chapter 1 that, according to the biblical view of human nature, human beings are fallen creatures. Although we were made in the image of God, we sinned and "all our righteousness is like filthy rags." We deserve God's wrath; or, if one does not believe in God, we do not deserve an idyllic life but, at best, to be left alone by others.

2. Life is tragic. Kant, though he was not conservative, echoed this idea when he rhetorically asked, "Out of the crooked timber of mankind, can any straight thing be built?" Conservatives tend to be pessimistic about the human condition. Because we are fundamentally egoists, all our projects will be corrupted by the ego. We may make progress in one realm, but there are always costs. More peace must mean less freedom. Human nature is fixed, so most of our ideas of progress are illusory. As long as we live, we suffer and finally die. All life is predatory and dies. We shall return to this idea in chapter 9, on Schopenhauer, a 19th-century conservative.

3. Morality and government are necessary for peace, security, and happiness. While not all conservatives are religious, a major theme is their adherence to the notion that humans are basically selfish or corrupted, so they need moral constraints and government to keep them all in check. Hobbes preferred a Leviathan, an absolute government; but the founding fathers of America were conservatives who preferred representational government with checks and balances in order to prevent the abuse of power. We need strong government to protect us from external threats as well as from each other, but government should be minimal, confining itself to those functions necessary to prevent the state of nature and to perform those functions which private individuals cannot conveniently carry out on their own (e.g., building a national highway system or protecting the environment).

Jean-Jacques Rousseau: a Liberal Theory of Human Nature

Man is born free but is everywhere in chains. *(Rousseau,* The Social Contract)

Introduction

It was said that the only time Immanuel Kant missed his 4-o'clock walk was when he was reading Rousseau's *Social Contract.* The influence of Rousseau on moral and political philosophy is revolutionary: Kant's political theory, Robespierre and other leaders in the French Revolution, socialist thought, Karl Marx's philosophy, and the student revolutions in Europe and America in the 1960s all can trace their roots to Rousseau's thought. *The Social Contract,* banned by the monarchy, became the bible of the French Revolution. Both Maximilien Robespierre and Thomas Paine were inspired and guided by his ideas.

Jean-Jacques Rousseau was born in Calvinist Geneva, Switzerland, on June 28, 1712, the son of a sentimental watchmaker. His mother died 9 days after Jean-Jacques' birth. His father and the local pastor educated him in classical literature, and at 13 he became an apprentice to an engraver. At 17 he was taken into the care of Madame de Warens, who persuaded him to convert to Catholicism and, a few years later, to visit her bed. Rousseau identified Madame de Warens with his long-lost mother and, consequently, felt "as though I had committed incest." A series of odd jobs took him away from Madame de Warens, and by the age of 20 he found himself in Paris, where he met a number of prominent philosophers, including

Voltaire and Diderot. Soon afterward, he married Thérèse Lavasseur, with whom he had five children, all of whom he turned over to foundling homes.

He launched his philosophical and writing career in 1750 by responding to a contest of the Academy of Dijon to write an essay on the question of whether the arts and sciences contributed to the purification or corruptions of morals. Filled with passion, he wrote a brilliant, award-winning essay, taking the unconventional positive side of the question. Most of the knowledge given by the arts and sciences is useless, he wrote. They had corrupted us. "Astronomy was born of superstition; eloquence of ambition, hatred, falsehood, and flattery; geometry of avarice; physics of an idle curiosity; and even moral philosophy of human pride."[6] We would be better off without such vanity and pretension. A human being is born innocent, naturally good. He is a Noble Savage, blissful in his ignorance and innocence, living in a simple, rustic Garden of Eden. "It is by his institutions alone that men become corrupt." The arts and sciences actually cause human degeneracy. "Nature made man happy and good, but . . . society depraves him and makes him miserable."[7] Rousseau's positive view of human nature is based on two psychological propositions: (1) humans are self-interested beings who care about their own happiness and (2) they have a natural repugnance at "seeing any being perish or suffer." Thus, their egoism is balanced by sympathy, which under the proper circumstances can override selfishness. Left to her- or himself, compassion will play a dominant role in relations with others; but in artificial society, education and the legislator must intervene to insure that compassion triumphs. Rousseau would rather not have an artificial society, but he realized that we cannot turn the clock backward and return to Eden. We must make the best of our sorry state. To this end, he wrote *The Social Contract* (1762) as a prescription for legitimate government and social relations. As he grew famous, he rethought his religious beliefs and left the Catholic Church, reaffirming his Protestant heritage. He felt that the doctrines of free will, immortality, and the existence of God were true but gave no arguments for them. In 1762, the French king Louis XV banned Rousseau's books and issued a warrant for his arrest. He fled to England, where he was received by David Hume and given a state pension by the British government. Rousseau appears to have become paranoid during this period, accusing Hume of plotting against him. He returned to Paris, where he died in poverty in 1778.

Human Nature Is Good

The fundamental principle of all morality, about which I have reasoned in all my works . . . is that man is a naturally good creature, who loves justice and order; that there is no original perversity in the human heart, and that the first movements of nature are always right.[8]

In his next essay, *Discourse on the Origin and the Foundations of Inequality* (1755), Rousseau sums up his view of human nature.

That men are actually wicked, a sad and continual experience of them proves beyond doubt: but, all the same, I think I have shown that man is *naturally good*.

What then can have depraved him to such an extent, except the changes that have happened in his constitution, the advances he has made, and the knowledge he has acquired? We may admire human society as much as we please; it will be none the less true that it necessarily leads men to hate each other in proportion as their interests clash, and to do one another apparent services, while they are really doing every imaginable mischief. What can be thought of a relation, in which the interest of every individual dictates rules directly opposite to those the public reason dictates to the community in general—in which every man finds his profit in the misfortunes of his neighbor?[9]

This second discourse brought Rousseau to prominence as France's foremost social critic. It offers us a picture of humans as healthy, happy individuals in a state of nature, which is the very opposite of Hobbes' violent version of that state being "solitary, poor, nasty, brutish and short." On the contrary, Rousseau urged, individuals in a state of nature were healthy, happy, peace-loving animals who wandered freely over the face of the earth, picking up plentiful food as they had need, sleeping at night wherever they desired to lay their heads. No one owned anything, though we each possessed freedom to do what we wanted to do. It is because of the lust for property that organized society became necessary.

> The first man who, having enclosed a piece of ground, bethought himself of saying *This is mine,* and found people simple enough to believe him, was the real founder of civil society. From how many crimes, wars and murders, from how many horrors and misfortunes might not any one have saved mankind, by pulling up the stakes, or filling up the ditch, and crying to his fellows, "Beware of listening to this impostor; you are undone if you once forget that the fruits of the earth belong to us all, and the earth itself to nobody." (*Discourse on the Origin and Foundations of Inequality,* p. 170)

In the state of nature, people were self-sufficient; but when a greedy few appropriated the wealth that God had created for the benefit of all, inequality and difference of power arose. The process is thus: private property causes inequalities and the need for government to protect property, and with government regulations (laws), comes the need to restrict our freedom. Inevitably, property causes inequalities and inequalities cause resentment. The state must use its force to protect property rights against the resentful poor. The enforcement of inequalities over property rights in turn leads to violence and great suffering, eventually to the relationship of master and slave. This is against **natural law** and so must not be allowed.

Rousseau concludes with an egalitarian prescription:

> I have tried to trace the origin and progress of inequality, and the institution and abuse of political societies, as far as these are capable of being deduced from the nature of man merely by the light of reason, and independently of those sacred dogmas which give the sanction of divine right to sovereign authority. It follows from this survey that, as there is hardly any inequality in the state of nature, all the

inequality which now prevails owes its strength and growth to the development of our faculties and the advance of the human mind, and becomes at last permanent and legitimate by the establishment of property and laws. Secondly, it follows that moral inequality, authorised by positive right alone, clashes with natural right, whenever it is not proportionate to physical inequality; a distinction which sufficiently determines what we ought to think of that species of inequality which prevails in all civilized, countries; since it is plainly contrary to the *law of nature,* however defined, that children should command old men, fools wise men, and that the privileged few should gorge themselves with superfluities, while the starving multitude are in want of the bare necessities of life.[10]

The state must enforce relative equality, one way or another. However, a social contract is required to carry out this egalitarian program.

The Social Contract

"Man is born free but is everywhere in chains," Rousseau laments at the beginning of his *Social Contract* (1762). People are essentially good and of equal worth.[11] In a state of nature, they were free and equal. Civilization has been a step backward, for with it we lost our essential equality and untrammeled freedom. He mocks Hobbes' claim that we accept the state for the sake of tranquility: "Tranquillity is found also in dungeons; but is that enough to make them desirable places to live in? The Greeks imprisoned in the cave of the Cyclops lived there very tranquilly, while they were awaiting their turn to be devoured."[12]

Although we were better off in the idyllic state of nature, we cannot return to it. So we build a new social contract, not based on protecting private property (though that may be tolerated) but as a means of "giving the law to ourselves" and thereby elevating us from mere men to the morally noble status of citizens, a compromise that leads to the situation where no one is master and no one is slave. Once people get a taste of property, they covet it, which Rousseau sees as an evil— but an evil with certain benefits. Part of the state's justification is to protect its members and their property from external and internal threats, but Rousseau lays down Lockean-like constraints on the acquisition of property: *(1)* the land may not be occupied by anyone, *(2)* one may not take more than one needs to subsist, and *(3)* one may take possession of it, not by staking a claim but by "working and cultivating it."

Rousseau modifies his strict egalitarianism and allows some discrepancies of wealth, just so long as they are not extreme.

I have already defined civil liberty; by equality, we should understand, not that the degrees of power and riches are to be absolutely identical for everybody; but that power shall never be great enough for violence, and shall always be exercised by virtue of rank and law; and that, in respect of riches, no citizen shall ever be wealthy enough to buy another, and none poor enough to be forced to sell himself; which implies, on the part of the great, moderation in goods and position, and, on the side of the common sort, moderation in avarice and covetousness.[13]

The limits to acquisition are when virtual slavery is possible, when people are forced to sell themselves to the rich.

In the ideal, republican government, the individual blends his or her identity with the good of the whole, the *commonweal*. Rousseau's state is not a representative government with a senate and judiciary but a pure democracy with a sovereign executive branch to carry out the will of the people. Every issue must be voted on, and the majority vote becomes the will of everyone, the general will; it becomes the will of each and every individual, whether he or she realizes it or not. If someone is blind to the general will, the entire body will force him or her to obey. Because this will is really that of the blind person (since he or she is an inextricable part of the group), the group is not doing anything against his or her true interest. The blind person is only being "forced to be free."[14]

Being a legislator in the government means not only passing laws in accordance with the will of the people but changing human nature itself, transforming one from an individual concerned only with his or her own interests into one that sees his or her identity as indistinguishable from the commonweal.

> He who dares to undertake the making of a people's institutions ought to feel himself capable, so to speak, of changing human nature, of transforming each individual, who is by himself a complete and solitary whole, into part of a greater whole from which he in a manner receives his life and being; of altering man's constitution for the purpose of strengthening it; and of substituting a partial and moral existence for the physical and independent existence nature has conferred on us all. He must, in a word, take away from man his own resources and give him instead new ones alien to him, and incapable of being made use of without the help of other men. The more completely these natural resources are annihilated, the greater and the more lasting are those which he acquires, and the more stable and perfect the new institutions; so that if each citizen is nothing and can do nothing without the rest, and the resources acquired by the whole are equal or superior to the aggregate of the resources of all the individuals, it may be said that legislation is at the highest possible point of perfection.[15]

The Noble Savage and *Emile*

I am as free as Nature first made man,
Ere the base laws of servitude began,
When wild in woods the noble savage ran.[16]

The idea of the noble savage, the innocent human uncorrupted by society, is highlighted in Rousseau's long treatise on education, *Emile*. In this work, he describes the education of a boy from birth until manhood. An idyllic, bucolic existence is described. The child must be allowed to roam freely like an animal in the country and not in the city, where artificial constraints would hamper his will. He is to be loved by his mother and taught by his father, who should be the dominant educator in his life. No man should beget children who is not prepared to educate them himself, advice Rousseau himself did not follow. Although free to explore nature, the child must be accountable, living under strict authority and allowed to suffer. The parents or tutor must avoid the two extremes of being too harsh, on the one hand, and too soft, on the other. Spoiling the child is the worst thing they can do to him. Parents must not overprotect the child. He must be allowed to face hardship and make mistakes, even if that leads to his death. We must not overvalue life. We all must die and better to die young, acting adventurously, than to live to old age a coward, afraid of risk. Emile must be allowed to fail. Rousseau would keep the child from learning to read until he is nearly a teenager, for books are a poor substitute for experience. The only book he should read as a child is *Robinson Crusoe*, Daniel Defoe's famous novel, for it promotes self-reliance. He must not learn foreign languages, for they are useless to his basic development as an autonomous being. Indeed, although a consummate dramatist, Rousseau is repelled by the theater, an allegory of the falseness of social life. Instead of hiding its head in shame, the theater celebrates its falseness. Emile will not be allowed to visit the theater.

Conclusion to Rousseau

Rousseau is one of the most influential writers in world history. Many believe his work inspired Robespierre and his radical colleagues in the French Revolution. He certainly inspired Kant and other liberal political philosophers.

The most perplexing thing about Rousseau's philosophy of human nature is his notion of being "forced to be free." It seems to be an oxymoron. Let us examine it more closely. Isaiah Berlin distinguishes between two kinds of liberty, negative and positive. *Negative liberty* is simply the absence of using coercion to influence a person. Coercion "implies the deliberate interference of other human beings."[17] Negative liberty is the freedom to do whatever we want without the interference of others. *Positive liberty*, on the other hand, is the genuine freedom to become your real or rational self. "The 'positive' sense of the word 'liberty' derives from the wish on the part of the individual to be his own master. I wish my life and decisions to depend on myself, not on external forces." At a minimum, this is what we call "autonomy." This is what Rousseau means by one's "true self," the ideal self which is our proper goal. However, Rousseau goes so far as to endorse society's right to "force people to become free.""Whoever refuses to obey the *general will* will be forced to do so by the entire body. This means that he will be *forced to be free.*"[18] It seems a contradiction in terms to say one can be "coerced to be free." Perhaps we ought not call "positive liberty" liberty at all but something else. As Berlin notes, "Liberty is liberty, not equality or fairness or justice or culture or human happiness or a quiet conscience." We ought not to conflate or confuse these two types of liberty. Political liberty should concentrate on negative liberty, but positive liberty does convey a useful concept and should be kept. Perhaps, it would be better to label it "autonomy."

Rousseau is correct in valuing autonomy, but he goes wrong in believing that the state can procure autonomy through force. Autonomy is produced by a good upbringing, socialization, and education.

Bertrand Russell points out that *The Social Contract* became the bible of most of the leaders in the French Revolution, and its doctrines of the general will and coercing people to be free became the basis for the guillotine.[19] These pernicious doctrines were appropriated by the Bolshevik revolutionaries in the Soviet Union to justify the reeducation centers and extermination camps of the Gulag Archipelago. No doubt, Rousseau would have been horrified by such a (mis)use of his theory, but his rhetoric may have gotten the best of him and carried over to the abuse of his own ideas.

The more general and important question is whether Rousseau's theory of human nature is true. Are human beings basically good (noble savages)? Is society the corrupter of our nature? Rousseau is often rich in rhetoric but poor in argument. He neither tells us how the evil of acquisitiveness arose in the halcyon state of nature nor provides evidence that such a paradisiacal state ever existed.

Perhaps the most favorable interpretation of Rousseau is as an idealist who urges us to find an innate goodness and compassion within each of us and to build a society on that goodness. Philosophers like Kant and John Rawls seem to have read him this way.

Summary: A Comparison Between Conservative and Liberal Perspectives

Whereas Hobbes viewed the state as a buffer against the deplorable anarchy of the state of nature, Rousseau saw the state and society in general as the corruption of the noble savage. Hobbes and Rousseau have opposite positions on human nature. For Hobbes, humans are psychological egoists who cannot act altruistically but are rescued by the Leviathan. For Rousseau, humans are innately good, noble savages who are corrupted by society. Left alone in nature, like Robinson Crusoe, humans would flourish. While Rousseau acknowledges that we cannot recover the Garden of Eden, he thinks we must get closer to nature. For Hobbes, we are determined to follow our instincts; free will is a myth, at best, the last impulse after deliberation. For Rousseau, we are truly free and can change our lives and our world. Here, Rousseau follows John Locke (1632–1704), who held that babies were born with a *tabula rasa,* a mental blank slate, so that education makes all the difference. In other words, nurture, not nature, is decisive in forming the human mind.[20] Rousseau holds to the Lockean faith in education, only he also believes that we are naturally good. For Hobbes, humans are naturally egoists and need government to rein them in. Government is top-down; whatever it decides is legitimate. For Rousseau, government must be bottom-up, from the people and for the people; but when the people do not see their true interest, the general will, they can be "forced to be free."

Hobbes is a pessimist, whereas Rousseau is an optimist. Hobbes thinks government is necessary to prevent chaos in the state of nature. Rousseau sees the state as a necessary evil, given our development as acquisitive beings who value property; but he finally gives the state as much power as Hobbes gives the "Leviathan." So long as it is justified in the name of the general will, the true interests of the people, the government can do what it wants.

There is a debate among ethologists as to whether humans, as descended from primates, are more like aggressive, violent chimpanzees or the more gregarious, pleasure-seeking bonobos: according to Hobbesians, we are more like chimpanzees; according to Rousseaueans, we are more like bonobos.

Although many conservatives would reject the idea of the Leviathan (or at least modify it), Hobbes' pessimistic view of human nature and skepticism about utopias are characteristics of conservatism. His tragic vision of human nature is echoed by Kant (see chapter 8), who wrote "From the crooked timber of humanity no truly straight thing can be made;" Edmund Burke (1729–1797); writers of the U.S. constitution Alexander Hamilton (1755–1804) and James Madison (1751–1836); the economist Frederick Hayek (1899–1992); and philosophers Arthur Schopenhauer (see chapter 9), Isaiah Berlin (1909–1997), Karl Popper (1902–1994), and Anthony Quinton.

While many liberals and socialists would reject some of the ideas about the general will and forcing people to be free, Rousseau's optimism about human nature and the egalitarian society resonate among liberals. Let us call Rousseau's ideal the "utopian vision." G. W. F. Hegel (1770–1831), Thomas Paine (1737–1809), John Stuart Mill (1806–1873), Karl Marx (see chapter 10), the famous Russian anarchist Peter Kropotkin (1841–1921), Leo Tolstoy (1828–1910), Herbert Marcuse (1899–1979), and, to a degree, John Rawls (1921–2002) and Ronald Dworkin (1931–) are heirs to Rousseau's optimism,[21] as are the radicals of the 1960s. During the revolutionary days in April 1968, I recall sitting in an SDS[22] rally at Columbia University, New York, in which radical students called for burning down the university so that, phoenix-like, the "People's University" could rise from the ashes. One student waved a banner on which the slogan "Utopia Is Right Around the Corner" was written. Unfortunately for them, the Leviathan's police were right around the corner, so the revolution never materialized. Rousseau and Marx were the heroes of many of my fellow students.

Conservatives are pessimistic about human nature and the prospects of radical improvement of the human condition. Human nature has been corrupted by original sin or at least endowed with a deep tendency toward perversity. Conservatives point to the experiments by Philip Zimbardo at Stanford University in the 1970s. Researchers created a simulated prison and randomly assigned 24 students to be either guards or prisoners for 2 weeks. Within days the "guards" had begun to engage in sadistic behavior, abusing prisoners. As I write this chapter in May 2004, American M.P.s and National Guard personnel have been accused of abusing Iraqi prisoners, forcing them to commit shameful sexual acts and masturbate in public. Conservatives, following the Old Testament and Hobbes, maintain that we need strong government with enforced penalties to hold sin in check. Human nature holds constant over time. We are just lucky that we did not live in Nazi Germany, for it is likely we would have succumbed to "the banality of evil," to use Hannah Arendt's words. We should have learned from the past what lurks in the recesses of the human heart. The best we can do is trust in a higher divine power and follow the proven principles and procedures that served us well in the past. Conservatives tend to be political and religious traditionalists, who value their heritage. "People will not look forward to posterity who do not look backward to their ancestors," Edmund Burke wrote.[23] They are skeptical of big government, the welfare state, and social engineering. They tend to be meritocrats (as opposed to egalitarians) and to emphasize moral responsibility.

Liberals, on the other hand, tend to be more hopeful on the prospects for human improvement. They tend to accept Locke's claim that at birth the mind is a blank slate and that culture and education may write on it what they will. Humans are very plastic, so environment counts much more than heredity. We should dream new dreams and aim high, believing that if we aim at nothing, we are sure to hit it. Human beings are malleable and can be improved through education and socialization. Liberals are more willing to accept big government to solve human problems, to redistribute wealth to where it will do more good. Need and equality tend to trump merit in arranging social institutions. This is epitomized in the socialist motto "From each according to his ability, to each according to his need."

Conservatives and Marxists both attack Rousseauean liberalism as naive. They produce as evidence against Rousseau's thesis the failure of benign anarchy, people living peacefully without the protection of government. There are enough opportunistic, aggressive people everywhere to take advantage of innocence and weakness. Anyone who has ever lived in a commune knows that the group must constantly struggle with freeloaders and cheaters.

The radical socialist George Manbiot tells of his experience with tribes in northwestern Kenya. He was delayed in a visit to a cattle camp in the region. When he arrived, all that remained were the skulls and clothes of the inhabitants, for they had been raided by warriors of a neighboring tribe. These warriors used modern weapons. In another region, the Maasai, armed only with spears and knives, seized almost all of the grazing area of what is now southern and central Kenya.[24] Liberals may respond that they do take into account human aggressivity, that some people, mainly unsocialized males, will be aggressive toward others. They simply maintain that goodness has been corrupted by poor environmental factors. This leads us to the question of gender roles.

One area of significant difference between conservatives and liberals is the issue of the role of women. Conservatives emphasize gender differences, believe that these differences are grounded in biology, and conclude that women have distinctive roles to play in nurturing their husbands and children. Steven Goldberg's *Why Men Rule: A Theory of Male Dominance* (1993) is a good example of this view.[25] He provides data showing that males have always dominated society. Although males and females are on average equally intelligent, universally females are more nurturing and males, more aggressive. Studies show that males have higher average mathematical and spatial aptitudes and females, better linguistic skills; but exceptions exist where women excel in mathematics and science and males, in language ability. In this regard, Carol Gilligan argues, contrary to mainline liberal thinking, that with regard to moral development girls develop differently from boys.[26]

Liberals, on the other hand, emphasize the similarities between males and females, holding that only their reproductive organs are different. They tend to hold that psychological differences, described in Gilligan's moral development theory, are social constructions. Liberal and radical feminists reject the status quo in gender relations as immoral male dominance and call for programs and policies that will produce equal results or at least more equal opportunity for women. They reject the work of scholars like Goldberg in favor of Margaret Mead and others who present data of more pacific female-led societies.[27] Whereas conservatives tend to emphasize biological factors in explaining human difference, liberals tend to explain all psychological differences in terms of environmental factors, such as upbringing and sociological conditions. This dichotomy of perspective can be traced back to Hobbes, on the one hand, and Locke (with the idea of a blank slate at birth) and Rousseau, on the other hand.

There is also a compromise position between the Tragic Vision and the Utopian Vision. The truth may be somewhere in the middle, and most people contain elements of both the Hobbesian right and the Rousseauean left. Hobbes and Rousseau serve as polar opposites, whose ideas help us to contrast the essential conservative and liberal positions on the nature and destiny of human beings.

Study Questions

1. Hobbes wrote "The utility of morality and civil philosophy is to be estimated, not so much by the commodities we have by knowing these sciences, as by the calamities we receive from not knowing them." What does he mean by this, and does the chapter selection illustrate it?

2. What does Hobbes mean by a "state of nature"? Can you think of illustrations of Hobbes' state of nature? If you have read William Golding's novel *Lord of the Flies,* can you apply Hobbes' analysis to it?

3. Is Hobbes' view of human nature accurate? Do we always act out of the motivations of fear and distrust? Are people entirely self-interested egoists? Is psychological egoism, the view that we always do what we perceive to be in our best interest, too bleak and one-sided?

4. Hobbes thought that only an absolute sovereign could establish or ensure peace and civil society. Is he correct? What would be his estimation of democracy? Could democratic society make use of his analysis? How would democrats modify Hobbes' theory?

5. What is Rousseau's view of human nature? How accurate is it?

6. What is Rousseau's concept of the general will? Is it a utilitarian principle? What are its strengths and weaknesses?

7. What does Rousseau mean by saying one may be "forced to be free"?

8. Compare Hobbes' and Rousseau's views on human nature. Are we more like chimpanzees or bonobos?

9. Identify Hobbesian and Rousseauean motifs in contemporary society.

10. Does history tend to confirm the liberal or conservative thesis on human nature?

Notes

1. All quotations in this section are from Thomas Hobbes, *Leviathan* (1651; Penguin Books, 1988, reprint).
2.f. C. Hood, *The Divine Politics of Thomas Hobbes* (Oxford University Press, 1964).
3. Hobbes describes the contract thus:

   The Mutual transferring of right, is that which men call CONTRACT. There is a difference between transferring of right to the thing; and transferring, or tradition, that is delivery of the thing itself. For the thing may be delivered together with the translation of the right; as in buying and selling with ready money; or exchange of goods, or lands: and it may be delivered some time after. (L, chapter 14)

4. E. L. Epstein, "Notes on *Lord of The Flies*," in William Golding, *Lord of the Flies* (Putnam, 1959).
5. Marianne Wiggins, *John Dollar* (Simon & Schuster, 1989). Note also the book Golding was responding to, *The Coral Island*, by R. M. Ballantyne (1858), which portrayed a group of virtuous boys who create a good society. Golding thought that Ballantyne had an all-too-rosy view of human nature, neglecting original sin. Might the same be said of those who generalize the contrast between virtuous women and vicious males?
6. Rousseau, *Discourse on the Arts and Science* (1750), part 2.
7. Roger Masters and Christopher Kelly, eds., *The Collected Works of Rousseau* (University Press of New England, 1992), vol. 1, p. 213.
8. Quoted in Timothy O'Hagan, *Rousseau* (Routledge, 1999), p. 15.
9. Rousseau, *The First and Second Discourses*, trans. Victor Gourevitch (Harper & Row, 1986), p. 209.
10. Ibid.
11. In *Social Contract*, he argues against Aristotle's claim that some people are natural slaves. Aristotle mistakenly "took the effect for the cause." Slavery is the effect of unequal, corrupt society, not of nature (book 1, chapter 2).
12. Ibid., book 1, chapter 4.
13. Ibid., book 1, chapter 11.
14. Ibid., book 1, chapter 7.
15. Ibid., book 2, chapter 7.
16. The idea of the "noble savage" first appears in John Dryden's *The Conquest of Granada* (1670), but the romantic idea seems to fit Rousseau's theory of human nature.
17. Isaiah Berlin, "Two Concepts of Liberty," in *Four Essays on Liberty* (Oxford University Press, 1969). Reprinted in L. P. Pojman, ed., *Modern and Contemporary Political Philosophy* (McGraw-Hill, 2002).

18. Rousseau, *Social Contract*, book 1, chapter 7.
19. Bertrand Russell, *A History of Western Philosophy* (Simon & Schuster, 1945), p. 700.
20. Locke wrote

> Let us then suppose the mind to be, as we say, white paper, void of all characters, without any ideas; how comes it to be furnished? Whence comes it by that vast store which the busy and boundless fancy of man has painted on it with an almost endless variety? Whence has it all the materials of reason and knowledge? To this I answer, in one word, from experience; in all that our knowledge is founded, and from that it ultimately derives itself. Our observation employed either about external sensible objects, or about the internal operations of our minds, perceived and reflected on by ourselves, is that which supplies our understandings with all the materials of thinking. These two are the fountains of knowledge, from whence all the ideas we have, or can naturally have, do spring. (*An Essay Concerning Human Understanding* [1689], book II, chapter 2)

21. John Locke, who preceded Rousseau, especially with his notion of the blank slate and the plasticity of human nature, should be included in the liberal camp, as should the whole Whig tradition in Great Britain. The Tory tradition represents the conservative tradition. See Steven Pinker, *The Blank Slate* (Simon & Schuster, 2002), for a good discussion of these issues.
22. SDS stood for Students for a Democratic Society. At this rally, the radical comedian Abby Hoffman urged students to overthrow the old repressive order and bring in a new democratic university for all the people, where everyone was free. Some students took him seriously and appeared to be copulating on the right corner of the stage.
23. Edmund Burke, *Reflections on the Revolution in France* (1790; Oxford University Press, 1999, reprint, ed. L. G. Mitchell).
24. George Monbiot, *Manifesto for a New World Order* (New Press, 2003), p. 39f.
25. Steven Goldberg, *Why Men Rule: A Theory of Male Dominance* (Open Court Publishing, 1993).
26. Carol Gilligan, *In a Different Voice* (Harvard University Press, 1982).
27. Margaret Mead, *Coming of Age in Samoa: A Psychological Study of Primitive Youth for Western Civilization* (Blue Ribbon Books, 1928), and *Sex and Temperament in Three Primitive Societies* (William Morrow, 1935). Mead's work has been challenged by Derek Freeman, *The Fateful Hoaxing of Margaret Mead* (Westview Press, 1999).

For Further Reading

Cranston, Maurice, and Richard Peters, eds., *Hobbes and Rousseau: A Collection of Critical Essays* (Doubleday, 1972).

Gilligan, Carol, *In a Different Voice* (Harvard University Press, 1982).

Goldberg, Steven, *Why Men Rule: A Theory of Male Dominance* (Open Court Publishing, 1993).

Hampton, Jean, *Hobbes and the Social Contract* (Cambridge University Press, 1986).

Hobbes, Thomas, *Leviathan* (Penguin Books, 1986). Introduction by C. B. MacPherson. A useful introduction in an inexpensive edition.

Hocutt, Max, "Compassion without Charity; Freedom without Liberty: The Political Fantasies of Jean-Jacques Rousseau," *The Independent Review,* vol. VIII. 2 (Fall 2003), pp. 165–191. A highly critical essay on Rousseau.

Kavka, Gregory, *Hobbesian Moral and Political Theory* (Princeton University Press, 1986). An advanced, thorough work.

Masters, Roger, and Christopher Kelly, eds., *The Collected Works of Rousseau* (University Press of New England, 1992).

Peters, Richard, *Hobbes* (Penguin Books, 1956). A clear exposition of Hobbes' ideas.

Pinker, Steven, *The Blank Slate* (Simon & Schuster, 2002).

Rousseau, Jean-Jacques, *Emile,* trans. Barbara Foxley (Dutton, 1974).

———, *On the Social Contract,* trans. Donald A. Cress (Hackett, 1987).

———, *The First and Second Discourses,* trans. Victor Gourevitch (Harper & Row, 1986).

Turnbull, Colin, *The Mountain People* (Simon & Schuster, 1972). A poignant account of a displaced people in northern Uganda whose social conditions reflect a Hobbesian state of nature.

Wolin, Sheldon S., *Politics and Vision* (Little, Brown, 1960). A perceptive history of Western political thought, with a good chapter on Hobbes.

CHAPTER 8

Immanuel Kant's Copernican Revolution

The Kantian Epistemic Revolution

Immanuel Kant (1724–1804), who was born into a deeply pietistic Lutheran family in Königsberg, Germany, lived in that town his entire life and taught at the University of Königsberg. He lived a duty-bound, methodical life, so regular that citizens were said to have set their clocks by his walks. Kant is one of the premier philosophers in the Western tradition, the last philosopher over whose greatness there is virtually universal consensus. In his monumental work *The Critique of Pure Reason* (1781, henceforth CPR), he inaugurated a revolution in the theory of knowledge, a revolution that completely reversed our orientation to reality in a manner analogous to the great Copernican revolution in 1543, when the Polish priest–scientist Nicolaus Copernicus (1473–1543) undermined the traditional view that the Sun revolves around the Earth and replaced it with the radical view that the Earth and the other planets revolved around the Sun. Like Copernicus' theory in astronomy, Kant's ideas have had abiding and powerful influence in the history of Western philosophy.

John Locke and the empiricists had claimed that the mind was a *tabula rasa*, a blank slate, upon which experience writes in a thousand ways until sensation begets memory and memory begets ideas. The idealist tradition from whence Kant came rejected the blank slate doctrine and posited innate ideas in the mind. The mind is not a passive tablet but an active organ which molds and coordinates sensations into ideas. The idealist tradition held that our innate ideas would enable us to uncover metaphysical truth about God, causality, free will, and immortality. However, upon reading Hume, Kant was struck with the cogency of his skeptical arguments on the nature of perception and causality. Hume "woke me from my dogmatic slumbers," Kant wrote and henceforth modified his views, combining a type of idealism with the empiricist doctrine that all our knowledge begins with experience.

That all our knowledge begins with experience there can be no doubt. For how is it possible that the faculty of cognition should be awakened into exercise otherwise

than by means of objects which affect our senses, and partly of themselves produce
representations, partly rouse our powers of understanding into activity, to compare,
to connect, or to separate these, and so to convert the raw material of our sensuous
impressions into a knowledge of objects, which is called experience? In respect
of time, therefore, no knowledge of ours is antecedent to experience, but begins
with it.

But, though all our knowledge begins with experience, it by no means follows
that all arises out of experience. For, on the contrary, it is quite possible that our
empirical knowledge is a compound of that which we receive through impressions,
and that which the faculty of cognition supplies from itself (sensuous impressions
giving merely the occasion), an addition which we cannot distinguish from the original element given by sense, till long practice has made us attentive to, and skilful
in separating it. It is, therefore, a question which requires close investigation, and
not to be answered at first sight, whether there exists a knowledge altogether independent of experience, and even of all sensuous impressions. Knowledge of this
kind is called *a priori,* in contradistinction to empirical knowledge, which has its
sources *a posteriori,* that is, in experience. (CPR, p. 41)[1]

However, Kant thought that Hume had made an invalid inference in concluding
that all knowledge arises from experience. Kant sought to demonstrate that the
rationalists had an invaluable insight, which had been lost in their flamboyant
speculation, that something determinate in the mind causes us to know what we
know.

Kant argued that the mind is so structured and empowered that it imposes
interpretive categories onto our experience, so we do not simply experience the
world, as the empiricists alleged, but interpret it through the constitutive mechanisms of the mind. This is sometimes called Kant's Copernican revolution. Until
now, we have assumed that all our knowledge must conform to objects:

> But every attempt to extend our knowledge of objects by establishing something in
> regard to them *a priori,* by means of concepts, has, on this assumption, ended in fail-
> ure. Therefore, we must see whether we may have better success in our metaphys-
> ical task if we begin with the assumption that objects must conform to our knowl-
> edge. In this way we would have knowledge of objects *a priori.* We should then be
> proceeding in the same way as Copernicus in his revolutionary hypothesis. After he
> failed to make progress in explaining the movements of the heavenly bodies on the
> supposition that they all revolved around the observer, he decided to reverse the
> relationship and made the observer revolve around the heavenly body, the sun,
> which was at rest. A similar experiment can be done in metaphysics with regard to
> the intuition of objects. If our intuition must conform to the constitution of the
> object, I do not see how we could know anything of the object *a priori,* but if the
> object of sense must conform to the constitution of our faculty of intuition, then *a
> priori* knowledge is possible.[2]

Our fundamental categories of thinking, space, time, and causality do not exist in
the world but are part of the necessary interpretive structure of our minds, analogous to wearing red-tinted glasses, which imposes spatial, temporal, and causal

order onto the manifold of experience.* Behind the phenomena which we perceive lies the noumenal world, the thing-in-itself (*ding an sich*), which we cannot know in any pure form but only as mediated through the categories of the mind.

In the paragraph just quoted, Kant makes his famous distinction between a priori and a posteriori knowledge: *a priori knowledge* is what we know prior to experience; it is opposed to *a posteriori knowledge,* which is based on experience. For Hume, all knowledge of matters of fact is a posteriori and only analytical statements (e.g., mathematical truths or statements such as "All mothers are women") are known a priori. Kant rejects this formula. For him, it is possible to have a priori knowledge of matters of fact. "But though all our knowledge begins with experience, it does not follow that it all arises out of experience." Indeed, Kant thinks that mathematical truth is not analytic but synthetic (the predicate adds something to the subject) and that there is other synthetic a priori knowledge, such as our knowledge of time, space, causality, and the moral law. The schema looks like this:

A PRIORI	A POSTERIORI
Analytic Tautologies and entailments ("All bachelors are unmarried")	None
Synthetic Causality, space, and time ($5 + 7 = 12$, the moral law)	Empirical judgments ("There are people in this room")

Kant gives two criteria for a priori judgments: necessity and universality. These two criteria seem to coalesce into the concept of "necessity," in that by "universality" he simply means that a universal proposition has no conceivable exception. After all, an empirical judgment could be universally true but not true by necessity. As examples of synthetic a priori judgments, he offers "$7 + 5 = 12$," "every event has a cause," and "everything occurs in time."

Although the idea of analytic a posteriori knowledge is not discussed in Kant's work, it seems clear that he rejected the idea because it was contradictory. That is, the idea of an analytic judgment, which depends solely on the relations of the concepts involved, makes no essential reference to experience, whereas a posteriori knowledge depends on experience.

The essential claim of those who recognize synthetic a priori knowledge is that the mind is able to grasp connections between concepts that are not analytically related. For example, we simply know upon reflection that all events have causes: "For every change there is an antecedent event which is necessarily connected with it." Similarly, we need not consult our senses to tell us that space is something that exists independently of matter. "If we remove from our empirical con-

---

The New Shorter Oxford English Dictionary defines *manifold* as follows: "That which is manifold; *specific in Kantian philosophy,* the sum of the particulars furnished by sense before they have been unified by the synthesis of the understanding."

cept of a body, one by one, every feature in it which is [merely] empirical, the color, the hardness or softness, the weight, even the impenetrability, there still remains the space which the body (now entirely vanished) occupied, and this cannot be removed" (CPR, Introduction, B 14). Kant, as we have noted, also thought our knowledge of mathematical truths was really synthetic a priori, rather than analytic. Time and space are the other two fundamental categories which our minds impose on all experience.

We can imagine a world with different physical laws—where Einstein's laws do not govern, where water is not wet nor fire hot, where mice are smarter than humans, and babies are born from elephants—but we cannot imagine a world without time. Yet, we have no argument that establishes time's reality. It is a given in all our experience, a lens through which we see the world. It may not be real, but we cannot live without assuming its reality.

Time, space, and causality are categories of the mind which we impose on phenomena, on the world as we perceive it; but we can never get behind the phenomena and synthetic a priori knowledge to the *ding an sich*, to the world as it really is. Similarly, we know only our empirical self, not our true essence, our noumenal self, the transcendent ego. We can infer that we have such a self, for it is the only satisfying explanation of why we have perceptions at all.

Kant's Moral Theory: The Categorical Imperative

In the 18th century, the rationalists and empiricists carried on a debate on the basis of moral knowledge. The rationalists, following Plato (see chapter 3), claimed that our knowledge of moral principles is a type of metaphysical knowledge, implanted in us by a transcendent reality, such as God, and discoverable by reason as it deduces general principles about human nature. On the other hand, the Scottish empiricists, especially Francis Hutcheson, David Hume, and Adam Smith, argued that morality is founded entirely on the contingencies of human nature and based on desire. Morality concerns making people happy, fulfilling their reflected desires; and reason is just a practical means of helping them fulfill their desires. There is nothing of special importance in reason in its own right. It is mainly a rationalizer and servant of the passions ("a pimp of the passions"). As Hume said, "Reason is and ought only to be a slave of the passions and can never pretend to any other office than to serve and obey them."[3] Morality is founded on our feeling of sympathy with other people's sufferings, on fellow feeling. For such empiricists, then, morality is contingent upon human nature:

Human nature → Feelings and desires → Moral principles

If we had a different nature, then we would have different feelings and desires and, hence, different moral principles.

Kant rejected the ideas of Hutcheson, Hume, and Smith. He was outraged by the thought that morality should depend on human nature and be subject to the fortunes of change and the luck of empirical discovery. Morality is not contingent but necessary. It would be no less binding on us if our feelings were different from what they are:

> Every empirical element is not only quite incapable of being an aid to the principle of morality, but is even highly prejudicial to the purity of morals; for the proper and inestimable worth of an absolutely good will consists just in this, that the principle of action is free from all influence of contingent grounds, which alone experience can furnish. We cannot too much or too often repeat our warning against this lax and even mean habit of thought which seeks for its principle amongst empirical motives and laws; for human reason in its weariness is glad to rest on this pillow, and in a dream of sweet illusions it substitutes for morality a bastard patched up from limbs of various derivation, which looks like anything one chooses to see in it; only not like virtue to one who has once beheld her in her true form.[4]

Kant said that it is not our desires that ground morality but our rational will. Reason is sufficient for establishing the moral law as something transcendent and universally binding on all rational creatures.

As we have noted, Kant wanted to remove moral truth from the zone of contingency and empirical observation and place it securely in the area of necessary, absolute, universal truth. Morality's value is not based on the fact that it has instrumental value, that it often secures nonmoral goods such as happiness. Rather, morality is valuable in its own right:

> Nothing can possibly be conceived in the world, or even out of it, which can be called good without qualification, except the Good Will. Intelligence, wit, judgment, and the other *talents* of the mind, however they may be named, or courage, resolution, perseverance, as qualities of temperament, as undoubtedly good and desirable in many respects; but these gifts of nature also may become extremely bad and mischievous if the will which is to make use of them, and which, therefore constitutes what is called *character* is not good. . . . Even if it should happen that, owing to special disfavor of fortune, or the stingy provision of a step-motherly nature, this Good Will should wholly lack power to accomplish its purpose, if with its greatest efforts it should yet achieve nothing, and there should remain only the Good Will, then, like a jewel, it would still shine by its own light, as a thing which has its whole value in itself. Its usefulness or fruitfulness can neither add to nor take away anything from this value.[5]

The only thing that is absolutely good, good in itself and without qualification, is the good will. All the other intrinsic goods, both intellectual and moral, can serve the vicious will and thus contribute to evil. They are only morally valuable if accompanied by a good will. Even success and happiness are not good in themselves. Honor can lead to pride. Happiness without good will is undeserved luck, ill-gotten gain. Nor is **utilitarianism** (the doctrine that morality consists in producing the greatest happiness for the greatest number of people) plausible, for if we have a quantity of happiness to distribute, is it just to distribute it equally, regardless of virtue? Should we not distribute it discriminately, according to moral goodness? Happiness should be distributed in proportion to people's moral worth.

We may question Kant's claims about the good will. Could we imagine a world where people always and necessarily put nonmoral virtues to good use, where it is simply impossible to use a virtue such as intelligence for evil? Is happiness any less good simply because one can distribute it incorrectly? Can't one put the good will itself to bad use, as the misguided do-gooder might? As the aphorism goes, "The road to hell is paved with good intentions." Could Hitler have had good intentions in carrying out his dastardly programs? Can't the good will have bad effects?

While we may agree that the good will is a great good, it is not obvious that Kant's account is correct, that it is the only inherently good thing. For even as intelligence, courage, and happiness can be put to bad uses or have bad effects, so can the good will; and even as it does not seem to count against the good will that it can be put to bad uses, so it should not count against the other virtues that they can be put to bad uses. The good will may be a necessary element to any morally good action, but whether the good will is also a sufficient condition to moral goodness is another question.

Nonetheless, perhaps we can reinterpret Kant so as to preserve his central insight. There does seem to be something morally valuable about the good will, apart from any consequences. Consider the following illustration. Two soldiers volunteer to cross enemy lines to contact their allies on the other side. Both start off and do their best to get through the enemy area. One succeeds; the other does not and is captured. However, aren't they both morally praiseworthy? The success of one in no way detracts from the goodness of the other. Judged from a commonsense moral point of view, their actions are equally good; judged from a utilitarian or consequentialist view, the successful act is far more valuable than the unsuccessful one. Here, we can distinguish the agent's worth from the value of the consequences and make two separate, nonconflicting judgments.

All mention of duties (or obligations) can be translated into the language of imperatives, or commands. As such, moral duties can be said to have imperative force. Kant distinguishes two kinds of imperative: hypothetical and categorical. The formula for a **hypothetical imperative** is "If you want A, then do B" (e.g., "If you want a good job, then get a good education," or "If you want to be happy, then stay sober and live a balanced life"). The formula for a **categorical imperative** is simply "Do B!" (i.e., do what reason discloses to be the intrinsically right thing to do, such as "Tell the truth!"). Hypothetical, or means/ends, imperatives are not the kind of imperatives that characterize moral actions. Categorical, or unqualified, imperatives are the right kind of imperatives, for they show proper recognition of the imperial status of moral obligations. Such imperatives are intuitive, immediate, absolute injunctions that all rational agents understand by virtue of their rationality.

One must perform one's moral duty solely for its own sake ("duty for duty's sake"). Some people conform to the moral law because they deem it in their own enlightened self-interest to be moral, but they are not truly moral because they do not act for the sake of the moral law. For example, a businessman may believe that "honesty is the best policy"; that is, he may judge that it is conducive to good business to give his customers correct change and high-quality products. However, unless he performs these acts because they are his duty, he is not acting morally, even though his acts are the same ones they would be if he were acting morally.[6]

The kind of imperative that fits Kant's scheme as a product of reason is one that universalizes principles of conduct. He names it the categorical imperative (CI): "Act only according to that maxim by which you can at the same time will that it would become a universal law." He elaborates: you must act "as though the maxim of your action were by your will to become a universal law of nature," analogous to the laws of physics.[7] He gives this as the criterion (or second-order principle) by which to judge all other principles.

By "maxim" Kant means the general rule in accordance with which the agent intends to act, and by "law" he means an objective principle, a maxim that passes the test of **universalizability.** The categorical imperative is the way to apply the universalizability test. It enables us to stand outside our personal maxims and estimate impartially and impersonally whether they are suitable as principles for all of us to live by. If you could consistently will that everyone would act on a given maxim, then there is an application of the categorical imperative showing the moral permissibility of action. If you cannot consistently will that everyone would act on the maxim, then that type of action is morally wrong. The maxim must be rejected as self-defeated. The formula looks like this:

$$\text{Maxim (M)}$$
$$\downarrow$$

$$\text{Second-order principle (CI)} \rightarrow \text{rejected maxims}$$
$$\downarrow$$

$$\text{First-order principle (the successful maxim)}$$

Kant gives several examples of the rational test for permissible actions. Suppose you want to make a lying promise. You promise to give me \$1,000 for my car. I give you my car, but you purposefully fail to pay me the money. What would universalizing the maxim of this action come to? "Whenever I can profit from making a lying promise, I should do so." Then what would happen to the practice of promising? It would be worthless. I cannot rationally will the practice of making lying promises. A similar logic applies to stealing and lying, but does it apply to every moral action? Could a fanatic will that all people of a certain race or religion be exterminated? Of course, to be consistent, that person would have to will that he or she be exterminated if it was discovered that he or she was a member of that race.

Kant offered three formulations of the categorical imperative. We have already discussed the first formulation; now, we will consider the second, referred to as the "kingdom of ends": "So act as to treat humanity, whether in your own person or in that of any other, in every case as an end and never as merely a means." Each person qua rational has dignity and profound worth, which entails that he or she must never be exploited, manipulated, or merely used as a means to our idea of what is for the general good (or to any other end).

What is Kant's argument for viewing rational beings as having ultimate **value?** It goes like this: in valuing anything, I endow it with value; it can have no value apart from someone's valuing it. As a valued object, it has conditional worth, which is derived from my valuation. On the other hand, the person who values the object is the ultimate source of the object and, as such, belongs to a different sphere of beings. We, as valuers, must conceive of ourselves as having unconditional worth. We cannot think of our personhood as a mere thing, for then we would have to judge it to be without any value except that given to it by the estimation of someone else. Then, that person would be the source of value, and there is no reason to suppose that one person should have unconditional worth and not another who is relevantly similar. Therefore, we are not mere objects. We have unconditional worth and so must treat all such value-givers as valuable in themselves—as ends, not merely means. I leave it to you to evaluate the validity of this argument, but most of us do hold that there is something exceedingly valuable about human life.

Kant thought that this formulation, the principle of ends, was substantively identical with his first formulation of the categorical imperative, but most scholars disagree with him. It seems better to treat this principle as a supplement to the first, adding content to the purely formal categorical imperative. In this way, Kant would limit the kinds of maxim that could be universalized. Egoism and the principle enjoining the killing of all Americans (or some other national group) would be ruled out at the very outset since they involve a violation of the dignity of rational persons. The process would be as follows:

1. Maxim (M) formulated
2. Ends test (Does the maxim involve violating the dignity of rational beings?)
3. Categorical imperative (Can the maxim be universalized?)
4. Successful moral principles survive both tests

Several questions arise regarding Kant's second formulation. Does the principle of treating persons as ends in themselves fare better than the original version of the **categorical imperative?** Why does reason and only reason have **intrinsic worth?** Who gives this worth or value to rational beings, and how do we know that they have it? What if we believe that reason has only instrumental value?

Kant's notion of the high inherent value of reason will be more plausible to those who believe that humans are made in the image of God and who interpret that (as has the mainstream of the Judeo–Christian tradition, see chapter 1) as entailing that our rational capabilities are the essence of being created in God's image: we have value because God created us with worth, that is, with reason. However, even nontheists may be persuaded that Kant is correct in seeing rationality as inherently good. It is one of the things rational beings value more than virtually anything else, and it is a necessary condition to whatever we judge to be a good life or an ideal life (a truly happy life).

Kant seems to be correct in valuing rationality. It does enable us to engage in deliberate and moral reasoning, and it lifts us above lower animals. Where he may have gone wrong is in neglecting other values or states of being that may have moral significance. For example, he believed that humans have no obligations to other animals since they are not rational; but surely the utilitarians are correct when they insist that the fact that none human animals can suffer should constrain our behavior toward them: we ought not cause unnecessary harm. Perhaps Kantians can supplement their system to accommodate this objection.

Kant's Transcendental Apperception: The Elusive Self

Hume, like the Buddha before him, had reduced the self to a series of perceptions, a succession of awareness, thus eliminating any basis for an essential self behind appearances. Kant thinks he can go beyond Hume. He argues that the "The manifold of the representation would never form a [coherent] whole" if there were no unifying self behind the appearances.

> All necessity, without exception is grounded in a transcendental condition. There must, therefore, be a transcendental ground of the unity of consciousness in the synthesis of the manifold of all our intuitions, and consequently also of the concepts of objects in general, and so of all objects of experience, a ground without which it would be impossible to think any object for our intuitions; for this object is no more than that something, the concept of which expresses such a necessity of synthesis.
>
> This original and transcendental condition is no other than *transcendental apperception.* Consciousness of self according to the determinations of our state in inner perception is merely empirical, and always changing. No fixed and abiding self can present itself in this flux of inner appearances. Such consciousness is usually named *inner sense,* or *empirical apperception.* What has *necessarily* to be represented as numerically identical cannot be thought as such through empirical data. To render such a transcendental presupposition valid, there must be a condition which precedes all experience, and which makes experience itself possible. There can be in us no modes of knowledge, no connection or unity of one mode of knowledge with another, without that unity of consciousness which precedes all data of intuitions, and by relation to which representation of objects is alone possible. This pure original unchangeable consciousness I shall name *transcendental apperception.* (CPR, pp. 134–138, A104–A109)

So although we can never reach our essential self directly, through *transcendental apperception,* or higher synthesizing of perception, we can know we have a transcendental self, a noumenal self, beyond appearances; otherwise, we could not hold the manifold of perceptions together. Instead of Hume's succession of awareness, we have an awareness of succession, a unifying transcendent self behind and beyond the empirical self. We cannot know much about this noumenal self, only that it exists. We do possess an essential beyond the changing flux of appearances.

Freedom of the Will

In the section on the Antimonies of Reason in the *Critique of Pure Reason* (which shows how reason sets forth opposite conclusions on metaphysical matters), Kant applies his doctrine of pure apperception to freedom of the will:

Man is one of the appearances of the sensible world, and in so far as he is one of the natural causes the causality of which must stand under empirical laws. Like all other things in nature, he must have an empirical character. This character we come to know through the powers and faculties which he reveals in his actions. In lifeless, or merely animal, nature we find no ground for thinking that any faculty is conditioned otherwise than in a merely sensible manner. Man, however, who knows all the rest of nature solely through the senses, knows himself also through *pure apperception;* and this, indeed, in acts and inner determinations which he cannot regard as impressions of the senses. He is thus to himself, on the one hand *phenomenon,* and on the other hand, in respect of certain faculties the action of which cannot be ascribed to the receptivity of sensibility, a *purely intelligible object.* We entitle these faculties understanding and reason. The latter, in particular, we distinguish in a quite peculiar and especial way from all empirically conditioned powers. For it views its objects exclusively in the light of ideas, and in accordance with them determines the understanding, which then proceeds to make an empirical use of its own similarly pure concepts. That our reason has causality, or that we at least represent it to ourselves as having causality, is evident from the *imperatives* which in all matters of conduct we impose as rules upon our active powers. *"Ought"* expresses a kind of necessity and of connection with grounds which is found nowhere else in the whole of nature. The understanding can know in nature only what is, what has been, or what will be. We cannot say that anything in nature *ought to be* other than what in all these time-relations it actually is. When we have the course of nature alone in view, *"ought"* has no meaning whatsoever. It is just as absurd to ask what ought to happen in the natural world as to ask what properties a circle ought to have. All that we are justified in asking is: what happens in nature? what are the properties of the circle?

This *"ought"* expresses a possible action the ground of which cannot be anything but a mere concept; whereas in the case of a merely natural action the ground must always be an appearance. The action to which the *"ought"* applies must indeed be possible under natural conditions. These conditions, however, do not play any part in determining the will itself, but only in determining the effect and its consequences in the [field of] appearance. No matter how many natural grounds or how many sensuous impulses may impel me to *will,* they can never give rise to the *"ought,"* but only to a willing which, while very far from being necessary, is always conditioned; and the *"ought"* pronounced by reason confronts such willing with a limit and an end—nay more, forbids or authorizes it. Whether what is willed be an object of mere sensibility (the pleasant) or of pure reason (the good), reason will not give way to any ground which is empirically given. Reason does not here follow the order of things as they present themselves in appearance, but frames to itself with perfect spontaneity an order of its own according to ideas, to which it adapts the empirical conditions, and according to which it declares actions to be necessary, even although they have never taken place, and perhaps never will take place. And at the same time reason also presupposes that it can have causality in regard to all these actions, since otherwise no empirical effects could be expected from its ideas. (CPR, pp. 472–473, A546–A548/B574–B576)

On the one hand, a person, as an appearance, our **empirical self,** comes under the ordinary laws of nature, that is, under the domain of causality. On the other hand, we can introspect and know that we are free, that we have an inner pure apperception of our self-determination. To be morally responsible one must be free to do either the right or wrong act, so it follows for Kant that, since morality is true, we must be free to do otherwise.

On God and Immortality

Kant argues that all so-called proofs for the existence of God and immortality are "altogether fruitless and by their nature null and void" (CPR, A636); but proofs against the existence of God and immortality are equally unsound. We simply cannot be dogmatic either way. What does Kant's theory advise in such a predicament?

> The positive value of the critical principles of pure reason in relation to the conception of God and of the simple nature of the soul, admits of a similar exemplification; but on this point I shall not dwell. I cannot even make the assumption—as the practical interests of morality require—of God, freedom, and immortality, if I do not deprive speculative reason of its pretensions to transcendent insight. For to arrive at these, it must make use of principles which, in fact, extend only to the objects of possible experience, and which cannot be applied to objects beyond this sphere without converting them into phenomena, and thus rendering the practical extension of pure reason impossible. *I must, therefore, deny knowledge, to make room for faith.* The dogmatism of metaphysics, that is, the presumption that it is possible to advance in metaphysics without previous criticism, is the true source of the unbelief (always dogmatic) which militates against morality. (CPR, Preface)

Kant was a Christian who believed that there were practical, moral reasons for believing in God and immortality. God and immortality are necessary postulates of ethics. Immortality is necessary in this way: according to Kant, the moral law commands us to be morally perfect. Since *ought* implies *can*, we must be able to reach moral perfection. However, we cannot attain perfection in this life, for the task is infinite. So there must be an afterlife in which we continue progressing toward this ideal.

God is a necessary postulate in that morality requires someone to enforce the moral law. That is, in order for the moral law to be completely justified, there must finally be a just recompense of happiness in accordance with virtue. We must get what we deserve. The good must be rewarded by happiness in proportion to their virtue, and the evil must be punished in proportion to their vice. This harmonious correlation of virtue and happiness does not happen in this life, so it must happen in the next life. Thus, there must be a God, acting as judge and enforcer of the moral law, without which the moral law would be unjustified.

Kant is not saying that we can prove that God exists or that we ought to be moral in order to be happy. Rather, the idea of God serves as a completion of our ordinary ideas of ethics.

Summary

Kant's view of human nature centers around three deep philosophical questions:

1. *What can I know?* Our knowledge is structured by synthetic a priori categories of space, time, and causality so that we know only appearances, never the noumenal world, the thing-in-itself. However, we are not confined to complete skepticism. Through transcendental reasoning, we can know that we have an essential self which exists beyond appearances, and we can know or have good reason to believe that the self is free to act morally or immorally.

2. *What ought I do?* Kant thought the practical side of reason was decisive, entailing that the most important thing in life was morality, acting out of a purely good will ("the only thing good in itself"). We ought to act morally, simply because it is right to do so, and we deserve to be treated on the basis of our moral character and actions. Immoral people forfeit their rights, so a murderer ought to be executed for his or her crime.

3. *What may I hope?* I may hope in God and immortality. Although we can neither prove the existence or nonexistence of God and immortality, we may hope in them. (I must, therefore, deny knowledge, to make room for faith.) Faith in God for Kant was a keystone to morality and meaning in life, without which neither morality nor a meaningful life was truly complete or fully justified.

Although Kant's theory of human nature is epistemically pessimistic (we can never reach the real world, the thing-in-itself), he is basically an optimist: humans, as rational beings, have inherent dignity through reason and thereby can know the moral law. We can reject Hume's skepticism about the self and via transcendental reason infer both an essential noumenal self and freedom of the will. Moreover, we ought to postulate the existence of God as the assumption necessary to justify the moral law. We can hope in God and immortality in spite of a paucity of rational evidence. This is the high watermark of philosophical optimism. We will see how the Kantian revolution, in the hands of the children of the revolution, resulted in a more pessimistic view of human nature.

Study Questions

1. What is Kant's Copernican revolution? How does it relate to earlier epistemologies?

2. What is synthetic a priori knowledge? Explain.

3. What is the phenomena/noumena distinction in Kant? Can we know the world as it really is?

4. What, according to Kant, are our notions of time, space, and causality?

5. What is Kant's moral theory? What is the Categorical Imperative?

6. Explain Kant's notion of the transcendental apperception of transcendent self? Compare it with the Buddhist notion of *an-atman* and Hume's view of personal identity.

7. Examine Kant's theory of free will. How cogent is his reasoning?

8. Kant claims that God is a necessary postulate in that morality requires someone to enforce the moral law. Is Kant right about this?

9. Kant's philosophy of human nature strives to combine the most rigorous rational analysis with the most hopeful moral conclusions. The question is, is he successful?

Notes

1. Immanuel Kant, *Critique of Pure Reason*, trans. Norman Kemp Smith (1781; St. Martin's Press, 1969, reprint), p. 41.
2. From the preface of Kant's *Critique of Pure Reason* (1781), my translation.
3. David Hume, *A Treatise of Human Nature*, book III, part III, section 3 (originally published in 1739–40; Oxford University Press, 1888, reprint), p. 415.
4. Immanuel Kant, *Fundamental Principles of the Metaphysics of Ethics*, trans. T. K. Abbott (Longman's, 1965), section 1, pp. 10–11. I have slightly revised the translation.
5. Ibid., p. 6.
6. Ibid., p. 46.
7. Ibid.

For Further Reading

Acton, Harry, *Kant's Moral Philosophy* (Macmillan, 1970).

Allison, Henry, *Kant's Transcendental Idealism* (Yale University Press, 1983).

Beck, Lewis White, *A Commentary on Kant's Critique of Practical Reason* (University of Chicago, 1960).

Beck, Lewis White, ed., *Studies in the Philosophy of Kant* (Bobbs-Merrill, 1965).

Ewing, A. C., *A Short Commentary on Kant's Critique of Pure Reason* (Methuen, 1950).

Guyer, Paul, *Kant and the Claims of Knowledge* (Cambridge University Press, 1987).

Kant, Immanuel, *Critique of Pure Reason*, trans. Norman Kemp Smith (St. Martin's Press, 1969).

Kemp, John, *The Philosophy of Kant* (Oxford University Press, 1968).

Kemp Smith, Norman, *A Commentary to Kant's "Critique of Pure Reason"* (Humanities Press, 1962).

Louden, Robert, *Morality and Moral Theory* (Oxford University Press, 1991).

O'Neill, Onora, *Acting on Principle: An Essay on Kantian Ethics* (Columbia University Press, 1975).

Ross, W. D., *Kant's Ethical Theory* (Clarendon Press, 1954).

Strawson, P. F., *The Bounds of Sense: An Essay on Kant's Critique of Pure Reason* (Methuen, 1966).

Walker, Ralph C. S., *Kant: The Arguments of the Philosophers* (Routledge & Kegan Paul, 1978).

Walker, Ralph C. S., ed., *Kant on Pure Reason* (Oxford University Press, 1982).

Werkmeister, W. H., *Kant* (Open Court, 1980).

Wolff, Robert Paul., ed., *Kant* (Doubleday, 1967).

CHAPTER 9

〜〜〜〜

Arthur Schopenhauer's Pessimistic Idealism

Kant speaks much of the dignity of man. I have never seen it. It seems to me that the notion of dignity can be applied to man only in an ironical sense. His will is sinful. His intellect is limited. His body is weak and perishable. How shall a man have dignity whose conception is a crime, whose birth is a penalty, whose life is toil, whose death is a necessity?

Human life must be some kind of mistake. Else why is man a compound of needs and necessities so hard to satisfy? And why, if perchance they should be satisfied, is he thereby abandoned to boredom? This is the direct proof that existence has no real value. For what is boredom but the feeling of the emptiness of life? The fact that this most perfect manifestation of life, the human organism, with the infinite cunning and complex working of its machinery, must oscillate between need and boredom and finally fall to dust and extinction, this fact, I say, is eloquent to him who has the mind to understand it. *(Schopenhauer,* Parega and Paralipomena*)*

Introduction

Schopenhauer's idealist view of human nature combines ideas from four of the theories we have already studied: Plato, Hinduism, Buddhism, and Kant. It is within the idealist tradition, but unlike Plato and Kant, though like Hinduism, it is pessimistic, as the above epigraph indicates.

Arthur Schopenhauer (1788–1860) saw himself as the philosopher who alone developed Kant's Copernican revolution to its correct conclusion. A genius who wrote his major work, *The World as Will and Representation*, while still in his mid-twenties, a pessimist who thought that life was meaningless, and the first Western philosopher to be deeply influenced by Eastern religion, Schopenhauer believed that all individual wills are mere manifestations of a cosmic Will. He was ferociously contentious, cantankerous,[1] cynical, irascible, obstinate, pessimistic, and egotistic, but also generous, kind, witty, charming, and prodigiously energetic—a genius. He was depressed by the suffering in the world as well as by his own disappointments in life. He was a renaissance man, a polymath, mastering several intellectual subjects. He studied all morning and played the flute every afternoon. His mental energy was phenomenal, as was his philosophical acumen. Modeling his style on that of the Scottish philosopher David Hume, he, more than any other philosopher, proved that German philosophy could be written in a clear and interesting manner. No German philosopher has ever exceeded his clear and scintillating style.

Schopenhauer was born to a wealthy cosmopolitan business family in the free city of Danzig in 1788. He was educated in Germany, France, and England and was fluent in each of these country's languages. Although prepared by his father for a career in international business, young Arthur detested that vocation and, after his father's death in 1805, was allowed by his mother to pursue a career in philosophy. Studying under the eminent German philosophers Johann Fichte (1762–1814) and Friedrich Schleiermacher (1768–1834), Schopenhauer was soon recognized as a brilliant student. He wrote his doctoral dissertation "On the Fourfold Root of the Principle of Sufficient Reason," a development of the idea, set forth by Leibniz and developed by Kant, that every object and event in the world has an explanation, a sufficient reason for why it exists or happened. After his father's death, he moved to Weimar with his novelist mother who opened a literary salon wherein Schopenhauer met some of the most famous people of the age, among them the greatest poet of his time, Goethe (1749–1832), with whom he became friends. However, Schopenhauer and his mother quarreled, and he moved into his own apartment. In 1813 he was introduced to Hinduism and began reading the Upanishads (see chapter 6). From that day on he derived comfort and spiritual sustenance from these ancient Scriptures. From 1814 to 1818 he wrote his *magnum opus, The World as Will and Representation,* a work ingeniously combining Kant's transcendental idealism with Hindu monism. His hopes for the book were soon dashed to the ground as the intellectual and literary world ignored it. Undaunted by this poor reception, Schopenhauer obtained permission to lecture at the University of Berlin where he unwisely scheduled his lectures at the same hour as the most renowned philosopher of his day, G. W. F. Hegel (1779–1830), whose work Schopenhauer despised as a fraud and a betrayal of Kant, was lecturing.[2] No one attended Schopenhauer's lectures, and his academic career abruptly ended.

For the next two decades Schopenhauer traveled and wrote singularly lucid essays on ethics and freedom of the will. In 1844 Schopenhauer wrote a second volume to *The World as Will and Representation,* developing the earlier work in a coherent manner. Finally, in 1853 an English literary journal, *The Westminster Review,* published an anonymous critical review of Schopenhauer's writings that began to stir up interest in his unconventional work. Seeing fame finally in the offing, Schopenhauer published a new edition of his major treatise. His final work was a set of short essays and aphorisms, written in 1851 and entitled, *Parega and Paralipomena.* He died of a heart attack in Frankfurt on September 21, 1860. His work influenced Søren Kierkegaard, Friedrich Nietzsche, Thomas Mann, and Sigmund Freud. Even Adolf Hitler claimed Schopenhauer as his inspiration.[3]

The World as Idea

Schopenhauer saw himself as a child of Kant's Copernican revolution, alone in carrying out his master's project to its logical conclusion. Kant had argued that there is an epistemic distinction between the world we experience, the world of appearances, and the real world, the *ding an sich*. We do not experience the world as it is but only impose the categories of the mind onto it, the categories of space, time, and causality. Whereas Kant thought he had denied reason to make way for faith, Schopenhauer remained an atheist, deeming Kant's departure from his own logic an unknowable flight into "Cloud-Cuckooland." The idea of a First Cause, which is what God would be, simply violates the Kantian principle of causality, that everything must have a cause, so even a God must have one. All we have are ideas or representations (*vorstellung*). "The world is my representation," Schopenhauer writes.

Volume 1 of *The World as Will and Representation* (hereafter abbreviated as W)[4] is divided into four books, with an appendix on Kant's philosophy. The first book presents the world as representation, as the manner in which we experience it. The second book deals with the world as will, how we must understand our wills as parts of a universal will. This doctrine is the answer to Kant's *ding an sich:* the thing in itself is the universal will. The third book shows that aesthetic contemplation is a means of making sense of the world. The fourth book, exemplifying Schopenhauer's pessimism, advocates resignation as the means of overcoming the perennial suffering in the world and the meaninglessness of life.

Schopenhauer begins Book 1 of volume 1 with the words "The world is my idea." Every living being receives information, representations of the world in temporal–spatial categories. All we know is this world of ideas. Matter does not exist, except as a confused idea.

> "The world is my idea."—this is a truth which holds good for everything that lives and knows, though man alone can bring it into reflective and abstract consciousness: If he really does this, he has attained to philosophical wisdom. It then becomes clear and certain to him that what he knows is not a sun and an earth, but only an eye that sees a sun, a hand that feels the earth; that the world which surrounds him is there only as idea, i.e., only in relation to something else, the consciousness, which is himself. If any truth can be asserted a priori, it is this: for it is the expression of the most general form of all possible and thinkable experience: a form which is more general than time, or space, or causality, for they all presuppose it; and each of these, which we have seen to be just so many modes of the principle of sufficient reason, is valid only for a particular class of ideas; whereas the antithesis of object and subject is the common form of all these classes, is that form under which alone any idea of whatever kind it may be, abstract or intuitive, pure or empirical, is possible and thinkable. No truth therefore is more certain, more independent of all others, and less in need of proof than this, that all that exists for knowledge and therefore this

whole world, is only object in relation to subject, perception of a perceiver, in a word, idea. This is obviously true of the past and the future, as well as of the present, of what is furthest off, as of what is near; for it is true of time and space themselves, in which alone these distinctions arise. All that in any way belongs or can belong to the world is inevitably thus conditioned through the subject, and exists only for the subject. The world is idea. (W, vol. 1, p. 3)

This theory of ideas was first positively set forth in the West by Bishop Berkeley. It is found in Vedanta Hinduism (chapter 6), which consigns the world of appearances to *maya,* the world of illusions.

His nearest antecedent, one which Schopenhauer deeply, though critically admired, is Kant's transcendental idealism, and in particular Kant's Copernican revolution (the categories of time, space, and causality are not in the world but part of our understanding). All these philosophies are versions of transcendentalism, meaning that reality transcends our comprehension; but Schopenhauer's version rejects Kant's and Berkeley's theism. With Kant, Schopenhauer holds that space, time, and causality are categories of understanding, not part of reality. We never experience the world as it is in itself but only as it appears to us through the categories of the mind.

This phenomenon of representations constitutes one of two essential aspects of the world. The other, to be dealt with below, is what Kant called *ding an sich,* which Schopenhauer will identify as the cosmic will to live. All other supposed philosophical realisms which hold that we have direct (e.g., Aristotle) or indirect (e.g., Galileo, Descartes, and Locke) access to "reality" are "the phantom of a dream, and its acceptance is an *ignis fatuus* (i.e., a foolish fire) in philosophy."

As noted, so far we have mainly a review of the idealist tradition from Plato and Hinduism to Berkeley and Kant. Schopenhauer argued along Kantian lines that space, time, and causality are inherently unstable concepts. We cannot formulate a clear idea of time having a beginning, nor can we grasp the idea of beginningless time. We cannot formulate the notion of space having boundaries, but neither can we imagine boundless space. We cannot form the notion of an infinite set of causes, but neither can we conceive of a first cause. The theological doctrine of God as the eternal, nonspatial, first cause, which Berkeley and others resort to as the solution of these problems, must be rejected for it violates the principle of causality ("every object and event must have a cause") and so raises the question, What caused God? He chides Kant for the inconsistency of both denying causality as part of the noumenal world and then implying that the noumenal world causes us to have the perceptions we have. So far Schopenhauer is simply correcting the idealist tradition. Now, in book 2 Schopenhauer makes an advance on transcendental idealism.

The Will to Live

Schopenhauer believed he had solved the riddle of the *ding an sich,* Kant's noumenal world which is behind appearance. He criticized Kant for making the noumenon an unperceptible but ultimately real substratum of everything there is, but he seemed to do so himself, only calling it "Will." He begins by showing that we can never get at ultimate reality simply by examining representations.

> Here we already see that we can never get at the inner nature of things *from without*. However much we may investigate, we obtain nothing but images and names. We are like a man who goes round a castle, looking in vain for an entrance, and sometimes sketching the facades. Yet this is the path that all philosophers before me have followed. (W, vol. 1, p. 99)

Schopenhauer will perform his own revolution by locating the *ding an sich* within the world, within our consciousness. We do not have to find a door into the castle, for we are already within it.

> The meaning that I am looking for of the world that stands before me simply as my representation, or the transition from it as mere representation of the knowing subject to whatever it may be besides this, could never be found if the investigator himself were nothing more than the purely knowing subject (a winged cherub without a body). But he himself is rooted in that world; and thus he finds himself in it as an *individual*, in other words, his knowledge, which is the conditional supporter of the whole world as representation, is nevertheless given entirely through the medium of a body, and the affections of this body are, as we have shown, the starting-point for the understanding in its perception of this world. For the purely knowing subject as such, this body is a representation like any other, an object among objects. Its movements and actions are so far known to him in just the same way as the changes of all other objects of perception; and they would be equally strange and incomprehensible to him, if their meaning were not unravelled for him in an entirely different way. Otherwise, he would see his conduct follow on presented motives with the constancy of a law of nature, just as the changes of other objects follow upon causes, stimuli, and motives. But he would be no nearer to understanding the influence of the motives than he is to understanding the connexion with its cause of any other effect that appears before him. (W, vol. 1, p. 99)

We know our bodies as appearances, as we know other objects in the world. But this is not the whole story. We are not simply representations. Our description of the world and human nature is only half done.

> All this, however, is not the case; on the contrary, the answer to the riddle is given to the subject of knowledge appearing as individual, and this answer is given in the word *Will*. This and this alone gives him the key to his own phenomenon, reveals to him the significance and shows him the inner mechanism of his being, his actions, his movements. To the subject of knowing, who appears as an individual only through his identity with the body, this body is given in two entirely different ways. It is given in intelligent perception as representation, as an object among objects, liable to the laws of these objects. But it is also given in quite a different way, namely as what is known immediately to everyone, and is denoted by the word *will*. (W, vol. 1, p. 100)

The will is inside our reality. It encompasses all intentional activity, including desires, wantings, fearings, hatings, strivings, hopings, and mere wishings. It includes a general will to live, found also in plants, as well as subconscious and conscious desires of humans and other animals. It is the inner force of nature, in stones, sand, water, and air. Schopenhauer writes, "I teach that the inner nature of everything is will."

Schopenhauer is a monist. The world is one, but there are two aspects, an outer, the representations, and an inner, the will. The will is identified with our bodies.

> Every true act of his will is also at once and inevitably a movement of his body; he cannot actually will the act without at the same time being aware that it appears as a movement of the body. The act of will and the action of the body are not two different states objectively known connected by the bond of causality; they do not stand in the relation of cause and effect, but are one and the same thing, though given in two entirely different ways, first quite directly, and then in perception for the understanding. The action of the body is nothing but the act of will objectified, i.e., translated into perception. (W, vol. 1, p. 100)

My body and my will are really one unity:

> We can turn the expression of this truth in different ways and say: My body and my will are one; or, What as representation of perception I call my body, I call my will in so far as I am conscious of it in an entirely different way comparable with no other; or, My body is the objectivity of my will; or, Apart from the fact that my body is my representation, it is still my will, and so on. (W, vol. 1, p. 103)

We have immediate knowledge of our bodies, which are the incarnations of will, our intentional stances. We do not infer our volitions from our bodily movements but intuit that the two are aspects of one another. Schopenhauer now brings the two aspects of our knowledge together:

> The double knowledge which we have of the nature and action of our own body, and which is given in two completely different ways, has now been clearly brought out. Accordingly, we shall use it further as a key to the inner being of every phenomenon in nature. We shall judge all objects which are not our own body, and therefore are given to our consciousness not in the double way, but only as representations, according to the analogy of this body. We shall therefore assume that as, on the one hand, they are representation, just like our body, and are in this respect homogeneous with it, so on the other hand, if we set aside their existence as the subject's representation, what still remains over must be, according to its inner nature, the same as what in ourselves we call *will*. For what other kind of existence or reality could we attribute to the rest of the material world? From what source could we take the elements out of which we construct such a world? Besides the will and the representation, there is absolutely nothing known or conceivable for us. If we wish to attribute the greatest known reality to the material world, which immediately exists only in our representation, then we give it that reality which our own body has for each of us, for to each of us this is the most real of things. But if now we ana-

lyze the reality of this body and its actions, then, beyond the fact that it is our representation, we find nothing in it but the will; with this even its reality is exhausted. Therefore we can nowhere find another kind of reality to attribute to the material world. If, therefore, the material world is to be something more than our mere representation, we must say that, besides being the representation, and hence in itself and of its *inmost nature*, it is what we find immediately in ourselves as will. . . . Therefore, if I say that the force which attracts a stone to the earth is of its nature, in itself, and apart from all representation, will, then no one will attach to this proposition the absurd meaning that the stone moves itself according to a known motive, because it is thus that the will appears in man.

The will considered purely in itself is devoid of knowledge, and is only a blind irresistible cure, as we see it appear in inorganic and vegetable nature and in their laws, and also in the vegetative part of our own life. Through the addition of the world as representation, developed for its service, the will obtains knowledge of its own willing and what it wills, namely that this is nothing but this world, life, precisely as it exists. We have heretofore called the phenomenal world the mirror, the objectivity of the will; and as what the will wills is always life, just because this is nothing but the presentation of that willing for the representation, it is immaterial and a mere pleonasm if, instead of simply saying "the will" we say "the will-to-live." (W, vol. 1, pp. 104–105)

Will is the force behind all nature, the energy of existence, of which my body is a manifestation. The secret behind the universe, the *ding an sich,* is "the will to live."

As the will is the thing-in-itself, the inner content, the essence of the world, but life, the visible world, the phenomenon, is only the mirror of the will, this world will accompany the will as inseparably as a body is accompanied by its shadow; and if will exists, then life, the world, will exist. Therefore life is certain to the will-to-live, and as long as we are filled with the will-to-live, we need not be apprehensive for our existence, even at the sight of death. It is true that we see the individual come into being and pass away; but the individual is only phenomenon, exists only for knowledge involved in the principle of sufficient reason, in the *principium individuationis.* Naturally, for this knowledge, the individual receives his life as a gift, rises out of nothing, and then suffers the loss of this gift through death, and returns to nothing. (W, vol. 1, p. 275)

The representations of our spatial–temporal selves, our egoistic identities, which Schopenhauer, borrowing a medieval formula, labels *principium individuationis* (i.e., individuating principle), are illusory and the loci of suffering. The idea that out existence is one of suffering is Eastern more than Western, focusing more on sin and seeing suffering as a symptom of sin.

Salvation from the Sufferings of Existence

For Schopenhauer, reality is will—spiritual, not material—but the will is the cause of suffering. Because our wills are insatiable, because we continuously desire, moving from one desire to another, we are doomed to suffering. Deep suffering is the common lot of human beings—the more sensitive, the more painful.

Human life must be some kind of mistake. Else why is man a compound of needs and necessities so hard to satisfy? And why, if perchance they should be satisfied, is he thereby abandoned to boredom? This is the direct proof that existence has no real value. For what is boredom but the feeling of the emptiness of life? The fact that this most perfect manifestation of life, the human organism, with the infinite cunning and complex working of its machinery, must oscillate between need and boredom and finally fall to dust and extinction, this fact, I say, is eloquent to him who has the mind to understand it.

Unless suffering is the direct and immediate object of life, our existence must entirely fail of its aim. It is absurd to look upon the enormous amount of pain that abounds everywhere in the world, originating in needs and necessities inseparable from life, as serving no purpose, as being the result of mere chance.

Let us consider the human race. Here life presents itself as a task to be performed. Here we see, in great and small, universal need, ceaseless wars, compulsory activity, extreme exertion of mind and body. Millions united into nations, striving for a common good, each individual on account of his own. But thousands are sacrificed. Now silly delusions, now intriguing politics, excite them to wars. Then sweat and blood must flow to carry out someone's ideas or expiate someone's folly. In peace time it is industry and trade. Inventions work miracles, seas are navigated, delicacies are brought from the ends of the earth, waves engulf thousands. The tumult passes description. And all to what end? To sustain life through a brief span, and then to reproduce and begin again.

From whence did Dante take the materials for his hell but from our actual world? And a very proper hell he was able to make of it. When, on the other hand, he came to describe heaven and its delights, he was confronted with difficulty, for our world affords no material for this.[5]

All of creation, as containing the cosmic will, suffers, especially human beings, and among humans, especially the most intelligent and sensitive, for they are able to feel joys and disappointments more keenly than the dull and stupid.

What can be done to liberate us? Schopenhauer offers two ways, a lesser and a greater means of salvation. In book 3 of his *magnum opus,* he describes the lesser, incidental mode, aesthetic contemplation. Aesthetic pleasure or beauty takes us beyond our banal existence for the moment and delights us. This transcendent moment is the highest state we can attain in life. Aesthetic contemplation raises the individual to a will-less, painless, atemporal mode of being, beyond the chains of egoism and illusion. However, few of us can maintain this level of aesthetic consciousness for more than a very short time, so it is not a means of salvation open to most of us or a complete means of salvation for anyone.

The greater, more permanent mode is described in book 4.

We, however, wish to consider life philosophically, that is to say, according to its Ideas, and then we shall find that neither the will, the thing-in-itself in all phenom-

ena, nor the subject of knowing, the spectator of all phenomena, is in any way
affected by birth and death. Birth and death belong only to the phenomenon of the
will, and hence to life; and it is essential to this that it manifest itself in individuals
that come into being and pass away, as fleeting phenomena, appearing in the form
of time, of that which in itself knows no time, but must be manifested precisely in the
way aforesaid in order to objectify its real nature. Birth and death belong equally to
life, and hold the balance as mutual conditions of each other, or, if the expression be
preferred, as poles of the whole phenomenon of life. The wisest of all mythologies,
the Indian, expresses this by giving to the very god who symbolizes destruction and
death. . . . i.e., to Shiva as an attribute not only the necklace of skulls, but also the
lingam,* that symbol of generation which appears as the counterpart of death. In this
way it is intimated that generation and death are essential correlatives which recip-
rocally neutralize and eliminate each other. It was precisely the same sentiment that
prompted the Greeks and Romans to adorn the costly sarcophags, just as we still see
them, with feasts, dances, marriages, hunts, fights between wild beasts, bacchanalia,
that is, with presentations of life's most powerful urge. This they present to us not
only through such diversions and merriments, but even in sensual groups, to the
point of showing us the sexual intercourse between satyrs and goats. The object was
obviously to indicate with the greatest emphasis from the death of the mourned individual the immortal life of nature, and thus to intimate, although without abstract
knowledge, that the whole of nature is the phenomenon, and also the fulfillment, of
the will-to-live. The form of this phenomenon is time, space, and causality, and
through these, individuation, which requires that the individual must come into
being and pass away. But this no more disturbs the will-to-live—the individual being
only a particular example or specimen, so to speak, of the phenomenon of the will—
than does the death of an individual injure the whole of nature. For it is not the individual that nature cares for, but only the species; and in all seriousness she urges
the preservation of the species, since she provides for this so lavishly through the
immense surplus of the seed and the great strength of the fructifying impulse. The
individual, on the contrary, has no value for nature, and can have none for infinite
time, infinite space, and the infinite number of possible individuals therein are her
kingdom. Therefore nature is always ready to let the individual fall, and the individual is accordingly not only exposed to destruction in a thousand ways from the
most insignificant accidents, but is even destined for this and is led toward it by
nature herself, from the moment that individual has served the maintenance of the
species. In this way, nature united openly expresses the great truth that only Ideas,
not individuals, have the highest reality proper, in other words are a complete objectivity of the will. Now man is nature herself, and indeed nature at the highest grade
of her self-consciousness, but nature is only the objectified will-to-live; the person
who has grasped and retained this point of view may certainly and justly console
himself for his own death and for that of his friends by looking back on the immortal life of nature, which he himself is. (W, vol. 1, pp. 275f)

The way of salvation is Hindu–Stoical resignation, surrendering one's individual
will with all its desires, thus freeing oneself from illusion and suffering. In ascetic

---

*The phallus or penis, worshipped as the symbol of the god Shiva.

self-denial, one renounces one's particular will and merges with the reality of the *ding-an-sich*, the ultimately real cosmic will to live. "What remains after the complete abolition of the will is, for all who are still full of the will, assuredly nothing. But also conversely, to those in whom the will has turned and denied itself, this very real world of ours with all its suns and galaxies, is—nothing" (W, vol. 1, p. 412).[6] That is, the solution of the problem of the suffering will is to give up one's egoistic will and surrender to the cosmic will to live.

Morality

Schopenhauer rejects **deontic,** or rule-governed, morality, believing it to be a confusion or built on false assumption. In his *On the Basis of Morality* (1841), he first subjects Kant's moral theory to a blistering attack. Kant, while correct in rejecting self-interested morality as a sham, is, nevertheless, guilty of transposing his idea of a noumenal realm from its appropriate context in epistemology to an inappropriate context in morality. All rule-governed approaches owe their authority to an enforcing mechanism, either God or positive law. To speak of an "absolute ought" or "the moral law," as Kant does, is a stupendous category mistake; that is, it transfers an idea from one context to another, inappropriate one. In revering the categorical imperative the way he does, Kant shows his theological roots. He is really a Christian in disguise.

Schopenhauer rejects Kant's second formulation of the categorical imperative: treat rational beings always as ends in themselves, never as mere means. He thinks the expression "ends in themselves" is meaningless rhetoric, a roundabout way of appealing to a religious view of humanity, namely, that humans are made in the image of God, with honor and dignity. Schopenhauer does not see much of this in the average human.

> Kant speaks much of the dignity of man. I have never seen it. It seems to me that the notion of dignity can be applied to man only in an ironical sense. His will is sinful. His intellect is limited. His body is weak and perishable. How shall a man have dignity whose conception is a crime, whose birth is a penalty, whose life is toil, whose death is a necessity?[7]

In place of rule-governed ethics, Schopenhauer substitutes an ethic of character. People act from what they really are. Moral philosophy is impotent to effect goodness. The only general rule in morality is "Do not harm anyone, but help everyone as much as you can." Beyond that, the ideal of love and compassion that we find in the New Testament is the one true ethical system, though we must divorce it from the superstitious idea of God. Altruism, the disinterested love of others, is the highest morality we can attain.

Schopenhauer argues that all animals, including humans, start out as egoists ("Let the world perish, so long as I survive"). As they become more socialized, their ethics becomes one of enlightened self-interest based on reciprocity ("I'll scratch your back if you scratch mine"). However, a moral miracle sometimes occurs in which people realize their cosmic identity (in the Hindu Vedas, *tat tvam asi*, "that art thou"), and we reach the highest realm of human existence.

Perhaps the following illustration will help make this idea clearer and link it up with the idea of salvation through cosmic identity discussed above. An incident reported by the religious scholar Joseph Campbell illustrates Schopenhauer's theory. One day, two policemen were driving up a road in Hawaii when they noticed, just beyond the railing that keeps the cars from rolling over, a young man preparing to jump. The police car stopped, and the policeman on the right jumped out to grab the man but caught him just as he jumped and was himself being pulled over when the second cop arrived in time and pulled the two of them back. Campbell writes,

> Do you realize what had suddenly happened to that policeman who had given himself to death with that unknown youth? Everything else in his life had dropped off—his duty to his family, his duty to his job, his duty to his own life—all of his wishes and hopes for his lifetime had just disappeared. He was about to die. Later, a newspaper reporter asked him, "Why didn't you let go? You would have been killed." And his reported answer was "I couldn't let go. If I had let that young man go, I couldn't have lived another day of my life." How come?[8]

Arthur Schopenhauer's answer is that such a psychological crisis represents the breakthrough of a metaphysical realization, which is that you and the other are one, that you are two aspects of the one life, and that your apparent separateness is but an effect of the way we experience the eternal forms under the conditions of space and time. "Our true reality is in our identity and unity with all life. This is a metaphysical truth which may become spontaneously realized under circumstances of crisis. For it is, according to Schopenhauer, the truth of your life."[9] Joseph Campbell comments on this:

> The hero is the one who has given his physical life to some order of realization of that truth. The concept of love your neighbor is to put you in tune with this fact. But whether you love your neighbor or not, when the realization grabs you, you may risk your life. That Hawaiian policeman didn't know who the young man was to whom he had given himself. Schopenhauer declares that in small ways you can see this happening every day, all the time, moving life in the world, people doing selfless things to and for each other.[10]

What Campbell calls the "hero," Schopenhauer calls the "moral person." "Boundless compassion for all living beings is the firmest and surest guarantee of pure moral conduct, and needs no casuistry" (i.e., no subtle hairsplitting distinctions).[11]

Schopenhauer, Sex, and Psychoanalysis

Schopenhauer articulated a number of doctrines later to be used as the basis of Freud's psychoanalysis. Schopenhauer's concept of the will contains the rudi-

ments of Freud's concepts of the unconscious and the id (see chapter 11). Schopenhauer's writings on madness anticipate Freud's theory of repression and his first
theory of the etiology of neurosis. Schopenhauer's work contains aspects of what
would become the theory of free association. Most importantly, Schopenhauer
articulates major parts of the Freudian theory of sexuality.

Schopenhauer thought that the will itself is unconscious but that it manifests
itself in sexual desire and the "love of life" in human beings. The latter are both
manifestations of an underlying will to live. Freud took over this whole picture of
dual instincts rooted in a single will to live and preserved it unchanged until at
least 1923. For both of them, the sex drive was by far the stronger of the two, "the
most perfect manifestation of the will to live" (W, vol. 2, p. 514). Again, he writes,

> The sexual impulse is the most vehement of all craving, the desire of desires, the
> concentration of all our willing. This . . . is the piquant element and the jest of the
> world, that the chief concern of all men is pursued secretly and ostensibly ignored
> as much as possible. But, in fact, at every moment we see it seat itself as the real and
> hereditary lord of the world, out of the fullness of its own strength, on the ancestral
> throne, and looking down from thence with scornful glances, laugh at the prepara-
> tions which have been made to subdue it, to imprison it, or at least to limit it and if
> possible to keep it concealed, or indeed so to master it that it shall only appear as a
> subordinate, secondary concern of life. (W, vol. 2, p. 513)

Schopenhauer anticipated Freud's emphasis on sexuality as our strongest drive.
It is tied to the desire to reproduce oneself, a bit like Dawkins' idea of the selfish
gene (see chapter 13), "the most complete manifestation of the will-to-live, its
most distinctly expressed type" (W, vol. 2, p. 513). For Schopenhauer, we know sex
to be the "decided and strongest affirmation of life by the fact that for man in the
natural state, as for the animal, it is his life's final end and highest goal." Because
the sexual drive is the strongest affirmation of life and the most complete manifestation of the will to live, Schopenhauer refers to the genitals as "the real focus
of the will," i.e., the clearest physical manifestation that the will manages to
achieve in the physical world. The sexual drive "springs from the depths of our
nature" (W, vol. 2, p. 511).[12]

Summary

Schopenhauer thought of his philosophy as continuing the Kantian epistemic revolution to its logical conclusion. He answers Kant's riddle on the *ding an sich*, arguing that we have knowledge of the noumenal world. He combines the Kantian
Copernican revolution in epistemology with Berkeley's theory of perception, with
Plato's metaphysical doctrine of the Forms or ideas and with Eastern (Hindu)
metaphysical teachings about *maya* and the sufferings of humanity. Representations and will to life or power are the two aspects of our world. They are the objective and subjective aspects of the world, combined in a harmonious synthesis.
"Will to power is to the mind like a strong blind man who carries on his shoulders

a lame man who can see." We have seen that he anticipates Freud's pansexuality and the idea of the id.

However, our individual wills lead us inevitably to disappointment and frustration, for they can never be satisfied but only continuously led on by fresh desires. Our lot in life is suffering—pervasive, penetrating, and painful. Aesthetic contemplation can enable us temporarily to transcend suffering, but the deepest and only abiding salvation comes in resigning one's self to the oceanic body of the world-soul. Morality must arise from good character in a life lived in love for all creatures.

Many find Schopenhauer's transcendental idealism implausible. The criticism goes like this: at least Plato had a larger metaphysical theory of the Forms and Berkeley had God to keep the college quad in existence when no conscious animal or human was present to perceive it. However, what accounts for the world when no cosmic mind is present? Science tells us that the universe existed for billions of years before we had any representation of it. How can Schopenhauer's theory account for that fact? What is this cosmic will to live except the physical force of energy? Isn't it an instance of what Alfred North Whitehead called the fallacy of misplaced concreteness: to subsume our individual conscious identities under the metaphor of physical energy? Even if our consciousness is an emergent property of energy states, it seems more than a mere energy state. These are the kinds of challenges Schopenhauer's transcendental idealism faces. I leave them for your consideration.

Study Questions

1. How does Schopenhauer carry on Kant's Copernican revolution?

2. What are the two aspects of the world that we experience according to Schopenhauer?

3. Explain Schopenhauer's doctrine of the will to live.

4. What is the relationship between our body and the will?

5. What is the human condition according to Schopenhauer? Do you agree with him?

6. How may we find liberation from the suffering and meaninglessness of existence?

7. According to Schopenhauer, what should be our attitude toward our death?

8. Examine Schopenhauer's closing statement (of his book): "What remains after the complete abolition of the will is, for all who are still full of the will, assuredly nothing. But also conversely, to those in whom the will has turned and denied itself, this very real world of ours with all its suns and galaxies, is—nothing." What does he mean?

9. What is the meaning of Joseph Campbell's illustration of the policeman risking his life for the man who attempted suicide?

10. Discuss Schopenhauer's ethics. What are its strengths and weaknesses?

11. Assess Schopenhauer's philosophy. How plausible is it? Discuss the problems with his system. What are its strengths and weaknesses?

Notes

1. Once when he quarreled with his landlady, he threw her down the stairs, seriously injuring her. She sued and won a settlement. When she died, Schopenhauer wrote "Obit anus, abit onus" ("The old woman dies, the burden departs").
2. Schopenhauer referred to Hegel as an "intellectual Caliban," a "philosophical creature of ministries ... manufactured from above with a political but miscalculated purpose; a flat, commonplace, repulsive, ignorant charlatan, who, with unparalleled presumption, conceit, and absurdity, pasted together a system which was trumpeted by his venal adherents as immortal wisdom." (*The Wisdom of Life and Other Essays,* trans. T. Bailey Saunders and E. B. Bax [Walter Dunne, 1901])
3. "Hitler's deadly seriousness, his singlemindedness and his commitment all issue from this notion of 'my adamant Will.' The origin of this notion and of its vocabulary in Schopenhauer and Nietzsche is a commonplace in the history of ideas ... although it is very unlikely that Hitler ever read Schopenhauer at all extensively (in spite of repeatedly claiming that 'in the trenches I read and re-read the little volumes until they fell apart')." (J. P. Stern, *Hitler* [1975], quoted in Arthur Schopenhauer, *The World as Will and Idea,* ed. David Berman, trans. Jill Berman [Everyman, 1995], p. 281)
4. All quotations from *The World as Will and Representation* are translations by E. J. Payne (Dover; 1969).
5. Schopenhauer, *Parega and Paralipomena.,* trans. E. Payne (Oxford University Press, 1974).
6. This is the conclusion of the book: it all comes down to nothing.
7. Schopenhauer, *Parega and Paralipomena.*
8. Joseph Campbell, *The Power of Myth* (Anchor Books, 1988), p. 138. I am indebted to Sterling Harwood for bringing this text to my attention.
9. Ibid., pp. 138–139.
10. Ibid.
11. Schopenhauer, *The Basis of Morality,* trans. E. J. Payne (Bobbs-Merrill, 1965), p. 172.
12. Freud acknowledged Schopenhauer's insights, but I suspect Schopenhauer's thought influenced Freud's theory. In *Freud's New Introductory Lectures* (1933), xxxii, Freud writes, "You may perhaps shrug your shoulders and say 'that [theory of the death instinct] isn't natural science, it's Schopenhauer's philosophy!' But, Ladies and Gentlemen, why should not a bold thinker have guessed something that is afterwards confirmed by sober and painstaking detailed research?" (quoted in Arthur Schopenhauer, *The World as Will and Idea,* p. 279).

For Further Reading

Atwell, J., *Schopenhauer: The Human Character* (Temple University Press, 1990).

———, *Schopenhauer on the Character of the World* (University of California Press 1995).

Copleston, F., *Arthur Schopenhauer: Philosopher of Pessimism* (Barnes and Noble, 1975).

Gardiner, P., *Schopenhauer* (Penguin Books, 1967).

Hamlyn, D. W., *Schopenhauer* (Routledge & Kegan Paul, 1980).

Jacquette, D., ed., *Schopenhauer, Philosophy and the Arts* (Cambridge University Press, 1996).

Janaway, C., ed., *The Cambridge Companion to Schopenhauer* (Cambridge University Press, 1999).

Janaway, Christopher, *Schopenhauer* (Oxford University Press, 1994).

Magee, Bryan, *The Philosophy of Schopenhauer* (Oxford University Press, 1997).

Schopenhauer, Arthur, *The World as Will and Representation*, trans. E. F. J. Payne (1819; Dover, 1969, reprint).

———. *Essays and Aphorisms*, trans. R. J. Holingdale (Penguin, 1970).

CHAPTER 10

Karl Marx's Theory of Human Nature

In the social production of their life, men enter into definite relations that are indispensable and independent of their will, relations of production which correspond to a definite stage of
development of their material productive forces. The sum total
of these relations of production constitutes the economic structure of society—the real basis, on which rises a legal and political superstructure, and to which correspond definite forms of
social consciousness. The mode of production of material life
conditions the social, political, and intellectual life process in
general. It is not the consciousness of men that determines their
being, but on the contrary, their social being that determines
their consciousness. *(Marx,* Critique of Political Economy, *1859)*

The philosophers have only interpreted the world, in various
ways; the point is to change it. *(Marx,* Ten Theses on Feuerbach, *1845)*

Introduction

In this chapter, we examine the work of the founders of Marxism, Karl Marx and
Friedrich Engels. Friedrich Engels (1820–1895) was born the son of a German
industrialist who moved to Manchester, England. He had considerable experience
of the workings of British industry during the Industrial Revolution and was able
to provide Marx with a firsthand insight of industrial realities. Harold Laski
describes the cofounder of the Marxist movement:

Aways friendly, usually optimistic, with great gifts both for practical action and for
getting on with others. . . . Widely read, with a very real talent for moving rapidly
through a great mass of material, he was facile rather than profound. He was utterly
devoid of jealousy or vanity. He had a happy nature which never agonized over the
difficulty of thought. . . . It never occurred to him, during the friendship of forty
years, marked only by one brief misunderstanding, to question his duty to serve
Marx in every way he could.[1]

Karl Marx (1818–1883) was born in Trier, Germany, into a Jewish family which had converted to Protestantism. He was educated in Catholic schools and at the University of Berlin, where he studied Hegel's philosophy and became a materialist. He received his doctorate from the University of Jena in 1841. As a youth, Marx was a devout Christian, but upon finishing gymnasium (the German high school) he became an atheist. He began his career in 1842 as a journalist for the liberal *Rheinische Zeitung* and soon distinguished himself as a brilliant and radical thinker. In 1843 he married Jenny Westphalen, the close friend of his boyhood. Later that year, he and Jenny moved to Paris, where he studied French **communism** and met Engels, who became his lifelong friend and benefactor. Being exiled from Paris for radical activities in 1849, he found political asylum in London, where he spent the rest of his life in research and writing and in organizing the First International Workingmen's Association. He was described by a contemporary as follows: "He combines the deepest philosophical seriousness with the most biting wit. Imagine Rousseau, Voltaire, Holbach, Lessing, Heine, and Hegel fused into one person—I say fused, not juxtaposed—and you have Dr. Marx."[2] He made a powerful impression on his contemporaries, often intimidating them with his rapier intellect and volcanic passion for his ideas. His principal works are *Economic and Philosophical Manuscripts of 1844*, *Manifesto of the Communist Party* (with Friedrich Engels, 1848), and *Capital* (3 volumes: 1867, 1885, 1895).

As a young man, Marx wrote "Hitherto, the various philosophies have only interpreted the world in various ways; the point is to change it." *The Communist Manifesto*, the most famous of his writings, embodies that thesis. It combines socioeconomic analysis of the class struggle with a plan of action for overthrowing the existing oppressive conditions. Marx argues that the struggle between classes is the essential catalyst of historical change: in earlier times, the structure of society was a complicated arrangement of hierarchical classes, but in the present period of the bourgeoisie, the social structure is developing toward a simple division of two classes, the ruling class, the bourgeoisie, owners of the means of production, and the proletariat, the worker-slaves. The proletariat are fast becoming self-conscious of their exploited state, and an international drama is unfolding in which they will create a violent revolution, throwing off their chains and, as new dictators, instantiating a new era of justice, an egalitarian, classless society "in which the free development of each is the condition for the free development of all."[3]

The attraction of Marxism is that it appeals to a set of simple theses and gives low-paid workers, the proletariat, a feeling of hope and power, a sense that history is ineluctably on their side in the fight for justice. Perhaps the best way of understanding Marxism is to examine the basic ideas. We turn to a brief analysis of his philosophy of human nature, consisting of ten theses.

Ten Marxist Theses

1. *Historical Materialist Determinism:* Like Hobbes, Schopenhauer, and Freud, whom we have already studied, Marx believed in **determinism,** though the

emphasis was on historical determinism rather than individual determinism. Socialism is inevitable. Insofar as Marx did discuss the individual, he espoused a materialist **epiphenomenalist** view of the mind's activities. He held that "conceiving, thinking, the mental intercourse of men, appear at the [earliest stages] as the direct efflux of their material behavior."[4] Analogous to his view of the mind is his epiphenomenal view of culture and consciousness. Economic factors determine the individual consciousness, not vice versa. Necessary economic laws will lead inevitably to communistic economic laws, which in turn determine history. Economic determination causes a dialectical process in which internal contradictions lead to the self-destruction of each stage of social history and the creation of a new economic stage—until the end of history—in the creation of the communist state. Note well that this is a one-directional and totally materialistic order. The causal process is entirely from the economic infrastructure (foundations) to the cultural superstructure (the walls, frame, and ceiling of the social edifice). The religion, law, morality, philosophy, and cultural artifacts are completely determined by the economic, materialist base; but they have no effect on the materialist order.[5] Law and morality are totally relativistic, the creation of the dominant class, and their validity is limited to the culture itself. In a capitalist society, morality and laws are the creation of the bourgeoisie and reflect their interests. Depending on the economic base and ruling class, morality changes its content, so what is moral in one society may well be immoral in another where the material conditions are different.

Some Marxists hold that in the final communist state, where class interest is abolished, a true morality will arise. The argument goes as follows:

1. Whatever is contained in the state of the true destiny of humanity is the true morality.
2. The communist state represents the true historical destiny of humanity.
3. Therefore, the communist state contains the true morality.

What are we to make of this argument? It has valid form, but are its premises true? There are three problems with it, which must be addressed before we can accept it. *(1)* Is it true that the communist state is the true destiny of humanity? Although Marx believed it was, it needs to be argued. Many philosophers do not believe it is the true destiny, and until we discover an argument for it, we may doubt the second premise. *(2)* Even if the second premise is true, how do we know what kind of morality it will produce? Also, even if we had some idea of that morality, we would not be required to live by that morality now in the time before the communist state. The morality for us now is that which our culture determines. *(3)* In speaking of the true destiny of humanity, the argument seems to presuppose an essential human nature. However, Marx denied that we have an essential human nature. He wrote "All history is but a continuous transformation of human nature."[6] Perhaps Marx is wrong about there not being a common basic human nature, but if there isn't, we cannot make sense of a true historical destiny of humanity.

The determinism thesis has the virtue of appearing to make the goal of communism as inevitable as the physical laws of nature. Its liability is that the same logic would seem to entail that we do not have free will and that we are pawns in history's dialectical struggle.

2. *Organicism:* For Marx, as for Rousseau (see chapter 7), individuality is subordinate to the organic whole. "Man is a species being. . . . Individuals are dealt with only in so far as they are personifications of economic categories, embodiments of particular class relations and class interests."[7] Individuals are replaceable. The material forces of history are inexorable, moving like a torrent on its predetermined path. If individuals get in the way, they must be sacrificed to the grander forces for the good of the whole. Marxists have prided themselves on their willingness to die for their cause, confident that history would confirm the allegiance. They have also been willing to kill in the name of Marx, as witnessed by the Stalinist purges in the 1930s and Mao Tse Tung's ruthless elimination of political enemies. The idea of human rights is a bourgeois fetish. As a collective group, it is the class that is preeminent.

3. *Class Struggle:* The driving determinist force in history is that of class struggle. People identify primarily with their socioeconomic class (not race, gender, or religion), and each class is antagonistic toward the others. Marx divided the history of humankind into five separate epochs: *(1)* the primitive communal society, *(2)* the slave society, *(3)* the feudal society, *(4)* the capitalist society, and, still to come, *(5)* the communist society. He argued that each of the first four phases has inner contradictions, or antagonisms, that lead to the next phase of history. As lords struggled against the bourgeoisie in feudalism, the bourgeoisie is presently pitted against the proletariat in capitalism.

We see this point in the opening lines of *Manifesto of the Communist Party,* in the section entitled "Bourgeois and Proletarians."

> The history of all hitherto existing society is the history of class struggles. Freemen and slaves, patrician and plebeian, lord and serf, guild-master and journeyman, in a word, oppressors and oppressed, stood in constant opposition to one another, carried on an uninterrupted, now hidden, now open fight, a fight that each time ended, either in a revolutionary re-constitution of society at large, or in the common ruin of the contending classes.
>
> In the earlier epochs of history, we find almost everywhere a complicated arrangement of society into various orders, a manifold gradation of social rank. In ancient Rome we have patricians, knights, plebeians, slaves; in the Middle Ages, feudal lords, vassals, guild-masters, journeymen, apprentices, serfs; in almost all of these classes, again subordinate gradations. The modern bourgeois society that has sprouted from the ruins of feudal society has not done away with class antagonisms. It has but established new classes, new conditions of oppression, new forms of struggle in place of the old ones.
>
> Our epoch, the epoch of the bourgeoisie, possesses, however, the distinctive feature: it has simplified the class antagonisms. Society as a whole is more and more splitting up into two great hostile camps, into two great classes directly facing each other: Bourgeoisie and Proletariat.[8]

Marx claims that in order to understand human nature and human history we must understand class antagonisms, especially the relations of oppressed to oppressors, for these forces have developed into "two contemporary classes: bourgeoisie and proletarian—those who own the means of production and those who are wage earners."[9]

4. *The Pivotal Role of Capitalism:* On the one hand, capitalism breaks the feudal hold over humanity, liberating it from the tyranny of the medieval feudal system, freeing the bourgeoisie and the serf on the manor. It creates the possibility of surplus and "rescues a considerable part of the population from the idiocy of rural life."[10] On the other hand, it enslaves people again as wage-slaves to industry. Working on commodities, the worker becomes a commodity in the hands of capitalism (see the discussion of thesis 6, alienation). As a system of exploitation, capitalism so degrades the individual, so frustrates his or her potentialities for creative development, that life under it is hell on earth, a mockery of all the ethical commands associated with the Christian–liberal tradition. By means of ever-increasing overproduction, improved technology, and cheaper labor forces abroad, capitalism displaces workers and increases misery in the world. As monopolies extend their tentacles, the competition is destroyed and more and more people find themselves oppressed. This internal antagonism between the capitalists and the workers will eventually come to a crisis wherein capitalism will be overthrown. As Marx writes, "The weapons with which the bourgeoisie felled feudalism to the ground are now turned against the bourgeoisie itself."

5. *Value Theory:* The worker (proletariat) creates value for the capitalist, but the capitalist does not reciprocate. Marx's theory of value is really a version of the classic notion of justice as desert. Workers are unjustly treated by not receiving what they deserve.

Many people think that Karl Marx was an opponent of merit or justice based on desert since he famously uttered the formula for distributive justice, "From each according to his ability, to each according to his need." However, this is a misinterpretation of Marx, who actually defends the classic notion of justice. In his *Critique of the Gotha Program,* Marx attacks utopian communists like Ferdinand Lassalle (1825–1864) for uncritically adopting the need-based motto. Distribution according to need should only take place in the ideal communist society, where everyone is equally deserving, since all contribute according to their maximal ability. Until that time, in the socialist society, the motto must be "From each according to his ability, to each according to his contribution."[11] Indeed, Marx's condemnation of capitalism is based on the classical idea of justice as desert. His *labor theory of value* condemns capitalists as vampires and parasites for stealing and exploiting the workers. Say that a worker makes a chair with a certain labor value, deriving from the worker's skill and labor, and we give it a value of 100, translating that into monetary terms, $100. The capitalist pays the worker only a fraction of the value, say $25, keeping the rest and, thus, growing rich on such exploitive thefts. Of course, the capitalist has a right to deduct overhead costs from the total value, the costs of the raw material and machines used, say $10, and to make a modest profit; but he goes far beyond that and robs the worker of the remainder, the other $65. This is unjust, claims Marx, for the worker deserves far more than what is received. Exploitation involves giving people less than they deserve, less than they are owed. Getting only half the value, the proletariats are robbed, and because they have no other options in an industrial society, in effect, become wage-slaves.

Although Marx seems to be a moral relativist, he treats justice, giving people what they deserve, as a moral absolute, binding on the bourgeoisie in a capitalist society.

6. *Alienation:* As industrial technology has radically expanded, it has changed the nature of work. Unlike in rural and hunter–gatherer societies, work in a modern industrial society is fragmented and meaningless. For the greater part of human history, work has been a physically demanding activity, requiring manual dexterity and personal ingenuity sufficient to cope with the fluctuations of the natural environment and culminating in a clearly identifiable end product, such as harvested wheat or corn, a successfully hunted deer, or artifacts (e.g., wheels, shoes, or cloth). The Industrial Revolution, beginning in the late 18th century, changed all this. Increasingly, work became a series of repetitive movements that, however exhausting after a full day, seldom used more than a fraction of a person's full muscular and mental ability. In place of the judgment and aptitude required to meet the variations of nature and basic human needs, factory work demanded only the ability to repeat a single task adapted to a changeless workplace. In regimented assembly lines, the worker contributes his or her specialized product to the total production. That small product is contributed with a monotonous repetitiveness that invites ennui and listlessness. Here is how one automobile-plant worker describes it:

> I work on a small conveyor which goes around in a circle. We call it a "merry-go-round." I make up zigzag springs for front seats. Every couple of feet on the conveyor there is a form for the pieces that make up the seat springs. As that form goes by me, I clip several pieces together, using a clip gun. I then put the pieces on the form, and it goes around to where other men clip more pieces together. . . . The only operation I do is work the clip gun. It takes just a couple of seconds to shoot six or eight clips into the spring and I do it as I walk a few steps. Then I start right over again.[12]

The assembly-line worker, with his or her dull and repetitive maneuvers, becomes the symbol of the fragmented and frustrated human being. Alienated from the fruit of his or her labor, the worker loses a sense of humanity, beats his or her spouse, tyrannizes his or her children, and becomes filled with self-loathing. Over 200 years ago, Adam Smith observed that a person who endlessly performed the same task "generally becomes as stupid and ignorant as it is possible for a human creature to become."[13] Here is Marx's description:

> The worker is related to the product of his labor as to an alien object. The object he produces does not belong to him, dominates him, and only serves in the long run to increase his poverty. Alienation appears not only in the result, but also in the process of production and productive activity itself. The worker is not at home in his work which he views only as a means of satisfying other needs. It is an activity

directed against himself, that is independent of him and does not belong to him. Thirdly, alienated labor succeeds in alienating man from his species. Species life, productive life, life creating life, turns into a mere means of sustaining the worker's individual existence, and man is alienated from his fellow man. Finally, nature itself is alienated from man, who thus loses his own inorganic body.[14]

7. *Oppression:* In discussing Marx's labor theory of value, we noted that capitalism exploits workers by not giving them the full value of the labor. The rich capitalist parasitically feeds off the poor, downtrodden proletariat. Eventually, the rich will get richer and the poor, poorer as the capitalists drive each other out of business and more and more people become proletariats, suffering oppression under the tyranny of capitalism. Overproduction and improved technology lead to redundancy and unemployment. Unemployed workers will suffer in poverty while the capitalists dine in opulence.

This yawning gap between the poor and the rich has inspired many people to identify with the Marxist cause even when they did not understand or agree with Marxist theory. Liberation groups such as the Sandinistas in Nicaragua and international feminist groups have found affinity with Marx's eloquent charge against the bourgeoisie. One recalls Edwin Markham's famous poem "The Man with a Hoe":

Bowed by the weight of centuries he leans
Upon his hoe and gazes on the ground,
The emptiness of ages in his face,
And on his back the burden of the world.
Who made him dead to rapture and despair,
A thing that grieves not and that never hopes,
Stolid and stunned, a brother to the ox?
Who loosened and let down this brutal jaw?
Whose breath blew out the light within this brain?

What gulfs between him and the seraphim!
Slave of the wheel of labor, what to him
Are Plato and the swing of Pleides?
What the long reaches of the peaks of song.
Through this dread shape the suffering ages look;
Time's tragedy is that aching stoop;
Through this dread shape humanity's betrayed,
plundered, profaned and disinherited,
Cries protest to the powers that made the world,
A protest that is also prophecy.

O master, lord and rulers in all lands,
How will the future reckon with this Man?
How answer his brute question in that hour
When whirlwinds of rebellion shake all shores?
How will it be with kingdoms and with kings—
With those who shaped him to the thing he is—
When this dumb Terror shall rise to judge the world,
After the silence of the centuries?[15]

8. *Revolution:* Finally, the workers of the world will unite (communist unions and intellectuals leading the way), overthrowing the capitalist lords in a grand revolution. Unfortunately, this will necessitate violence, not because the communists desire violence but because the capitalist rulers will not relinquish power voluntarily and peacefully. No ruling class ever surrenders power voluntarily. It must be wrested from the rulers at gunpoint, and this lamentably requires great violence. It is inevitable.

9. *Dictatorship:* There will be a short-lived socialist dictatorship of the proletariat necessary during the transition to communism. In this dictatorship, the capitalists will be punished and the workers will take over control of the factories and redistribute the property of the capitalists. Such a proletarian dictatorship took place in Russia in 1917 under Lenin. It lasted until 1991.

10. *Communism:* Soon, all oppressive capitalist institutions, classes, and inequalities will be abolished and a reign of peace and prosperity will ensue in which crime and greed will disappear since the causes of crime and greed—scarcity, private property, and oppression—will be exterminated. In this utopian state, physical and intellectual work are joined. Here shall the communist motto become a reality: From Each According to His Ability, to Each According to His Need. That is, one will work for the good of all to the best of his or her ability, for one knows that all of his or her needs will be met by the society as a whole. The Marxist utopia will come about, consisting of solidarity with and among the masses, altruism, and goodwill:

> Man will become immeasurably stronger, wiser, and subtler; his body will become more harmonized, his movements more rhythmic, his voice more musical. The forms of life will become dynamically dramatic. The average human type will rise to the heights of an Aristotle, a Goethe, or a Marx. And above this ridge new peaks will rise.[16]

Finally, the state will wither away and in its place will be a utopia, in which the workers' rule will be From Each According to His Ability, to Each According to His Need.

These ten theses outline the essential Marxist theory. Humans have their identity within classes and cultures produced by productive economic forces. The class struggle will come to a head and explode in a violent revolution in which the proletariat will be victorious and transform society into the utopian communist state. However, other aspects of human beings in society are parts of Marx's overall theory of human nature.

Secularity and Religion

Marx, rejecting the Christian faith of his youth, thought he could build his state on a secular, humanistic, naturalistic philosophy. Religion, a distorted expression of human alienation, was a threat to human progress and must be abolished. Here is a classic passage.

Man, who has found in the fantastic reality of heaven, where he sought a supernatural being, only his own reflection, will no longer be tempted to find only the *semblance* of himself—a non-human being—where he seeks and must seek his true reality.

The basis of irreligious criticism is this: *man makes religion;* religion does not make man. Religion is indeed man's self-consciousness and self-awareness so long as he has not found himself or has lost himself again. But *man* is not an abstract being, squatting outside the world. Man is *the human world,* the state, society. This state, this society, produce religion which is an *inverted world consciousness,* because they are an *inverted world.* Religion is the general theory of this world, its encyclopedic compendium, its logic in popular form, its spiritual *point d'honneur,* its enthusiasm, its moral sanction, its solemn complement, its general basis of consolation and justification. It is *the fantastic realization* of the human being inasmuch as the *human being* possesses no true reality. The struggle against religion is, therefore, indirectly a struggle against *that world* whose spiritual *aroma* is religion.

Religious suffering is at the same time an *expression* of real suffering and a *protest* against real suffering. Religion is the sigh of the oppressed creature, the sentiment of a heartless world, and the soul of soulless conditions. It is the *opium* of the people.

The abolition of religion as the *illusory* happiness of men, is a demand for their *real* happiness. The call to abandon their illusions about their condition is a *call to abandon a condition which requires illusions.* The criticism of religion is, therefore, *the embryonic criticism of this vale of tears* of which religion is the *halo.*

Criticism has plucked the imaginary flowers from the chain, not in order that man shall bear the chain without caprice or consolation but so that he shall cast off the chain and pluck the living flower. The criticism of religion disillusions man so that he will think, act and fashion his reality as a man who has lost his illusions *and* regained his reason; so that he will revolve about himself as his own true sun. Religion is only the illusory sun about which man revolves so long as he does not revolve about himself.

It is the *task of history,* therefore, once the *other-world of truth* has vanished, to establish the *truth of this world.* The immediate *task of philosophy,* which is in the service of history, is to unmask human self-alienation in its *secular form* now that it has been unmasked in its *sacred form.* Thus the criticism of heaven is transformed into the criticism of earth, the *criticism of religion* into the *criticism of law,* and the *criticism of theology* into the *criticism of politics.*[17]

In other words, a humanistic naturalism based on universal camaraderie must replace religion. Can one reject Marx's ideas on religion and still support much else of his theory? Many Christians in Latin America, including "liberationist theologians," sometimes refer to themselves as Marxist Christians. Is this a contradiction in terms, (an oxymoron) or can we modify Marxism to make it compatible with forms of religion that emphasize social justice?

A Manifesto for a Revolutionary Program

Marx together with his friend and benefactor Engels set forth an outline of these points in their classic revolutionary work *Manifesto of the Communist Party,* excerpted below and hereafter abbreviated M.

It has become evident, that the bourgeoisie is unfit any longer to be the ruling class in society, and to impose its conditions of existence upon society as an overriding law. It is unfit to rule because it is incompetent to assure an existence to its slave within his slavery, because it cannot help letting him sink into such a state, that it has to feed him, instead of being fed by him. Society can no longer live under this bourgeoisie, in other words, its existence is no longer compatible with society. (M, section I)

The struggle between the bourgeois class and the proletariat will reach a crisis point, erupting in revolution. The bourgeoisie has created the very conditions of modern industry which will result in its downfall. "The development of modern industry, therefore, cuts from under its feet the very foundation on which the bourgeoisie produces and appropriates products. What the bourgeoisie therefore produces, above all, are its own gravediggers. Its fall and the victory of the proletariat are equally inevitable." (M, section I).

Private property must be abolished. Rousseau said property was the beginning of our downfall as noble savages, and Pierre-Joseph Proudhon (1809–1865) said in 1840 in his *What is Property?* "Property is theft." Marx agrees.

All property relations in the past have continually been subject to historical change consequent upon the change in historical conditions. The French Revolution, for example, abolished feudal property in favor of bourgeois property.

The distinguishing feature of communism is not the abolition of property generally, but the abolition of bourgeois property. But modern bourgeois private property is the final and most complete expression of the system of producing and appropriating products that is based on class antagonisms, on the exploitation of the many by the few.

In this sense, the theory of the Communists may be summed up in the single sentence: Abolition of private property. (M, section II)

Communists have been accused of advocating the elimination of all property, including that of the proletariat; but Marx makes an exception for the "Hard-won, self-acquired, self-earned property . . . of the petty artisan and of the small peasant, a form of property that preceded the bourgeois form" (M, section II). That sort of possession is part of the labor theory of value. They deserve that property. He means only modern bourgeois private property.

Communism deprives no man of the power to appropriate the products of society; all that it does is to deprive him of the power to subjugate the labor of others by means of such appropriation. (M, section II)

According to Marx, the charges against communism made from a religious, philosophical, and, generally, ideological standpoint are not deserving of serious examination.

Marx believes the revolution is inevitable. The history of economics proves that intellectual production changes character as the material production is altered.

In depicting the most general phases of the development of the proletariat, we traced the more or less veiled civil war, raging within existing society, up to the point where that war breaks out into open revolution, and where the violent overthrow of the bourgeoisie lays the foundation for the sway of the proletariat.

Hitherto, every form of society has been based, as we have already seen, on the antagonism of oppressing and oppressed classes. But in order to oppress a class, certain conditions must be assured to it under which it can, at least, continue its slavish existence. The serf, in the period of serfdom, raised himself to membership in the commune, just as the petty bourgeois, under the yoke of feudal absolutism, managed to develop into a bourgeois. The modern laborer, on the contrary, instead of rising with the progress of industry, sinks deeper and deeper below the conditions of existence of his own class. He becomes a pauper, and pauperism develops more rapidly than population and wealth. And here it becomes evident that the bourgeoisie is unfit any longer to be the ruling class in society, and to impose its conditions of existence upon society as an overriding law. . . .

What the bourgeoisie, therefore, produces, above all, is its own gravediggers. Its fall and the victory of the proletariat are equally inevitable. (M, section I)

Marx and Engels now lay down their basic ten-point program, to be tailored to the particular conditions of the country in question. In the most advanced countries, the following will be pretty generally applicable.

1. Abolition of property in land and application of all rents of land to public purposes.
2. A heavy progressive or graduated income tax.
3. Abolition of all right of inheritance.
4. Confiscation of the property of all emigrants and rebels.
5. Centralization of credit in the hands of the State by means of a national bank with the State holding an exclusive monopoly on capital.
6. Centralization of the means of communication and transport in the hands of the State.
7. Extension of factories and instruments of production owned by the State; the bringing into cultivation of waste-land, and the improvement of the soil, generally in accordance with a common plan.
8. Equal liability of all to labor. Establishment of industrial armies, especially for agriculture.
9. Combination of agriculture with manufacturing industries; gradual abolition of the distinction between town and country, by a more equable distribution of the population over the country.
10. Free education for all children in public schools. Abolition of children's factory labor in its present form. Combination of education with industrial production. (M, section II)

Some of these points, like progressive income tax and free public education for all children, have been adopted and no longer seem revolutionary. The controversial

points have to do with the abolition of property and the establishment of industrial armies.

Marx and Engels believed that historical **dialectical materialism** was guaranteed the last word, complete victory. They felt sure that the revolution would
break out in industrialized countries such as Germany, England, and France.
When this finally succeeds, the class struggle as well as divisions will dissolve.
However, in the initial stage, the proletariat will temporarily take over the means
of production.

> When, in the course of development, class distinctions have disappeared, and all
> production has been concentrated in the hands of a vast association of the whole
> nation, the public power will lose its political character. Political power, properly so
> called, is merely the organized power of one class for oppressing another. If the pro-
> letariat during its contest with the bourgeoisie is compelled, by the force of circum-
> stances, to organize itself as a class; if, by means of a revolution, it makes itself the
> ruling class, and, as such, sweeps away by force the old conditions of production,
> then it will, along with these conditions, have swept away the conditions for the
> existence of class antagonisms and of classes generally, and will thereby have abol-
> ished its own supremacy as a class.
>
> In place of the old bourgeois society, with its classes and class antagonisms, we
> shall have an association, in which the free development of each is the condition for
> the free development of all. . . .
>
> The Communists disdain to conceal their views and aims. They openly declare
> that their ends can be attained only by the forcible overthrow of all existing social
> conditions. Let the ruling classes tremble at a Communistic revolution. The prole-
> tarians have nothing to lose but their chains. They have a world to win.
>
> Workers of All Countries, Unite! (M, section IV)

Conclusion

Marxism has inspired millions to fight for social and economic change. The Russian Revolution in October 1917, the Chinese Marxist movement under Mao Tse
Tung, Castro's Cuba—to name a few governments dedicated to Marxist principles—and political parties that have been influenced by Marx's thought, including the Labor Party in Great Britain and the Social Democratic Party in Germany
reflect the widespread and profound influence of Marxist thought on human society. Perhaps no single political–economic doctrine has so influenced the course of
human history during the past 150 years. Even the success of capitalism in the
West may be in part attributed to reading and heeding Marx's dire warnings and
correcting some of capitalism's more degrading features.

On the other hand, Marx was mistaken on some things. He thought that his theory would precipitate a revolution in European industrialized countries, not Russia. The fact that communism did not arise as he expected and that it proved a failure in Eastern Europe and the Soviet Union must give one pause. Nonetheless, it
could still be true that its time is yet to come. We must evaluate it on its own merits.

Two of the many questions that may be asked of Marxism are the following: (1)
Is its unidirectional determinism correct? Are history and culture nothing but the

products of economic factors, or could it be the case that spiritual and cultural ideas actually influence the economic development of a society? For example, could a nation's religious tradition affect its economic–political development? (2) Is class antagonism a sufficient factor to explain all historical development? It is generally agreed that class is an important feature in understanding history, but whether it is the only feature is a matter of controversy. One may also question whether the dictatorship of the working class (the proletariat) is a necessary phase for social–political development. Why can social progress not proceed without the transition state of a dictatorship?

Marx believed that human history was explained by the existence of class conflict and that class conflict reflected the particular historical phases of economic production. He believed that the superstructure—philosophy, morality, law, and all culture—was a product of class orientation and that class struggle would inevitably lead to the dictatorship of the proletariat, which in turn would lead to the abolition of all classes, to a classless and radically egalitarian society "in which the free development of each is the condition for the free development of all." A problem with his philosophy is that if all philosophy is relative to its economic condition, so is Marx's. It too is only a projection of the economic conditions in which he lived. It is only relatively true, true at a certain time and place, but not objectively true.

Summary

Karl Marx developed a powerful, comprehensive theory of human nature based on economic progression from the hunter–gatherer society to capitalism and on to communism. It was based on historical materialist determinism, which defined culture and morality as functions of economics and described communism as inevitable. The class struggle between the bourgeoisie and the proletariat would intensify the gap between the rich property class and the poor workers until the workers, having nothing to lose but their chains, would revolt and overthrow the ruling class, becoming themselves the new ruling class. The dictatorship of the proletariat would then develop into the communist state, where "each would contribute according to his ability and each would receive according to his need." Here, alienation would end and human beings would live together in happiness. Marx thought that religion, being the "opium of the people," consisted in false consciousness. Human consciousness does not determine economic–social conditions, but economic conditions determine social consciousness.

Study Questions

Reread the selections from Marx's writings in this chapter and see if you can answer the following questions.

1. Explain historical materialist determinism.

2. Explain Marx's *organicism*. What does he mean by that term?

3. What is the significance of the class struggle in Marx's philosophy?

4. What do Marx and Engels predict as the future course of the class struggle?

5. What is the relationship between the Communist Party and the proletariat?

6. What will be the result of the proletarian revolution?

7. What are some of the specific social changes that will occur in the most advanced countries? To what degree have their predictions been realized?

8. Do you agree with Engels and Marx that the cultural values, including moral ideals and laws, of a society are always the reflection of the ruling class? Does this make all values relative?

9. If all ideas, including theoretical ideas, are relative to economic conditions, isn't Marxist theory also simply relative to the economic conditions of Marx's time? If they are just ideas that the economic conditions of a time determine what some people will have, why should we think they are valid or true? Why accept them if we don't like them? What is their authority over us? Was not Marx, then, just determined to write what he did by his economic position?

10. What is Marx's view of morality? Is Marx a moral relativist? Does he treat justice as an absolute?

11. What are the strengths and weaknesses of the Marxist theory of human nature?

12. Compare Marx and Engels with Hobbes and Rousseau (chapter 7). Which view is closer to the truth?

13. What is Marx's analysis of religion? Is it valid? Explain.

Notes

1. Harold Laski, Introduction, in *The Communist Manifesto* (Random House, 1967).
2. Cited in David McClellan's *Karl Marx* (Viking Press, 1975), p. 3.
3. Karl Marx and Friedrich Engels, *Manifesto of the Communist Party,* trans. Samuel Moore, ed. Friedrich Engels (Progress Publishers 1888 from orig. German text of 1848).
4. Karl Marx and Friedrich Engels, *The German Ideology* (International Publishers, 1947), p. 14.
5. In the passage quoted at the head of the chapter, Marx is more qualified than elsewhere, saying that economic relations condition the superstructure. Marx, always rhetorically impressive, is not always clear or precise.
6. Marx, *The Poverty of Philosophy* (Prometheus, 1847), chapter 2.
7. Marx, *Basic Writings on Politics and Philosophy* (Doubleday, 1959), p. 136.
8. Karl Marx and Friedrich Engels, *Manifesto of the Communist Party.*
9. Ibid.

10. Ibid.

11. Karl Marx, *Critique of the Gotha Program,* in *Karl Marx: Selected Writings,* ed. D. McLellan (Oxford University Press, 1977), pp. 566f.

12. Charles R. Walker and Robert H. Guest, *The Man on the Assembly Line* (Harvard University Press, 1952), p. 46.

13. Adam Smith, *The Wealth of Nations* (1776; Modern Library, 1937), p. 734.

14. Karl Marx, *Early Texts,* ed. David McClellan (Blackwell, 1971) p. 137f.

15. Edwin Markham, "The Man with a Hoe" (1899). Markham (1852–1940) was inspired to write the poem after viewing a painting of the same name by French painter Jean-Francois Millet. The complete poem can be found at www.poetry-archive.com/m/the_man_with_the_hoe.html, reprinted from *The Little Book of Modern Verse,* ed. Jessie B. Rittenhouse (Houghton Mifflin Company, 1917).

16. Leon Trotsky, *Literature and Revolution,* cited in Robert Nozick, *Anarchy, State and Utopia* (Basic Books, 1974), p. 241.

17. Karl Marx, "Critique of Hegel's Philosophy of Right," in *Karl Marx: Early Writings,* trans., ed. T. B. Bottomore (McGraw-Hill, 1963).

For Further Reading

Berlin, Isaiah, *Karl Marx* (Oxford University Press, 1959).

Forman, James, *Communism* (Dell, 1972). An accessible survey.

Lictheim, George, *A Short History of Socialism* (Praeger, 1970). A useful survey of the subject.

Mandel, Ernest, *An Introduction to Marxist Economic Theory* (Pathfinder Press, 1969).

Marx, Karl, *Capital* (Dent, 1957).

———, *The Early Writings,* trans. and ed. T. Bottomore (McGraw-Hill, 1963). The best collection of the early writings.

———, *Early Writings,* trans. Lucio Colletti (Penguin Books, 1974). A good, inexpensive edition of Marx's early work.

———, *Selected Writings,* trans. and ed. David McClellan (Oxford University Press, 1977).

McLellan, David, *The Thought of Karl Marx: An Introduction* (Harper Torchbooks, 1971). A good introduction.

McMurtry, John, *The Structure of Marx's World-View* (Princeton University Press, 1978). A helpful, sympathetic interpretation.

Popper, Karl, *The Open Society and Its Enemies,* vol. 2 (Routledge, 1966). A critique from a classical liberal democratic perspective.

Tucker, Robert, *Philosophy and Myth in Karl Marx* (Transaction Press, 2000). Approaches the religious dimension in Marx.

CHAPTER 11

Sigmund Freud's Theory of Human Nature:
Pansexuality and Psychoanalysis

The dance of sex. If one had no other reason for choosing to sub-
scribe to Freud, what could be more charming than to believe
that the whole vaudeville of the world, the entire dizzy circus of
history, is but a fancy mating dance, that dictators burn Jews and
businessmen vote Republican, that helmsmen steer ships and
ladies play bridge, that girls study grammar and boys engineering all at the behest of the Absolute Genital? When the synthesizing mood is upon one, what is more soothing than to assert
that this one simple yen of humankind, poor little coitus, alone
gives rise to cities and monasteries, paragraphs, and poems, foot
races and battle tactics, metaphysics and hydroponics, trade
unions, and universities? Who would not delight in telling some
extragalactic tourist, "On our planet, sir, males and females copulate. Moreover, they enjoy copulating. But for various reasons
they cannot do this whenever, wherever, and with whomever
they choose. Hence, all this running around that you observe.
Hence the world"? A therapeutic notion! *(John Barth,* End of the Road)[1]

Introduction

Freud inaugurated the sexual revolution. Whatever one thinks of his theory, he
was an innovative thinker who created a paradigm shift in Western thought. He
challenged the philosophical ideal of the "rational man" that dominated from
Socrates to Bertrand Russell, asserting that prerational, unconscious forces determined our behavior. Psychoanalysis and the recognition of an unconscious,
whence arise desire and action, are part of the repertoire of our intellectual life
because of Freud's creative genius.

Sigmund Freud was born in Freiburg, Moravia,* on May 6, 1856, and died in

---

*Now part of the Czech Republic.

London in 1939. He was a precocious child and a brilliant student, on whom his family laid high expectations. He spent most of his life in Vienna, where his Jewish family moved when he was 3. In that same year (1859), Darwin published his *Origin of Species* (see chapter 13). Before Darwin, human beings were viewed as special, semi-divine beings, set apart from nature by the fact that they had immortal souls. Darwin's dangerous idea was that humans are animals and, as such, may be the subject of scientific study, that is, studied along naturalistic lines.

A year after Darwin's daunting publication, in 1860, Gustav Fechner (1801–1887), the German philosopher, published his classic *Elements of Psycho Physics*, a book that marks the beginning of the science of psychology, setting forth evidence that the mind can be studied scientifically and measured quantitatively.[2] About that same time, Herman von Helmholz (1821–1894) formulated the principles of the conservation of energy, which stated that energy is a quantity just as mass is. It can be transformed but not destroyed. When energy disappears from one place, it appears in another. Helmholz's discovery led to the field of dynamics, which in turn led to thermodynamics and Einstein's theory of relativity.

As a young scientist doing biological research in the 1870s and 1880s, Freud was aware of the sciences of psychology and dynamics. Freud's genius was to apply these studies to the human personality, creating a dynamic psychology, one which transforms energy within the personality. He called his new science "psychoanalysis."

As a scientist of the mind, Freud thought that he could eventually quantify the mind's working. He was a determinist who believed that all behavior is caused by antecedent states of affairs. Free will is an illusion. Slips of the tongue, dreaming, hallucinating, repressing memories, neurosis, and psychosis are all caused by forces within the mind in relation to one's environment. The trick is to discover the nature of those causes. Freud saw this as his task and believed that by understanding the causal mechanisms, the therapist could enter as a causal force to effect changes for the better. His theory suggests that the patient is not morally responsible for his or her neurosis. Our mental states are simply the result of the influences upon us.

After receiving his medical degree from the University of Vienna in 1881, Freud began to specialize in the treatment of nervous disorders. He married Martha Bernays and set up his medical practice, caring for primarily neurotic middle-class women. In the late 19th century, many of the symptoms presented by women were referred to as "hysteria" and often thought to be caused by an imbalance of the uterus. The French psychologist Jean Charcot was having success in treating hysteria with hypnosis. Freud learned the method but concluded that it offered only a temporary cure. From an Austrian colleague, Joseph Breuer, he learned the cathartic method of therapy, listening to the patient talk about his or her malady, thereby enabling the patient to find release from tension by ventilating his or her feelings.

In the 1890s, Freud began to analyze himself, examining first his dreams and allowing himself to freely associate. Based on this self-analysis as well as his clinical experience, he wrote his first book, *The Interpretation of Dreams* (1900). The book, ignored by scientists of the time, is now generally considered one of the classics of psychology. In it he argued that dreams are a form of wish fulfillment and, suitably interpreted, reveal deep desires and secrets locked in the unconscious. They usually have a sexual dimension. A series of brilliant books followed, culminating in *Three Essays on the Theory of Sexuality* (1905), where he developed his views on the development of the sex drive (German *trieb*), earning his theory the label of "pansexuality" (i.e., everything in life is caused by our sexual instincts). While Freud never argued that everything can be reduced to sex, he argued that sex, in one form or another, plays such a dominant role that the term *pansexuality* may serve as a rough characterization of his theory. "Whatever case and whatever symptom we take as our point of departure, in the end we infallibly come to the field of sexual experience."[3] He calls his discovery that *"premature sexual experience lies at the bottom of every case of hysteria . . . a caput Nili* [the source of the Nile] in neuropathology."[4]

During this period, Freud's fame spread throughout Europe, and he drew many disciples to himself, the most illustrious being Carl Jung and Alfred Adler, both of whom eventually broke with Freud and founded rival schools of their own. Freud was deeply hurt by these ruptures of relationships, especially Jung's, for he had hoped this highly personable, Protestant disciple would spread his theories to the wider gentile European community, increasing their credibility. Although Freud was a generous man of integrity, he tended to be introverted, impersonal, and "anal-retentive" by his own admission. He was generally pessimistic about humanity. "I have found little that is good about human beings on the whole. In my experience, most of them are trash."[5] Jung seems to be one of the rare exceptions to this dire assessment. He regarded Jung's break with him as a betrayal.

Following World War I, psychoanalysis became the rage of the West, its influence being felt in every sphere of life, from literature, drama, art, and religion to morality, education, and the social sciences. It became fashionable to be psychoanalyzed. In the 1920s, Freud further developed his theory of personality, centering it around the trinity of ego, **id,** and **superego.** In 1936, when the Nazis took over Austria, Freud emigrated to London, where he continued to write until his death in 1939.

The Trinity of Personality

According to traditional Christianity, a person is made up of three components: body, soul, and spirit. For Freud, the three components of personality are id, ego, and superego. In the mentally healthy person, the components form a unified system and work in harmony, thus enabling the individual to function efficiently in his or her environment, performing transactions with the environment which fulfill his or her needs and desires. However when the components are in tension, in disharmony, he or she becomes maladjusted, with a subsequent decrease in efficiency.

Id

The function of the id is to provide for the release of energy in the system. As we noted at the end of chapter 9, Schopenhauer anticipated Freud's principle with his notion of the ubiquitous will to live. Freud develops Schopenhauer's idea of a blind powerful force, linking it to the pleasure principle. The aim of the pleasure principle is to rid the person of tension or at least to reduce the amount of tension to a low level so that it can be kept under control. Tension is experienced as pain or discomfort, while relief is experienced as pleasure or satisfaction. The aim of the pleasure principle is a special case of the universal tendency found in all matter to maintain homeostasis in the face of internal and external disturbances of the organism. For example, when an infant is hungry and food is not immediately available, contractions in the stomach produce pain, which causes restlessness and crying, which typically cause the parents to produce food to quell the pain, which in turn causes pleasure.

The *id* is the primary source of psychic energy and the instincts. Using a hydraulic metaphor, it is a force that creates pressure on the entire system for release. It is a blind, potentially destructive force, like water pressure. It is in closer touch with the body and its transactions with the world than the ego or superego. It discharges tension by increasing motor activity and image formation, that is, bodily movement and projecting images such as wishes, desires, and dreams, which are a form of wish fulfillment.

> The id is . . . a chaos, a cauldron of seething excitement. We suppose that it is somewhere in direct contact with somatic processes, and takes over from them instinctual needs and gives them mental expression, but we cannot say in what substratum this contact is made. These instincts fill it with energy, but it has no organization and no unified will, only an impulsion to obtain satisfaction for the instinctual needs, in accordance with the pleasure-principle. The laws of logic—above all, the law of contradiction—do not hold for processes in the id. Contradictory impulses exist side by side without neutralizing each other or drawing apart; at most they combine in compromise formations under the overpowering economic pressure towards discharging their energy.[6]

Ego

The ego is the executive of the personality system, which aims at controlling and ruling the id and maintaining communication with the external world. When the ego is functioning properly, harmony and efficiency result. When it allows either the id or the superego to overwhelm it, disharmony and inefficiency result and the personality becomes maladjusted to the environment. Whereas the id is governed by the pleasure principle, the ego is governed by the reality principle. For example, the child has to learn to discriminate over what he or she puts into the mouth, accepting food and drink but not razor blades and poison. He or she has to learn to tolerate some tension, to postpone pleasure, to finish a task before resting, playing, or eating. Similarly the person must learn to sublimate or postpone his or her sexual drives until appropriate times. The ego is the center of rational thinking, learning, and wisdom. Its capacity is laid down by heredity but developed by socialization and education. The properly functioning ego informs us of the likely success of alternate behavioral patterns. It gives us a firm grip on reality and channels the id's drives in ways most likely to produce happiness.

Superego

The superego is the legislative–judicial branch of the personality. It represents the ideal patterns and principles of behavior. Whereas the ego focuses on reality (what is the case), the superego focuses on ideality (what ought to be the case). It is the source of morality and law. Its goal is not pleasure but perfection or, at least, moral goodness. Whereas the reality principle informs the person that stealing or cheating might bring great success in reaching a goal, the superego would veto the proposal, prescribing adherence to a set of moral principles. According to Freud, children internalize the principles their parents communicate by word and deed. The superego is constituted by two subsystems, the ego-ideal and conscience. The *ego-ideal* corresponds to the child's conception of his parents' values, which they communicate by rewards and punishments. If a child is consistently punished for lying and rewarded for truthfulness, honesty is likely to be one of his ideals. *Conscience* corresponds to the child's feeling regarding his success in living by the ego-ideals. It produces a discomforting feeling of guilt whenever one violates an ego-ideal but a feeling of satisfaction whenever one adheres to one's ideals.

The superego serves to control behavior so that personalities can live together in peace and harmony. It places inner constraints on the id and ego, harnessing the sexual and aggressive drives which would endanger the stability of society. The id is a product of biological evolution, something hereditary; the ego is a product of one's interface with the world; and the superego is the product of socialization and culture.

When the flow of instinctual energy is blocked by the ego or superego, it tries to break through the constraining walls and discharge itself in fantasy or action. When the breakthrough is successful, the ego's rational governance is undermined. The person may make mistakes in speaking, writing ("Freudian slips"), perceiving, and remembering, and may have accidents because he or she becomes confused and loses contact with reality. The ability to solve problems and discover reality is diminished by the interference of impulsive wishes. For example, one has a hard time keeping one's mind on one's work when one is hungry, sexually excited, or angry.

Sexuality

As Schopenhauer noted, but Freud emphasized, the sex drive is the most powerful drive in humans, a sort of psychological hydraulic pressure which seems to burst through the mental pipes and cisterns at times. Freud believed that people varied in their sexual drives. For some, the drive is so strong that they cannot sublimate all of its impulses in socially useful action. Some of these people simply refuse to conform to society's mores and act out in unsocial behavior, such as rape, seduction, and promiscuity. Others repress the impulses, turning the drives inward, usually resulting in psychoneurosis.

In his article "'Civilized' Sexual Morality and Modern Nervous Illness" (1908), Freud argued that while women have weaker sexual drives than men, they tend to contract more psychoneurotic illness, partly because fewer opportunities for sublimation were open to them and partly because they were more involved in families than men. "In many families the men are healthy, but from a social point of view, immoral to an undesirable degree, while the women are high-minded and over-refined, but severely neurotic."[7]

Freud believed that children go through various stages of development, beginning with the oral stage, where sucking at the mother's breast dominates. The baby first seeks gratification orally through the mother's breast, an object for which other surrogates can later be provided. Initially unable to distinguish between the self and the breast, the infant soon becomes aware of the mother as the first external love object. After this oral phase, during the second year, the child's erotic focus shifts to its anus, caused in part by the challenge of toilet training. During the anal phase the child's pleasure in defecation is at odds with its need for self-control. People who are fastidious or obsessive are fixated in this stage. Freud felt he was an anal-type personality. The third phase, lasting from about age 3 to 6, is the phallic phase. During the phallic stage boys and girls are fascinated by genitalia, the boys priding themselves on their penis and the girls wishing they had one. They have "penis envy." Boys often believe that both their parents have penises and that their sisters have yet to grow theirs.

Boys and girls at an early age typically become attached to the parent of the opposite sex. Freud calls this the "Oedipus complex," named after the hero of Sophocles' play *Oedipus Rex,* in which Oedipus, orphaned as a baby, grows up to become a dashing young man who unwittingly kills his biological father, King Laius, and unsuspectingly marries his biological mother, Queen Jocasta. When he discovers his crime, he gouges out his eyes and wanders blindly for the rest of his life. Analogously, boys become emotionally attached to their mothers and subconsciously wish their fathers out of the way. They feel intense hostility toward competing males. Girls go through analogous relations with their fathers. Jung gave the name "Electra complex" to this relationship, after the daughter of Agamemnon, sister of Orestes, who kills their mother Clytemnestra in Aeschylus' trilogy the *Oresteia.* Freud centers his analysis on male sexual development, arguing that as the boy matures (as a response to the imagined threat of castration by others), he makes a transition from hatred toward the father to identification with him. He is warned not to play with his penis and, above all, not to masturbate; he might be punished by having his organ dismembered and becoming like his sister. To avoid such an outcome, the ego reasons that it is wise to make peace with the father and anyone else who has power over him. The identification with the father dissolves the Oedipus complex, and the boy typically grows into a normal male.

In his paper "Female Sexuality" (1931), Freud argues that the castration complex occurs differently in girls.

> The girl acknowledges the fact of her castration, and with it too, the superiority of the male and her own inferiority; but she rebels against this unwelcome state of affairs. From this divided attitude three lines open up. The first leads to a general

revulsion from sexuality. The little girl, frightened by the comparison with boys, grows dissatisfied with her clitoris, and gives up her phallic activity and with it her sexuality in general as well as a good part of her masculinity in other fields. The second line leads her to cling with defiant self-assertiveness to her threatened masculinity. To an incredibly late age she clings to the hope of getting a penis some time. That hope becomes her life's aim; and the phantasy of being a man in spite of everything often persists as a formative factor over long periods. This "masculinity complex" in women can only result in a manifest homosexual choice of object. Only if her development follows the third, very circuitous, path does she reach the final normal female attitude, in which she takes her father as her object and so finds her way to the feminine form of the Oedipus complex.[8]

Most girls take the third alternative and grow into healthy women.

Freud's shocking, libidinous message to his Victorian contemporaries was that we are fundamentally sexual beings. The theory that sexuality defines our being immediately drew the wrath of the Catholic Church, and many politicians and women were offended by his theory. Even his erstwhile disciple, Carl Jung, criticized it as too rigid and untrue. Jung argued that Freud overemphasized sexual energy and transformed Freud's idea into a broader "libidinous energy," emphasizing that male and female traits (*anima* and *animus*) were in everyone to differing degrees. Members of the women's movement often rejected Freud's theory as sexist, taking particular offense at the idea of penis envy. The Nazis burnt his books for being politically unsavory, and the Communist Party in the Soviet Union rejected them as bourgeois and reactionary.

Consciousness and the Unconscious

Freud holds an iceberg model of consciousness. We are conscious of only a small part of our experience, the tip of the iceberg. Most of our beliefs, desires, and phobias are beneath the surface of consciousness. Freud wrote that "scientific work in psychology will consist in translating unconscious processes into conscious ones, and thus filling in the gaps in conscious perceptions."[9] The unconscious always seeks to maximize pleasure and minimize pain. Psychoneuroses, such as obsessive–compulsiveness, paranoia, and narcissism, are caused by unresolved problems in psychosexual development, such as failure to progress satisfactorily from the oral or anal stage or to resolve one's Oedipal relationship.

Psychotherapy, the prescriptive element of psychoanalysis, aims at delving into the unconscious. It consists in letting the patient talk about his or her dreams or experiences in such a way that the analyst can interpret them. By understanding their origins, the patient will find a cure through coming to terms with his or her past. Freud believed that the therapist must become the surrogate problematic parent with whom the patient has had an arrested relationship. The patient transfers, or projects, the emotions toward the parent to the therapist and reenacts the childhood urges which now are invested on the new object, the therapist. In this way, feelings long repressed can be ventilated, a catharsis takes place, and the patient comes to understand his or her problems and emotionally comes to terms with them. The therapist must remain neutral, nonjudgmental, and detached in the process. Freud had his patient relax on a couch while undergoing therapy in order to facilitate the process.

Dreams as Wish Fulfillment

Dream therapy was Freud's favorite mode of analysis. "The interpretation of dreams is the royal road to knowledge of the unconscious activities of the mind. . . . A dream is a (disguised) fulfillment of a (suppressed or repressed) wish."[10]

> A wish-fulfillment must bring pleasure, but the question then arises, "To whom?" to the person who has the wish, of course. But as we know, a dreamer's relation to his wish is a quite peculiar one. He repudiates them and censors them—he has no liking for them, in short.[11]

Freud distinguished the satisfaction of the person from the satisfaction of the wish. The wish may be fulfilled but not the person who has the dream-wish. Secondly, he distinguished the "manifest content" of the dream from its "latent content." The *manifest content* is what the dreamer remembers of the dream. The *latent content* is the hidden content, that which gives the dream its meaning. The psychoanalyst's task is to reveal the deeper latent content of the dream so that the patient can come to terms with his or her unresolved problems.

Let us look at one of Freud's examples. A young woman patient, who had married very early in life and been married for several years, told of the following incident:

> She was at the theater with her husband. One side of the stalls was completely empty. Her husband told her that Elise L. and her fiancé had wanted to go too, but had only been able to get bad seats—three for 1 florin 50 kreuzer—and of course they could not take those. She thought it would not really have done any harm if they had.[12]

On the day of the dream, her husband had told her that her friend and contemporary Elise L. had just become engaged. The patient then related this dream to that fact and others. The week before, she had wanted to go to a particular play and had bought tickets early, so early that she had to pay a booking fee. Then, on arrival at the theater, one whole side of the stalls was seen to be empty, and her husband had teased her for her anxiety in purchasing the tickets so early. The sum of 1 florin 50 kreuzer reminded her of another sum, a present of 150 florins which her sister-in-law had been given by her husband and which she had rushed off to exchange for a piece of jewelry. In connection with the word *three*, introduced in a context where we would expect *two*, all the dreamer could think of was that Elise, though she had married 10 years later than the patient, was only 3 months younger than she. However, she could not explain the meaning of getting three tickets for two persons.

Freud was impressed by the large number of associations embedded in this dream and reconstructed the dream thusly: "Really it was absurd of me to be in such a hurry to get married. I can see from Elise's example that I could have got a husband later." Regarding the ratio of the two sums of money (1 florin 50 kreuzer to 150 florins), Freud surmises that she means "and I could have got one a hundred times better with the money, i.e., my dowry."

The question immediately arises, How does Freud know that his interpretation is the correct one? One can imagine a hundred other interpretations of the dream or even that the dream lacks any deeper meaning but is simply a series of associations. Apparently, the response is that dream interpretation is an art which the skilled therapist has mastered with practice.

One general puzzle about Freud's theory of mind, or psyche, has to do with the fact that he claims to be a materialist who denies the existence of a separate soul but whose description of the mind treats it as having a life of its own. One would think that Freud is an epiphenomenalist (see chapter 14). **Epiphenomenalism** holds that mental events are caused by brain events but have no causal efficacy of their own, but Freud's treatment of the mind would suggest the very opposite, that it has a rich life of its own.

Religion

In *The Future of an Illusion* (1927), Freud said that religion is an illusion, a projection of the father image. Little children grow up thinking their parents, often the father, is god-like and very powerful. They stand in reverent awe of his grandeur and look to him for providential support. When they become teens, they realize that their fathers are also mortal and not especially powerful, but they still have this inclination to worship the kind of being that they revered as small children. Hence we have the projection on the empty heavens of a father image, a God made in the father's image. Religion, as illusory, would evaporate when people became autonomous, that is, understood their primal urges and became liberated from atavistic myths.

> A special importance attaches to the case in which this attempt to procure a certainty of happiness and a protection against suffering through a delusional remolding of reality is made by a considerable number of people in common. The religions of mankind must be classed among the mass-delusions of this kind.[13]

Some religious people have rejected Freud's theory of psychoanalysis as well as his view of religion as an illusion; they suggest that his *Future of an Illusion* is really simply the "illusion of the future." Responding to Freud's claim that God is the projection of the father image, theists offer the hypothesis that the relation to one's (hopefully benevolent) parents is God's way of teaching us about his love for us.

Civilization and Its Discontents

Freud follows Hobbes, rather than Rousseau, in depicting human nature as violent and unstable.

> Men are not gentle, friendly creatures wishing for love, who simply defend themselves if they are attacked, but that a powerful measure of desire for aggression has to be reckoned as part of their instinctual endowment. The result is that their neighbor is to them not only a possible helper or sexual object, but also a temptation to them to gratify their aggressiveness on him, to exploit his capacity for work without recompense, to use him sexually without his consent, to seize his possessions, to humiliate him, to cause him pain, to torture and to kill him. *Homo homini lupus* [man is a wolf to man]; who has the courage to dispute it in the face of all the evidence in his own life and in history?[14]

Nevertheless, in the state of nature people are inhibited, whereas in civilization they are repressed. Freud argued that we have paid a huge price for civilization. On the one hand, civilization, because it organizes our energies in purposeful manners, offers many benefits, including those of physical and social mobility, efficient communication, medicine, a longer life span, and institutions which enable us to resolve conflicts peacefully. On the other hand, it causes enormous frustration of our id. We must control our passions and live within a moral straightjacket—our superego.

> We come upon a contention which is so astonishing that we must dwell upon it. This contention holds that what we call our civilization is largely responsible for our misery, and that we should be much happier if we gave it up and returned to primitive conditions. I call this contention astonishing because, in whatever way we may define the concept of civilization, it is a certain fact that all the things with which we seek to protect ourselves against the threats that emanate from the sources of suffering are part of that very civilization.[15]

Such frustration has caused neurosis.

> It arose when people came to know about the mechanism of the neuroses, which threaten to undermine the modicum of happiness enjoyed by civilized men. It was discovered that a person becomes neurotic because he cannot tolerate the amount of frustration which society imposes on him in the service of its cultural ideals, and it was inferred from this that the abolition or reduction of those demands would result in a return to possibilities of happiness.[16]

The result of human socialization in civilized society is guilt. Guilt is an internal authority, a product of the superego, which takes the place of the external authority, the overseeing parents and police. We now feel guilty for having our natural instincts, sexual and aggressive drives.

Happiness becomes very difficult, if not impossible, to sustain. A few, like St. Francis of Assisi, can sublimate their ids and live a life of love for others; but the vast majority cannot. There seems to be some truth in Freud's contention. We think that we would be happier if our every whim was satisfied. However, on second thought, the idea of continual sense-gratification seems a delusion. In the state of nature, life can be "solitary, poor, nasty, brutish and short." Our desires are insatiable, for as soon as one is satisfied, another takes its place. Part of the secret of happiness is to learn to be content with what one has, not to seek for more than life can offer. John Stuart Mill seems wiser than either the Epicureans or Freud:

> Happiness . . . [is] not a life of rapture; but moments of such, in an existence made up of few and transitory pains, many and various pleasures, with a decided predominance of the active over the passive, and having as the foundation of the whole, not to expect more from life than it is capable of bestowing.[17]

Rival Psychoanalytic Theories

Several of Freud's disciples broke from him and started schools of their own. The most famous of these were Carl Gustav Jung (1875–1961) and Alfred Adler (1870–1937) both of whom broke with the master because of what they felt was his fixation with sex.

Adler, born and trained in Vienna, broke with Freud in 1911. In 1932 he traveled to the United States, where he taught for the last 5 years of his life. He held that self-realization or self-worth was at the heart of human predicament, so that every person needed to strive for his own perfection in his own way. The personality type is formed in childhood and partly determined by what particular inferiority affects the person most deeply during those formative years. Neurosis is largely a result of failing to overcome one's innate sense of inferiority (Adler coined the term "inferiority complex"). We spend our lives trying to overcome our feeling of inferiority, seeking power and self-worth. He held that the so-called feminine traits were not innate but products of socialization. The therapist's task is to help the patient realize his potential. Adler earned a reputation for being commonsensical.

Jung, the Swiss-born son of a Protestant minister, thought Freud misunderstood and underestimated the power of religion and overestimated the role of sex in one's life and broke with him in 1913. He seemed to believe in a spiritual force like the soul that is independent of the body. His work often reads more like a metaphysical system than a scientific one. He held to the idea of a collective unconscious, which penetrated each individual unconscious and which the therapist must help the patient to uncover. This unconscious was populated with cosmic *archetypes* (universal symbols; e.g., the image of the snake biting its own tail as a symbol of the eternal completeness of life; the god-figure as the source of all reality, etc.). For Freud, all symbols, whether in dreams, myths, or art, are essentially sexual. Caves, pits, bottles, and holes represent the vagina; swords, guns, sticks, pencils, and spears are phallic representations. Freud's direction is from general ideas and types of objects to the particular (the sexual symbol). Jung's theory goes in the opposite direction, form the particular to the general, much like Platonic Forms. "Behind the particularized mother's womb lies the archetypal womb of the great Mother of all living; behind the physical father the archetypal Father, behind the child, the [pure eternity]; behind the particular manifestation of the procreative sexual libido lies the universal creative and re-creative Spirit."[18] *(1)* These archetypes point to a transcendent and mysterious dimension in life. *(2)* The individual unconscious mind contains not only those primitive experiences which have been repressed but also aspects of mental life which have been neglected in the course of one's development. In this regard, Jung held that each person is androgynous, having a female and a male dimension (the animus and anima), and, in order to find spiritual wholeness, must focus on the neglected aspect of the pair as he or she matures. Many scientists, including Darwin, and philosophers have remarked that in the pursuit of their analytical skills they lost an appreciation of and facility with poetry and literature. There is a danger of the paralysis of analysis that often accompanies intense concentration on philosophy, math, or science. Psychological health in adults involves not so much regressing to infantile phases of life but coming to terms with the fullness of one's personality, both the male and female dimensions. *(3)* The personal unconscious becomes much less important than in Freud's theory. Jung, contrary to his teacher, held that some experiences can be completely erased from memory because they have "lost a certain energic value."

Jung's theory contains three levels of consciousness: *(1)* present consciousness; *(2)* the personal unconscious, what is temporarily forgotten but accessible through superficial stimulation; and *(3)* the deep collective unconscious. As evidence for this deeper universal unconscious, he pointed to the "extraordinary" unanimity of archetypes in the mythologies of different cultures and claimed that the mental repertoires of his patients contained such archetypes deep within them. Like Adler, but unlike Freud, Jung's theory is future-oriented and devalues past experiences. The goal is to become psychologically healthy, to live a happy, fulfilled, worthwhile life. By recognizing the universal archetypes within and by filling out one's personality, one can attain such a fulfilled, happy life. Jung is more optimistic about the prospects for happiness than Freud. Recalling the metaphors of chapter 7, Freud is closer to the tragic vision and Jung, to the utopian vision of life.

Summary

Freud's theory of psychoanalysis, with its concept of the unconscious, focuses on the sex drive, and progression in the child's personality, has deeply influenced the way we look at ourselves and life in general. A scandal to his Victorian contemporaries, his ideas, or psychomythology, have influenced our vocabulary to the extent that we find it natural to describe the self in terms of the tripartite ego, id, and superego, rather than as body, soul, and spirit. The quote from John Barth at the beginning of this chapter describes the influence of Freud on our culture. The "dance of sex" profoundly influences, if not defines, many of our lives, especially in adolescence and young adulthood. Every advertiser and pornographic entrepreneur knows this: sex sells.

Nonetheless, the question is, Is Freud's theory true or at least plausible? We may wonder whether Freud's theory is autobiographical. He notes his ambivalent relationship with his father and inordinate love for his mother, which may have caused him to overgeneralize. His claim that girls are filled with penis envy seems another exaggeration. The idea of dreams always being instances of sexual wish fulfillment seems implausible. My nightmares don't seem to be, nor do dreams of food when one is hungry or dreams recalling actual events, such as a recent horrendous bombing or the happy occasion of winning a sports event or prize.

Some psychological incidents do seem to lend themselves to Freudian interpretation. Here is one example given by Thomas Nagel:

> At a dinner party, an elderly man of independent means, who had spent his life as a private scholar without an academic position, challenged a psychiatrist who was present to explain why, whenever he listened to the news on the radio, he fell asleep just at the point when the stock market report came on. The psychiatrist, knowing these facts, replied that it probably expressed difficult feelings about his father. "My *father!*" said the man incredulously, "My father has been dead for fifty years!" The conversation then went on to other things, but the next day, the man telephoned the psychiatrist to report that later in the evening the memory had come flooding back to him that when, in his youth, he had resisted going into the family business, his father had made him promise at least to listen to the stock market report on the radio every day.[19]

That some of our behavior is explained by the fact that we have repressed certain memories, desires, or fears is very likely correct; but a single valid insight does not validate an entire theory, one made up of constituent parts such as ego, id, and superego and applicable to every human action by everyone.

Perhaps the most general criticism is that his theory is nonfalsifiable. How could we objectively test it so that we would know what could count against it? When one disagrees with a favored analysis of a dream, the analyst simply claims that the objector has misinterpreted the dream. However, what are the criteria for correct interpretation? Isn't the analyst simply appealing to authority? "Trust me, I'm an expert, so I know the latent content of your dream."

Several years before I became a philosopher, I took training under a Jungian therapist; but I interacted with Freudians and Adlerians. I noted that Freudian analysts put a decided sexual interpretation, Jungians a religious interpretation, and Adlerians a self-assertion, power-based interpretation on the same dreams. Suppose Joe wants to quit his job for another one. Joe's conscious reason is simply that this new job is more interesting, but psychoanalytical theories may disagree, seeking a deeper unconscious reason. The Freudian might interpret his act as arising from an unconscious Oedipal wish to win his mother's sexual favor. The Adlerian might interpret this as an attempt to overcome a feeling of inferiority or a quest for power. The Jungian might interpret it as an endeavor to discover the true meaning of life in an ideal life. These are fascinating, creative interpretations, but they are different self-contained systems offering no independent criteria for sorting out the myth from the truth. How can one test them? It struck me that these psychoanalytical theories, with their different methods of salvation, were perhaps new quasi-religious faiths, fascinating but unfalsifiable.

Finally, there is a self-referential problem with each psychoanalytic theory. If Freud's theory is a product of unresolved unconscious desires, of an Oedipal complex, why should we believe it is true? If Adler's theory is simply the product of the will to power, of the attempt to overcome the inferiority complex, why should we believe it is true? If Jung's theory is the result of coming to terms with his anima, his feminine self, why should we believe it is true? Or should we give up the quest for objective truth in favor of a relative, subjective notion?

Study Questions

1. Describe Freud's psychoanalytic theory. What are its salient points?

2. Examine John Barth's characterization (the epigraph at the head of this chapter) of Freud's theory as pansexuality. Is it an accurate characterization?

3. What are the weakest points of Freud's system? Can they be met?

4. Discuss Freud's contention that neurosis is the price we pay for civilization and that we cannot be happy because it requires that we frustrate our id.

5. How does Freud explain religion? How plausible is his thesis? What are the arguments against his view? What do you think?

6. Compare Freud's theory with Adler's and Jung's theories of human nature.

7. Compare Freud's theory of human nature with Schopenhauer's (chapter 9).

8. Discuss the self-referential problem discussed in the last paragraph of this chapter.

Notes

1. John Barth, *End of the Road* (Bantam, 1981).
2. Fechner called his theory "psychophysics." His methods are still used in experimental psychology.
3. *The Complete Psychological Works of Sigmund Freud,* trans. and ed. James Strachey (Macmillan, 1974), vol. III, p. 199.
4. Ibid., p. 203.
5. Freud, *Psychoanalysis and Faith,* quoted in Anthony Storr, *Freud: A Very Short Introduction* (Oxford University Press, 1989), p. 13.
6. Freud, *New Introductory Lectures on Psychoanalysis,* trans. W. J. H. Sprott (Norton, 1933).
7. Freud, "'Civilized' Sexual Morality and Modern Nervous Illness" in *The Pelican Freud Library* (Penguin, 1977), vol. 9, p. 61.
8. Freud, "Female Sexuality," in *The Pelican Freud Library,* vol. 7, p. 376.

9. Freud, "Some Elementary Lessons in Psycho-analysis," in *Collected Papers,* (Hogarth Press, 1949), vol. V, p. 382.
10. Freud, *The Complete Psychological Works of Sigmund Freud,* vol. V, p. 608.
11. Ibid., vol. XV, p. 215.
12. Ibid., p. 122. Quoted in Richard Wollheim, *Sigmund Freud* (Cambridge University Press, 1990), p. 75. I follow Wollheim in my discussion of Freud's theory of dreams.
13. Freud, *Civilization and Its Discontents,* trans. James Strachey (Norton, 1962), chapter II.
14. Ibid., chapter V.
15. Ibid., chapter III.
16. Ibid.
17. Mill, *Utilitarianism* (1861), chapter 2.
18. Quoted in J. A. C. Brown, *Freud and the Post-Freudians* (Penguin, 1977), p. 44.
19. Thomas Nagel, "Freud's Permanent Revolution," in *New York Review of Books* (May 12, 1994).

For Further Reading

Adler, Alfred, *Problems of Neurosis* (Cosmopolitan Book, 1930).

Brown, J. A. C., *Freud and the Post-Freudians* (Penguin, 1977).

Chodorow, Nancy, *The Reproduction of Mothering* (University of California Press, 1978).

Dinnerstein, Dorothy, *The Mermaid and the Minotaur: Sexual Arangements and Human Malaise* (Harper & Row, 1977).

Flanagan, Owen, *Freud's Dreams* (Oxford University Press, 2000).

Freud, Sigmund, *The Complete Psychological Works of Sigmund Freud* (Macmillan, 1974).

———, *The Pelican Freud Library* (Penguin, 1977), 9 vols.

———, *The Basic Writings of Sigmund Freud,* ed. A. A. Brill (Random House, 1938).

———, *Civilization and Its Discontents,* trans. James Strachey (Norton, 1962).

Jones, Ernest, *The Life and Work of Sigmund Freud* (Penguin, 1961).

Jung, C. G., *Analytical Psychology* (Vintage Books, 1968).

Midgley, Mary, *The Ethical Primate* (Routledge, 1994).

Nagel, Thomas, "Freud's Permanent Revolution," *New York Review of Books* (May 12, 1994).

Nye, Robert, *Three Views of Man* (Wadsworth, 1975).

Storr, Anthony, *Freud: A Very Short Introduction* (Oxford Univeristy University Press, 1989).

Wollheim, Richard, *Sigmund Freud* (Cambridge University Press, 1990).

CHAPTER 12

The Existentialist Theory of Human Nature: Kierkegaard, Nietzsche, and Sartre

Man would rather have the Void for his purpose than be void of purpose. *(Nietzsche,* Genealogy of Morals*)*

We are condemned to freedom. *(Sartre,* Existenialism in Humanism*)*

Introduction

There was once a young student of philosophy and theology who mastered all the philosophical positions of his time, who patiently worked through one system of knowledge after another, memorizing, analyzing, refuting, revising, and amalgamating the theses of learned men. His one aim was to find the *truth,* not simply empirical truth, factual knowledge, but a truth for which there was not yet a name, a sort of inner truth, a spiritual ideal for which he could live and die, an ideology that either proceeded from the heart or found a resounding echo of affirmation in the heart. The student wrote in his diary:

What I really lack is to be clear in my mind what *I am to do,* not what I must know— except that a certain amount of knowledge is presupposed in every action. I need to understand my purpose in life, to see what God wants me to do, and this means that I must find a truth which is true for me, that I must find *that idea for which I can live and die.*[1]

He then criticizes his whole academic career as largely superfluous:

What would be the use of discovering so called "objective" truth, of working through all the systems of philosophy and of being able to review them all and show up the inconsistencies within each system? What good would it do me to be able to develop a political theory and combine all the intricate details of politics into a complete system, and so construct a world for the exhibition of others but in which I did not live; what would it profit me if I developed the correct interpretation of Christianity in which I resolved all the internal problems, if it had no deeper significance *for me and for my life;* what would it profit me if truth stood before me cold and naked, indifferent to whether I recognized her, creating in me paroxysms of anxiety rather than trusting devotion?

He then asks "What is truth but to live for an idea? Ultimately everything must rest on a hypothesis but the moment it is no longer outside him, but he lives in it, then and only then does it cease to be merely a hypothesis for him."[2] It becomes the *lived truth,* subjective truth.

The student graduated from the university with honors but was unable to obtain a teaching position, so he began to write, developing the sort of thoughts expressed in the sentences you have just read—only he didn't write in the usual philosophical style. Instead, he told stories and wrote witty aphorisms and essays about literature, music, the aesthetic life, morality, and religion in which the flow of the discourse was arranged so as to awaken the conscience, compelling the reader to ask questions about the meaning and purpose of life. His first books were best sellers—only no one knew who this mysterious author was, for he didn't sign his name to his books. Instead, he used pseudonyms: Victor Eremita, Johannes de Silentio, Vigilius Haufniensis, Nicolas Notabene, Constantine Constantius, Johannes Climacus, and so forth. All these Latin pseudonyms had symbolic meaning. Translated, they read "The Victorious Hermit," "John Who Is Silent," "The Vigilant Watchman of the Harbor" (he lived in a harbor town), "Nicolas Note Well," "Constant Constantine," and "John Who Is Trying to Climb" to heaven, respectively. The author's reasons for not including his own name were complex, but the main reason was his desire to draw attention to the ideas contained in his books and to the reader's personal relationship with these ideas, often written on several levels: an innocent story, a message to his ex-fianceé, a philosophical discourse, a call to "subjective truth." He was prolific, producing 18 books in 5 years, publishing completely at his own expense and losing money in the venture.

His life was filled with constant and intense suffering. He was frustrated in love, frustrated in his vocational aspirations, frustrated by his physical liabilities—especially by his severe back ailment that eventually led to a premature death. He opposed the journalistic corruption of his day, incurring the wrath of the avant-garde press, which mocked him almost daily. One cartoon depicts him standing in the center of the universe with the Sun, Moon, stars, and all else revolving around him, suggesting that he was an egomaniac. Eventually, his reputation was ruined, and he became undeservedly the laughingstock of his community. He felt a mission to teach the common folk but was even rejected by them. They began to name their dogs after him. He was deeply religious, devoutly Christian; but in his quest for integrity he felt compelled to reject the established church of his land as anti-Christian and joined the Atheist Society in protest to the spiritual deadness of the church. The established church responded in kind, hurling abuse his way. An intense controversy erupted between him and the church.

As a religion [organized Christianity], as it is now practiced, is just about as genuine as tea made from a bit of paper which once lay in a drawer beside another bit of paper which once had been used to wrap up a few dried tea leaves from which tea had already been made three times.[3]

In the midst of his battle with the church, he collapsed on the main street of his city, Copenhagen, and was taken to the hospital. Some days later, a priest came to administer last rites, the Eucharist (Holy Communion), advising him that he was dying. Our subject brushed the priest aside, exclaiming "No, I will not accept the body and blood of my Lord and Savior from the hands of a lackey of the state! Send an unpaid layman and I will partake." A few days later, without having received the Eucharist, he died at the age of 42. Thus ended the life of the father of existentialism, Søren Aabye Kierkegaard (May 5, 1813–November 11, 1855).

This was the beginning of existentialism as a philosophical movement. For about 50 years, Kierkegaard's name and ideas were almost entirely forgotten in the intellectual world. His books fell out of print and his private papers were stowed away in a dusty closet. Then, suddenly, early in the 20th century, his ideas exploded like a time bomb. Rediscovered first in Germany, his thoughts were initially linked with those of Friedrich Nietzsche (1844–1900).

Nietzsche held that the fundamental creative force that motivates all creation is the will to power. We all seek to affirm ourselves, to flourish, and to dominate. Since we are essentially unequal in ability, it follows that the fittest will survive and be victorious in the contest with the weaker and baser. There is great aesthetic beauty in the noble spirit coming to fruition, but this process is hampered by Judeo–Christian morality, which Nietzsche labeled "slave morality." Slave morality, which is the invention of jealous priests, envious and resentful of the power of the noble, prescribes that we give up the will to power and excellence and become meek and mild, that we believe the lie that all humans are of equal worth. Of course, the herd really subscribes to the will to power as much as anyone: railing against it is a symptom of the will to power. Nietzsche also referred to this in his private papers as the ethics of resentment [my translation].

The baseness of some people suddenly spurts up like dirty water when some holy vessel, some precious thing from a locked shrine, some book with the marks of a great destiny, is carried past; and on the other hand there is a reflex of silence, a hesitation of the eye, a cessation of all gestures that express how a soul *feels* the proximity of the most venerable.

Thus, similarly, the superiority of the noble souls engenders envious hate in the herd, in the ignoble. There is an age-old platitude, going at least as far back as the Roman historian Livy, which says "the tallest blades of grass get cut first." Nietzsche's inegalitarianism is based partly on Darwin's evolution and the idea of the survival of the fittest, partly on Schopenhauer's will to power, and partly on the vacuum left by the "death of God." Nietzsche expresses his thesis in a famous, dramatic passage called "The Madman."

Have you ever heard of the madman who on a bright morning lighted a lantern and ran to the market-place calling out unceasingly: "I seek God! I seek God!"—As there were many people standing about who did not believe in God, he caused a great deal of amusement. Why! is he lost? said one. Has he strayed away like a child? said another. Or does he keep himself hidden? Is he afraid of us? Has he taken a sea voyage? Has he emigrated?—the people cried out laughingly, all in a hubbub. The insane man jumped into their midst and transfixed them with his glances. "Where is God gone?" he called out. "I mean to tell you! *We have killed him,*—you and I! We are all his murderers! But how have we done it? How were we able to drink up the sea? Who gave us the sponge to wipe away the whole horizon? What did we do when we loosened this earth from its sun? Whither does it now move? Whither do we move? Away from all suns? Do we not dash on unceasingly? Backwards, sideways, forewards, in all directions? Is there still an above and below? Do we not stray, as through infinite nothingness? Does not empty space breathe upon us? Has it not become colder? Does not night come on continually, darker and darker? Shall we not have to light lanterns in the morning? Do we not hear the noise of the gravediggers who are burying God? Do we not smell the divine putrefaction?—for even Gods putrefy! God is dead! God remains dead! And we have killed him! How shall we console ourselves, the most murderous of all murderers? The holiest and the mightiest that the world has hitherto possessed, has bled to death under our knife,—who will wipe the blood from us? With what water could we cleanse ourselves? What lustrums, what sacred games shall we have to devise? Is not the magnitude of this deed too great for us? Shall we not ourselves have to become Gods, merely to seem worthy of it? There never was a greater event,—and on account of it, all who are born after us belong to a higher history than any history hitherto!"— Here the madman was silent and looked again at his hearers; they also were silent and looked at him in surprise. At last he threw his lantern on the ground, so that it broke in pieces and was extinguished. "I come too early," he then said, "I am not yet at the right time. This prodigious event is still on its way, and is travelling,—it has not yet reached men's ears. Lightning and thunder need time, the light of the stars needs time, deeds need time, even after they are done, to be seen and heard. This deed is as yet further from them than the furthest star,—*and yet they have done it!*"— It is further stated that the madman made his way into different churches on the same day, and there intoned his *Requiem aeternam deo.* When led out and called to account, he always gave the reply: "What are these churches now, if they are not the tombs and monuments of God?"[4]

God plays no vital role in our culture—except as a protector of the slave morality, including the idea of equal worth of all persons. If we recognize that there is no rational basis for believing in God, we will see that the whole edifice of slave morality must crumble and with it the notion of equal worth. Nietzsche believed that the world was void of intrinsic value or meaning. We must impose our own value upon it. In place of God and intrinsic value, we must create our own value. We must become Supermen (*Ubermenschen*). The morality will be the creation of these Supermen, based on the virtues of high courage, discipline, and intelligence, in the pursuit of self-affirmation and excellence. They will oppose the slave (Christian) morality of the mediocre herd, and the herd will envy and hate these superior beings. Nietzsche agrees with Plato and Aristotle that the masses are worthless and believes that new Supermen will overcome the herd. Some have claimed that Nietzsche inspired the Nazi leaders, but Nietzsche would have considered Hitler an embodiment of the herd mentality. He was against mediocrity, not humans as such. He did make some intemperate statements which could be interpreted as nihilistic or anti-women. He thought women were inferior. "Are you going to a woman? Do not forget your whip!"[5]

> One half of mankind is weak, typically sick, changeable, inconsistent . . . she needs a religion of weakness that glorifies being weak, loving and being humble as divine. . . . Woman has always conspired with types of decadence, the priests, against the "powerful," the "strong" the "men."[6]

Nietzsche is not a typical philosopher, for he uses few arguments, preferring aphorisms and sarcasm to drive home his fragmented ideas. Aesthetic sensibility seems to replace religion and morality for him. "We must agree to the cruel sounding truth that slavery belongs to the essence of culture; the wretchedness of struggling men grows still greater in order to make possible the production of a world of art for a small number of Olympian men."[7]

Thus, existentialism, as the thoughts of the Christian Kierkegaard and the atheist Nietzsche were linked together, entered the world as a two-pronged fork, disturbing the intellectual soil throughout Europe. First, it was the theologians, such as Karl Barth, Rudolf Bultmann, Paul Tillich, and Reinhold Niebuhr, who welcomed Kierkegaard's thoughts. Soon, novelists and poets became infected with these new ideas: Fyodor Dostoevsky, Franz Kafka, Hermann Hesse, T. S. Eliot, and W. H. Auden and later Saul Bellow, Norman Mailer, John Barth, Walker Percy, and John Updike.

A new breed of philosophers sprang up, the existentialists, among whom are Martin Buber, Martin Heidegger, Jean-Paul Sartre, and José Ortega y Gassett. Before long, existentialism had permeated the intellectual world everywhere. It was at first condemned by both the communist Soviet Union as bourgeois subjectivism and by the Roman Catholic Church as dangerous individualism, though before long Catholics had appropriated many of its ideas.

What exactly was this new philosophy? What was its purpose and mission? Well, to touch the spirit of Kierkegaard's and existentialism's ideas, let me tell a story.

There was once a man who discovered his shadow. Watching its lithe motion, he assumed that it was alive. Because it followed him so faithfully, he decided that he was its master and that it was his servant. Gradually, he began to believe that it was the shadow that was initiating the action and that the shadow was his irreplaceable guide and companion. He took increasing account of its comfort and welfare. He awkwardly maneuvered himself in order that it might sit in a chair or lie in bed. The importance of the shadow to the man grew to such an extent that finally the man became, in effect, "the shadow of his shadow"!

Existentialism is a call to look inward, to develop one's own personal philosophy of life, to get one's priorities right. Kierkegaard, Nietzsche, and Martin Heidegger (1889–1976) deplored the tendency of humanity to become slaves of their

FRIEDRICH NIETZSCHE

Friedrich Nietzsche (1844–1900), a German existentialist, has played a major role in contemporary intellectual development. Descending through both his parents from Christian ministers, Nietzsche was brought up in a pious German Lutheran home and was known as the little Jesus by his schoolmates. He studied theology at the University of Bonn and philology at Leipzig, becoming an atheist in the process. At the age of 24, he was appointed professor of classical philology at the University of Basel in Switzerland, where he taught for 10 years until forced by ill health to retire. Eventually, he became mentally ill and spent the last 10 years of his life in a mental institution. He died August 25, 1900.

Thoughts on the Meaning of Life

Man would sooner have the Void for his purpose than be void of Purpose. (*Genealogy of Morals*)

Hegel says, "That at the bottom of history, and particularly of world history, there is a final aim, and that this has actually been realized in it and is being realized—the plan of Providence—that there is a reason in history: that is to be shown philosophically and this as altogether necessary." (This is balderdash.) My life has no aim and this is evident even from the accidental nature of its origin. That I can posit an aim for myself is another matter. But a state has no aim; we alone give it an aim.

Whatever does not kill me makes me stronger.

Truth and Untruth

A belief, however necessary it may be for the preservation of a species, has nothing to do with truth. (*Beyond Good and Evil*)

The falseness of a judgment is not for us necessarily an objection to a judgment. The question is to what extent it is life-promoting, life-preserving, species-preserving, perhaps even species-cultivating. To recognize untruth as a condition of life—that certainly means resisting accustomed value feelings in a dangerous way; and a philosophy that risks this would by that token alone place itself beyond good and evil. (*Beyond Good and Evil*)

Beyond Right and Wrong

To speak of right and wrong per se makes no sense at all. No act of violence, rape, exploitation, destruction, is intrinsically unjust, since life itself is violent, rapacious, exploitative, and destructive and cannot be conceived otherwise. (*Genealogy of Morals*)

Will to Power

What is Good? All that enhances the feeling of power, the Will to Power, and the power itself in man. What is Bad?—All that proceeds from weakness. What is happiness?—the feeling that power is increasing—that resistance has been overcome.

Not contentment, but more power; not peace at any price but war; not virtue, but competence (virtue in the Renaissance sense, virtue, free from moralistic acid). The first principle of our humanism: The weak and the failures shall perish. They ought even to be helped to perish.

What is more harmful than any vice?—Practical sympathy and pity for all the failures and the weak: Christianity. (*Will to Power*)

Style and Character

One thing is needful,—To give style to one's character—a great and rare art! It is practiced by those who survey all the strengths and weaknesses of their nature and then fit them into an artist plan until every one of them appears as art and reason and even weaknesses delight the eye. Here a large mass of second nature has been added; there a piece of original nature has been removed—both times through long practice and daily work at it. Here the ugly that could not be removed is concealed; there it has been reinterpreted and made sublime. Much that is vague and resisted shaping has been saved and exploited for distant views. . . . In the end, when the work is finished, it becomes evident how the constraint of a single taste governed and formed everything large and small. Whether this taste was good or bad is less important than one might suppose, if only it was a single taste! (*Joyful Wisdom*)

The Ubermensch (Superman)

We immoralists make it a point of honor to be affirmers. More and more our eyes have opened to that economy which needs and knows how to utilize all that the holy witlessness of the priest, of the diseased reason of the priest, rejects—that economy in the law of life which finds an advantage even in the disgusting species of the prigs, the priests, the virtuous. What advantage? Be ourselves, we immoralists are the answer. (*Thus Spoke Zarathustra*)

technologies, "shadows of their shadows." They decried the herd mentality of modern people, their susceptibility to peer pressure, what others think. Kierkegaard warned in his journals in the 1840s, long before the advent of television, that there would come a time when people would stare mesmerized into a box that would inform them on what to believe. The true individual must stand alone, deriving his or her ideals from within, not from without. The eternity that dwells within the heart is a neglected treasure by most people. Each of us has a duty to work out his or her own salvation with fear and trembling, to find a personal truth for which he or she can live and die.

Three Theses of Existentialism

Existentialism contains radical views on human nature. Three theses, embraced in one way or another by virtually all members of this movement, predominate: *(1)* existence precedes essence, *(2)* the absurdity of existence, and *(3)* radical freedom. Let us examine each of these.

1. *Existence precedes essence.* In classical philosophy, notably that of Plato and Aristotle, we find the concept that essence precedes existence. Truth is eternal, unchangeable, absolute, and the central goal of philosophy. For Plato, as we saw in chapter 3, the Forms or essences exist in a transcendent dimension, and our job is to discover them through philosophical contemplation, through reason. Human beings have a common eternal ("essentialist") nature defined by reason ("Humans are rational animals"). As Aristotle said,

> Reason is the true self of every person, since it is the supreme and better part. It will be strange, then, if he should choose not his own life, but some other's. . . . What is naturally proper to every creature is the highest and pleasantest for him. And so, to man, this will be the life of Reason, since Reason is, in the highest sense, a man's self.[8]

In one way or another, all the major philosophical systems from Plato through the Middle Ages down to Descartes, Leibniz, Kant, and Hegel carried on this essentialist tradition. Truth is outside of us, and our job is to use reason to discover it.

Existentialism denies the priority of objective truth. What is important is what we do about ourselves, how we live within the light we have, the decisions we make. We find ourselves "thrown" into existence, afloat over 70 fathoms of ocean water, and we must somehow keep afloat (or drown). A key question becomes, Why not drown? However, the urgency of finding a purpose to life radically transforms the relationship between objective truth and subjective apprehension. Sartre says, "There is no human nature. . . . Man is nothing else but what he makes of himself."[9] We must invent ourselves. For Kierkegaard, this thesis is set forth in his dictum that "subjectivity is Truth."

All existential problems are passionate ones, for when existence is interpreted with reflection, it generates passion. To think about existential problems without passion is tantamount to not thinking about them at all since it is to forget the point—that the thinker is himself an existing individual. Passion is the way to truth, and the way may be more valuable than the end.

A precursor of existentialism, the German philosopher Gotthold Lessing (1729–1781), said, "If God set forth before me the Eternal, unchangeable Truth in his right hand and the eternal quest for Truth in his left hand and said, 'Choose,' I would point to the left hand and say, 'Father, give me this, for the eternal unchangeable Truth belongs to you alone.'" The quest for truth is appropriate to the dynamics of people still growing, still in need of spiritual development. The reason that God can truly possess absolute truth is that he is pure subjectivity (pure love), but we are sinful, selfish, ignorant, and alienated from the ground of our being; the way to overcome this alienation (for Kierkegaard it is equivalent to sin) is to delve deep and act from our inner resources, listening to the still, small voice within rather than the roar of the crowd or the imperious voice of authority.

In this regard, the precursor of existentialism, Blaise Pascal (1623–1662), wrote "The heart has reasons which the mind knows nothing of."[10] Kierkegaard disagreed with Aristotle about the supremacy of reason within us: "In existence rational thought is by no means higher than imagination and feeling, but coordinate. In existence all factors must be co-present." The passions, feelings, intuitions, and imagination have been neglected by philosophers, but they are just as valuable as reason and also define our being:

> When the question of truth is put forward in an objective manner, reflection is directed objectively to the truth as an object to which the knower is related. The reflection is not on the relationship but on whether he is related to the truth. If that which he is related to is the truth, the subject is in the truth. When the question of truth is put forward in a subjective manner, the reflection is directed subjectively to the individual's relationship. If the relation's HOW is in truth, the individual is in truth, even if the WHAT to which he is related is not true.[11]

Kierkegaard calls this other valuable attitude **subjective truth.** It characterizes our passionate concern to live according to our lights. He illustrates this with the parable of the two worshipers.

> We may illustrate this by examining the knowledge of God. Objectively, the reflection is on whether the object is the true God; subjectively, the reflection is on whether the individual is related to a *what* in such a way that his relationship is a God-relationship.
>
> If one who lives in a Christian culture goes up to God's house, the house of the true God, with a true conception of God, with knowledge of God and prays—but prays in a false spirit; and one who lives in an idolatrous land prays with the total passion of the infinite, although his eyes rest on the image of an idol; where is there most truth? The one prays in truth to God, although he worships an idol. The other prays in untruth to the true God and therefore really worships an idol.
>
> Here is a definition of Truth: An objective uncertainty held fast in an approximation process of the most passionate inwardness is the truth, the highest truth attainable for an existing individual. . . . The above definition is an equivalent expression for faith. Without risk there is no faith. Faith is precisely the contradiction between the infinite passion of the individual's inwardness and the objective uncertainty. If I am capable of grasping God objectively, I do not believe, but precisely because I cannot do this I must believe . . . so as to remain out upon the deep, over seventy fathoms of water, still preserving my faith.[12]

We find ourselves thrown out into a sea of unknowing:

> Sitting quietly in a ship while the weather is calm is not a picture of faith; but when the ship has sprung a leak, enthusiastically to keep the ship afloat by pumping while yet not seeking the harbor; this is the picture. And if the picture involves an impossibility in the long run, that is but the imperfection of the picture.[13]

Existence is a task filled with paradoxes and never completed. It demands our passionate interest, and reason must take its proper place as a servant of the inner promptings of a passionate heart. The value of life is in the process, not reaching the end. In the end, we all die.

2. *The absurdity of existence.* In his autobiography, Count Leo Tolstoy (1828–1910) tells the story of a traveler fleeing an infuriated animal. Attempting to save himself from the beast, the man runs toward a well and begins to climb down, when to his distress he spies a dragon at the bottom of the well. The dragon is waiting with open jaws, ready to eat him. The poor fellow is caught in a dilemma. He dares not drop into the well for fear of the dragon, but he dares not climb out of the well for fear of the beast. So he clutches a branch of a bush growing in the cleft of the well and hangs onto it for dear life. His hands grow weak, and he feels that soon he will have to give in to his grim fate; but he still holds on desperately. As he grasps the branch for his salvation, he notices that two mice, one white and one black, are nibbling away at the main trunk of the branch onto which he is clinging. Soon, they will dislodge the branch.

The traveler is you and I, and his plight is yours and mine, the danger of our demise on every hand. The white mouse represents our days and the black, our nights. Together they are nibbling away at the three-score years and ten, which make up our branch of life. Inevitably all will be over, and what have we to show for it? Is this all there is? Can this brief moment in the history of the universe have significance? What gives life value or importance?

The certainty of death heightens the question of the meaning of life. Like a prisoner sentenced to death or a patient with a terminal illness, we know that, in a sense, we are all sentenced to death and are terminally ill, but we flee the thought in a thousand ways. What is the purpose of life?

The French existentialist Albert Camus (1913–1960), in his youthful work *The Myth of Sisyphus*, looks at existence as an objectively meaningless event and is forced to conclude the following:

> There is but one truly serious philosophical problem, and that is suicide. Judging whether life is or is not worth living amounts to answering the fundamental question of philosophy. All the rest—whether or not the world has three dimensions, whether the mind has nine or twelve categories—comes afterwards. These are games.[14]

With life at stake, Camus begins an inquiry into the absurdity of existence. Here is his description of the state of mind that leads to the thought of voluntary death.

> Suicide has never been dealt with except as a social phenomenon. On the contrary, we are concerned here, at the outset, with the relationship between individual thought and suicide. An act like this is prepared within the silence of the heart, as is a great work of art. The man himself is ignorant of it. One evening he pulls the trigger or jumps. Of an apartment-building manager who had killed himself I was told that he had lost his daughter five years before, that he had changed greatly since, and that experience had "undermined" him. A more exact word cannot be imagined. Beginning to think is beginning to be undermined. Society has but little connection with such beginnings. The worm is in man's heart. That is where it must be sought. One must follow and understand this fatal game that leads from lucidity in the face of existence to flight from light.[15]

Even for the more fortunate, life is never easy, but at various moments we sense that the whole state of existence "is not worth the trouble."

> What, then, is that incalculable feeling that deprives the mind of the sleep necessary to life? A world that can be explained even with bad reasons is a familiar world. But, on the other hand, in a universe suddenly divested of illusions and lights, man feels an alien, a stranger. His exile is without remedy since he is deprived of the memory of a lost home or the hope of a promised land. This divorce between man and his life, the actor and his setting, is properly the feeling of absurdity. All healthy men having thought of their own suicide, it can be seen, without further explanation, that there is a direct connection between this feeling and the longing for death.
>
> The subject of this essay is precisely this relationship between the absurd and suicide, the exact degree to which suicide is a solution to the absurd. The principle can be established that for a man who does not cheat, what he believes to be true must determine his action. Belief in the absurdity of existence must then dictate his conduct. It is legitimate to wonder, clearly and without false pathos, whether a conclusion of this importance requires forsaking as rapidly as possible an incomprehensible condition. I am speaking, of course, of men inclined to be in harmony with themselves. . . .
>
> It happens that the stage sets collapse. Rising, streetcar, four hours in the office or the factory, meal, streetcar, four hours of work, meal, sleep, and Monday Tuesday Wednesday Thursday Friday and Saturday according to the same rhythm—this path is easily followed most of the time. But one day the "why" arises and everything begins in that weariness tinged with amazement. "Begins"—this is important. Weariness comes at the end of the acts of a mechanical life, but at the same time it inaugurates the impulse of consciousness. It awakens consciousness and provokes what follows. What follows is the gradual return into the chain or it is the definitive awakening. At the end of the awakening comes, in time, the consequence: suicide or recovery. In itself weariness has something sickening about it. Here, I must conclude that it is good. For everything begins with consciousness and nothing is worth anything except through it. . . .
>
> Knowing whether or not one can live *without appeal* is all that interests me. I do not want to get out of my depth. This aspect of life being given me, can I adapt myself to it? Now, faced with this particular concern, belief in the absurd is tantamount to substituting the quantity of experiences for the quality. If I convince myself that this life has no other aspect than that of the absurd, if I feel that its whole equilibrium depends on that perpetual opposition between my conscious revolt and the darkness in which it struggles, if I admit that my freedom has no meaning except in relation to its limited fate, then I must say that what counts is not the best of living but the most living. . . . [16]

Does Camus have an answer to these questions? Why not suicide? Why accept the absurdity of existence? He seems to give no good answer to the question other than a determination to maximize the quantity of experiences.

> On the one hand the absurd teaches that all experiences are unimportant, and on the other it urges toward the greatest quantity of experiences. How, then, can one fail to

do as so many of those men I was speaking of earlier—choose the form of life that brings us the most possible of that human matter, thereby introducing a scale of values that on the other hand one claims to reject?

But again it is the absurd and its contradictory life that teaches us. For the mistake is thinking that the quantity of experiences depends on the circumstances of our life when it depends solely on us. Here we have to be over-simple. To two men living the same number of years, the world always provides the same sum of experiences. It is up to us to be conscious of them. Being aware of one's life, one's revolt, one's freedom, and to the maximum, is living, and to the maximum. Where lucidity dominates, the scale of values becomes useless.[17]

What does life mean in such a universe? Nothing else for the moment but indifference to the future and a desire to use up everything that is given. Belief in the meaning of life always implies a scale of values, a choice, our preferences. Belief in the **absurd,** however, teaches the contrary; but this is worth examining.

Camus compares our existence to that of Sisyphus in Greek mythology. Sisyphus was condemned by the gods for disobedience. His punishment consisted in rolling a huge boulder up the side of a mountain until it reaches the top, whereupon the boulder rolls down to the bottom and Sisyphus must follow its course and retrieve it. He goes through this process again and again for all eternity. Tedious, boring, meaningless, such is the process of our never-ending toil. Consider the average person in our society. One Monday morning, a man or woman gets up early in the morning, washes, dresses, goes to the toilet, and eats breakfast. Another hour or so is spent mindlessly commuting to a job whose work, when looked at with a lucid eye, is ultimately purposeless. Were it not for the grim need to earn a livelihood, sane people would laugh at such behavior. Then, return: a mindless commute to a mindless evening before a mindless entertainment box and then to a mindless sleep. The sorry saga is repeated Tuesday, Wednesday, Thursday, and Friday for over 40 years until the person retires, too old to discover the vacuity of his or her existence. Saturday he or she spends recovering from the exhaustion of the first 5 mindless days, and on Sunday he or she is bored at the home of relatives or else enjoys inconsequential gossip about others, wrings his or her hands at the downward course of the world (especially the young), or mindlessly watches a football game on TV. Occasionally, to relieve the pain of existence, the person gets drunk, takes drugs, or soothes his or her raging hormones in an act that any animal can perform. What is the goal of such mortals but to generate and rear children so that they can perpetuate this farce?

Is this what life is all about?

Kierkegaard, being religious, agrees with such sentiments to the extent that life for most people is absurd; but he argues that our very alienation from what we inwardly sense to be a higher self is a hint of God's voice, a holy hypochondria, calling us back, inwardly, to God. Not rational demonstration, not the philosophical proofs of God's existence, but the inner turmoil of the soul in the absurdity of existence leads us to make a leap of faith into a religious mode of existence. Absurdity is not an objective but a subjective problem that calls for a subjective response, a decision in passion.

Only those who have felt the contradictions of life, the inner alienation, the dread and despair connected with self-realization can appreciate religion; but to have experienced the absurd in life is to be a candidate for the religious quest:

> In this manner God certainly becomes a hypothesis, but not in the useless, passionless way this word is generally used. The only way that an individual can come into a relation with God is when the dialectical contradiction brings his passion to the point of despair, and helps him to embrace God with the "category of despair"—faith. Then the hypothesis that God exists becomes far from arbitrary or detached but a life-necessity. It is not so much that God becomes a hypothesis as that the individual's hypothesis of God becomes necessary.[18]

Ultimately, Kierkegaard believes that Christianity, with its doctrine of the Incarnation, wherein God becomes human in Christ, is the proper fit for the passions of the heart:

> Subjectivity culminates in passion, Christianity [through the doctrine of the Incarnation] is the paradox, paradox and passion are a mutual fit, and the paradox is altogether suited to one whose situation is, to be in the extremity of existence. Aye, never in all the world could there be found two lovers so wholly suited to one another as paradox and passion.[19]

3. *Freedom*. Jean-Paul Sartre (1905–1980) has emphasized this aspect of our being more than anyone. We "are condemned to freedom." Sartre connects the notion of freedom with the idea that existence precedes essence. Imagine an idea of the most magnificent house in the world, your dream house. You decide to build it and call an architect to design the plans. Then, you hire a builder who constructs the house according to your plans. Now you have an existing house to serve your purpose. The essence (or idea) precedes the existence of the house.

Traditionally, this is how humans have viewed the relation between essence and existence. There was a God who had an idea of man and woman and who created them in his image. They, like the house, had a definite nature and a purpose. Their being was defined as a rational, immortal soul. Existence was merely the living out of this essence.

But now, take away God. For the atheist (like Sartre or Camus), there is no ideal mind that defines our being. We are not like the house that has been designed for a purpose with a definite nature. We are just born. We find ourselves conscious beings without definite nature or purpose but completely free to determine our nature. We must create our essence:

> The child takes his parents for gods. Their actions like their judgments are absolute. They are the incarnation of universal Reason, law, the meaning and purpose of the world. When the eye of these divine beings is turned on him, their look is enough to justify him at once to the very roots of his existence. It confers on him a definite, sacred character. Since they are infallible, it follows that they see him as he really is. There is no room in his mind for hesitation or doubt. True, all that he sees of himself

is the vague success of his moods, but the gods have made themselves the guardians of his eternal essence. He knows that it exists. Even though he can have no direct experience of it, he realizes that his truth does not consist in what he can know of himself, but that it is hidden in the large, terrible yet gentle eyes which are turned towards him. He is a real essence among other real essences; he has his place in the world—an absolute place in an absolute world.[20]

As the child grows, he or she discovers that his parents are fallible, that they are neither gods nor viceroys of God, that the whole phenomenon of the essence-granting process is a charade. There is no God, no essence, no absolute place in the universe for us, no absolute determinants whatsoever. We are free to create our own essence; we are condemned to **absolute freedom.**

Sartre tells a story to illustrate how even our morality is relative to our free, creative invention. During World War II, a student came to Sartre in order to ask for advice. Should he fight for his country by fleeing France and crossing the channel to England, where de Gaulle's Free French Army was preparing for a battle with the Vichy government? Or should he stay home and care for his ailing mother? What does morality require of me? he asked Sartre. Sartre told him that he could not give advice, that morality did not require anything as such, but that he, the student, must create his own morality. He must decide which principle to live by and universalize it for all people. Even morality is a function of our freedom.

For Kierkegaard, even faith itself is a function of freedom. Reason is a whore for the highest bidder: "If I really have reason and am in the situation in which I must act decisively, my reason will put forth as many possibilities *pro* and *contra*, exactly as many." Reason always leads to skepticism, leaving all important issues in doubt; so faith must take over where reason leaves off. Through freedom the leap of faith comes into play. You are responsible even for what you believe!

We usually think of freedom as a very positive, salutary trait, one that all adolescents crave; but, according to the existentialists, it is at least as negative as it is positive. It is a dreadful burden, imposing a heavy responsibility on us, for with it we cannot get off the hook of existence. We are totally responsible for our actions, for what we become.

The experience of freedom is not that of fear. It is inappropriate to say that we fear freedom. We dread it. It causes deep anxiety within.

Imagine that you are walking along a narrow ridge overlooking two precipices on either side, with no guard rail to hold onto. You might fear that you will slip on a stone and be hurled over into the abyss or that the earth will give way beneath you, but you might also experience anguish at the vertigo, or dizziness, of looking over the cliff, which could result in your falling into the abyss. You might be numbly aware of a certain attraction for the abyss, which calls to you from below, to which you might respond by casting yourself into its deep bosom. Fear is caused by the world, by an external object that we would avoid; but dread or anxiety is not caused by the world but by ourselves, by something within our nature. We would like to ensure our beings against the contingency of freedom, but we can't. No guarantee is given against our destructive use of freedom. It is ominous, pervading our entire being, pushing us at every moment. In dreadful freedom we

JEAN-PAUL SARTRE

Jean-Paul Sartre was born in 1905 into the home of a historic Swiss–French Protestant family, the Schweitzers. He was the second cousin of Albert Schweitzer. His father died when he was 1 year old, so he was brought up by his young mother Anne Marie, who was more like his playmate and worshiper than parent, and his maternal grandfather in Alsace. Of his childhood he wrote, "I had no rights because I was overwhelmed with love. I had no duties because I did everything through love." His godlike grandfather spoke to him once about being a writer. Sartre mistook it for a divine command and spent the rest of his life in obedience. He sometimes wrote 10,000 words a day. In 1945 Sartre launched his new literary review, Les Temps Modernes *(named after Charlie Chaplin's famous film) and was about to give one of the most famous speeches in modern cultural history.*

This is what the historian of ideas, Paul Johnson, had to say about Sartre:

> October 29, 1945 is the turning point in French culture. Shortly after the end of World War II a beleaguered and exhausted France is trying to recover from defeat and four years of German occupation. A lecture was to be given at the Club Maintenant. Everyone came, fights broke out, people went hysterical trying to get into the hall, which was packed to capacity. Frenchmen and women fought each other for chairs and with chairs, smashing 30 of them before the lecture. Men and women fainted in the fray, as they were crushed against one another. When the celebrated speaker arrived, the mob in the street was so large, he thought that he was witnessing a demonstration organized by the Communist Party. His friends had to force an entrance for him. Meanwhile, the theaters in Paris were deserted. A leading speaker addressed an all but empty hall. All Paris had gone to hear a short (5'2"), squinty, bespectacled mole of a man give a lecture entitled "Existentialism Is a Humanism." Who was this man and what caused this astonishing spectacle?
>
> A new literary and philosophical hero had emerged from the war with a new philosophy in tune with the times, which accepted the dark tragedy of defeat and war and the absurdity of the human condition. A secular priest was offering a secular gospel, Existentialism, which was neither Christian nor Communist, to make sense of a senseless world. This editor, philosopher, novelist, and playwright, who would soon be referred to as the "Eiffel Tower of French Culture," would dominate the intellectual life of Europe for the next 25 years. At his funeral April 19, 1980, 50,000 French people would converge in procession on the Montparnasse Cemetery. Sartre's press coverage defied the wildest dreams. Several newspapers carried every word of the long lecture. The Catholic daily *La Croix* called Sartre's existentialism "a greater danger than eighteenth-century rationalism or nineteenth-century positivism." Soon all his books were placed on the Roman Catholic Index [list of censored books], which greatly increased their sales. The Communist *L'Humanité* called Sartre an enemy of society, and Stalin's cultural commissar, Alexander Fadayev, called him "a Jackal with a typewriter, a hyena with a fountain pen." It was the greatest intellectual promotion scheme of the century. "Existentialism Is a Humanism" sold over ½ million copies in the first month alone.[21]

shape our essence. We said before that, for the existentialists, humans lack an essence; but we could say that freedom is our essence.

In Sartre's most famous play *No Exit*, three people sit in hell, torturing one another, each believing that fate has conspired against them and that they are damned to torment one another for eternity. "Hell is other people." One can question exactly what Sartre means by this, but, at any rate, at the end of the play we see that the door next to them has always been unlocked. They endure damnation by their own volition. Similarly, you are responsible for what you do and what you become. You are free to change just as soon as you decide to do so.

Sartre's theory of freedom is at the heart of his ethics. One must choose what one will become, but the ethical choice is one of universalization of one's actions. He quotes Dostoevsky's *Possessed*: "If God doesn't exist, everything is possible." It would be comforting if God did exist, but since he does not, we must invent ourselves and our ethics. We may do anything we wish, so long as we take responsibility for it and universalize it. Thus, Sartre could not give advice to his student faced with the dilemma of either staying with his invalid mother or joining the Free French forces in England. He alone must choose and take responsibility for his choice.

This theme of inventing ourselves and morality is reminiscent of Nietzsche, who in his famous "Death of God" passage wrote "We must ourselves become gods to be worthy of this deed." For Nietzsche, Western civilization had eliminated the practical need for God, so now we face the terrifying prospect of having to figure out how to live for ourselves. Nietzsche, like Schopenhauer (see chapter 9), is cynical about moral rules. The herd, the mediocre majority, uses the rules to hold down the superior souls, the *ubermenschen*, who could crush these spiritual weaklings, the masses, if the masses had not united against them, pulling them down to mediocrity. The superior souls are aesthetically better than the masses, and for Nietzsche, that seems to justify their exploiting the masses. A true aristocracy is its own legitimization, the highest justification of society.

> Its fundamental belief must be precisely that society is not allowed to exist for its own sake, but only as a foundation and scaffolding, by means of which a select class of beings may be able to elevate themselves to their higher duties . . . to a higher existence: like those sun-seeking climbing plants in Java—they are called *Sipo Matador*—which encircle an oak so long and so often with their arms, until at last, high above it, but supported by it, they can unfold their tops in the open light, and exhibit their happiness.[22]

For Kierkegaard, ethics is a necessary, but not a sufficient, condition for the highest life possible for human beings. It makes up the second stage of existence, the highest being the religious–existential life, which we described above. Within the religious life, love predominates as the motive-force of action.[23]

For none of the major existentialists is ethics important in itself. It is, at best, an expression of one's authentic choices and a measure of one's absolute responsibility. Only Kierkegaard seems to hold a strong view of objective goodness, and that is rooted in love for God and one's fellow human beings.

An Assessment of Existentialism

Existentialism is a reaction to the influence of science and technology on our self-understanding. The existentialist philosophers have attempted to serve as an important corrective to what they perceive as overly rationalistic and reductivist views of human nature that tend to leave out an appreciation of the arts, imagination, passions, and emotions. Perhaps certain classical and medieval systems were guilty of that. Kierkegaard thought that the German idealist philosopher George W. F. Hegel (1770–1831) was the major villain of his day. Hegel, Kierkegaard contended, erected marvelous castles in the ethereal heavens of thought while he himself lived in an existential doghouse. Take care, philosopher, how you live!

Each of us must come to terms with his or her personal existence. Kierkegaard is correct. Philosophy must become personal. We must work out the meaning of our lives, not once but continually. Actually, I think many philosophers before Kierkegaard, Nietzsche, Sartre, and Camus said as much. Socrates sought to make philosophy practical and personal. St. Augustine recognized the inward element of philosophical endeavor. René Descartes threw off all previous authority in order to work out a new and vibrant system of thought. David Hume recognized the role of the passions and emotions, stating that "reason is and ought only to be a slave of the passions, and can never pretend to any other office than to serve them."[24]

Camus states that the only important question in philosophy is, Should I commit suicide?—since life has no meaning but is absurd. Victor Frankl, who survived more than 3 years in Nazi concentration camps, the originator of "logotherapy," began his psychotherapy by asking his patients why they do not commit suicide. In facing that question, one begins to see one's values and whatever goals one has in life.[25] Frankl discovered that the difference between surviving and not surviving the tortures of the concentration camp lay in being able to give a satisfactory answer to that question. Even a bad meaning may enhance survival better than no meaning. To quote Nietzsche again, "Man would sooner have the Void for his purpose than be void of Purpose."

Perhaps it is mainly in its emphasis on the subjective, on freedom, that existentialists tend to distinguish themselves; but this is just where the criticism of existentialism starts. Does it not overemphasize the role and reality of freedom and undermine the reality of determinate structures and the role of reason? Many think it does.

Sartre, in his passion for freedom, goes so far as to reject the reality of the unconscious! Apparently, even our dreams are freely chosen. However, psychologists, if not the Bible and common sense, have taught us that we are not always aware of our deepest motives, that we deceive ourselves, that early experiences, long buried in our subconscious, incline our behavior. Indeed, whether and to what extent we are free is itself a deeply philosophical problem, as we have seen in other chapters. Reason is the means by which we discover whether and to what extent we are free.

The emphasis on subjectivity and freedom easily slides into an overemphasis on *individualism,* tending toward a solipsism where the self becomes a world entire to itself, cut off from other selves. To quote from John Donne's 1624 poem *"Devotions upon Emergent occasions,"* "No man is an island." Men and women are social beings, connected to one another in interpersonal relations, through such institutions as family, school, club, business, community, city, and state. We are all in one another's debt so that we must come out of ourselves, communicate with others, reason together, and strive for an interpersonal moral code.

For Kierkegaard, no moral rule was fully binding. God could at any moment call on people to sacrifice their loved ones as he once called Abraham to do. Notice Sartre's description of his student's dilemma over whether to leave his mother and join the Free French forces or remain with her. Is this not a dilemma just because two recognizably valid values are at stake: loyalty to family and devotion to justice? What if the student had come to Sartre and said "I have a dilemma. I want to know whether I should rape my mother or take care of her"? Would Sartre have nothing more to say than "Morality requires nothing. You must choose your own morality and universalize it for all others"! If so, then we can only say that he misunderstands the social function of morality, which in part is to procure human flourishing and the resolution of conflicts of interest. The mistake of existentialism is to suppose that every moral decision has the same status as a genuine dilemma; but if everything is a dilemma, then nothing is, for nothing matters. It is only because morality has a rational structure where universal values inhere that we can rightly realize that sometimes we are placed in situations where two values compete or where whatever we do will be an evil of sorts and so choose the lesser of evils.

So we might recommend a rationalized, socialized, moral existentialism or, what comes to much the same thing, an analytical philosophy that recognizes the need for autonomy and subjective depth. Reason is a higher value than existentialists sometimes allow, but the passions, imagination, and personal adaptation of ideas are also important, more so than traditional philosophy has sometimes recognized. We are by nature feeling creatures, but so are other animals. What sets us apart is largely our ability to reason and deliberate on our desires and emotions and to act on those deliberations. Then, of course, we can reason about the reasoning that went into the earlier reasons and deliberations. We can judge, compare, and communicate our reasons to others in argument; revise our conclusions in light of their rational critiques; and generally make progress toward being wiser, more understanding persons.

Summary

Existentialism is a type of philosophy of human nature that is rooted in lived experience ("existence precedes essence"), concerned with human freedom and purpose in the midst of the apparent absurdity of life. Both religious and secular versions emphasize the need for personal decision, freedom, and the contingent. Kierkegaard, the father of existentialism, thought that the quest for meaning would lead to religion; but secular existentialists—Nietzsche, Heidegger, Sartre, and Camus—reject religion as a viable option and call on humans to live without objective meaning or religion. We noted the criticisms of existentialism—that it tends to be overly individualistic and may become irrational. However, it may serve as an important, imaginative corrective to purely abstract impersonal (essentialist) philosophies.

Study Questions

1. Discuss the main ideas of existentialism. How valid are they? Assess the strengths and weaknesses of this view of human nature.

2. Do you agree with Sartre that there is no objective purpose in life but that each of us must give our lives a purpose? Or are there objective purposes already present that we need only discover? Explain.

3. Some people say that life is made meaningful by ameliorating the suffering in society and/or by bringing revolutionary changes into being. As a youth, the English philosopher John Stuart Mill had such a view. In his Autobiography, Mill describes the crisis of meaning that took place in his twenty-second year of life. Following the English utilitarian reformer Jeremy Bentham, his whole life had been dedicated to social reform; and as long as he could see the world improving, he felt satisfaction and even happiness. However, a crisis arose in 1826. He was in "a dull state of nerves, such as everybody is occasionally liable to," when the following question occurred to him:

   > Suppose that all your objects in life were realized; that all the changes in institutions and opinions which you are looking forward to, could be completely effected at this very instant: would this be a great joy and happiness to you? An irrepressible self-consciousness distinctly answered, "No!" At this my heart sank within me: the whole foundation on which my life was constructed fell down. All my happiness was to have been founded in the continual pursuit of this end. The end had ceased to charm, and how could there ever again be any interest in the means? I seemed to have nothing left to live for.[26]

   Mill went through a deep depression that lasted several months in which he came close to suicide. Ask yourself the same question as he did. What would your answer be? What is the significance of your answer?

4. What gives you meaning in life? Kierkegaard defined *subjective truth* as that for which you are willing to live and die. For what are you willing to live and die?

5. Examine Lessing's quotation, cited by Kierkegaard as the theme of his philosophy: "If God set forth before me the Eternal, unchangeable Truth in his right hand and the eternal quest for Truth in his left hand and said, 'Choose,' I would point to the left hand and say, 'Father, give me this, for the eternal unchangeable Truth belongs to you alone.'" What does this mean?

6. Do you agree with the existentialists, especially Sartre, that we are "condemned to freedom"? Are we responsible for what we do with our lives, or do chance

and circumstances have more to do with what we become than the existentialists assert?

7. What does Nietzsche mean by the death of God? Is he correct?

8. What does Sartre mean by saying "existence precedes essence"?

9. What are the various existentialists' attitudes toward ethics? Compare
Kierkegaard with Nietzsche and Sartre.

Notes

1. Søren Kierkegaard, *Papirer,* vol. 1, eds. P. A. Heiberg and Victor Kuhr (Gyldendals, 1909). My translation.
2. Ibid.
3. My translation from his private papers.
4. Friedrich Nietzsche, *Joyful Wisdom* (Frederick Unger, 1958), p. 125. Book is also called *The Gay Science.*
5. *Thus Spoke Zarathustra,* in *The Portable Nietzsche,* trans. Walter Kaufman (Viking Press, 1966) p. 179.
6. *The Will to Power,* section 864. Nietzsche sometimes gives the impression that he is a nihilist. For interpretations that combat this negative view, see Michael Tanner, *A Very Short Introduction to Nietzsche* (Oxford University Press, 1987), and Alexander Nehamas, *Life as Literature* (Harvard University Press, 1987).
7. Quoted in Bruce Detwiler, *Nietzsche and the Politics of Aristocratic Radicalism* (University of Chicago Press, 1990), p. 106.
8. Aristotle, *Nicomachean Ethics,* I.7.
9. Jean-Paul Sartre, *Existentialism,* trans. Bernard Fechtman (Philosophical Library, 1948).
10. Pascal, *Pensees* (1677), no. 277.
11. Søren Kierkegaard, *Samlede Vaerker,* vol. 7, ed. A. B. Drachmann, J. L. Heiberg, and H. O. Lange (Gyldendals, 1901). My translation.
12. Ibid.
13. Ibid.
14. Albert Camus, *The Myth of Sysyphus,* trans. Justin O'Brien (Vintage, 1960), p. 3.
15. Ibid.
16. Ibid.
17. Ibid.
18. Kierkegaard, *Samlede Vaerker.*
19. Ibid.
20. Jean-Paul Sartre, *Words,* trans. B. Frechtman (Braziller, 1964), p. 3.
21. Paul Johnson, *Modern Times* (Harper & Row, 1983).
22. Friedrich Nietzsche, *Beyond Good and Evil,* trans. R. J. Hollingdale (Penguin, 1973), p. 193.
23. Kierkegaard, *Works of Love,* trans. Howard & Edna Hong (Harper, 1962).
24. David Hume, *Treatise on Human Nature* (1739), p. 415.
25. Victor Frankl, *Man's Search for Meaning* (Simon & Schuster, 1959).
26. John Stuart Mill, *Autobiography* (1873).

For Further Reading

Barrett, William, *Irrational Man* (Doubleday, 1958). Still the best introduction to existentialism.

Bretall, Robert, ed., *A Kierkegaard Anthology* (Princeton University Press, 1946). A good collection.

Camus, Albert, *The Plague* (Random House, 1948). Deals poignantly with existentialism and the problem of evil.

———, *The Myth of Sisyphus and Other Essays*, trans. J. O. O'Brien (Random House, 1955). Camus' youthful, brilliant essay.

Frankl, Victor, *Man's Search for Meaning* (Beacon Press, 1963). An important work in existential psychology.

Kaufmann, Walter, ed. and trans., *A Portable Nietzsche* (Viking Press, 1954). A good collection.

———, *Existentialism from Dostoevsky to Sartre* (New American Library, 1975). A good anthology.

Kierkegaard, Søren, *Fear and Trembling*, trans. Walter Lowrie (Princeton University Press, 1954). One of Kierkegaard's most important works.

Klemke, E. D., *The Meaning of Life* (Oxford University Press, 1981). A good collection.

Nehamas, Alexander, *Life as Literature* (Harvard University Press, 1987).

Nietzsche, Friedrich, *Beyond Good and Evil*, trans. Walter Kaufmann (Random House, 1966). A classic.

———, *On the Genealogy of Morals* and *Ecce Homo*, trans. Walter Kaufmann (Random House, 1967). Nietzsche's critique of the history of Western moral philosophy.

Oaklander, Nathan, ed., *Existentialist Philosophy* (Prentice Hall, 1992). An excellent anthology with important introductory essays.

Pojman, Louis P., *The Logic of Subjectivity: Kierkegaard's Philosophy of Religion* (International Scholars Publications, 1999). A critical examination of Kierkegaard's existentialism.

Sartre, Jean-Paul, *Existentialism*, trans. Bernard Fechtman (Philosophical Library, 1948). A classic in modern existentialism.

Tanner, Michael, *A Very Short Introduction to Nietzsche* (Oxford University Press, 1987). Gives a more positive interpretation of Nietzsche's thought.

CHAPTER 13

The Darwinian Theory of Human Nature

Great minds shape the thinking of successive historical periods. Luther and Calvin inspired the Reformation; Locke, Leibniz, Voltaire and Rousseau, the Enlightenment. Modern thought is most dependent on the influence of Charles Darwin. (*Ernst Mayer in a speech to the Swedish Royal Academy of Science, Sept 23, 1999*)

Introduction: The Shaking of the Foundations

No event has done more to alter our self-understanding, our theory of ourselves in the last three or four hundred years than the publication of Charles Darwin's *Origin of Species by Means of Natural Selection* in 1859. It disrupted the overlapping consensus of cosmic teleology, which reigned from the ancient Hebrew and Greeks to the mid-19th century, and in its place put chance and necessity. The creationist–evolution debate has wrought havoc in American schools and communities for over eight decades with no let-up in sight. Disturbed by evolutionary claims that dinosaurs ruled the earth for thousands of years before humans evolved, which feature prominently at Disney world, creationists have even begun their own theme parks, which depict dinosaurs living on earth 6,000 years ago.[1] Darwinism may also have implications for our social–political culture, to the effect that our biological makeup may constrain our social experience. We shall never be the same again, for every generation after Darwin's work must come to terms with his prodigious undertaking, his shaking of the foundations of Western philosophy, sociology, and religion.

The idea of evolution was not new in Darwin's time. The pre-Socratic Greek philosopher Anaximander (ca. 610–546 B.C.E.) speculated that human beings arose from fish-like creatures in the sea. In the French Enlightenment, Maupertius, Diderot, and Lamarck set forth versions of evolution. Jean-Baptiste Pierre Lamarck (1744–1879) after whom the designation "Lamarckism" was coined, was the most notable, holding that acquired traits, such as the giraffe's long neck and a weightlifter's musculature, were passed on to their progeny. However, these versions were taken as mere thought-experiments and not a threat to faith and morals. Darwin's theory of natural selection was a threat, what Daniel Dennett calls his "dangerous idea" (See *Darwin's Dangerous Idea*, Penguin, 1996).

Shortly after the publication of *Origin of the Species*, a debate was held at Oxford University between Bishop Samuel Wilberforce and Darwin's disciple T. H. Huxley, on the thesis that humans evolved via natural selection from lower organisms, such as apes. When the future British prime minister Benjamin Disraeli, then at Oxford, heard the question "Is man an ape or an angel?" he responded "My Lord, I am on the side of the angels."

This debate over the origins of humanity has continued ever since. While Darwin's theory of evolution did not establish atheism, it made it possible to be a self-respecting atheist. Before Darwin, the orderliness of nature and its wonders, from the eye of a bird to the brain of a human, called for a grand designer who created the world. After Darwin, an alternative paradigm was available, evolution of species via chance and the inexorable laws of nature.

Charles Darwin (1809–1882) was born in Shrewsbury, England, the son of one of the most successful physicians in England and grandson of the great physician Erasmus Darwin. After his mother died, when Charles was 8, he was sent to a boarding school, where he was bored. In order to pass the time, he occupied himself with collecting insects, especially beetles. Eventually, he entered Cambridge University in order to prepare for the Anglican ministry. However, he was more interested in natural history (geography and biology) than theology and distinguished himself in the natural sciences. Upon graduation, his mentors recommended him for the post of unpaid naturalist aboard the HMS *Beagle,* a ship whose charge was to survey the east and west coasts of South America and which would circumnavigate the globe, a voyage that would last 5 years (1831–1836). It was while collecting and examining the exotic species in South America and on the Galapagos Islands that the idea of natural selection occurred to him.

When Darwin returned to England, he went to work writing up an account of his voyage but also writing up his notes on the theory of evolution and natural selection. Initially, he showed his writings to no one, least of all his beloved wife Emma, whose devout faith he deeply respected and did not wish to disturb. In 1838 he read Thomas Malthus' *Essay on the Principle of Population,* in which Malthus argued that population growth was always geometric while food supply increases arithmetically, so that weaker people would be culled in a struggle for survival. It suddenly dawned on Darwin that this was the way evolution worked, selecting those more suitable to survive in a general struggle for survival, thus gradually creating new species. He had found his mechanism for evolutionary development, natural selection under conditions of scarcity. He began to write up his theory but was reluctant to publish it; for one thing, he did not understand the mechanism in the organism by which change occurred, and for another, he feared his theory would have a deleterious effect on the public and disturb his devout wife Emma, causing religious doubt.

An event occurred that was to force Darwin's hand. A young biologist, Alfred Russell Wallace, sent Darwin an essay describing in marvelous detail the theory of natural selection which he had independently discovered. Darwin was shaken to the foundations by this essay, for it eloquently described his own theory. With the help of the prominent geologist Charles Lyell, both Wallace's and Darwin's articles on natural selection were published in 1858. Then, Darwin wrote his masterpiece, *Origin of the Species,* which was published the following year. The book immediately became a lightning rod of debate over evolutionary theory and changed the course of history.

Darwin's earthshaking discovery was his theory of natural selection in Malthusian situations of scarcity, thereby producing new species. Darwin assembled a large amount of circumstantial evidence to support his theory: the fossil record, showing gradual development from simple life forms to more complex ones; the homologous structure of life forms; vestigial organs, such as the appendix and tailbone; and geographical similarities (e.g., similar species dwell in proximity to one another). He also demonstrated how selective breeding of plants and animals resulted in better types. None of these arguments proved evolution, but they established a cumulative case for naturalistic evolution which seemed to explain the facts of life better than traditional creationist accounts of the world.

Darwin never knew the mechanism whereby natural selection takes place. Not until the revival of Gregor Mendel's theory of selective character traits, confirmed by William Bateson's work in the 1890s, the gradual falsification of Darwin's rival Lamarckism. Hugo De Vries' theory of genetic mutation in 1900, and Ronald Aylmer Fisher's comprehensive *Genetical Theory of Natural Selection* in 1930 was the mechanism identified. Hermann Muller in 1927 demonstrated artificial mutation produced by X-rays, showing that genes could be mutated by natural causes, thus leading to genetic variation on which natural selection could work. In 1954 James Watson and Francis Crick discovered the structure of DNA, the chemical substance of the gene, the ultimate constituents of heredity, which confirmed the genetic theory of natural selection.[2]

Darwinian Evolution

The theory held by Jews and Christians in the West (see chapter 1) was that God created the universe from nothing (*ex nihilo*) in 6 days, creating humanity on the sixth day. The Hebrew–Christian Bible (as well as the Muslim Koran) proclaims a special creation of the heavens and earth, plants and animals, as well as human beings, about 6,000 years ago (around 4,004 B.C.E.). The Scriptures maintain that God created two historical persons, Adam and Eve, from the dust of the earth and that all human beings are descendants of these two original persons.

Biological science holds, to the contrary, that there was no such special creation of each species, let alone one Adam and Eve, but that all life forms evolved during a long period of about 3 or 4 billion years. All life forms are the result of natural selection, consisting of an abundance of individuals, some of whom are better fitted to survive in their environment, and mutations which sometimes produce advantage relative to an environment.

Naturalist evolutionary theory holds four theses which are either questioned or rejected by creationists:

1. *The ancient earth thesis.* The universe is about 15 billion years old and the Earth, about 4.5 billion years old, not 6,000 as the biblical genealogical record, first calculated by Bishop James Ussher in the 17th century, indicates. Many biblical scholars argue that we ought not take this record literally.

2. *The common ancestry thesis.* Life originated from nonliving matter over 3 billion years ago in a single place. As Stephen Jay Gould puts it, there is "a tree of evolutionary descent linking all organisms by ties of genealogy."

3. *The progression thesis.* Life, once originated, has progressed from relatively simple to relatively complex forms, from unicellular life to multicellular life (such as coral and fish), culminating in the most complex animal, *Homo sapiens.*

4. *The naturalistic selection thesis.* Natural selection took place by a chance process of genetic replication of species striving to survive by adapting to their environment and in the process developing mutations which favored some members over others. This natural selective process has no need for a divine hand to guide it, though it does not rule out that possibility. Although the process of evolution has created highly complex organs like the eye and brain and highly complex animals like whales and human beings, it presumably did so without a conscious watchmaker. It was the work of a "Blind Watchmaker" (to use the title of Richard Dawkins' illuminating book).

The question is, Is Darwinian evolution true, or was there a special creation, as described by the writer of Genesis?

Evolutionists, though they cannot at present replicate cross-species evolution, do cite a panoply of evidence, including *(1)* the fossil record (showing the gradual succession of life forms and the progression of species, including transitional forms such as sea-dwelling tetrapods, throughout the geological record), *(2)* embryonic replication (ontogeny recapitulates phylogeny, i.e., the individual embryo has traits inherent to earlier life forms), *(3)* vestigial organs (e.g., it seems hard to explain the presence of the appendix in humans, except as part of a degenerating legacy from our ancestors who had a much coarser diet; humans have inhospitable wisdom teeth or third molars, which in other primates are as fully developed as the rest of their teeth; gills appear in human fetuses; and rudimentary wings appear in flightless birds), and *(4)* biochemical characteristics. There is a close similarity in biochemical and molecular characteristics among members of a related group. Thus, homologous forms of hemoglobin and cytochrome c occur in humans, apes, and monkeys. Such similarities occur not only in proteins but also at the more fundamental level of RNA and DNA. Even more impressive is that the most critical molecules in living systems, such as DNA, RNA, and ATP (adenosine triphosphate), most of the small molecules of intermediary metabolism, and many proteins, such as cytochrome, occur throughout the living world. This is why we can make bacteria produce human insulin—they have the same machinery used by humans to make this protein. The genetic code of chimpanzees is 98% identical to the human genetic code. Genetic mutations occur constantly, causing heritable variability, which eventually gives rise to new species.

This is the basic idea: humanity gradually evolved over time by natural selection through chance (genetic mutation) and necessity from less developed life forms. While individual points of evolutionary theory are challenged and the exact formulations qualified, the edifice as a whole has withstood the assaults of criticism for nearly 150 years.

Darwin's theory of evolution has caused the cultural uproar that he feared (in his diary he self-deprecatingly refers to himself as "the devil's chaplain"). Many people have been shocked by its radical naturalistic implications. George Bernard Shaw wrote, in *Back to Methusala* (1921), "If it could be proved that the whole universe had been produced by . . . selection, only fools and rascals could bear to live." Writers like Arthur Koestler fear that Darwinism promotes vapid materialism, which is destroying our respect for human life.[3] Disraeli's choice (mentioned above) of the angels over the apes has been echoed thousands of time over the past 150 years. Both the religious right and the political left (for different reasons) have been repulsed by Darwin's "dangerous idea": the religious because it makes God unnecessary; the egalitarian left because it suggests that our social proclivities are rigorously constrained by biology. The main opponents in the United States of America are the Christian creationists, who hold to the account in the biblical book of Genesis that God created humanity in His image by a dramatic fiat. They challenge Darwinism at every point.

While creationists accept *microevolution* (evolution within a species), they reject *macroevolution* (evolution across species). They argue that the evidence for transitional species is misleading and that "vestigial organs" really had species-specific functions, so, all things considered, it is more reasonable to hold that such organs as the eye and the human brain were created by God in a special act than that they simply evolved by natural selection. They also point out that the fossil record fails to turn up a missing link between the ape and the human and that it is incredible to suppose that such complex organs as the eye or human brain developed gradually over time. There was not enough time for such incredibly intricate processes. Finally, the creationists point out that scientists have not been able to create life, so it is more reasonable to believe that the creation of life is a special act of God.[4] Duane Gish of the Creation Science Research Institute argues that the evidence, when impartially considered, favors the theory of special creation over Darwinian evolution.[5] Gish argues that since evolutionary theory has not been proved and has a rival, creation science, both should be presented in schools. The evidence for evolution is weak. We have not found the missing link. He points to problems with the fossil record. Why don't we find fossils before the Cambrian age? he asks. To claim that the eye and brain came about through chance is simply incredible. He argues that both creationism and Darwinian evolution are religious outlooks, defining *religion* broadly as a total worldview. A response to the creationists is given by David Kline, who defends evolution as the only truly scientific theory, supported by biological and fossil evidence.[6] The human eye is not unique, nor without inbuilt defects, but continuous with eyes in other animals and less acute than that of the eagle or falcon.

Evolutionists argue that, firstly, the idea of a species is vague and fraught with problems so that the demarcation between species is not clear and, secondly, the hypothesis of evolution of species or kingdoms is still the best explanation, given all the evidence available. They point out that "creation science" is not really a science since it sets forth no experimental data and never confirms its hypothesis but merely cites religious authority.

Alvin Plantinga constructs an argument to the effect that if we accept the hypothesis that our cognitive faculties are reliable, then we ought not to accept evolutionary naturalism.[7] However, if theism is true, God did design our cognitive faculties to be reliable. The argument is as follows:

1. Naturalistic evolution caused us to develop our cognitive faculties in ways conducive to survival, not truth.
2. If naturalistic evolution is true, there is no reason to believe that our cognitive faculties are reliable.
3. If you have used your cognitive faculties to come to believe in evolutionary naturalism, you have a defeater* for the conclusion that evolutionary naturalism is true.
4. Therefore, you ought not believe that evolutionary naturalism is true.

Plantinga argues that, while methodological naturalism is plausible, metaphysical naturalism is incoherent; at least we are never justified in believing it. Methodological naturalism stipulates that scientific examination must confine itself to natural causes and not metaphysics, but metaphysical naturalism draws metaphysical conclusions about the findings of science. It speculates that there is no place for a providential God in the order of nature, that the best explanation for life on earth is mere evolutionary chance and the laws of nature.

While Plantinga's argument is a legitimate challenge to metaphysical naturalism, the naturalist response is that it is simplistic and overlooks the possibility that theoretical truth may be a by-product of evolutionary development. While evolution selects primarily for survival, part of the noetic equipment developed in that process, larger brains, gives us the ability to deliberate and assess evidence and may enable us to engage in metaphysical contemplation. Reason, both inductive and deductive, is a meme (see p. 214) which has developed over time and enables us to set forth hypotheses as to why given events occur. We can test these hypotheses, verifying or falsifying them. While only mathematical and logical processes can yield absolute certainty, our hypotheses can survive crucial experiments and thus win out as the best explanation available for the events in question. Just as Sherlock Holmes can assemble circumstantial evidence and infer the criminal's identity, so scientists can assemble circumstantial evidence and infer a Darwinian naturalist hypothesis. Darwinian evolution, it is alleged, has survived systematic criticism, so it stands as the best explanation of how humanity originated.

On the other hand, theist evolutionists exist. Christian thinkers like Ernan McMullen of the University of Notre Dame, Langdon Gilkey, John Hick, and most notably, the Jesuit evolutionary paleontologist and priest, Teilhard de Chardin argue that God used evolution to create humanity. Hick and Chardin argue that humanity is still evolving toward perfection, toward an Omega point, where it will be fit for the Kingdom of God.[8]

---

*A defeater is a cogent reason for rejecting a theory or idea.

Evolution and Evil

Darwin himself, though trained as a clergyman, was deeply troubled by the problem of evil, which caused him to doubt his faith and eventually, but reluctantly, give up belief in God. His theory of natural selection can be seen as undermining theistic explanations with regard to evil. Evolution holds that evil is not the result of Satan's sin, Adam's Fall, or human misuse of free will but, rather, the consequence of the species developing adaptive strategies which tend to be accompanied by pain, suffering, unhappiness, and conflicts of interest, the major categories of evil. It is our evolution from nonsentient to sentient beings that enables us to experience pain. Pain serves as a warning mechanism, but extreme contingencies can trigger the capacity for no protective reason. The sensation of pain may cause us to withdraw our hand from a fire, but being immolated in a burning building serves no warning purpose at all and seems entirely gratuitous. Much of our physical suffering is simply the failure of evolution's adaptive strategies. For example, *bipedalism* (the ability to walk upright on two limbs) enables "higher" primates, including humans, to free up their forelimbs for other purposes, like grasping and thrusting; but it incurs several liabilities, including loss of the speed of its quadripedal ancestors and an increased likelihood of lower back pain, troublesome birth difficulties, and even stomach problems and herniation as the center of balance shifts and more pressure is placed on the abdominal region. Sickle-shaped red blood cells are adaptive in areas where malaria is rampant, but where it is not, they may be lethal: children born with sickle-cell anemia have only one-fifth the chance of children with normal cells of surviving to maturity. Similarly, human aggressivity may be adaptive in hunting and defending one's self against predators; but in social groups, in the face of conflicts of interest, it tends to be maladaptive, causing suffering, injury, and death. The use of reason is necessary for social cooperation and coexistence, but the instincts of our ancestor species are more reliable and efficient. Reason leads to institutions like morality and law, necessary for civilization; but these create their own liabilities in terms of guilt, shame, litigation, and frustration. No lion deliberates as to whether it should kill an antelope or copulate with an available lioness, nor are its forays followed by guilt or remorse. It enjoys its conquests without worrying about whether it has violated antelope rights. A lion simply follows its instincts and usually gets away with it; no police officer arrests it for violating the antelope's right to life.

The point is not that we should go back to the state of the *noble savage* (the primitive human who is innocent of evil), if such a being ever existed.[9] We cannot, even if we tried. The point is that each evolutionary adaptive strategy tends to incur a loss of some other virtue or capability, and this is what accounts for evil. What we call "moral evil" is simply part of the natural evolutionary process. Much, if not most, of moral or human-made evil is the "unintended" result of nature's making us creatures with insatiable wants but limited resources and sympathies (Tennyson called it "The Nature red in tooth and claw").[10]

This evolutionary account of the origins of evil fits within the broader framework of human biology and animal ethology. To that extent, it is confirmable by scientific research, whereas the religious accounts of the origin of evil have less impressive credentials. How do we recreate or confirm the record of the Fall of Adam and Eve? The naturalistic account holds that we do not need myths or dogmas about the Fall or original sin. Simply investigating evolutionary processes of adaptation is sufficient as an explanation for our greatest problems. Evil has a biological basis, being simply the inextricable comcomitant of characteristics that served (and still serve) an adaptive function.

Theists respond to this account of evil by either rejecting evolution in favor of a creationist account or absorbing the evolutionary account into a theistic framework. The first strategy seems a lost cause since evolution is supported by all we know about animal biology and genetics. The second strategy is more promising but haunted by problems of explaining why God was not more efficient and benevolent in developing the species. Couldn't he have avoided the waste (sacrificing the millions of less fit individuals and species) and done things more benevolently (e.g., made carnivorous animals herbivores and so avoided the predator–prey cycle of death and destruction)?

So the problem of evil persists in haunting theism, and theists continue to devise strategies to ward off the attacks. On which side do the best reasons lie?

Social Darwinism and Sociobiology

Darwin's doctrine places a great deal of weight on our biological origins as determining, or at least significantly influencing, who and what we are. Diametrically opposed to the existentialist philosophy of Sartre (see chapter 12), which holds that there is no human nature as such but we are free to invent ourselves, Darwinian thought emphasizes the thesis that our genetic makeup has evolved for millions of years, producing an essential nature and thereby severely constraining our behavioral options. There is no obvious place for freedom of the will. If human beings are the product of heredity and environmental conditioning, evolutionary theory puts the emphasis on the heredity factor. Most psychometricians today put the ratio of heredity to environment at between 6:4 and 7:3.[11]

In the 19th and early 20th centuries, Darwinian thought, supplemented by Herbert Spencer's notion of survival of the fittest, was used to justify *laissez-faire* economics, neglect of the poor, eugenics, racism, and imperialism. Called "social Darwinism," it reasoned that because nature's way was ruthless exploitation of the weak by the strong, we ought to condone the exploitation of weaker people by stronger, smarter ones, whether through ruthless capitalism or expansive colonialism. Nature's way is for the stronger and smarter to dominate the weak and stupid. Spencer put it this way,

> Unpitying as it looks, it is better to let the foolish man suffer the appointed penalty of his foolishness. For the pain—he must bear it as well as he can; for the experience—he must treasure it up, and act more rationally in the future. To others as well as to himself will his case be a warning. And by multiplication of such warnings,

there cannot fail to be generated in all men a caution corresponding to the danger to be shunned.[12]

Social Darwinism, although it may have contained some truth (that life is not fair and that we must pay for our foolish judgments), seems simplistic and self-serving today, for it pays insufficient attention to other human traits, such as sympathy, autonomy, environmental input, and the possibility of cultural improvement. Darwin noted that, from an evolutionary point of view, it is better that the strong and intelligent survive over the weak and stupid; the infirm or stupid should be sterilized so that their genes are not passed on. However, he recognized that compassion is a high value, which would militate against this evolutionary ruthlessness. Darwin, then, was not a full social darwinist. He argued that morality arises out of animal needs and behavior patterns but that it takes on a dynamic life of its own, hopefully resulting in an expanding circle, encompassing all creatures everywhere on earth.

> As man advances in civilization, and small tribes are united into larger communities, the simplest reason would tell each individual that he ought to extend his social instincts and sympathies to all the members of the same nation, though personally unknown to him. This point being once reached, there is only an artificial barrier to prevent his sympathies extending to the men of all nations and races. If, indeed, such men are separated from him by greater differences in appearance or habits, experience unfortunately shows us how long it is, before we look at them as our fellow-creatures. Sympathy beyond the confines of man, that is, humanity to the lower animals, seems to be one of the latest acquisitions. It is apparently unfelt by savages, except towards their pets. How little the old Romans knew of it is shown by their abhorrent gladiatorial exhibition. The very idea of humanity, as far as I could observe, was new to most of the Gauchos of the Pampas. This virtue, one of the noblest with which man is endowed, seems to arise incidentally from our sympathies becoming more tender and more widely diffused, until they are extended to all sentient beings. As soon as the virtue is honored and practiced by some few men, it spreads through instruction and example to the young, and eventually becomes incorporated in public opinion.[13]

A more sophisticated theory, holding to some of the same premises as social Darwinism, is sociobiology, first put forward by Edward O. Wilson in *Sociobiology: The New Synthesis* in 1975 and then in his more popular book *On Human Nature* in 1978. He begins the first book with a comparison of his theory with Camus' existentialism (see chapter 12).

> Camus said that the only serious philosophical question is suicide. That is wrong even in the strict sense intended. The biologist, who is concerned with questions of physiology and evolutionary history, realizes that self-knowledge is constrained and shaped by the emotional control centers in the hypothalamus and limbic system of the brain. These centers flood our consciousness with all the emotions—hate, love, guilt, fear, and others—that are consulted by ethical philosophers who wish to

intuit the standards of good and evil. What, we are then compelled to ask, made the hypothalamus and limbic system? They evolved by natural selection. That simple biological statement must be pursued to explain ethics and ethical philosophers, if not epistemology and epistemologists, at all depths. Self-existence, or the suicide that terminates it, is not the central question of philosophy.[14]

Natural selection, not existential choice, was the driving force of our personal and social existence. Ethics must recognize a set of givens rather than try to deny our biological determinants. The reaction by philosophers was swift and negative. Wilson, they claimed, had simply repeated the naturalistic fallacy that one cannot derive value statements from purely factual ones. However, gradually, many philosophers came to find some plausibility, if not cogency, in Wilson's contention.

The sociologist James Q. Wilson developed the sociobiological point that humans have a biologically based innate moral sense:

> If man is infinitely malleable, he is as much at risk from the various despotisms of this world as he would be if he were entirely shaped by some biochemical process. The anthropologist Robin Fox has put the matter well: "If, indeed, everything is learned, then surely men can be taught to live in any kind of society. Man is at the mercy of all the tyrants . . . who think they know what is best for him. And how can he plead that they are being inhuman if he doesn't know what being human is in the first place?" Despots are quite prepared to use whatever technology will enable them to dominate mankind; if science tells them that biology is nothing and environment everything, then they will put aside their eugenic surgery and selective breeding programs and take up instead the weapons of propaganda, mass advertising, and educational indoctrination. The Nazis left nothing to chance; they used all methods.
>
> Mankind's moral sense is not a strong beacon light, radiating outward to illuminate in sharp outline all that it touches. It is, rather, a small candle flame, casting vague and multiple shadows, flickering and sputtering in the strong winds of power and passion, greed and ideology. But brought close to the heart and cupped in one's hands, it dispels the darkness and warms the soul.[15]

The sociobiological thesis states that morality is the product of evolution and should be understood as a component of biology, making up the new field of sociobiology, the evolutionary emergence of social norms. Evolution explains not only our development as bipedal, big-brained mammals with opposable thumbs but also our social behavior, why males dominate females, why mothers nurture their offspring, as well as why we have an abhorrence for incest and infanticide. These tendencies have been favored by natural selection because, for example, mothers who so act would be more likely to rear their offspring to maturity and pass on their genes than those who neglected or killed their progeny; likewise, an abhorrence of incest would tend to protect offspring from disabilities that could be passed down by inbreeding, thus threatening genetic survival. Sociobiology rejects the androgynous model (that males and females are really similar except for reproductive functions), held by some feminists. It holds that not only do males and females play different roles but these roles generate different temperaments. Because women are limited in the number of children they can have, they tend to be more selective in their choice of sexual partners. Men, having billions of sperm, can potentially father thousands of children. Since attaining high status gives them more access to women, they are more likely to be status seekers than women. The fact that there are more male than female corporate executives is attributable to this feature.

Sociobiology asserts that our behavior is biologically influenced and, in some cases, even determined, so ethical principles and moral theory are little more than rationalizations of genetic programming. The fact that we are largely ignorant of this programming does not lessen their force. As Jonathan Harrison notes,

> Human beings no more need a rational appreciation of the advantages of morality in order to have it than birds need a rational appreciation of having wings in order to fly. People do not disapprove of incest for the conscious reason that it increases the probability of their producing deformed children or even for the reason that it would lead to the break up of the family. Although these would be good reasons for disapproving of it, most people do not know it has these tendencies. They disapprove of incest simply because they have been born to develop such a belief on attaining a certain age or with an innate tendency unreflectingly to copy other people's belief, produced for whatever reasons, however trivial, that incest is wrong.[16]

The foremost defender of sociobiology today is Richard Dawkins, who, in a series of books, the most prominent being *The Selfish Gene*,[17] puts forth the thesis that it is the gene, not the individual or group, that is the primary unit of natural selection, with the individual functioning as the vehicle for passing on the gene. Individuals live and die, but the gene carries on indefinitely. Consider this example. When a bird sees a hawk overhead, it will usually give an alarm call, warning its flock-mates of the danger of the predator. This instinctive "altruistic" behavior, while it enables the flock-mates to flee, decreases its own survival chances by calling attention to itself. Traditional Darwinian theory places the emphasis on the survival of the individual, but the selfish gene theory puts the emphasis on the gene. Since the flock-mates are likely to have the same genes as the alarm-sounding bird, including the gene for raising warning signals, the altruistic bird is actually indirectly enhancing the survival chances of its own genes. Conversely, birds without this alarm-sounding behavior would lessen the prospects for passing on their genes. Thus, altruism and egoism turn out to be compatible in this theory.

We are gene machines, but we are complicated gene machines, ones that have developed big brains, which in turn have created non-genetic replicators that Dawkins labels *memes*.* *Memes* are cultural artifacts—beliefs, ideas, theories, institutions, practices, reasoning patterns, fashions, and behavioral patterns—which may be transmitted through time and place. A language is an example of a meme.

---

*The *Oxford English Dictionary* defines *meme* as an element of a culture that may be considered to be passed on by non-genetic means, esp. imitation.

Once invented, it takes on a life of its own, grows, replicates, and embeds itself into the larger culture. Market exchange is an example of a meme which takes on a distinct life of its own, replicating wherever possible. Religion is another meme, an invention which is taken as reality and passed on from generation to generation. Memes tend to enhance the quality of our lives, working for the survival of individuals, but they sometimes get in the way of the gene's destiny. For example, contraceptive devices are memes that interfere with genetic transmission, and modern medicine is a set of memes that alter the evolutionary process, keeping alive those who would perish in a more primitive environment. A religious meme may enslave a person, causing him or her to live ascetically, say as a monk or nun, so that he or she fails to pass on his or her genes; or it may turn him or her into a suicide bomber in the belief that he or she will thereby earn a place in heaven. Thus, culture swamps nature and memes trump their originators, genes.

Memes are part of the construction of social reality. Certain facts are objectively true because people believe they are and act accordingly. For example, money does not exist in nature and is functional only because we all accept it. Checks are once-removed memes from money, and credit cards are even further removed from nature. Yet, all these inventions are basic to our social life. Similar statements can be made for our political institutions. Enough people are ready to obey laws and pay taxes so that the few outliers can be caught and punished. The U.S. Constitution, the fact that George W. Bush is the 43rd president of the United States, and the fact that the New England Patriots won the Super Bowl in 2004 are social facts which exist within a context of institutional memes.[18]

Not everyone accepts the idea of memes. They have been criticized for having insufficient copying fidelity, not being the kind of physical entity that can be replicated, and being vague on just how large or small a unit must be to deserve the name *meme.* The response to these charges is that one should not take the idea too rigidly but as a metaphor for cultural phenomena that can be passed on across generations and cultures.[19]

In a cautious, critical response to sociobiology, Elliott Sober argues that while evolutionary theory can contribute to an explanation of ethics, it has limited value in justifying our ethical principles.[20] Ethics has an autonomy of its own that evolutionary ethicists like E. O. Wilson, Richard Dawkins, and Michael Ruse fail to take adequately into consideration. The most passionate attack on sociobiology is R. C. Lewontin, Steven Rose, and Leon Kamin's book *Not in Our Genes,* in which they systematically assault genetic determinism and the related thesis that different races have different average intelligence.[21] Defending a socialist outlook on the world, they argue that sociobiological theory is really an arm of right-wing politics. Human beings are vastly more plastic than the sociobiologists aver, they argue, emphasizing environmental conditioning as the dominant cause for human inequality and difference. Wilson, Dawkins, and Steven Pinker have denied the charge of being genetic determinists and politically right-winged but have defended a strong relationship between genetics and human differences, while admitting that there is much all human beings have in common.[22]

Perhaps the most heated debate on the implications of sociobiology has to do with social engineering and the apparent differences in ability of different racial, ethnic, and gender groups. Scores on standard tests with regard to cognitive skills show significant average differences between groups. The average white and Asian scores 195 points higher on the SAT than the average black, and on virtually all IQ tests for the past seven or eight decades, the average black IQ is 85 as opposed to the average white and Asian IQ of over 100. Sociobiological proponents like Richard Herrnstein, Charles Murray, Arthur Jensen, and Michael Levin argue that these scores show significant differences in cognitive ability between races, so social engineering programs like a affirmative action are little more than procrustean manipulations which harm those of higher abilities.[23] Opponents like Lewontin, Rose, Kamin, and Gould argue that environmental factors are making the difference here, not native ability, and that our standardized tests do not accurately measure native ability.[24] The controversy tends to produce more heat than light, so many universities have prohibited research or discussion on the subject. On many campuses, it is politically incorrect to discuss such matters. Whatever the truth of the matter, the incendiary discussions over the issue demonstrate how divisive the possible implications of Darwin's dangerous idea can be.

In response to critics of sociobiology, Dawkins argues that his theory supports a wider view of evolutionary morality than his critics suppose, one that supports the rationality of moral principles. The selfish gene is not altogether selfish but gives rise to reciprocal altruism. This leads us to the prospect of an evolutionary morality.

The Darwinian sociobiological theory regarding human personality emphasizes the dominance of heredity over environment. Our genetic endowment is more important than our upbringing. For example, Steven Pinker argues that criminality is more a result of genetic makeup than poor environment.[25] Twin studies support these conclusions. Identical twins, even those raised apart, have very similar personalities, far more similar than siblings or "virtual twins" (unrelated siblings raised together).

> Identical twins think and feel in such similar ways that they sometimes suspect that they are linked by telepathy. When separated at birth and reunited as adults, they say they feel they have known each other all their lives. Testing confirms that identical twins, whether separated at birth or not, are eerily alike (though far from identical) in just about any trait one can measure. They are similar in verbal, mathematical, and general intelligence, in their degree of life satisfaction, and in personality traits such as introversion, agreeableness, neuroticism, conscientiousness, and openness to experience. They have similar attitudes toward controversial subjects such as the death penalty, religion, and modern music. They resemble each other not just in paper-and-pencil tests but in consequential behavior such as gambling, divorcing, committing crimes, getting into accidents and watching television. And they boast dozens of shared idiosyncrasies such as giggling incessantly, giving interminable answers to simple questions, dipping buttered toast in coffee, and—in the case of Abigail van Buren and Ann Landers—writing indistinguishable syndicated advice columns. The crags and valleys of their electroencephalograms (brain

waves) are as alike as those of a single person recorded on two occasions, and the wrinkles of their brains and distribution of gray matter across cortical areas are also similar.[26]

Opponents argue that one contributing reason identical twins are so similar is that they are typically raised in similar environments.

However, the evidence seems to be in the direction of a strong genetic component in personality development. The Minnesota Twin Studies, started in 1979 and led by Thomas J. Bouchard, indicate that about 70% of the variance in IQ is associated with genetic variation. Among *monozygotic* (identical) twins, remarkable similarities were found. Two 39-year-old British housewives raised apart were each found to have manicured hands and to wear seven rings and two bracelets on one wrist and a watch and a bracelet on the other. Two monozygotic men with very different upbringings had authoritarian personalities. Two others had similar endogenous depressions, and another pair had identical patterns of headache (a combination of tension headache and migraine). Another pair went into law enforcement, vacationed in Florida, and drove a Chevrolet. Another pair married and divorced women named Linda and then married women named Betty. One named his son James Allen and the other James Alan; they had identical smoking and drinking patterns and chewed their fingernails to the nubs. However, Bouchard and his colleagues are quick to point out that environment is also important. Like an acorn planted in a desert, without a suitable environment one's highest potential will not be reached, no matter how great the genetic endowment.[27]

Evolution and Ethics

Morality—that is, successful morality—can be seen as an evolutionary strategy for gene replication. Here is Dawkins' example in *The selfish bird*: birds are afflicted with life-endangering parasites. Because they lack limbs to enable them to pick the parasites off their heads, they—like much of the animal kingdom—depend on the ritual of mutual grooming. It turns out that nature has evolved two basic types of birds in this regard: those disposed to groom any other bird (the nonprejudiced type?) and those that refuse to groom others but present themselves for grooming. The former type of bird Dawkins calls "suckers" and the latter, "cheaters."

In a geographical area containing harmful parasites and where there are only suckers and cheaters, suckers will do fairly well but cheaters will not survive for want of cooperation. However, in a sucker population in which a mutant cheater arises, the cheater will prosper and the cheater gene type will multiply. As the suckers are exploited, they will gradually die out; but if and when they become too few to groom the cheaters, the cheaters will start to die off too and eventually become extinct.

Why don't birds all die off? Somehow, via a mutation, nature has come up with a third type, call them "grudgers." Grudgers groom all and only those that reciprocate in grooming them. They groom each other and suckers but not cheaters. In fact, once caught, a cheater is marked forever. There is no forgiveness. It turns out then that, unless there are a lot of suckers around, cheaters have a hard time of it, harder even than suckers. However, it is the grudgers that prosper. Unlike suckers, they do not waste time helping unappreciative cheaters, so they are not exploited and have ample energy to gather food and build better nests for their loved ones.

One of Dawkins' fellow atheist defenders, J. L. Mackie, argues that the real name for suckers is "Christian," one who believes in complete altruism, even turning the other cheek to one's assailant and loving one's enemy. Cheaters are ruthless egoists who can survive only if there are enough naive altruists around. Whereas grudgers are reciprocal altruists who have a rational morality based on cooperative self-interest, suckers, such as Socrates and Jesus, advocate "turning the other cheek and repaying evil with good." Instead of a Rule of Reciprocity ("I'll scratch your back if you'll scratch mine"), the extreme altruist substitutes the Golden Rule ("If you want the other fellow to scratch your back, you scratch his— even if he won't reciprocate").[28]

The moral of the story is this: altruist morality (so interpreted) is only rational given the payoff of eternal life (with a scorekeeper, as Woody Allen says). Take that away, and it looks like a sucker system. What replaces the "Christian" vision of submission and saintliness is the reciprocal altruist with a tit-for-tat morality, someone who is willing to share with those willing to cooperate.

In a recent groundbreaking work in evolution and psychology, Elliott Sober and David Sloan Wilson illustrate this point about reciprocal altruism via the system of distributing socially beneficial rewards and punishments. They take the case of the hunter, who spends an enormous amount of time hunting at great risk to himself but distributes food to all of the group, hunters and non-hunters alike. This seemingly altruistic, group-enhancing behavior is rewarded by the group:

> It turns out that women think that good hunters are sexy and have more children with them, both in and out of marriage. Good hunters also enjoy a high status among men, which leads to additional benefits. Finally, individuals do not share meat the way Mr. Rogers and Barney, and Dinosaur would, out of the goodness of their heart. Refusing to share is a serious breach of etiquette that provokes punishment. In this way sharing merges with taking. These new discoveries make you feel better, because the apparently altruistic behavior of sharing meat that would have been difficult to explain now seems to fit comfortably within the framework of individual selection theory.[29]

So, while sharing the spoils of hunting might at first sight appear to be an example of pure altruism, the rule of reciprocity comes into play, rewarding the hunter for his sacrifice and contribution to the group. Sober and Wilson call activities like hunting, which increase the relative fitness of the hunter, "primary behavior" and the rewards and punishment that others confer on the hunters "secondary behavior." "By itself, the primary behavior increases the fitness of the group and decreases the relative fitness of the hunters within the group. But the secondary behaviors offset the sacrifice and promote altruistic behavior, so that they may be called the amplification of altruism."[30]

This primitive notion of reciprocity seems to be necessary in a world like ours. One good deed deserves another (and *mutatis mutandis* with bad deeds). Reciprocity is the basis of desert—good deeds should be rewarded and bad deeds punished. We are grateful for favors rendered and, thereby have an impulse to return them; we resent harmful deeds and seek to pay the culprit back in kind ("an eye for an eye, a tooth for a tooth, a life for a life"). Put summarily, positive desert is gratitude universalized and punishment (negative desert) is resentment over harmful deeds universalized.

To be sure, there is a difference between high altruism and reciprocal altruism, which may simply be enlightened self-interest. The lesson to be drawn is that we should provide moral training so that children grow up to be spontaneously altruistic in a society which rewards such socially useful behavior. In this way, what is legitimate about egoism can be merged with altruism in a manner that produces deep individual flourishing.

Mackie may caricature the position of the religious altruist, but he misses the subtleties of wisdom involved (Jesus said "Be as wise as serpents but as harmless as doves" Mt. 10:16). Nevertheless, he does remind us that there is a difference between core morality and complete altruism. We have duties to cooperate and reciprocate but no duty to serve those who manipulate us, nor an obvious duty to sacrifice ourselves for people outside our domain of special responsibility. As we have noted, Darwin wrote of the expanding circle of our concern. We have a special duty of high altruism toward those in the close circle of our concern, namely, our family and friends. However, we have a duty to expand the circle of our moral concerns, wider and wider, eventually reaching all humanity, and even the animal kingdom.[31]

Sociobiologists may point to the fact that there is a basic common universal human nature, so the principle of reciprocity supplemented by rules of thumb like the Golden Rule (perhaps formalized in Kant's categorical imperative) will yield a common set of moral rules transcending specific cultures.

Summary

Toward the end of chapter 1 on the Hebrew–Christian (biblical) view of human nature, we noted the paradigmatic idea of the Great Chain of Being, which provided a cosmic map by which to steer our lives, a spiritual navigational tool which gave meaning to life from the biblical times until the modern times. The Copernican revolution first disrupted the chain and displaced humans from the pedestal in the center of the universe and put them in a sideshow on a minor planet orbiting around an average star in the midst of a minor galaxy. Darwin's revolution was an even more dangerous idea, challenging the entire paradigm by disrupting our picture of humanity as being created in the image of God, "a little lower than the angels," reducing it to the status of an animal, more like a chimpanzee than the angel Gabriel. We can appreciate Benjamin Disraeli's exclamation, "My Lord, I am on the side of the angels." Darwinism does seem to devalue our currency. It has offered an alternative paradigm to our understanding of human nature and our relationship to the universe. Chance and necessity have replaced God as the dominant concepts informing our public worldview. This paradigm shift has fed into the idea of the separation of church and state so that religious concepts have been pushed to the fringes of social life, into the private domain. The religious right recognizes how dangerous Darwin's ideas are and has opposed them at every point. Alvin Plantinga's self-refutation argument is the most sophisticated philosophical attack on them. Liberal religious theologians like Teilhard de Chardin have sought to come to terms with these dangerous ideas, developing such ideas as theistic evolution: God used evolution as his medium for creating humanity. However, many Darwinians, like Dawkins and Dennett, allege that it may not be possible to carry through such a reconciliation. The Great Chain of Being is broken, and there is no hope of reassembling the pieces.

While the religious right wing attacks the evolutionary view of human nature because of its threat to religion, the left wing attacks it (or some of its manifestations) because of its political implications. If biology is destiny, then our attempts at producing a socialist utopia or egalitarian society may be counterproductive or even impossible. If sociobiology is the correct interpretation, we must learn to live with some social inequalities. On the other hand, biology has endowed us with large, resourceful brains, which can enable us to construct a more just, peaceful society.

The work of evolutionists like Richard Dawkins and David Sloan Wilson, in reconciling genes with memes and egoism with reciprocal altruism, may provide a broad basis for a universal morality based on our common human nature.

Sociobiology offers exciting prospects for greater human understanding, which will bring moral challenges of their own. The Human Genome Project opens the possibility for detailed understanding of how our physical and psychological natures work. If this works out, we will have to decide to what extent we want to engage in genetic engineering and even eugenics. The challenges brought by Darwin's dangerous idea are mind-boggling. We must cautiously hope for the best. With this in mind, let us close with the concluding paragraph from Darwin's *Origin of the Species*.

> It is interesting to contemplate a tangled bank, clothed with many plants of many kinds, with birds singing on the bushes, with various insects flitting about, and with worms crawling through the damp earth, and to reflect that these elaborately constructed forms, so different from each other, and dependent upon each other in so complex a manner, have all been produced by laws acting around us. These laws, taken in the largest sense, being Growth with reproduction; Inheritance which is almost implied by reproduction; Variability from the indirect and direct action of the conditions of life, and from use and disuse; a Ratio of Increase so high as to lead to a Struggle for Life, and as a consequence to Natural Selection, entailing Divergence of Character and the Extinction of less improved forms. Thus, from the war

of nature, from famine and death, the most exalted object which we are capable of conceiving, namely, the production of the higher animals, directly follows. There is grandeur in this view of life, with its several powers, having been originally breathed by the Creator into a few forms or into one; and that, whilst this planet has gone circling on according to the fixed law of gravity, from so simple a beginning endless forms most beautiful and most wonderful have been, and are being evolved.[32]

Study Questions

1. What are the main features of Darwinian evolutionary theory?

2. What is the evidence for Darwinian evolution? Do you think macrolevel evolution is a fact or just a hypothesis? Explain your answer.

3. What is Plantinga's self-refuting argument against believing in evolution? How cogent is it?

4. How does evolutionary theory deal with the perennial problem of evil? Is it a more plausible explanation of evil than the religious explanations?

5. Why are Darwin's ideas seen as dangerous to both the political and religious right and left?

6. What is sociobiology? What are its strengths and weaknesses?

7. Darwin thought that humanity was still evolving, but he was a pessimist about our ultimate prospects. He wrote:

   Believing as I do that man in the distant future will be a far more perfect creature than he now is, it is an intolerable thought that he and all other sentient beings are doomed to complete annihilation after such long-continued slow progress.[33]

   Evaluate this thesis.

Notes

1. Abby Goodnough, "Darwin-Free Fun for Creationists," *New York Times* (May 1, 2004).
2. James Watson, *The Double Helix* (Penguin, 1969).
3. Arthur Koestler, *The Ghost and the Machine* trans. Daphene Hardy (Penguin, 1969).
4. Evolutionary biologists like John Jagger of the University of Texas at Dallas (personal correspondence, May 20, 2004) point out that we have created viruses and believe that biologists will soon create simple cell life forms.
5. Duane Gish, "Creation–Evolution" (Impact Article 4), reprinted in ed. L. Pojman, *Philosophy of Religion: An Anthology* (Wadsworth, 2003).
6. David Kline, "Theories, Facts and Gods: Philosophical Aspects of the Creation–Evolution Controversy," in *Did the Devil Make Darwin Do It?* ed. D. B. Wilson (Iowa State University Press, 1983).

7. Alvin Plantinga, *Warranted Christian Belief* (Oxford University Press, 2000), esp. pp. 227–240 and "The Christian Argument Against Evolutionary Naturalism," in ed. L. Pojman, *Philosophy of Religion: An Anthology.*

8. Teilhard de Chardin, *The Phenomenon of Man* (Harper & Row, 1955); Langdon Gilkey, "Darwin and Christian Thought," *Christian Century* (1960); and Nancy Murphy, *Theology in the Age of Scientific Reasoning* (Cornell University Press, 1990).

9. The idea of the noble savage first appears in John Dryden's *The Conquest of Granada* (1670):

> *I am as free as Nature first made man,*
> *Ere the base laws of servitude began,*
> *When wild in woods the noble savage ran.*

   The idea was made famous by Jean-Jacques Rousseau, who developed a romantic philosophy of humanity in the primitive state being good but corrupted by society.

10. Alfred Lord Tennyson, "In Memoriam A.H.H." (http://www.photoaspects.com/chesil/tennyson/memoriam4.html), LVI, lines 13–16. The poem was written between 1849–1850 and first published in 1869.

11. See T. Bouchard, "Genes, Environment, and Personality," *Science* (1994); and Michael Levin, *Why Race Matters* (Praeger, 1997), pp. 96ff.

12. Herbert Spencer, *Social Statics: or the Conditions Essential to Human Happiness Specified* (Chapman, 1851), p. 378.

13. Charles Darwin, *The Descent of Man* (Prometheus Books, 1998), chapter 3.

14. E. O. Wilson, *Sociobiology: The New Synthesis* (Harvard University Press, 1975), p. 3.

15. James Q. Wilson, *The Moral Sense* (Free Press, 1993), pp. 250–251.

16. Jonathan Harrison, *Challenges to Morality* (Macmillan, 1993), p. 27.

17. Richard Dawkins, *The Selfish Gene* (Oxford University Press, 1976).

18. See John Searle, *The Construction of Social Reality* (Free Press, 1995), for an excellent discussion of the construction of social facts, not to be confused with the social construction of reality.

19. See Richard Dawkins' foreword in Susan Blackmore's *The Meme Machine* (Oxford University Press, 1999), as well as Blackmore's discussion throughout her book. Some people have inferred from this claim that memes are not true. This is incorrect. The cultural artifacts they stand for are part of our social reality, but they may not have an independent ontological existence apart from our conventions.

20. Elliott Sober, "A Prospect for an Evolutionary Ethics," in ed. L. Pojman, *Ethical Theory* (Wadsworth, 2002).

21. R. C. Lewontin, Steven Rose, and Leon Kamin, *Not in Our Genes* (Penguin, 1984). In another attack on E. O. Wilson, "Against Sociobiology," *New York Review of Books* (1975), p. 22, E. Allen, Lewontin, Stephen Jay Gould, and others accuse the sociobiologists of seeking to preserve the status quo and compare their ideas to those that led to the "gas chambers of Nazi Germany."

22. See Steven Pinker, *The Blank Slate* (Viking, 2002), chapters 6 and 7, for a comprehensive discussion of this matter.

23. See Richard Herrnstein and Charles Murray, *The Bell Curve* (Free Press, 1994), esp. chapters 13 and 14; and Michael Levin, *Why Race Matters* (Praeger, 1997).

24. See Lewontin, et al., op. cit.; and Stephen Jay Gould, *The Mismeasure of Man* (Norton, 1981).

25. Steven Pinker, op. cit., pp. 50 ff, 176f. "Study after study has shown that a willingness to commit antisocial acts, including lying, stealing, starting fights, and destroying property, is partly heritable (though like all heritable traits it is exercised more in some environments than in others."

26. Steven Pinker, op. cit., p. 47.

27. Constance Holden, "Identical Twins Reared Apart," *Science,* vol. 207 (March 1980); Thomas J. Bouchard, et al., "Sources of Human Psychological Differences: The Minnesota Study of Twins Reared Apart," *Science* (12 October 1990).

28. J. L. Mackie, "The Law of the Jungle: Evolution and Morality," *Philosophy,* vol. 53 (1978). My own view is that we either are hard-wired for reciprocity or learn it very early in our psycho-social development.

29. Elliott Sober and David Sloan Wilson, *Unto Others: The Evolution and Psychology of Unselfish Behavior* (Harvard University Press, 1998), pp. 142–143.

30. Ibid.

31. Charles Darwin, *The Descent of Man* (Prometheus Books, 1998), chapter 3.

32. Charles Darwin, *Origin of the Species* (John Murray, 1859), chapter 16.

33. Charles Darwin, *The Autobiography of Charles Darwin,* ed. Nora Barlow (Collins, 1958), p. 92.

For Further Reading

Behe, Michael, *Darwin's Black Box* (Simon & Schuster, 1996).

Blackmore, Susan, *The Gene Machine* (Oxford University Press, 1999).

Bowler, Peter, *Evolution: The History of an Idea* (University of California Press, 1984).

Darwin, Charles, *Origin of the Species* (Harvard University Press, 1964).

———, *Descent of Man* (Prometheus Books, 1998).

Dawkins, Richard, *The Selfish Gene* (Oxford University Press, 1976).

Dennett, Daniel, *Darwin's Dangerous Idea* (Simon & Schuster, 1995).

Gould, Stephen Jay, *The Mismeasure of Man* (Norton, 1981).

———, *Wonderful Life* (Norton, 1989).

Harrison, Jonathan, *Challenges to Morality* (Macmillan, 1993).

Herrnstein, Richard, and Charles Murray, *The Bell Curve* (Free Press, 1994), especially chapters 13 and 14.

Kitcher, Philip, *Vaulting Ambition: Sociobiology and the Quest for Human Nature* (MIT Press, 1985).

Levin, Michael, *Why Race Matters* (Praeger, 1997).

Lewontin, R.C., Steven Rose, and Leon Kamin, *Not in Our Genes* (Penguin, 1984).

Mayr, Ernest, *One Long Argument: Charles Darwin and the Genesis of Modern Evolutionary Thought* (Harvard University Press, 1991).

Pinker, Steven, *The Blank Slate* (Free Press, 1999).

Plantinga, Alvin, *Warranted Christian Belief* (Oxford University Press, 2000).

Pojman, L. P., ed., *Philosophy of Religion: An Anthology* (Wadsworth, 2003), part 8.

Richard, Janet Radcliffe, *Human Nature after Darwin* (Routledge, 2002).

Ruse, Michael, *Taking Darwin Seriously* (Prometheus Books, 1998).

Sober, Elliott, and David Sloan Wilson, *Unto Others: The Evolution and Psychology of Unselfish Behavior* (Harvard University Press, 1998).

Spencer, Herbert, *Social Statics: Or the Conditions Essential to Human Happiness Specified* (Chapman, 1851).

Watson, James, *The Double Helix* (Atheneum, 1968).

Wilson, D. B., ed., *Did the Devil Make Darwin Do It?* (Iowa State University Press, 1983).

Wilson, E. O., *Sociobiology: The New Synthesis* (Harvard University Press, 1975).

———, *On Human Nature* (Harvard University Press, 1978).

Wilson, James Q., *The Moral Sense* (Free Press, 1993).

Wright, Robert, *The Moral Animal* (Little, Brown, 1994).

CHAPTER 14

Human Nature in Contemporary Theories of the Mind

The curiosity of Man and the cunning of his Reason have revealed much of what Nature held hidden. The structure of space–time, the constitution of matter, the many forms of energy, the nature of life itself; all of these mysteries have become open books to us. To be sure, deep questions remain unanswered and revolutions await us still, but it is difficult to exaggerate the explosion in scientific understanding we humans have fashioned over the past 500 years.

Despite this general advance, a central mystery remains largely a mystery: the nature of conscious intelligence. *(Paul Churchland,* Matter and Consciousness)[1]

One topic in philosophy that deals directly with the subject of human nature is the philosophy of the mind. Classical dualistic theories found in Plato, Augustine, and Descartes have been challenged by contemporary philosophers like Paul and Patricia Churchland and Daniel Dennett, who have put forth materialist theories of the mind that force us to reconsider our ideas of the self and human nature in general. In this chapter we will examine the debate between dualist and monist materialist theories of mind. We begin with an overview of the problem and a discussion of the traditional theory of dualistic interactionism. We then discuss materialist theories of the mind, followed by functionalist theories.

Dualistic Interactionism

The Classical Dualist Theory

Intuitively, there seem to be two different types of reality: material and mental. There are bodies and minds. Bodies are solid, material entities, extended in three-dimensional space, publicly observable, measurable, and capable of causing things to happen in accordance with invariant laws of mechanics.

A mind, on the other hand, has none of these properties. Consciousness is not solid or material, is not extended in three-dimensional space, does not occupy space at all, is directly observable only by the person who owns it, cannot be measured, and seems incapable of causing things to happen in accordance with invariant laws of mechanics. Only the individual can think his or her thoughts, feel his or her emotions, and suffer his or her pain. Although a neurosurgeon can open the skull and observe the brain, she or he cannot observe a person's mind or its beliefs, sensations, emotions, or desires.

Unlike physical bodies, mental entities have no shape, weight, length, width, height, color, mass, velocity, or temperature. It would sound odd indeed to speak of a belief weighing 10 pounds like a sack of potatoes, a feeling of love measuring 8 by 10 feet like a piece of carpet, a pain being as heavy as a cement bag, or a desire that was green and had a temperature of 103 degrees.

Yet, common sense tells us that these two entities somehow interact. We step on a nail, and it pierces our skin, sending a message through our nervous system that results in something altogether different from the shape or size of the nail or skin, something that does not possess size or shape and that cannot be seen, smelled, tasted, or heard—a feeling of distress or pain. Whereas the nail is public, the pain is private.

On the other hand, our mind informs us that it would be a good thing to get a bandage to put over the cut that has resulted from stepping on the nail (maybe a tetanus shot, too); thus, the mind causes us to move the body. Our legs carry us to the medicine cabinet, where we stop, raise our arms and with our hands take hold of the cabinet, open it, take the bandage out, and then apply it dexterously to the wound.

Here, we have an instance where the body affects the mind and the mind in turn affects the body. Common sense shows that a close interactive relationship exists between these two radically different entities. This position is called **dualistic interactionism,** the theory that the body and the mind are different substances that causally interact on each other. We can represent it pictorially in the following manner: let BS represent brain state, MS represent mental state, and the arrows represent causation. The dualistic interactive picture of reality looks like this:

For example, stepping on the nail causes the first brain state (BS_1), which in turn causes the first mental state (MS_1—the feeling of pain in one's foot), which in turn causes us (via a brain state) to decide to move our foot (BS_2), which in turn brings relief from the pain (MS_2) as well as the intention to get a bandage for our wound

TABLE 14.1

Idealism (Monistic Idealism)

Only the mental exists: minds and ideas. Matter is an illusion. This position is held by Hindus and Christian Scientists and received its fullest defense in the work of Bishop George Berkeley (1685–1753).

Dualism

Mind and brain interact. The Mind causes bodily motions and the body causes mental events.

Materialism (Physicalism)

Metaphysical Behaviorism

Metaphysical behaviorism denies either mental events or their importance in understanding behavior.

Reductive Materialism

Reductive materialism (identity theory) finds a one-to-one correlation between mental states and events and brain states and events. Beliefs, pains, and desires are mental events that occur in the brain—that is, they are happening in the brain.

Eliminative Materialism

Eliminative materialism, like reductive materialism, denies mental states but goes further and denies our way of characterizing mental events as beliefs, desires, pains, and the like. Our commonsense views of mental events constitute a faulty folk psychology that cannot stand up to inspection. A science of brain events should replace folk psychology. Eventually, we will not talk of pain but of a C fiber firing in a certain place.

Functionalism

Functionalism emphasizes the input–output relations of behavior. However, unlike behaviorism, it admits the importance of mental events (and of introspection). Against reductive materialism, it denies that just one type of brain state can always be correlated with a type of mental event. Just as a watch can be operated by a battery or springs, different material constructions could yield the same kind of mental event.

Neutral Monism

Neutral monism is a fourth type of position (neither idealism, dualism, nor materialism). It posits a third underlying reality, of which matter and mind are manifestations. The view was first put forward by Baruch Spinoza (1632–1677) and developed by William James (1842–1910).

(MS_3), leading to the third brain state (BS_3) that causes us to move toward the first-aid kit in the bathroom.

The following questions arise. Exactly *how* does this transaction between the mind and brain occur? *Where* does it occur? Could it be, as materialists contend, that the mind is really simply a function of the body, not a separate substance at all? Of could the idealist monists be correct in asserting that the body is really an illusion and that there is only one substance, the mind alone?

Table 14.1 shows schema of the three main types of position that may be useful. Both idealism and materialism are monisms, reducing all reality to one underlying substance. Dualism opposes both types of monism.

There are several types of dualism besides interactionism. The most notable is *epiphenomenalism*, which posits a one-way causal relationship: the body affects the mind, causing mental events, but the mind does not affect the body. Mental events are like the babbling of brooks, the exhaust from a car's engine, or the smoke from a train's chimney. They are effects of physical processes but do not themselves cause motion in the water, the car, or the train. Epiphenomenalism is represented in the following schema:

$$
\begin{array}{cccc}
MS_1 & MS_2 & MS_3 & MS_4 \\
\uparrow & \uparrow & \uparrow & \uparrow \\
BS_1 & BS_2 & BS_3 & BS_4
\end{array}
$$

Finally, there is a view called **panpsychism,** which holds that everything in nature has a mind or a soul. Panpsychism is a correlate to pantheism, which holds that everything is God or contains God. According to panpsychism, soul or mind is in the ultimate particles of physics and only because of it can we experience consciousness.

Materialism, the theory that matter and the law of physics constitute ultimate reality, has several versions. The simplest is metaphysical behaviorism, which denies either mental events or their importance in understanding behavior. Actually, **behaviorism** is not so much a theory about the mind–body problem but a theory about how to understand the language we use in describing mental events. All talk about beliefs, desires, and emotions should be set in terms of dispositions to behave. Metaphysical behaviorism was prominent in the first half of this century, but two strong objections have caused it to be virtually abandoned in the philosophy of the mind. First, a person is concerned not just with his or her outward behavior but with inner events as well. Patients undergoing operations who are given a paralyzing drug, such as curare, manifest no outward behavior yet feel pain. A traditional behaviorist model does not take such "nonbehavioral" states seriously. Second, the idea of "dispositions to behave" cannot easily be spelled out, for an infinite number of different conditions may be potential factors in a dispositional account.

The second version of materialism is **reductive materialism,** which attempts to find a one-to-one correlation between mental states and brain states and identifies the former with the latter. Beliefs, pains, and desires will turn out, on this account, to be simply brain states.

The third version is **functionalism,** which denies that there is any one type of brain state or event that can always be correlated with a type of mental event. For example, I may feel pain in my hand on two different occasions but may have two different areas of the brain activated. Actually, functionalism need not be materialist at all. It could be agnostic on the mind–body problem, confining itself to outputs of human activity. (We will examine functionalism later in this chapter; see p. 240).

The final version is **eliminative materialism,** which contends that our ordinary talk about mental events is mistaken. Our commonsense conceptual scheme is labeled **folk psychology** and includes the concepts of belief, desire, emotions, perceptions, and sensations. When we learn more about our brains and the way they work, we will be able to replace this subjectivist speech with a more scientific discourse. For example, instead of talking about a headache in my forehead, I might talk about certain C fibers firing in my brain. (We will examine reductive and eliminative materialism later in this chapter; see p. 234).

One other theory should be noted: *neutral monism,* the view that one common but unknown substance underlies all reality, matter, and mind. Baruch Spinoza (1632–1677) first put forth this position, though it was developed by William James (1842–1910) at the end of the 19th century. Although this may seem a suitable compromise between those who are attracted to monism and those who are inclined to dualism, neutral monism actually compounds the problem: now, not only do we not understand matter and mind but we also have a third mystery to worry about. If it is true, there seems little evidence for it. Yet, given the difficulties with the other positions, some may finally select it as the least objectionable of the lot.

The main historical debate has been between interactive dualism and two forms of materialism: reductive and eliminative. We will spend most of our time in this chapter and the next examining these three theories.

First, we turn to René Descartes' (1596–1650) classic rendition of interactive dualism (sometimes called "substance dualism"). Descartes, after doubting everything that it is possible to doubt, including that he had a body, asked "What am I?" and came to the conclusion that he was not essentially a body but a mind:

> I am not a collection of members which we call the human body: I am not a subtle air distributed through these members, I am not a wind, a fire, a vapor, a breath, nor anything at all which I can imagine or conceive; because I have assumed [through doubt] that all these were nothing.[2]

However, he cannot doubt that he himself, as a thinking thing, exists: "But what then am I? A thing which thinks. What is a thing which thinks? It is a thing which doubts, understands, conceives, affirms, denies, wills, refuses, which also imagines and feels."[3]

According to Descartes, three kinds of objects or substances exist in the universe: *(1)* the eternal substance, God; *(2)* his creation in terms of mind; *(3)* his creation in terms of matter. Humans are made up of the latter two types of substance. "We may thus easily have two clear and distinct notions or ideas, the one of created substance which thinks, and the other of corporeal substances, provided we carefully separate all the attributes of thought from those of extension."[4] That is, mind and matter have different properties, so they must be different substances.

We are thinking substances, or embodied minds,

> for I am not only lodged in my body as a pilot in a ship, but I am very closely united to it, and so to speak so intermingle with it that I seem to compose with it one whole. For if that were not the case, when my body is hurt, I, who am merely a thinking thing, should perceive this wound by the understanding only, just as the sailor perceives by sight when something is damaged in his vessel.[5]

The two kinds of substances that make us each a person intermingle in such a way that they causally act on each other. Although it might be that a mind interacts with each part of its body separately, Descartes' view is that the mind interacts only with the brain. The material event that causally stimulates one of our five senses (e.g., light hitting the retina of the eye) results in a chain of physical causation that leads to a certain brain process from which a certain sensation results. Then, in turn, being affected by the brain, the mind, through mental events, acts on the brain, which in turn affects the body. Descartes thought he could pinpoint the place in the brain where the interaction between mind and brain took place: "The part of the body in which the soul exercises its function immediately is in nowise the heart, nor the whole of the brain, but merely the most inward of all its parts, to wit, a certain very small gland which is situated in the middle of its substance."[6]

This gland, the pineal gland, is the seat of the mind. It functions as the intermediary that transmits the effects of the mind to the brain and the effects of the brain to the mind. There is no reason to believe that the pineal gland is the seat of the mind, and neuroscience has given a better explanation of its function. We will disregard Descartes' mistake about the pineal gland and accept the essential structure of his theory as the classic expression of dualistic interactionism.

Descartes' view seems close to what we arrive at through common sense. We seem to be aware of two different kinds of event, physical and mental, as was described earlier in this chapter. Mental events cause physical events, and physical events cause mental events. At this point, the interactionist argues that epiphenomenalism is mistaken in making the causal direction only one way. What evolutionary use is the mind if it does no work? It seems to violate Newton's dictum that "nature does nothing in vain." It is a useless fifth wheel. On the contrary, the dualist avers, our intuitions tell us that the reasons (grasped by the mind) initiate causal chains that result in physical actions and other mental events. For example, I may decide (a mental event) to imagine all the friends I have ever had and call them up to consciousness. The epiphenomenalist account glosses over the introspective process and states that all of these decisions and imaginings are simply the by-products of mysterious physical processes. With friends like that, the interactionist concludes, who needs materialist enemies?

Our mental states seem private and incorrigible, at least most of them. Only I can know whether I am really in pain, whether I really believe that God exists, whether I really intend to keep a promise or to be a moral person. True, perhaps I can misremember, be mistaken about a borderline feeling (is it a slight pain or a sharp tickle? lemon-flavored ice cream or a variety of orange-flavored ice cream?); but for a whole host of experiences, introspection is reliable. Folk psychology works.

A Critique of Dualistic Interactionism

Nonetheless, there are problems with dualistic interactionism. Here are the four most prominent ones:

1. Where does the interaction of the soul and body take place?
2. How does the interaction occur?
3. How can the idea of the mental causing the physical be reconciled with the principle of the conservation of energy?
4. How can the idea of two realities, body and mind, be reconciled with **Occam's Razor,** the principle of simplicity?

Let's take up each criticism in turn. First, where does the interaction take place? Descartes thought it took place in the pineal gland, but evidence does not show that it does or that the pineal gland has anything to do with consciousness. The problem is that whereas physical states have spatial location, mental states do not. Mental substance is not subject to the laws of physics (otherwise, we would conclude it was material). However, if we cannot speak of mental states having location, it seems odd to speak of a "where" in which they "touch" or "meet" or "interact" with physical objects.

This certainly raises an interesting puzzle. The dualist responds that we do not have to understand where the mind is located (that may be a nonsensical question) to be able to say that it affects the brain in the brain. That is, we posit that there are metaphysical laws in addition to physical laws. God, mind, and the realm of the spirit operate within the realm of the former kind of laws.

The second objection—how does the interaction occur?—is very similar to the first. How can physical states result in something wholly other, something mental? To move a stalled car, several people must push it. Force must be exerted in every physical change, and force is a product of mass and acceleration so that whatever exerts force must be capable of physical movement. However, nothing mental has mass or acceleration (mental objects do not travel through space from your hometown to the university), so nothing mental can exert physical force or be affected by force. Thus, nothing physical can be causally affected by anything mental, nor can anything mental be causally influenced by anything physical.

How might dualists reply to this difficult problem? One way might be to respond like Hamlet (in Act I.V of Shakespeare's *Hamlet*), that "there are more things in heaven and earth, Horatio, than is written in your philosophy." Why should we suppose that substances must be qualitatively similar before they can influence each other? Doesn't the very thought that someone is out to harm me cause a state of psychological and physical depression or fear? Also, doesn't that fear cause me to take action to protect myself? Isn't my decision to raise my hand obviously an example of the mind causing the body to move? Isn't agency itself testimony to the truth of interactionism?

Perhaps free agency, the source of the second example, is a myth or an illusion; but it cannot be dismissed out of hand. An argument is needed to exclude introspective reports for free will as evidence for dualistic interaction.

The third problem involves the principle of the conservation of energy. This principle states that the amount of energy in a closed physical system remains constant, so if there is causal interaction between mental events and physical events, the principle of conservation of energy is violated. Energy is a function of matter, not mind; but the dualist believes that my decision to pick up the book in front of me somehow creates the necessary energy to cause the book to rise. So, it would seem, on dualist premises, that the principle of the conservation of energy is violated.

Once again, dualists are faced with a formidable challenge. At least three options are open for them:

1. The principle of the conservation of energy applies only to closed systems, but the universe may be an open system. Energy may come and go at different points. The trouble with this answer is that contemporary physics operates on the assumption that the universe is a closed system. This has ramifications for the notion of divine intervention. The theist, believing that God sometimes intervenes in the universe, thus altering energy states from without, seems committed to an open universe.

2. There may be a replacement of energy within the closed system, so that when ten ergons appear via my decision to lift the book, ten ergons disappear in another place. This is possible, but, of course, it is just an ad hoc hypothesis necessary to save the theory.

3. It may not be necessary that mental causation involves a transfer of energy but only a harnessing or redirection of energies. The problem with the redirection hypothesis is that one would like to know how the mind can affect the direction of energy flow without itself being a form of energy. This brings us back to problem 2 discussed previously.

We turn to the fourth objection to dualism, which gets us into the arguments for materialist monism. The idea of two realities, body and mind, seems to violate **Occam's razor,** the principle of simplicity. The principle of simplicity is an abductive principle (i.e., one having to do with arriving at the best explanation) that claims we should prefer explanations that minimize the number of entities postulated. All things being equal, isn't it better to have one all-embracing explanation of several different events rather than two? Instead of the puzzle of substance interaction, wouldn't the posit of a single substance with a single set of laws have the advantage of giving us a unified picture of reality?

Imagine that two murders have been committed in a large nearby city, one in the southern part of town on Monday afternoon during rush hour and one in the northern part a half-hour later. In both cases, a woman has been killed by an assailant who sucks blood from her neck and leaves a picture of Dracula on the corpse. On the one hand, the evidence points to two murderers, committing the crimes independently, for no one could possibly get from the southern part of town to the northern part of town in a half-hour, especially during rush hour. However, it would greatly simplify the police's investigation if they could assume some way of traveling between the two places and so be on the lookout for one murderer instead of two. It would be too great a coincidence if two vampires acting independently should both strike in the same city within a half-hour of each other. The quest for economy and reduction to simpler basic units seems to be of great importance in explaining phenomena.

This is the commonsense motivation that informs the tendency toward monism. Unless there is a compelling reason not to do so, simplicity and economy of explanation, reducing differences to an underlying unity, are desirable for problem solving. The question is whether there is a compelling reason for not making a move to simplicity. Since the dualist's response at this point is global, having to do with the entire product of materialist monism, we might well postpone it until we see the case for materialism.

Finally, the dualist has difficulty explaining how we can know there are other minds besides our own. I am directly aware of my own mental events but no one else's. When I feel pain and pleasure and have fears and hopes, I know these inner states directly; but I never directly experience anyone else's mental states. When I hit my finger with a hammer, I feel excruciating pain; but when I hit your finger with the hammer, I do not feel anything. So how do I know you are feeling pain?

We can put the argument this way. Consider the three causal states in myself.

1. The initial modification in my body (the hammer hitting my finger)
2. My feeling pain caused by the hammer's blow on my finger
3. My subsequent bodily change (a scream, the contorted facial expression, and the sudden withdrawal of my finger)

When other people hit their fingers with a hammer, I behold the first and third conditions but not the second. I see the same kind of physical states that I experience in myself, but I do not experience the other person's pain. I can infer that the other person is in pain from the similarities of outward behavior (conditions 1 and 3). I infer that other people are relevantly similar to me, so they must also be experiencing pain (condition 2).

However, there are problems with this response. First, I cannot check on the correctness of the conclusion that the other body is experiencing feeling like my own. I can introspect into my own mind to see whether I am in pain or angry or fearful, but I cannot extrospect into my neighbor's mind to see whether he or she is in pain or angry or fearful.

The main problem with the argument for the inference to other minds is that this argument from analogy is a generalization from only one particular, my case. Normally, inductive reasoning goes from many particular instances to an inductive generalization, but the argument from analogy for other minds proceeds from only one instance, my own, to a generalization about all other living animals and human beings. This generalization seems unwarranted, as though a primitive being who has only seen one tree, a cherry tree, generalizes that all the trees in the world are cherry trees.

Since the argument for other minds is unsound, the dualist seems driven to *solipsism*, the view that only I (the experiencer) exist as a mental being. Everyone else may simply be robots or automatons mimicking my behavior. Of course, no one really believes this, but the logic of the dualist's argument from analogy tends in this direction.

Materialism

In the afternoon of September 13, 1848, in the Vermont countryside, an affable 25-year-old foreman, Phineas P. Gage, was leading a group of men in laying a new line of the Rutland and Burlington Railroad. They needed to blast a huge rock blocking their way, so Gage poured gunpowder into the narrow hole that had been drilled in the rock. Powder in place, the next step was to tamp down the charge, which Gage proceeded to do. However, the iron tamping rod rubbed against the side of the shaft, and a spark ignited the powder, causing an explosion. The iron rod—three and a half feet in length and an inch and a quarter in diameter—burst from the hole, struck Gage just beneath his left eye, tore through his skull, and landed 50 feet away.

Gage was thrown to the ground, his limbs twitching convulsively; but soon he was able to speak. He was taken to a hotel, where doctors were able to stop the bleeding. Amazingly, he lived; but he was transformed from a friendly, intelligent leader into an intemperate, unreliable, childish ox with the evil temper to match it.

Materialism says that what we call mind is really a function of the brain; that when the brain is injured, as was the case with Gage, or diseased, the effect is seen in behavior and impaired mental functioning. In Alzheimer's disease, for example, the cerebral cortex and the hippocampus contain abnormal, twisted tangles and filaments as well as abnormal neurons. The loss of neurons in the nucleus basalis results in a reduction of choline acetyltransferase, an enzyme needed for normal brain function. The result is the slow death of the brain. Without the brain (or some physical equivalent), no mental states are possible.

Cutting the corpus callosum, the thick band of nerves linking the two hemispheres of the cerebral cortex, can result in two separate centers of consciousness. Different parts of the brain are responsible for different mental operations. Over 30 years ago, the Canadian neurosurgeon Wilder Penfield conducted a set of experiments in which he used electrodes to stimulate the cerebral cortex of patients. They began to recall memories from the past and even sang lullabies learned in early childhood, which they had forgotten, lending support to the thesis that memories are stored in the neurons of the cerebral cortex.

Furthermore, a systematic correspondence seems to exist between the structure of different animals' brains and the sort of behavior they exhibit. Why do we need such a complex brain with billions of cells and trillions of connections if the mind is located in its own separate substance? If dualism is correct, this intricately constructed, complex brain is unnecessary baggage, superfluous machinery. All that the mind should require is some channel for linking the mental with the physical worlds.

Metaphysical materialism, the doctrine that matter and the laws of physics make up and govern the entire universe, has a long history. It was held by the first Greek cosmologists (discussed in chapter 2), expounded in greater detail by the Greek philosopher Democritus (ca. 460–370 B.C.E.) and the Roman atomist Lucretius (ca. 99–55 B.C.E.), and given still deeper expression in the work of Thomas Hobbes (see chapter 7). Hobbes was a theist materialist, who believed that all reality except God is material. God alone is spirit. We are entirely material beings:

> The world (the universe, that is the whole mass of all things that are) is corporeal, that is to say, body; and hath the dimensions of magnitude, namely, length, breadth, and depth; also every part of body, is likewise body, and hath the like dimensions; and consequently every part of the universe is body; and that which is not body, is not part of the universe. . . . Spirit, that which is incorporeal, is a term that rightly belongs to God himself, in whom we consider not what attribute expresses best his nature, which is incomprehensible, but that which best expresses our desire to honor him.[7]

Bringing the discussion into the present, the British philosopher Colin McGinn puts it this way:

> What we call mind is in fact made up of a great number of subcapacities, and each of these depends upon the functioning of the brain. [Neurology] compellingly demonstrates . . . that everything about the mind, from the sensory-motor periphery to the inner sense, is minutely controlled by the brain: if your brain lacks certain chemicals or gets locally damaged, your mind is apt to fall apart at the seams. . . . If parts of the mind depend for their existence upon parts of the brain, then the whole of the mind must so depend too. Hence the soul dies with the brain, which is to say it is mortal.[8]

By "materialism" neither Hobbes nor contemporary materialists like McGinn mean *value materialism*, the thesis that only money and the things money can buy have any value, nor do they necessarily rule out religion or the spiritual aspects of life. Indeed, some scholars interpret the biblical view of humanity as materialist rather than dualist (see chapter 1). The materialists mean simply that the physical system of the brain and the physical events that take place within it are the entirety of our conscious lives. There is no separate mental substance, and mental events are really physical events.

There are two central varieties of materialist monism: reductive and eliminative. Both distinguish themselves from metaphysical behaviorism, the view that denies or ignores mental events and describes the human condition in terms of dispositions to act. In this chapter, we will examine both forms of materialism.

Reductive materialism, sometimes known as the identity theory, admits mental events (but not a separate mental substance) but claims that each mental event is really a brain state or event. Our center of consciousness resides in the brain, probably about 2 inches behind the forehead. We are conscious of happenings in our cerebral cortex, even though they appear to be different from measurable brain states. Thus, a pain in my foot can be identified with a brain event—say, a C fiber firing—and a belief can be identified with certain sentences symbolically stored in some area of the cerebral cortex.

Eliminative materialism goes even further in rejecting dualism, calling on us to reject as false the whole folk psychology language that makes reference to pains, beliefs, and desires. Such language supposes that our introspective states are incorrigible or infallible reporters of our inner life. Psychological experiments seem to show that we can be mistaken about our introspective reports. So we should reject folk psychology for a richer scientific theory. Here is how Richard Rorty, one of the earliest proponents, puts it:

> A certain primitive tribe holds the view that illnesses are caused by demons—a different demon for each sort of illness. When asked what more is known about these demons than that they cause illness, they reply that certain members of the tribe— the witch-doctors—can see, after a meal of sacred mushrooms, various (intangible) humanoid forms on or near the bodies of patients. The witch-doctors have noted, for example, that a blue demon with a long nose accompanies epileptics, a fat red one accompanies sufferers from pneumonia, etc. They know such further facts as that the fat red demon dislikes a certain sort of mold which the witch-doctors give people who have pneumonia. If we encountered such a tribe, we would be inclined to tell them that there are no demons. We would tell them that diseases were caused by germs, viruses, and the like. We would add that the witch-doctors were not seeing demons, but merely having hallucinations.[9]

Rorty goes on to argue that this belief in demons is analogous to our belief that we have pains:

> The absurdity of saying, "Nobody has ever felt a pain" is no greater than that of saying "Nobody has ever seen a demon," if we have a suitable answer to the question, "What was I reporting when I said I felt a pain?" To this question, the science of the future may reply, "You were reporting the occurrence of a certain brain-process, and it would make life simpler for us if you would in the future, say 'My C-fibers are firing' instead of saying 'I'm in pain.'" In so saying, he has as good a prima facie case as the scientist who answers the witch-doctors' question, "What was I reporting when I reported a demon?" by saying, "You were reporting the content of your hallucination, and it would make life simpler if, in the future, you would describe your experience in those terms."[10]

If philosophers like Rorty are right, our folk psychology language is as superstitious and misleading as the witch doctors' belief that demons cause illness. Mental events like pains should not merely be identified with brain states (like C-fibers firing) but should be replaced by neurological language, which we might call "neurospeak." Instead of saying "I've a pain in my foot," neurospeak will say something like "A C-fiber is firing in quadrant A2 of brain LP" (it is unclear whether "persons" will survive neurospeak). Instead of saying "I believe that so and so will win the presidential election," neurospeak will tell us to say "The sentence S17 is manifesting itself in quadrant C56 of cerebral cortex LP."

Whatever the future prospects of eliminative materialism, at present it seems like science fiction or, at best, a research project to excite neuroscientists and their philosopher kin. However, we need not choose between reductive and eliminative materialism for our purposes. They both suppose a materialist monism, and the question is whether materialist monism is true.

The implications of materialism are far-reaching. We would have to eliminate not only the concepts of pain, belief, and desire but that of conscience as well. Guilt is merely the vestigial remnant of primitive neural configurations in the amygdala; love, a leftover of primate constructions in the hippocampus; and the moral sense, a survival of reptilian brain configurations. The implications are more radical than anything we have ever encountered in philosophy or in life itself. If these doctrines are true, not only is some of our folk psychology to be passed over but our notion of a self must be eliminated, and we must accept the Buddhist doctrine of the *an-atman* (see chapter 6).

The main criticism of such monism is that it is obvious on introspection that we have mental events and that any theory that would deny them has a strong presumption of self-evidence to overcome. The question is, How does something purely material, like neurons and glia, give rise to something that is nonmaterial, like consciousness? Reductivism, under the guise of reinterpreting mental events, claims it is not doing away with the events but only showing their true identity as physical events lodged in the brain.

The dualist's criticism of this identification rests on an appeal to **Leibniz's Law** (identity of indiscernibles): two things are numerically identical if and only if they have all the same properties in common. It can be expressed in the following formula (don't be afraid of the symbols):

$$\text{If } (x)(y)[(x = y), \text{ then } (P) \ (Px, \text{ if and only if } Py)]$$

That is, for any two entities x and y, if they really are the same, then if x has property P, y must also have it (and vice versa—if y has the property, x must also). For example, if Superman is really Clark Kent, then it could not be the case that if Superman is 6 feet tall, Clark Kent is 5 feet 9 inches tall. You certainly could not have Superman not being located in space!

The dualist points out that the mind has different properties from the body. The body occupies space and is subject to the laws of physics, whereas the mind does not occupy space and doesn't appear to be subject to the same laws. We might set forth the argument like this. Let M stand for mind, B for body, and P for property. Then,

1. B has property P (e.g., extension in space, so can be measured).
2. M lacks property P (so cannot be measured).
3. If B has P and M lacks P, then M is not identical with B.
4. Therefore, the mind is not identical with the brain.

As we noted earlier, bodies are solid, material entities, extended in three-dimensional space, publicly observable, and measurable, whereas minds have none of these properties. Consciousness is not solid or material, is not extended in three-dimensional space, does not occupy space at all, is directly observable only by the person who owns it, cannot be measured, and seems incapable of causing things to happen in accordance with invariant laws of physics. Only the person concerned can think his or her thoughts, feel his or her emotions, and suffer his or her pain.

How might the materialist respond to this? Materialists point out that what seems to be different is not always so. In times past, lightning was deemed a mysterious and spiritual force. The ancient Greeks thought that lightning was a thunderbolt of Zeus. Now we know that it is a luminous electrical discharge in the atmosphere, produced by the separation of electrical charges in thunderstorm clouds. Although it may not appear to us as electrical charges, physics assures us of that identity.

For eons the nature of life was held to be a mysterious *élan vital* (a spiritual substance that animated whatever was living). However, in this century, such vitalism was undermined by discoveries in molecular biology. Life is made up of the same basic elements as other material, nonliving things. The difference between living and nonliving things, biology tells us, is not in the kind of substance that underlies the two types of things but in the arrangement of those substances.

Similarly, water has different properties from hydrogen and oxygen (e.g., wetness) but is nevertheless nothing but H_2O. So, it could turn out that mental events are really physical events and states and nothing more. Materialists believe we are especially likely to be misled by thinking that consciousness has certain "phenomenological" properties it really does not. For instance, when we imagine a green apple, we are inclined to say that our memory image is green. However, nothing in our brain is green, so the critic of materialism triumphantly concludes that the mental image is not in our brain. The materialist replies that the image is not literally green and that, indeed, we do not literally have an image before our mind's eye, as we might literally have a picture of an apple before our physical eye in an art gallery. What is happening when we imagine an apple, according to the materialist, is that the same thing is going on in the brain as what goes on when we see a real green apple. We imagine seeing something green, and in that sense our imagination may be said to be green; but there is nothing literally green in our minds. So nothing impedes the identification of mental with physical processes.

The materialist points out that our increased understanding of brain behavior makes it a plausible hypothesis that conscious thought and feeling are simply phenomenological descriptions of that which neuroscience describes from an externalist point of view.

The goal is to have a unified, explanatory mind–brain theory in which both science and common sense can take satisfaction.

Where does this leave us? The materialist has a certain amount of empirical success to his or her credit, which should give the dualist pause. The more that neuroscience can explain, the more impressive the credentials of materialism become. However, can it really explain the self, consciousness, free will; or is there an element of hubris at the very core of the materialist project?

The dualist agrees with the materialist monist that a unified explanation would be a good thing if we could get it. The following questions, however, arise: Does something get left out in the shuffle? What is the price of such unity—free will, human dignity based on the idea of mental substance, God, or the spiritual order? If there is independent evidence for these things, then unity of explanation is not worth the price.

Thomas Nagel expresses nagging doubts about the attempt to capture the essence of humanness via a detached, scientific approach to the subject:

> There are things about the world and life and ourselves that cannot be adequately understood from a maximally objective standpoint, however much it may extend our understanding beyond the point from which we started. A great deal is essentially connected to a particular point of view . . . and the attempt to give a complete account of the world in objective terms detached from these perspectives inevitably leads to false reductions or to outright denials that certain patently real phenomena exist at all. . . . To the extent that such no-nonsense theories have an effect, they merely threaten to impoverish the intellectual landscape for a while by inhibiting the serious expression of certain questions. In the name of liberation, these movements have offered us intellectual repression.[11]

Each conscious being, like a bat, has a distinct, subjective feel which is not captured by physicalist descriptions of the bat or dolphin or human being. We do not know what it is like to be a bat because we haven't had the bat's peculiar experience. So experience, conscious experience, cannot be reduced to physicalist explanations.

Is Nagel right? The dualist believes that he is, whereas the materialist denies it. Paul Churchland responds that each sentient being has its own particular neuronal network so that it experiences reality in a unique way.

Perhaps the mind–body problem cannot be viewed in isolation from the rest of philosophy. What you decide regarding the theory of knowledge generally, the philosophy of religion, and the problem of free will and determinism will influence your conclusion on the mind–body problem. However, we should look at one more theory before we move on—that is, functionalism, a theory that claims to get around the problems inherent in reductivism.

Materialists are "exhilarated by the . . . [prospect of developing] an evolutionary explanation of the human intellect."[12] Why should we fear honest inquiry? they ask. Isn't the search for truth at the heart of science?

Reductive and eliminative materialism seem to satisfy the principle of simplicity and conform to a scientific view of the world. Eliminative materialism seems a promissory note that science will eventually reinterpret our experience in a new framework and language. As such, we probably should admit it is a possibility but not one for which there is presently much evidence. Reductive materialism is less radical, but it still faces problems, especially that of seeming to leave out of its account the phenomenology of conscious experience, of consciousness itself. Let us turn now to the third type of theory in the philosophy of mind.

Functionalism and Biological Naturalism

Consciousness: The having of perceptions, thoughts, and feelings; awareness. The term is impossible to define except in terms that are unintelligible without a grasp of what consciousness means. Many fall into the trap of confusing consciousness with self-consciousness—to be conscious it is only necessary to be aware of the external world. Consciousness is a fascinating but elusive phenomenon: it is impossible to specify what it is, what it does, or why it evolved. Nothing worth reading has been written about it. (*The International Dictionary of Psychology,* 1989)

At this point, you may be frustrated by the problems surrounding each theory that we have examined so far. The debates over whether we are made of one or two different substances, whether mental events can be reduced to brain events, and whether mental events exist at all seem fraught with insurmountable problems. "A plague on all your houses," we are tempted to shout, after working through these theories. There is a group of philosophers who feel exactly the same way. In the 1960s and early 1970s, philosophers like Jerry Fodor of The Massachusetts Institute of Technology and Hilary Putnam of Harvard criticized the current versions of materialist monism, the identity theory; and in its place they offered a new theory, functionalism.[13]

In this section, we will examine both the functionalist's critique of the identity theory and functionalism itself as a replacement of other theories. Then, we will look at criticisms of functionalism.

Functionalists take issue with aspects of the identity theory, the form of reductivism that identifies types of mental events with types of brain events, and with metaphysical behaviorism, which denies the reality of mental events. First, they argue against the behaviorists and those holding the identity theory that mental states and events must be accounted for. The behaviorist is interested in input and output states. Functionalism, which is the heir to behaviorism, argues that this formula leaves out the uniqueness of mental states. Not only must environmental input and behavioral output be accounted for, but a third factor, types of mental states, must be recognized (see Fig. 14.1).

A similar first criticism is leveled by the functionalists against the reductivists (or identity theory). Functionalists argue that, although it may or may not be the case that physical matter is the only substance of which we partake, mental events

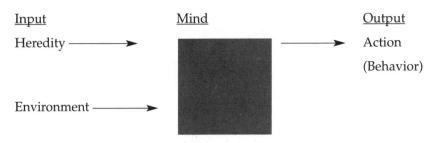

Figure 14.1

exist and must be accounted for. Second, they accuse reductivists of "chauvinism" for thinking that material brains like those found in humans and other animals are the only things that can account for mental events. Just as racism is chauvinism about race, sexism a prejudice about gender, and speciesism an unjustified view about one's own species, so reductivism is a chauvinism that unwarrantedly excludes all other forms of realization of mental events. "Just because Martians don't have brains like ours doesn't mean that they don't suffer or use reason!" the functionalist is apt to insist. Here, functionalism sets forth the doctrine of *multiple realizability*, the view that mental events could be realized in many different forms and structures.

Note that the identity theorists hold that mental events are reducible to types of brain events, that consciousness is really nothing but a brain state or event. It is this doctrine of type identity at which the functionalist aims his or her attack.

Functionalists draw their inspiration from Aristotle, who distinguished between form and matter, arguing that a form could be realized in many different ways, in different substances. For example, a statue of Abraham Lincoln could be made of marble, wood, clay, steel, aluminum, or paper mâché. That is, for Aristotle there is no single type of matter that defines an entity. The form of the substance, not the substance itself, is the defining feature.

The doctrine of multiple realizability applies this insight to mental events, interpreting them as functions. Let's illustrate the doctrine by applying it to an artifact. Consider the mousetrap. Here are five different examples of mousetraps:

1. A standard spring trap. Cheese is placed on a trigger; the mouse is attracted to the cheese and trips the trigger, which in turn releases a spring, causing a metal bar to come crashing down on the head or neck of the mouse.

2. Like the standard trap, only instead of a bar coming down, a rope is released by the trigger. It surrounds the neck of the mouse, tightens and at the same time pulls the mouse off the ground, hanging it.

3. A trapdoor mousetrap. When the mouse touches the cheese, a trapdoor opens, and the mouse falls into a shoot, leading directly to an incinerator.

4. A scented model of a mouse of the opposite sex is poisoned with a lethal perfume and left for the mouse to embrace. When it does so, the mouse imbibes the poison and soon expires.

5. An awesome model of a ferocious cat, which when seen by mice causes them to die of fright.

All these instruments qualify as mousetraps. They all have the same purpose or function. We could invent other ways of trapping mice. Enumerating the different types of mousetrap is not the way of accounting for the idea of a mousetrap, however. There is no single material feature that all and only mousetraps have in common. All that they have in common is the abstract idea that their purpose or function is to catch mice. They can realize that function in multiple ways—hence the name, the doctrine of multiple realizability.

Similarly, the functionalist hypothesizes that there is no reason to rule out the possibility that mental events are realized in different ways in different structures. They could be realized in brain tissue like ours or a different kind of tissue in other animals, in the silicon chips of computers, in some other structure of alien bodies, or in an unknown substance that makes up angels. From artificial intelligence to angels, all that counts is that mental events be the result and that these mental events be part of the causal process mediating environmental input and behavioral outputs.

Similarly, in different humans, there may be different ways in which the same function is realized. The cerebral cortex may have more than one type of structural mechanism that produces mental events, and two different people may function identically though they have different types of inward processes taking place.

At the core of the functionalist position is the idea that what makes a mental state like pain what it is, is its functional role: pain simply is whatever causes, for example, the rapid withdrawal of hands from the fire and whatever results from putting one's hand into the fire. So if a creature with entirely different wiring from ourselves was behaviorally isomorphic to ourselves, the inner states that mediated its behavior would be the same as our inner states because the essence of an inner state is the causes and effects it has.

Yet, this is just where functionalism runs into problems. If the processes that produce the same function are too different, couldn't functionalism be missing an important feature of mental events? The inverted-spectrum argument is offered to illustrate this point.

You have a particular type of sensation when you look at a red object and a different kind of sensation when you look at a green object. However, isn't it possible for someone else to have the reverse sensations? When another person looks at the green apple, he or she has a red sensation; and upon looking at the red apple, a green sensation.

His or her behavior, use of the words *red* and *green*, would be functionally identical with yours, and his or her sensations of seeing a "red" and "green" apple would be functionally identical with yours; however, the inner states are really different despite the functional equivalence. Would this show that functionalism has missed an essential feature in accounting for mental events? Would it show that it is not just the function that counts but the reality of what is going on inside of one's mind or brain? Functionalism concentrates on the input–output relationships: I step on a nail (the input), and that action sends a message to my brain that in turn causes me to cry "Ouch" (the output). Other people simply withdraw their feet. Some grimace, others cry out, and still others cry. Concentrating on the functional analysis of cause and effect, however, seems to have the defects of behaviorism (which functionalism was in part meant to answer). The functionalist account leaves out precisely what is important, the quality of the inner state. That is, it is not enough to say that there are functionally equivalent types of mental events in conscious beings; we must also pay attention to the conscious experience itself that could be of a different type despite functional identity.

The functionalist generally meets this objection by denying the possibility or likelihood of the inverted-spectrum case or radically different qualitative states given the same biological state, but they seem conceivable.

In the 1930s and 1940s, the British mathematician Alan Turing (1912–1954) devised an idealized finite calculating program to determine whether computers could think. Two rooms are equipped with input/output devices, both going to an experimenter in a third room. A human is placed in one room and a computer in the other, each communicating with the experimenter. By issuing instructions, asking questions, and receiving replies, the experimenter tries to determine which room has the human and which, the machine. If he or she cannot tell the difference, this constitutes strong evidence that computers can think. It turns out that under standard conditions the experimenter cannot tell the difference. Hence, many scientists and philosophers concluded that computers can think. The Turing machine supported the functionalist account of the philosophy of mind, which, for a time, became the dominant theory of the mind.

One philosopher demurred. John Searle of the University of California argued that the Turing test failed to prove that computers can think. He offered the following thought-experiment.[14] Suppose you are in a room with boxes filled with Chinese symbols, which you can identify by their shapes but have no understanding of their meaning. People in another room send questions written in Chinese to you with instructions in English on how to match the questions with the symbols in the box. Suppose further that after this first batch, you are given a second batch of Chinese writing along with rules (in English) for correlating the second batch with the first. Since you understand the rules, they enable you to correlate one set of formal symbols with another set of formal symbols. That is, you can identify the symbols entirely by their shapes.

After this, you are given a third batch of Chinese symbols together with some instructions in English that enable you to correlate elements of this third batch with those of the first two batches, and these rules instruct you how to give back certain Chinese symbols with certain sorts of shapes in response to certain sorts of shapes given to you in the third batch. Unknown to you, the people who are giving you all these symbols call the first batch "script," the second batch "story," and the third batch "questions." Furthermore they call the symbols you give back to them in response to the third batch "answers to the questions," and the set of rules in English that they gave you, they call the "program." Nobody just looking at your answers can tell that you do not speak a word of Chinese. You neither speak nor understand Chinese. All you have proved is that you can manipulate symbols.

Now imagine that these people also give you stories in English, which you understand, and that they ask you questions in English about these stories, and you give them back answers in English. Suppose also that after a while you get so good at following the instructions for manipulating the Chinese symbols and the programmers get so good at writing the programs that from the external point of view (i.e., someone outside the room) your answers to the questions are absolutely indistinguishable from those of native Chinese speakers. Nobody just looking at your answers can tell that you do not read a word of Chinese. Let us also suppose that your answers to the English questions are, as they no doubt would be, indistinguishable from those of other native English speakers, for the simple reason that you are a native English speaker. From the point of view of an observer, the answers to the Chinese questions and the English questions are equally good.

However, in the Chinese case, unlike the English case, you produce the answers by manipulating uninterpreted formal symbols; you simply behave like a computer performing computational operations on formally specified elements. You are "simply an instantiation of the computer program." You have inputs and outputs that are indistinguishable from a Chinese speaker, but you understand nothing.

Similarly, a computer can be programmed to manipulate symbols, but it, nevertheless, still lacks understanding of the meaning of what it is doing. So, Searle concludes, contrary to Tuning and his followers, the adherents of Strong Artificial Intelligence (AI), computers, unlike humans, cannot think. They lack consciousness, **intentionality,** and understanding. There are no grounds to suppose that robots or other types of artificial intelligence can understand, have feelings, have intentions, or perform mental acts. Do you agree? Can you think of a response that the functionalist might make to Searle's Chinese Room Objection? Whether functionalism is a significant advance over behaviorism, which it sought to replace, and whether it is superior to reductive materialism are highly controversial questions in contemporary philosophy of mind. What seems correct is the idea of multiple realizability. No reason has been given against the possibility that some types of behavioral or mental events have different types of structural accounts. The question is, Can some form of eliminative materialism or other theory account for this feature while giving a better account of how the various structures actually work? This is one of the exciting challenges of contemporary philosophy of mind, which I must leave you to ponder.

Meanwhile Searle has set forth a positive outline for a solution to the problem of consciousness. Consciousness is a biological property, one which emerges from lower-level neuronal functions in the cerebral cortex. Intentional properties, as well as consciousness itself, are simply aspects of biological events. Just as the molecular structure on the surface of a table gives rise to the property of smoothness (when in contact with our finger) and as a sufficient number of H_2O molecules give rise to the phenomenon of liquidity, so consciousness emerges on a higher level from the neuronal activity at lower levels of the cerebral cortex. The value of Searle's solution is that it takes consciousness seriously, rather than denying it, as the behaviorists and materialists do. It is a fundamental reality and not a mere epiphenomenon. However, in a sense, isn't it a type of materialism or physicalism or emergent biological materialism? For consciousness still is a property of the physical brain. This may be one of the most fascinating theories in the literature. Still, no one understands how consciousness arises, what causes the phenomenal feel or awareness that accompanies our every waking moment, and how consciousness unifies all our various experiences.

Dualism Revisited

Recently, David Chalmers has sought to defend dualist interactionism. His main argument, the *zombie argument*, is continued in the following passage from his book *The Conscious Mind:*

> Consider the logical possibility of a *zombie:* someone or something physically identical to me (or to any other conscious being), but lacking conscious experiences altogether. At the global level, we can consider the logical possibility of a *zombie world:* a world physically identical to ours, but in which there are no conscious experiences at all. In such a world, everybody is a zombie.
>
> So let us consider my zombie twin. This creature is molecule for molecule identical to me, and identical in all the low-level properties postulated by a completed physics, but he lacks conscious experience entirely. (Some might prefer to call a zombie "it," but I use the personal pronoun; I have grown quite fond of my zombie twin.) To fix ideas, we can imagine that right now I am gazing out the window, experiencing some nice green sensations from seeing the trees outside, having pleasant taste experiences through munching on a chocolate bar, and feeling a dull aching sensation in my right shoulder.
>
> What is going on in my zombie twin? He is physically identical to me, and we may as well suppose that he is embedded in an identical environment. He will certainly be identical to me *functionally:* he will be processing internal configurations being modified appropriately and with indistinguishable behavior resulting. He will be *psychologically* identical to me. . . . He will be perceiving the trees outside, in the functional sense, and tasting the chocolate, in the psychological sense. All of this follows logically from the fact that he is physically identical to me, by virtue of the functional analyses of psychological notions. . . . It is just that none of this functioning will be accompanied by any real conscious experience. There will be no phenomenal feel. There is nothing it is like to be a zombie.[15]

According to the zombie argument, then, it is logically possible that there be a world in which people are exactly like us in every physical detail but do not have experiences, or have experiences that are not like anything we have. These people would be indistinguishable from us in terms of behavior and physical structure down to the last detail. Chalmers thinks that since we can conceive of zombies who are physically identical to us but lacking consciousness—and, following Hume, whatever can be conceptually distinguished is different—we must have consciousness as a separate substance. We must be minds as well as physical bodies.

What do you make of Chalmers' theory? It has stirred up a lot of debate, but the essential problem is that it does not disprove that consciousness is a biological process, ontologically part of the brain's makeup and processes. The main objection is that it could well be that zombies are impossible. A being could not be exactly like us but lack conciousness. Interactive dualism is certainly a logical possibility, but so is epiphenomenalism. Also, some kind of materialism or functionalism could be the true explanation. One has to make a case that one theory is explanatorily richer than the others.

Summary

We have noted the strengths and weaknesses of functionalism, the theory that different structures could give rise to mental events and that we need not understand these processes to have a workable understanding of the workings of our mind. The strength of functionalism is that it improves on behaviorism by recognizing the reality of psychological states and events and keeps open the possibility of mental events in other types of structures (physical or nonphysical) different from ours. Its weakness is that, like its parent behaviorism, functionalism is essentially a black box theory, failing to recognize the reality of consciousness and intentionality. We have noted Searle's charge that computers cannot think so that strong artificial intelligence is a mistaken project, and we have noted his proposal of consciousness as a biological process.

You must ask yourself whether functionalism or any of its rivals give a satisfactory account of the central mystery of humanity, the conundrum of intelligent consciousness. Dualist interactionism preserves our intuition that conscious thought and intention affects the body, but it may be undermined by our theory of how the brain works. Material monism does justice to our understanding of neurology but seems to lose the self in a mass of neurons, Delta fibers and C-fibers. Epiphenomenalism does justice to the phenomena of physical behavior, recognizing that it causes mental events, but fails to do justice to our intuition that the mind also causes physical behavior. Functionalism is attractive because it leaves a lot of space for the internal workings of the mind but leaves all the fundamental causal questions unanswered. Panpsychism is an attractive placeholder for some because it puts mind into the heart of matter, but it does not explain anything. While it may be an exaggeration to say, as does *The International Dictionary of Psychology,* that "Nothing worth reading has been written about it," we have neither solved the mind–body problem nor learned how consciousness works. Perhaps we simply do not have enough information or understanding to solve this question. Perhaps we will never have the requisite capacity to understand how physical reality relates to mental reality. Whatever the answer, the questions about human nature and the mind–body problem are certainly the most interesting we can ask. Can you provide a rationally defensible answer for yourself?

Study Questions

1. What are the primary issues involved in the mind–body problem? How do the various theories discussed in this chapter throw light upon the question of human nature?

2. Examine the arguments for and against dualistic interactionism. How strong are the criticisms against this position? Can these criticisms be answered?

3. What is epiphenomenalism? What are its strengths and weaknesses?

4. What is the principle of simplicity, and how does it affect the discussion of dualism?

5. What is behaviorism? What are some problems with it?

6. What do you make of the story of Phineas Gage? Do such examples provide evidence that we are mistaken in supposing that the mind or consciousness is a separate reality?

7. If someone accepts materialism, is he or she thereby committed to determinism?

8. Examine the doctrines of reductive and eliminative materialism. What is the evidence for them? What is the evidence against these doctrines? If someone opts for materialism, which version (reductive or eliminative) is more plausible? How radical are these doctrines?

9. Jeffrey Olen offers the following analogy on the relation of interactive dualism, epiphenomenalism, and the identity theory:

> Some people who have never seen a watch find one alongside a road. They pick it up and examine it, noticing that the second hand makes a regular sweep around the watch's face. After some discussion, they conclude that the watch is run by a gremlin inside. They remove the back of the watch but cannot find the gremlin. After further discussion, they decide that it must be invisible. They also decide that it makes the hands go by running along the gears inside the watch. They replace the watch's back and take it home. The next day the watch stops. Someone suggests that the gremlin is dead.
>
> Someone else suggests that it's probably sleeping. They shake the watch to awaken the gremlin, but the watch remains stopped. Someone finally turns the stem. The second hand begins to move. The person who said that the gremlin was asleep smiles triumphantly. The winding has awakened it.
>
> For a long time the people hold the gremlin hypothesis, but finally an innovative citizen puts forth the hypothesis that the watch can work without a gremlin. He dismantles the watch and explains the movements of the inner parts. His fellows complain that he has left out the really important aspect, the gremlin. "Of course," they agree, "the winding contributes to the turning of the gears. But only because it wakes up the gremlin, which then resumes its running." But gradually the suggestion of the innovative citizen converts a number of others to his position. The gremlin is not vital to run the watch. Nevertheless, they are reluctant to reject the gremlin altogether. So they compromise and conclude that there is a gremlin inside, but he is not needed to run the watch.
>
> But the man who figured out that the watch worked without the intervention of a gremlin is dissatisfied. If we do not need the gremlin to explain how the watch works, why continue to believe that it exists? Isn't it simpler to say that it does not?[16]

Do you think that this is a good analogy of our views on the mind–body problem?

10. What are the advantages of functionalism? How plausible a theory is it? What does it do that the other theories do not? What does it leave out that is important? Can eliminative materialism answer the problems raised by functionalism?

11. Review the major theories discussed in this chapter. Assess their strengths and weaknesses. What is your conclusion?

12. Consider Searle's Chinese Room Objection. Is Searle's concept of understanding clear (see note 14)? Could you argue that we really understand in degrees, so that robots and computers simply have low-level understanding whereas we have high-level understanding?

Notes

1. Paul Churchland, *Matter and Consciousness* (MIT Press, 1990), p. 1.
2. René Descartes, *The Philosophical Works of Descartes,* vol. 1, trans. E. Haldane and G. R. T. Ross (Cambridge University Press, 1911), p. 152.
3. Ibid.
4. Ibid.
5. Ibid., p. 192.
6. Ibid, p. 345.
7. Thomas Hobbes, *Leviathan* (Penguin Books, 1986), chapter 46.
8. Colin McGinn, *London Review of Books* (January 23, 1986), 24f.
9. Richard Rorty, "Mind–Body Identity, Privacy, and Categories," *Review of Metaphysics* (1965), 28f.
10. Ibid., p. 30f.
11. Thomas Nagel, *A View from Nowhere* (Oxford University Press, 1986), p. 7.
12. Daniel Dennett, *The Intentional Stance* (MIT Press, 1987), p. 5.
13. See Jerry Fodor, *Psychological Explanations* (Random House, 1968); and Hilary Putnam, "The Nature of Mental States," in *Mind, Language and Reality* (Cambridge University Press, 1975). Both articles are found in Beakley and Ludlow's anthology and Rosenthal's anthology, both listed in For Further Reading.
14. John Searle, "Minds, Brains and Programs," *The Behavioral and Brain Sciences,* vol. 3 (1980). Searle describes *understanding* as "implying both the possession of mental (intentional) states and the truth (validity, success) of these states." *Intentionality* is that "feature of certain mental states by which they are directed at or about objects and states of affairs in the world. Thus, beliefs, desires, and intentions are intentional states; undirected forms of anxiety and depression are not."
15. David Chalmers, *The Conscious Mind: In Search of a Fundamental Theory* (Oxford University Press, 1996), pp. 94–95.
16. Jeffrey Olen, *Persons and Their Worlds* (Random House, 1983), p. 223.

For Further Reading

Beakley, Brian, and Peter Ludlow, eds., *The Philosophy of Mind: Classical Problems and Contemporary Issues* (MIT Press, 1992). An excellent anthology.

Chalmers, David, *The Conscious Mind* (Oxford University Press, 1996). The most thorough discussion of consciousness in the literature, from a dualist position.

Churchland, Paul, *Matter and Consciousness* (MIT Press, 1990). A superb introductory text from a materialist perspective.

Dennett, Daniel, *The Intentional Stance* (MIT Press, 1989). A brilliant discussion of the mental states.

———, *Consciousness Explained* (Brown & Co., 1991).

Levin, Michael E., *Metaphysics and the Mind–Body Problem* (Clarendon Press, 1979). An excellent defense of materialism. My illustration of the principle of simplicity was taken from this work.

Lycan, William, ed., *Mind and Cognition* (Blackwell, 1991). An excellent anthology.

McGinn, Colin, "Can We Solve the Mind–Body Problem?" *Mind*, vol. 98 (1989).

———, *The Character of Mind* (Oxford University Press, 1982). A rich, compact exposition of the major issues.

Moreland, J. P., *Scaling the Secular City* (Baker Books, 1987). Contains a defense of dualistic interactionism from a Christian perspective.

Rosenthal, David M., ed., *The Nature of Mind* (Oxford University Press, 1992). The best anthology of contemporary work available. Contains an excellent bibliography.

Searle, John, *Mind, Brains and Science* (Harvard University Press, 1984). A perceptive work, setting forth puzzles and providing a brilliant analysis of the issues.

———, *The Rediscovery of Mind* (MIT Press, 1992). A further development of Searle's ideas.

Stich, Stephen, *From Folk Psychology to Cognitive Science: The Case Against Belief* (MIT Press, 1983).

Turing, A., "Computing Machinery and Intelligence," *Mind*, vol. 59 (1950).

CHAPTER 15

The Paradox of Human Nature: Are We Free?

> If I were capable of correct reasoning, and if, at the same time, I had a complete knowledge both of his disposition and of all the events by which he was surrounded, I should be able to foresee the line of conduct which, in consequence of those events, he would adopt. *(H. T. Buckle,* History of Civilization in England, *1857)*

Free Will and Determinism

We have reached the end of our study of the various theories of human nature. We have examined several of the most prominent ones, assessing their strengths and weaknesses. Before I provide a brief summary of what has been covered, we need to look at one more issue.

Throughout this work, one issue that has come up over and over again is that of determinism versus free will. Philosophers like Augustine, Rousseau, Kierkegaard, and Sartre have asserted a strong version of free will and made moral responsibility depend on it. On the other hand, Hobbes, Schopenhauer, Marx, Freud, and the contemporary neuro-philosophers Dennett and Churchland deny it, holding to the **causal thesis,** that every act and event in the universe is caused by antecedent events. Science depends on this thesis. Moreover, we find it hard to think about actions in noncausal terms. If libertarian free will is true, it seems a mystery. Granted, we all feel free while acting; but if Freud is right, these feelings may be deceptive, masking unconscious causes. The main argument for freedom of the will is the argument from moral responsibility. We want something like free will to ensure moral responsibility. The question is whether one can be a determinist and consistently hold to moral responsibility. In this chapter, we examine the arguments for libertarianism and determinism and then explore the possibility of reconciling determinism with moral responsibility.

Determinists, as we have noted, believe the causal thesis. Carried to its logical conclusion, it would follow (as Buckle notes in the quotation above) that were I to know all the initial states in the universe and the laws of nature, I could predict all of the future events in the universe.

However, everyone, including determinists, feels resentment at others who purposefully step on their toes or cheat them or break a promise or lie to them. Moreover, we become grateful for favors rendered, admire the feats of our heroes, and celebrate acts of kindness and justice. Albert Schweitzer deserved our admiration for sacrificing the status and comforts of a socially and professionally successful musical and academic career in order to set up a medical clinic in French West Africa, serving the poor and needy the rest of his life. Conversely, racists who harm others deserve to be sanctioned and punished for their immoral acts. Adolf Hitler and his Nazi followers were responsible for heinous, terrible actions, for which they deserved punishment appropriate to their crimes. We cannot help but hold people responsible for their actions: they ought to be praised and rewarded for their virtuous actions and blamed and punished for their vicious actions. We may call this the responsibility thesis.[1] All socially mature persons, even determinists, have such reactive attitudes.

These theses, the causal thesis and the responsibility thesis, seem both true and diametrically opposed to one another. Each seems to entail the denial of the other. The responsibility thesis seems to entail freedom of the will, whereas the causal thesis seems to rest on a theory of determinism which excludes freedom of the will. Determinists like Schopenhauer, Buckle, Baron D'Holbach, and John Hospers before him argue that the causal thesis is true and excludes moral responsibility. Clarence Darrow used the determinist thesis to his advantage in getting lighter sentences for convicted criminals, arguing that they were merely the victims of forces over which they had no control.[2] In the words of Omar Khayyam, we are

But helpless pieces of the game He plays
Upon this Chequer-board of Nights and Days;
Hither and thither moves, and checks and slays,
And one by one back in the Closet lays.[3]

We may call Darrow's position hard determinism. It holds that determinism and moral responsibility are incompatible.

We want to hold onto moral responsibility. Libertarians claim that only the doctrine of libertarian free will can guarantee moral responsibility. So let us turn to libertarianism.

Libertarianism

Libertarianism is the theory that we do have free wills. It contends that, given the same antecedent (prior) conditions at time $t1$, an agent S could do either act $A1$ or $A2$. That is, it is up to S what the world will look like after $t1$, and his or her act is causally underdetermined, the self making the unexplained difference. Libertarians do not contend that all our actions are free, only some of them. Neither do they offer an explanatory theory of free will. Their arguments are indirect. They offer two main arguments for their position. The first is the argument from deliberation, and the second is the argument from moral responsibility.

The Argument from Deliberation

The position is nicely summed up in the words of Corliss Lamont:

> There is the unmistakable intuition of virtually every human being that he is free to make the choices he does and that the deliberations leading to those choices are also free flowing. The normal man feels too, after he has made a decision, that he could have decided differently. That is why regret or remorse for a past choice can be so disturbing.[4]

As an example, there is a difference between a knee jerk and purposefully kicking a football. In the first case, the behavior is involuntary, a reflex action. In the second case, we deliberate, notice that we have an alternative (viz., not kicking the ball), consciously choose to kick the ball, and if successful, find our body moving in the requisite manner so that the ball is kicked.

Deliberation may take a short or long time, be foolish or wise; but the process is a conscious one wherein we believe that we really can do either of the actions (or any of many possible actions). That is, in deliberating, we assume that we are free to choose between alternatives and that we are not determined to do simply one action. Otherwise, why deliberate? This should seem obvious to everyone who introspects on what it is to deliberate. Furthermore, there seems to be something psychologically lethal about accepting determinism in human relations; it tends to curtail deliberation and paralyze actions. If people really believe themselves totally determined, the tendency is for them to excuse their behavior. Human effort seems pointless. As Arthur Eddington put it, "What significance is there to my mental struggle tonight whether I shall or shall not give up smoking, if the laws which govern the matter of the physical universe already preordain for the morrow a configuration of matter consisting of pipe, tobacco, and smoke connected to my lips?"[5]

The Determinist's Objection to the Argument from Deliberation

The determinist responds to this by admitting that we often feel "free" and that we could do otherwise but that these feelings are illusory. The determinist may admit that at any given time *t1*, while deliberating, she or he feels free, at least on one level. However, on a higher level or after the deliberation process is over, she acknowledges that even the deliberation is the product of antecedent causes. Ledger Wood suggests that the libertarian argument from deliberation can be reduced to this formula: "I feel myself free, *therefore*, I am free." He analyzes the deliberative decision in three constituents: *(1)* the recognition of two or more incompatible courses of action, *(2)* the weighing of considerations favorable and unfavorable to each of the conflicting possibilities of action, and *(3)* the choice among the alternative possibilities. "At the moment of making the actual decision, the mind experiences a *feeling* of self-assertion and of independence both external and internal." However, Wood insists that the determinist can give a satisfactory account of this feeling, regarding it as "nothing but a sense of relief following upon earlier tension and indecision."

> After conflict and uncertainty, the pent-up energies of the mind—or rather of the underlying neural processes—are released and this process is accompanied by an inner sense of power. Thus the feeling of freedom or voluntary control over one's actions is a mere subjective illusion which cannot be considered evidence for psychological indeterminacy.[6]

Sometimes, the determinist will offer an account of action in terms of action being the result of the strongest motive. Adolf Grunbaum puts it this way:

> Let us carefully examine the content of the feeling that on a certain occasion we could have acted other than the way we did in fact act. What do we find? Does the feeling we have inform us that we could have acted otherwise under exactly the same external and internal motivational conditions? No, says the determinist, this feeling simply discloses that we were able to act in accord with our strongest desire at the time, and that we could indeed have acted otherwise if a different motive had prevailed at that time.[7]

We could break up the concept of motivation into two parts, that of belief and desire (or wants), resulting in the combination of a desire based on certain beliefs. If Mary strongly desires to fly to New York from Los Angeles at a certain time and believes that taking a certain American Air Lines flight is the best way to do this, she will, unless there are other intervening factors, take such a flight. There is no mystery about the decision. She may deliberate on whether she really wants to pay the $50 more on American than she would have to pay on a later economy flight, but once she realizes that she values getting to New York at a certain time more than saving $50, she will act accordingly. If Mary is rational, her wants and desires will function in a reliable pattern. Because wants and beliefs are not under our direct control, are not products of free choice, and the act is a product of desires and beliefs, the act is not a product of free choice either. The argument goes something like this:

1. Actions are the results of (are caused by) beliefs and desires.
2. We do not freely choose our beliefs and desires.
3. Beliefs and desires are thrust on us by our environment in conjunction with innate dispositions.
4. Therefore, we do not freely choose our actions, but our actions are caused by the causal processes that form our beliefs and desires.

If this is so, it is hard to see where free will comes into the picture. The controversial premise is probably premise 2, whether we choose our beliefs and desires.

The determinist would maintain that we do not choose our beliefs but that they, as truth-directed, are events in our lives, the way the world represents itself to us. That is, beliefs function as truth detectors; as it is not up to us what the truth is, so it is not up to us to form beliefs about the world. You can check this in a small way by asking why it is you believe that the world is spherical and not flat. Because of evidence, or because you choose to believe it? If the latter, could you give up the belief by simply deciding to do so? Neither do we choose our desires, but our desires simply formulate choices. We do not choose to be hungry or to love knowledge, although when we find ourselves in conflict between two conflicting desires (e.g., the desire to eat ice cream and the desire to lose weight), we have to adjudicate the difference. This decision is simply a process of allowing the strongest desire (or deepest desire—a deep dispositional desire could win out over a sharply felt occurrent desire) to win out. However, all this can be explained in a purely deterministic way, without resorting to a mysterious free act of the will.

The Libertarian Counterresponse: Agent Causation

Now, the libertarian objects that this is too simplistic a notion of action. We cannot isolate the desires and beliefs in such a rigid manner. There are intangibles at work here and they may be decisive in bringing all factors of desire and belief together and formulating the final decision. Some libertarians, such as Roderick Chisholm and Richard Taylor, respond to this view of motivation by putting forward an alternative picture of causation to account for actions. According to Chisholm and Taylor, it is sometimes the case that agents themselves are the cause of their own acts. That is, the agent causes actions without himself or herself changing in any essential way. No account need be given on how this is possible:

> The only conception of action that accords with our data is one according to which men . . . are sometimes, but of course not always, self-determining beings; that is, beings which are sometimes the causes of their own behavior. In the case of an action that is free, it must be such that it is caused by the agent who performs it, but such that no antecedent conditions were sufficient for his performing just that action. In the case of an action that is both free and rational, it must be that the agent who performed it did so for some reason, but this reason cannot have been the cause of it.[8]

This notion of the self as agent differs from the Humean notion that the self is simply a bundle of perceptions; instead, the self is a substance and a self-moving being. Human beings are not simply assemblages of material processes but complex wholes, with a different metaphysical status from physical objects. Furthermore, the self is a substance and not an event. It is a being that initiates action without being moved to act by antecedent causes. If I raise my hand, it is not the events leading up to the raising of my hand that cause this act, but I myself am the cause. In a sense, the self becomes a "god," creating ex nihilo, in that reasons may influence, but do not determine, the acts. In the words of Chisholm,

If we are responsible, and if what I have been trying to say [about agent causality] is true, then we have a prerogative which some would attribute only to God: each of us, when we act, is a prime mover unmoved. In doing what we do, we cause certain events to happen and nothing—or no one—causes us to cause those events to happen.[9]

Perhaps the libertarian draws some support for this thesis from Genesis 1:26, where God says "Let us make man in our image." The image of God may be our ability to make free, causally underdetermined decisions. In a sense, every libertarian believes in at least one "god" and in creative miracles. This theory, although attractive in that it preserves the notion of free agency, suffers from the fact that it leaves agent causation unexplained. The self is a mystery that is unexplained. Actions are seen as miracles that are unrelated to antecedent causal chains, detached from the laws of nature. Nevertheless, something like the argument from agency seems to be intuitively satisfying upon introspection. We do feel that we are free agents. Along these lines, the libertarian dismisses the determinist's hypothesis of a complete causal explanation based on a correlation of brain events with mental events. Memories are stored in the brain, but the self is not. Whether as an emergent property, a transcendent entity, or simply an unexplained mystery, the self must be regarded as primitive. In a Cartesian manner, it is to be accepted as more certain than anything else and the source of all other certainties.

Objection to Arguments from Introspection

The problem with the argument from introspection, which underlies the agency theory, is that our introspections and intuitions about our behavior are often misguided. Freudian psychology and common sense tell us that sometimes when we believe that we are acting from one motive, another hidden subconscious motive is really at play. The hypnotized person believes that she or he is free when she or he is uttering preordained speech, while the audience looks on knowingly. Dr. Chris Frederickson, a neurophysiologist at the University of Texas at Dallas, has told of experiments with electrodes that illustrate this point nicely. Patients with electrodes attached to their neocortex are set before a button, which sets off a bell. The patients are told that they may press the button whenever they like. The patients proceed to press the buttons and ring the bells. They report that they are entirely free in doing this. However, the monitoring of the brain shows that an impulse is started in the cerebral cortex before they become aware of their desire and decision to press the button, and when this impulse reaches a certain level, the patients feel the volition and press the button. Is it fair to suppose that all our behavior may follow this model? Do we only become conscious of the workings of our subconscious at discrete moments? Notice in this regard that often we seem to have unconsciously formulated our speech before we are conscious of what we are saying. The words flow naturally, as though some inner speech writer were working them out beforehand. It seems, then, that our introspective reports must be regarded as providing very little evidence in favor of free will in the libertarian sense. As Baruch Spinoza (1632–1677) said, if a stone hurled through the air were to become conscious, it would probably deem itself free.

The Argument from Quantum Physics (A Peephole of Free Will)

At this point, libertarians sometimes refer to an argument from quantum mechanics in order to defend themselves against the insistence of determinists that science is on their side in their espousal of universal causality. The argument from quantum mechanics is negative and indirectly supports the libertarian thesis. According to quantum mechanics as developed by Niels Bohr (1885–1962) and Max Born (1882–1970), subatomic particles do not follow causal processes but instead yield only statistically predictable behavior. That is, we cannot predict the motions of individual particles, but we can successfully predict the percentage that will act in certain ways. A certain randomness seems to operate on the subatomic level. Hence, there is a case for indeterminacy. This thesis of quantum mechanics is controversial. Albert Einstein (1879–1955) never accepted it. "God doesn't play dice!" he said. Quantum physics may only indicate the fact that we do not know the operative causes at the subatomic level. After all, we are only in the kindergarten of subatomic physics. So the indeterminist may be committing the fallacy of ignorance in reading too much into the inability of quantum physicists to give causal explanations of subatomic behavior. On the other hand, perhaps quantum physics should make impartial persons reconsider what they mean by "causality" and whether it could be the case that it is an unclear concept in the first place. The fact that our notion of causality is vague and unanalyzed was pointed out long ago by David Hume (1711–1776) and reiterated in the 20th century by William James (1842–1910):

> The principle of causality . . . —what is it but a postulate, an empty name covering simply a demand that the sequence of events shall some day manifest a deeper kind of belonging of one thing with another than the mere arbitrary juxtaposition which now phenomenally appears? It is as much an altar to an unknown god as the one that Saint Paul found at Athens. All our scientific and philosophic ideas are altars to unknown gods.[10]

Recent work by philosophers on the subject of causality has not substantially improved this state of affairs. The notion, although enjoying an intuitively privileged position in our noetic structure, is still an enigma. Nevertheless, although the quantum theory and doubts about causality may cause us to loosen our grip on the notion of universal causality, it does not help the libertarians in any positive way, for it only shows at best that there is randomness in the world, not that there is purposeful free agency. Uncaused behavior suggests erratic, impulsive, reflex motion without any rhyme or reason, the behavior of the maniac, lacking all predictability and explanation, behavior out of our rational control. However, free action must be under my control if it is to be counted as my behavior. That is, the thesis of libertarianism is that the agent is underdetermined when he makes a purposeful, rational decision. All that quantum mechanics entails is that there are random events in the brain (or wherever) that yield unpredictable behavior for which the agent is not responsible.

The Argument from Moral Responsibility

Determinism seems to conflict with the thesis that we have moral responsibilities, for responsibility implies that we could have done otherwise than we did. We do not hold a dog responsible for chewing up our philosophy book or a 1-month-old baby for crying because they could not help it, but we do hold a 20-year-old student responsible for cheating because (we believe) she or he could have done otherwise. Black-backed seagulls will tear apart a stray herring seagull baby without the slightest suspicion that their act may be immoral, but if humans lack this sense, we judge the behavior as pathological, as substandard. Moral responsibility is something that we take very seriously. We believe that we do have duties, "oughts," over which we feel rational guilt at our failure to perform; but there can be no such thing as duties, praise, blame, or rational guilt if we are not essentially free. The argument form is as follows:

1. If determinism is true and our actions are merely the product of the laws of nature and antecedent states of affairs, then it is not up to us to choose what we do.
2. But if it is not up to us to choose what we do, we cannot be said to be responsible for what we do.
3. So if determinism is true, we are not responsible for what we do.
4. But our belief in moral responsibility is self-evident, at least as strong as our belief in universal causality.
5. So if we believe that we have moral responsibilities, determinism cannot be accepted.

We must reject the notion of determinism even if we cannot give a full explanatory account of how agents choose. Here, the determinist bites the bullet and admits that we do not have moral responsibilities and that it is just an illusion that we do. However, we are determined to have such an illusion, so there is nothing we can do about it. Perhaps we cannot consciously live as determinists, in the sense that when we act we cannot help feel that we are free to do otherwise, but why should we think that we can? We are finite and fallible creatures, driven by causal laws, but with self-consciousness that makes us aware of part (but only a part) of the process that governs our behavior. We can accept determinism, realize that we are not really free, and take account of this in our institutional arrangements—perhaps by basing punishment on the principles of deterrence, prevention, and rehabilitation, rather than on desert and responsibility. The libertarian will not accept this reply as an adequate answer because determinism seems to make us into robots who respond to forces beyond our control—the antecendent determining factors. However, there is another response to the problem of free will and determinism, which claims to save both the notion of determinism and the notion of moral responsibility. To this reconciling project, called compatibilism, we turn.

Metaphysical Compatibilism

Some philosophers, namely David Hume, John Stuart Mill (1806–1873), Walter Stace (1886–1967), and Harry Frankfurt argue that we can reconcile the causal thesis with the responsibility thesis. This is called metaphysical compatibilism, or simply **compatibilism,** sometimes also referred to as soft determinism. The difference between these two designations is that whereas the soft determinist holds to the truth of determinism, the compatibilist maintains that even if determinism is true, moral responsibility is not denied. On the other hand, metaphysical libertarians, like William James and others holding to contracausal freedom of the will, agree with determinists that if the causal thesis is true, moral responsibility does not exist. They are called incompatibilists. Let us examine the case for compatibilism.

A leading compatibilist, Walter Stace, has argued that the problem of freedom and determinism is really only a semantic one, a dispute about the meanings of words. Freedom has to do with acts done voluntarily, and determinism has to do with the causal processes that underlie all behavior and events. These need not be incompatible. Mahatma Gandhi (1869–1948) fasted because he wanted to free India from colonial rule and so performed a voluntary or free act, whereas a man starving in the desert is not giving up food voluntarily or as a free act. A thief purposefully and voluntarily steals, whereas a kleptomaniac cannot help stealing. In both cases, each act or event has causal antecedents, but the former in each set are free, whereas the latter are unfree: "Acts freely done are those whose immediate causes are psychological states in the agent. Acts not freely done are those whose immediate causes are states of affairs external to the agent."[11]

Sometimes the compatibilist position is put in terms of reasons for actions. An agent is free just in case he or she acts according to reasons rather than from either internal neurotic or external coercive pressures. However our reasons are not things we choose but wants and beliefs with which we find ourselves. Since free actions are caused by that which is not a free act, we can see that our free actions are in a sense determined. The argument for compatibilism can be formulated like this:

1. The reasons R that someone S has for performing act A are not themselves actions.
2. S could not help having R.
3. Act A could nevertheless be free because it was not coerced by external causes.
4. Therefore, an action may result from having a reason that one could not help having—that is, a reason that one was not free not to have—and yet the action might nevertheless be free.
5. Therefore, we obtain the collapse of the argument for the incompatibility of free action and determinism.

The compatibilist challenges the libertarian to produce an action that does not fit this formula. Consider the act of raising my hand at time *t1*. Why do I do it? Well, if it is a rational (i.e., free) act, it's because I have a reason for raising my hand. For example, at *t1* I wish to vote for Joan to be president of our club. I deliberate on whom to vote for (i.e., allow the options to present themselves before my mind), decide that Joan is the best candidate, and raise my hand in response to that judgment. It is a free act, but all the features can be accommodated within causal explanatory theory. Reasons function as causes here.

What kind of free act would not be determined by reasons? Consider the situation of coming to a fork in the road with no obvious reason to take either one (or go back, for that matter). If there are no reasons to do one thing more than another, I have no basis for choice. However, I may still believe that doing something is better than just standing still, so I flip a coin in order to decide. This belief functions as my reason for flipping the coin. Similarly, I may flip a "mental coin" by letting the internal devices of my subconscious make an arbitrary decision. The alternative to these arbitrary "flips of the coin" is to be in the same position as Buridan's ass, who starved to death while he was an equal distance between two luscious bales of hay because there was no more reason to choose one bale over the other! So, the objection runs, all rational action is determined by reason, and libertarianism turns out to be incoherent. The compatibilist joins with the determinist to the extent that he or she asserts that all actions have a sufficient causal explanation. Free actions are caused by reasons the person has, and unfree actions are caused by nonrational coercion. What would it mean to act freely without reasons? What kind of freedom would that be? Would it not turn out to be irrational, hence arbitrary or unconsciously motivated action? If our free acts are the acts that we do voluntarily because we have reasons for them, we can be held accountable for them. We identify with the springs of those actions and so may be said to have produced them in a way that we do not produce involuntary actions. We could have avoided those actions if we had chosen to do so. Hence, we are responsible for them.

One particularly sophisticated version of this position is that of Harry Frankfurt, who argues that what is important about freedom of the will is not any contracausal notions but the manner in which the will is structured. What distinguishes persons from other conscious beings (which he calls "wantons") are the second-order desires that they have. All conscious beings have first-order desires, but persons have attitudes about those first-order desires. They either want it to be the case that their first-order desires motivate them to action or that they do not motivate them to action: "Someone has a desire of the second order either when he wants simply to have a certain desire or when he wants a certain desire to be his will. In situations of the latter kind, I shall call his second-order desires 'second-order volitions.'"[12]

A nicotine addict may very well desire that his first-order desire for a cigarette be frustrated or overcome, whereas a wife unable to feel certain sentiments toward her husband may have a second-order desire that she would come to have feelings of affection for her husband. Nevertheless, we should not confuse free will with free action:

We do not suppose that animals enjoy freedom of the will, although we recognize that an animal may be free to run in whatever direction it wants. Thus, having the freedom to do what one wants to do is not a sufficient condition of having a free will. It is not a necessary condition either. For to deprive someone of his freedom of action is not necessarily to undermine the freedom of his will. When an agent is aware that there are certain things he is not free to do, this doubtless affects his desires and limits the range of choices he can make. But suppose someone, without being aware of it, has in fact lost or been deprived of his freedom of action. Even though he is no longer free to do what he wants to do, his will may remain as free as it was before. Despite the fact that he is not free to translate his desires into actions or to act according to the determinations of his will, he may still form those desires and make those determinations as freely as if his freedom of action had not been impaired.[13]

Hence, it makes no sense to define free will as the libertarians do, as those actions that originate in ways underdetermined by antecedent causes. A person's will is free just in case she or he is free to have the will she or he wants, whether or not she or he is able to act.

Libertarians are not satisfied with the compatibilist thesis. William James called it a "quagmire of evasion."[14] As Peter van Inwagen of the University of Notre Dame has noted, if determinism is true, then our acts are the consequences of the laws of nature and events in the remote past. However, it is not up to us what went on before we were born, and neither is it up to us what the laws of nature are. Therefore, the consequences of these things (including our present acts) are not up to us.[15] The compatibilist responds that just so long as our actions were done voluntarily, we may be held accountable for them.

You may have already noticed that the libertarian theory cannot be proven and the determinist thesis cannot be falsified. Simply not finding the cause of some event E does not mean there is none, any more than not finding the murderer of some victim does not mean there is none. However, a theory that is unfalsifiable is a poor scientific theory. We want to know what would count against the theory in order to be able to test it.

We should make one more point about the debate over free will and determinism. The theory of naturalistic evolution tells us that wholly deterministic and physicalistic processes are responsible for whatever we are. However, we are self-conscious beings whose inner experiences are not physicalist. They are mental. Hence, as we saw in chapter 14, the fundamental mystery is how something as physicalistic as evolutionary processes could result in something nonphysical—consciousness—from which freedom of the will emerges. Although the determinist cannot explain consciousness or how the physical results in and causes the mental, the libertarian is no better off, for no one has successfully explained how the mental can affect the physical. How does the mind make contact with the body in order to move it to action? Where are its points of contact, its hooks that pull on our brains and/or limbs? In the end, perhaps the best we can do is to be aware of the fascinating mystery of the problem of free will and determinism and admit our ignorance about a solution. If we look at ourselves through the eyes of science and neurophysiology, we will no doubt regard ourselves as determined. If we look at ourselves from the perspective of morality, as subjective deliberators, we must view ourselves as having free will. As philosophers—which we all are, like it or not—we stand in wonder at the dualism that forces us to take both an objective/determinist and a subjective/libertarian perspective of conscious behavior. This dichotomy seems unsatisfactory, incompatible, and yet inescapable.

Given the dilemma of determinism, perhaps the best way to preserve moral responsibility is to adopt a disjunctive strategy. We can hold that either libertarianism or compatibilism is true. It may be hedging our bet, but the strategy gives us what we want, responsibility.

Summary

The debate over freedom and determinism is one of the most intractable in philosophy. We feel that we are free and need an idea of free will to ensure moral responsibility. Yet science seems to presuppose metaphysical determinism, the doctrine that every event and state of affairs in the universe has a sufficient cause. Some object that quantum mechanics shows that determinism is false, but even if that is so, it does not show that we have free will, only that the universe might behave in a random manner. The compatibilist tries to reconcile free will and determinism by redefining responsibility in terms of voluntary action. Whether this succeeds is an open question.

Study Questions

1. Go over the two major theories (determinism and libertarianism). What are the strengths and weaknesses of each theory? Which do you think is the best answer, and why?

2. It is often claimed that our moral intuitions—that we are responsible for our actions and have duties, that people should be praised or blamed and punished or rewarded for their actions—turn out to be illusory if the libertarian answer is not true. The argument, which we noted above, goes as follows:

   1. If determinism is true and our actions are merely the product of the laws of nature and antecedent states of affairs, then it is not up to us to choose what we do.
   2. However, if it is not up to us to choose what we do, we cannot be said to be responsible for what we do.
   3. So if determinism is true, we are not responsible for what we do.
   4. However, our belief in moral responsibility is self-evident, at least as strong as our belief in universal causality.
   5. So if we believe that we have moral responsibilities, determinism cannot be accepted.

   We must reject the notion of determinism even if we cannot give a full explanatory account of how agents choose. Of course, even if this is a sound argument, the determinist can bite the bullet and admit that we do not have moral responsibilities and that it is just an illusion that we do. We are determined to have such an illusion, so there is nothing we can do about it. Evaluate this argument and the determinist response. How would the compatibilist respond to it? Discuss your answer.

3. Jean-Paul Sartre wrote "We are condemned to freedom." Explain.

4. Discuss the problem of punishment. How would a determinist, a libertarian, and a compatibilist defend the practice of punishing criminals?

5. Examine the following quotation by Thomas Nagel:

> If one cannot be responsible for consequences of one's acts due to factors beyond one's control, or for antecedents of one's acts that are properties of temperament not subject to one's will, or for the circumstances that pose one's moral choices, then how can one be responsible even for the stripped-down acts of the will itself, if *they* are the product of antecedent circumstances outside of the will's control? The area of genuine agency, and therefore of legitimate moral judgment, seems to shrink under this scrutiny to an extensionless point.[16]

What is your response to Nagel's argument?

Notes

1. Although the term *responsibility* is used in various ways, we may define *moral responsibility* as equivalent to deserving praise or blame for actions. To be legally responsible is to fulfill standard conditions or requirements determined by the law. To be morally responsible is to fulfill standard conditions determined by morality. *The Oxford Companion to Philosophy* defines it as "covering (i) having a moral obligation and (ii) the fulfilment of the criteria for deserving blame or praise (punishment or reward) for a morally significant act or omission." Responsibility seems closely allied with the concept of autonomy, the ability to deliberate and make choices. The feature distinguishes us from most nonhuman animals—the ability to reflect and decide on actions. How we choose and what we do determine the quality of our responsibility.
2. Clarence Darrow, *Attorney for the Damned* (Simon & Schuster, 1957).
3. Omar Khayyam, *Rubaiyat,* trans. Edward Fitzgerald (Random House, 1947, quatrain 69). Khayyam (ca. 1047–1123) originally wrote in Persian, in present-day Iran.
4. Corliss Lamont, *Freedom of Choice Affirmed* (Horizon, 1967), p. 3.
5. Arthur Eddington, *The Nature of the Physical World* (Macmillan, 1928).
6. Ledger Wood, "The Free Will Controversy," *Philosophy,* vol. 16 (1941), p. 386.
7. Adolf Grunbaum, "Causality and the Science of Human Behavior," in *Philosophical Problems,* ed. M. Mandelbaum (Macmillan, 1957), p. 336.
8. Richard Taylor, *Metaphysics* (Prentice-Hall, 1974), p. 54.
9. Roderick Chisholm, "Human Freedom and the Self," in *Free Will,* ed. Gary Watson (Oxford University Press), p. 32.
10. William James, "The Dilemma of Determinism," in *Essays on Faith and Morals* (World Press, 1962).
11. Walter Stace, *Religion and the Modern Mind* (Lippincott, 1952).

12. Harry Frankfurt, "Freedom of the Will and the Concept of a Person," in *Free Will*, ed. Gary Watson (Clarendon Press, 1982), pp. 81–95.
13. Ibid., p. 90.
14. James, op. cit.
15. Peter van Inwagen, *An Essay on Free Will* (Clarendon Press, 1983), p. 16.
16. Thomas Nagel, *Mortal Questions* (Cambridge University Press, 1979), p. 35.

For Further Reading

Dennett, Daniel, *Elbow Room: The Varieties of Free Will Worth Wanting* (MIT Press, 1984). A well-argued defense of compatibilism.

Lehrer, Keith, and James Cornman, *Philosophical Problems and Argument,* 3rd ed. (Macmillan, 1982). Lehrer's essay in chapter 3 is excellent.

Stace, Walter T., *Religion and the Modern Mind* (Lippincott, 1952). Contains a lucid account of compatibilism.

Trustead, Jennifer, *Free Will and Responsibility* (Oxford University Press, 1984). A clear, accessible introduction to the subject.

van Inwagen, Peter, *An Essay on Free Will* (Clarendon Press, 1983). A highly original study, criticizing compatibilism.

Watson, Gary, ed., *Free Will* (Clarendon Press, 1982). Contains important articles, especially those by Frankfurt, van Inwagen, and Watson himself.

Conclusion

What is man in nature? A Nothing in comparison with the Infinite, an All in comparison with the Nothing, a mean between nothing and everything. Since he is infinitely removed from comprehending the extremes, the end of things and their beginning are hopelessly hidden from him in an impenetrable secret; he is equally incapable of seeing the Nothing from which he was made, and the Infinite in which he is swallowed up.

What will he do then, but perceive the appearance of the middle of things, in an eternal despair of knowing either their beginning or their end. All things proceed from the Nothing, and are borne towards the Infinite. Who will follow these marvelous processes? The Author of these wonders understands them. None other can do so. *(Pascal,* Pensees, *199)*

We have examined several theories of human nature, viewing a vast amount of diversity and genius. A vast number of fascinating hypotheses abound, paying tribute to the fecundity of the human mind or, possibly, divine revelation. In this conclusion, we bring together our findings. In our introduction, we asked eight questions regarding human nature. Let us see how the various theories answered those questions.

What Is the Truth About Human Nature?

Of what are we made? Is our nature monistic (totally mental or totally material) or dualistic (both mental and material)? Are we spiritual beings, made in the image of God, as the Bible states,[1] or divine sparks, as the Eastern religions teach and Plato believed? Or, are we wholly material beings, as Hobbes, Marx, and contemporary neuroscience hold? We examined dualist theories, such as Augustine, Descartes, and Kierkegaard hold; epiphenomenal theories, like those of Marx and

Freud; and materialist theories, like those of Hobbes, Darwin, and the neurophilosophers. The body–mind problem deals with the form of our nature.

Going deeper, into the content of human nature, we may ask, What is humanity's essence? Religions hold that we are made in the image of God and so have divine essence in our hearts, which gives us infinite dignity and equal worth. However, they also teach that we have sinned and fallen short of the glory of God and are in need of salvation. The three Western religions, Judaism, Christianity, and Islam, are ethical monotheisms, viewing God as an all-powerful, benevolent being who will judge individuals according to their deserts, Judaism emphasizing the keeping of the kosher laws, Christianity emphasizing salvation by grace through faith (in Christ), and Islam highlighting the five pillars of faith (i.e., belief in the oneness of God, praying five times a day, fasting during Ramadan, making a pilgrimage to Mecca, and almsgiving) and applying religious law (*sharia*). All three accept the Genesis account of creation, the Fall of Adam and Eve, and the goal of living in fellowship with God forever.

Plato, Aristotle, and Kant hold that reason is our essence, while Schopenhauer, Kierkegaard, and Nietzsche hold that it is our will. Hobbes held that we are psychological egoists, inordinately selfish, whereas Rousseau held just the opposite, that in the state of nature we were good (noble savages) and that civilization has corrupted us. Marx believed that human nature was plastic, so economic processes were constantly changing our essence. The economic base of society creates class consciousness and determines the entire superstructure of society. Darwin held that we are simply animals with big brains, who, like other animals, must struggle for survival. Freud held that our essence is our sexuality, especially our unconscious libido. Sartre says we have no essence but must freely invent one; we are condemned to freedom.

Historically, the Christian tradition posited a Great Chain of Being, reaching from God to the tiniest molecule, on the other side of which was nothingness—the absence of being. The chain was a great solace because it linked all reality into one coherent system with a benevolent God controlling the maintenance of the whole. It gave people meaning and a purpose for which to live. However, the enlightenment movement, highlighted by the Copernican, Kantian, Darwinian, and Freudian revolutions, put enormous stress on the links so that the chain was strained, if not broken. We seem to have lost our bearings and have a sinking, sickening sensation of falling into the abyss of nothingness. Nietzsche captures our experience:

What did we do when we loosened this earth from its sun? Whither does it now move? Whither do we move? Away from all suns? Do we not dash on unceasingly? Backwards, sideways, forwards, in all directions? Is there still an above and below? Do we not stray, as through infinite nothingness? Does not empty space breathe upon us? Has it not become colder? Does not night come on continually, darker and darker? Shall we not have to light lanterns in the morning? Do we not hear the noise of the grave-diggers who are burying God? Do we not smell the divine putrefaction?—for even Gods putrefy! God is dead! God remains dead! And we have killed him! How shall we console ourselves, the most murderous of all murderers?[2]

Do We Have Free Will or Are We Wholly Determined by Antecedent Causes?

Can we transcend the chain of event-causation and act as free agents? We have seen that the Judeo–Christian tradition from the Hebrew Bible through the New Testament, St. Augustine, and Kierkegaard hold to the idea of libertarian free will. Otherwise, God would be responsible for evil, not humanity. Jean-Jacques Rousseau, Jean-Paul Sartre, and Roderick Chisholm also embrace it. Free will is not discussed by Plato and discussed only indirectly by Aristotle, but they assume that we are morally accountable. Philosophers like Hobbes, Schopenhauer, Freud, Marx, and the neuro-philosophers discussed in chapter 14 seem to believe in hard determinism. As we discovered in chapter 15, philosophers like Kant, Hume, Stace, and Frankfurt adhere to compatibilism, reconciling determinism with moral responsibility. Without a notion of moral responsibility, it is hard to see how we could live together. The reactive attitudes of praising and blaming seem to entail a notion of responsibility. However, we could be deceived. Freud argues that a deeply embedded id lies within the unconscious, which deceives us into doing things whose springs of action are hidden from us. Could we be deceived about our principle of free will? Could all our actions be wholly determined by antecedent forces? Even if this turned out to be true, could we live by the doctrine of determinism?

What Is Our *Telos* or Destiny?

Where are we heading? Is there life after death, or do we just rot and disintegrate? Is our destiny to love God and enjoy him forever, as the Judeo–Christian tradition holds? We saw that materialists like Schopenhauer, Nietzsche, Marx, Darwin, Freud, Sartre, and the modern materialists believe that this life is the only one we will ever know and that the idea of immortality is an illusion invented for our comfort but without any serious evidence whatsoever. It is simply a myth like "pie in the sky by and by." Others, like Kant, argue that while we cannot know there is an afterlife, we can hope for it. Hinduism holds to reincarnation and the absorption into Brahma in nirvana. Buddhism holds that we can reach an afterlife, even nirvana, without a notion of God. If one is religious, one may be disposed to believe in life after death; but then the question shifts to whether one's religion has sufficient supporting evidence. If it does, well and good. That gives it grounds for belief. If it does not, then we are suffering from just another nice illusion or imbibing the "opium of the people," to quote Marx.

What Can We Know?

Plato believed we could have eternal a priori knowledge. Plato and Aristotle believed that we can know the truth about ultimate reality (chapters 3 and 4).

Empiricists like Locke, Mill, and the behaviorists believed that at birth our minds were a blank slate (*tabula rasa*), so everything we know we learn from our environment. The corollary of the blank slate thesis is that humans can be molded by culture and education into whatever form they choose. We are plastic (chapter 7). Marx agreed and held that our perspective is determined by the ruling class and our specific class consciousness, so what counts for knowledge is relative to our socioeconomic class. He believed religion was an opiate to compensate the oppressed for their suffering. Darwinians hold that we are animals with big brains who have been selected for survival skills, not metaphysical knowledge. Alvin Plantinga argued that since naturalistic evolution is a metaphysical system, if it is true, we probably are not justified in believing it (chapter 13). Sociobiologists hold that our genetic endowment largely determines who we are and how we will perceive the world.

Kant's Copernican revolution reversed the direction of knowledge. We do not see the world as it is in itself but only as we impose a priori categories (ideas of space, time, and causality) upon it. Schopenhauer took Kant's insight and elaborated upon it, setting forth the will to live as the thing in itself, the ultimate ground of our being. He thus anticipated Freud's idea of the unconscious id, the sexual drive, which drives all human life. Jung rejected Freud's pansexuality in favor of a Platonic repertoire of eternal archetypes. Kierkegaard held, with Kant, that since we cannot have knowledge of metaphysical truth, we must live by faith, trusting where we cannot see. Freud, Adler, and Jung said that we need to undergo psychoanalysis to discover our true selves, to know who we really are. From Plato and Hinduism to neuroscience, there are a plethora of theories claiming to uncover the Truth. How do we know which theory of knowledge is the correct one? How can we test the many theories that make claims to being the way to Truth?

Ludwig Wittgenstein, one of the greatest philosophers of the 20th century, wrote, "We feel that even when all possible scientific questions have been answered, the problems of life remain completely untouched. Of course there are then no questions left, and this itself is the answer."[3]

Wittgenstein is assuming that unless science can answer a question, it is not a legitimate question. Is this really so? Why can't there be questions without our being able to answer them with certainty? Perhaps science will never be able to completely solve the body–mind problem (why is the consciousness?) or how the universe came into being. Does that mean no answer exists? I doubt it. Wittgenstein admitted a "mystical" tendency in humans.[4] We raise these questions even though science cannot answer them. Here, religion comes in to try to make sense of these transnatural concerns. Science, for all its wonders and benefits, does not give meaning to our lives. We need philosophy and maybe even religion to do that. The major religions, such as Hinduism, Buddhism, Judaism, Christianity, and Islam, do this in various ways. Philosophical movements such as Platonism, Aristotelianism, Stoicism, Kantianism, and Existentialism also attempt to fulfill this task. Granted, some of these answers are less appealing than others. Nietzsche rightly said "Man would rather have the Void for his purpose than be void of pur-

pose." The point is not to dismiss cosmological questions as ill-formed or illegiti-
mate but to seek the most comprehensive and coherent theory that answers them,
even if we can never achieve absolute certainty about the answers.

How Shall We Live?

What is the best or right way to carry on our daily activities? This question equiv-
ocates between two interpretations: (1) How can we find happiness and fulfilment? (2) What is the best way for us to live together? For Socrates and Plato, these
sub-questions yield identical answers. Since the good is good for you, it is always
in your interest to live morally. Christianity and Hinduism come to the same conclusion but for different reasons. Christians hold that God sees all and will reward
and punish us according to our moral deserts. Hinduism and Buddhism hold that
the law of karma guarantees that what you sow in this life you will reap in a reincarnated future existence. Plato argues in the *Republic* that the moral person is 732
times happier than the immoral. Deep philosophical reasoning will enable us to
throw off our chains of ignorance and escape from the cave of illusions and shadows to the sun's light, where we will be free. Jesus said "The truth shall make you
free" and claimed to be both the truth and the way to it. Hindus, Buddhists, and
Schopenhauer argue that it is by giving up desire and the empirical self that we
may find fulfilment. Aristotle said that since we are social animals we must live
together in communities in order to be happy and that in the good society the virtuous will fare better than the vicious. Regarding the first question, Freud said that
we must undergo psychoanalysis to find fulfillment, while religions say we must
have faith in God in order to be saved and find happiness. Regarding the second
question, Dostoevsky thought that without God morality did not exist: "If there is
no God, all things are permissible," claims Ivan in *Brothers Karamazov*.[5] Augustine
(chapter 5) believed that no true happiness can be found outside of God, nor can
humans, infected by original sin, truly be good without grace.

Aristotle thought the best life was one of moderation, following the Golden
Mean, but one also needed a little bit of luck, like being born into a good family in
a resourceful community and having good friends. Kant thought that an objective
set of moral principles could be discovered by using the Categorical Imperative
("Always act in such a way that you can will the maxim of your action could be a
universal law of nature"). Kant and Mill held that we can find happiness and live
a moral life simply by reason alone without recurring to authority. The Eastern
religions and Schopenhauer hold that in order to find nirvana (even in this life) we
must give up desire and the idea of an individual self and be merged in the Whole.
On the other hand, Marx, following the Sophists, thought that morality was relative to the ruling class—might makes right. Yet, we saw how he inconsistently
held that justice was giving workers what they deserve and condemned the capitalists for exploiting the workers. Darwin and the sociobiologists hold that morality evolves as rational humans seek to realize their inclinations as social animals
in a community. James Q. Wilson sums up the thesis of an innate moral sense:

Mankind's moral sense is not a strong beacon light, radiating outward to illuminate in sharp outline all that it touches. It is, rather, a small candle flame, casting vague and multiple shadows, flickering and sputtering in the strong winds of power and passion, greed and ideology. But brought close to the heart and cupped in one's hands, it dispels the darkness and warms the soul.[6]

On the opposite end of the scale, rejecting the idea of an essential human nature, Sartre held that we invent morality then universalize it, taking responsibility for all people. It is part of being condemned to freedom.

From our study we can conclude that a basic similarity exists between all humans in all cultures so that at the core of social existence is a common morality. Social life requires certain universals, such as not intentionally taking innocent life, keeping promises, avoiding harm to others, and the like. As Stuart Hampshire has noted, "There is nothing . . . culture bound in the great evils of human experience, reaffirmed in every age and in every written history and in every tragedy and fic-tion: murder and the destruction of life, imprisonment, enslavement, poverty, physical pain, and torture, homelessness and friendlessness."[7] These great evils are universally recognized, and from the basis of moral argument in every culture and every epoch, regardless of how much cultures may differ religiously and with regard to their further positive ideals and conceptions of the good.

An auxiliary to the first question is how we should organize society so that our nature can flourish. What kind of economic–political policy should we instantiate in order to provide the best context for human flourishing? Plato advocated a mer-itocratic aristocracy, open to members of both sexes, led by philosophers as kings. He eschewed democracy as mediocrity and leading to tyranny of the ignorant masses. Aristotle followed him in embracing aristocracy but excluded women from positions of leadership and was more tolerant toward democracy. Marx developed a communist state as the only answer to human misery, while Hobbes developed a strong form of contractual authoritarianism where the Leviathan state rules. Rousseau outlined a form of participatory democracy, where the majority, not the monarch or Leviathan, reigns but where the outliers can "be forced to be free." Conservatives like Hobbes, Burke, Schopenhauer, and Freud set forth a tragic vision of life and generally advise us to trust tradition. Liberals like Rousseau and radicals like Marx set forth a hopeful vision of life and call on us to overthrow the rotten decadence of oppressive regimes and build a better, more egalitarian world. However, if conservativism often tolerates and supports an unjust status quo, Rousseauean socialism and Marxist radicalism often result in a reign of terror or the Soviet gulag archipelago or Mao Tse Tung's Red Guard movement in the 1970s, which persecuted and executed intellectuals and nonconformists.

How Are the Two Sexes Related?

Are men and women essentially the same except for reproductive organs, or do their natures differ fundamentally? Plato was the first gender egalitarian, who proposed the then radical idea of equal opportunity for women. Women should have equal opportunity, he thought, but not be guaranteed equal results. This is today's liberal position, developed by Mary Wollstonecraft and John Stuart Mill in the late 18th and 19th centuries.[8] Plato's disciple, Aristotle, thought women were less rational and should be ruled by men, even as they should rule slaves and children. Conservatives, following Aristotle, and contemporary sociobiologists hold that there are fundamental differences between males and females. Men are by nature (on average) more aggressive, while women are more nurturing and suited to child-rearing. A third group, Marxist feminists, hold that only when bourgeois society is replaced by a communist, classless society can women and men be truly free. A fourth group, androgynous feminists, agree with Plato that the two sexes are basically equal in ability and should be expected to compete equally in every dimension of life. Some feminists hold that gender differences (as opposed to physiological differences) are cultural constructs. A fifth group, radical feminists, believes that all Western societies are oppressive to women and need to be radically changed.[9] At the extreme end of this group are those who believe that women are not just equal but superior to men, that women need men like they need a brain tumor.[10] A sixth group, difference feminists, like Carol Gilligan and Nel Nodding, agree with conservatives that women develop differently from men.[11] Our differences should be recognized and respected. People are often deeply divided on this issue, frequently with considerable emotion.

Finally, we may ask whether a greater openness to the female aspect of human personality, including promoting women to leadership positions, would result in a less violent, more peaceful world. Males have dominated positions of leadership since time immemorial and have been the cause of wars with untold casualties. Would women leaders be more pacific? Naysayers point to Margaret Thatcher, Golda Meir, Winnie Mandela, Jiang Qing (the wife of Mao Tse Tung), and Indira Gandhi as examples of women who have been every bit as aggressive as most men; but perhaps this is because the kind of leaders we choose replicate the male model. Some feminist critics have argued that Golding's Hobbesian novel *Lord of the Flies,* in which a group of boys become depraved cannibals, is too artificial for moral instruction. That society is an anomaly, consisting only of preadolescent boys uprooted from home and community. If girls or adults were introduced into the story, they argue, it would make it different. Similarly, they contend, a group of girls would behave less violently. However, Marianne Wiggins' novel *John Dollar* portrays a group of girls stranded on an island who also engage in some vicious behavior, including cannibalism.[12]

The larger question is, Can men and women together create what William James called a "moral equivalent of war," a more benign channeling of human aggressivity? The celebrated war veteran Glenn Gray has written:

> How deeply is this impulse to destroy rooted and persistent in human nature? Are the imaginative visions of Empedocles and Freud true in conceiving that the destructive element in man and nature is as strong and recurrent as the conserving, erotic element? Or can our delight in destruction be channeled into other activities than the traditional one of warfare? We are not far advanced on the way to these

answers. We do not know whether a peaceful society can be made attractive enough to wean men away from the appeals of battle. Today we are seeking to make war so horrible that men will be frightened away from it. But this is hardly likely to be more fruitful in the future than it has been in the past. More productive will certainly be our efforts to eliminate the social, economic, and political injustices that are always the immediate occasion of hostilities. Even then, we shall be confronted with the spiritual emptiness and inner hunger that impel many men toward combat. Our society has not begun to wrestle with this problem of how to provide fulfillment of human life, to which war is so often an illusory path.[13]

What Is More Fundamental, the Individual or the Group?

In the Old Testament, the sins of one man (e.g., Achan in Jos. 7:18) are passed down to the whole society, Israel; and in the New Testament, Paul writes that because of Adam's disobedience, the whole world is condemned (Rom. 5:12). In ancient Greece, we see an emphasis on the community as more important than the individual. This idea is also reflected in Plato (chapter 3) and Aristotle (chapter 4), who emphasize the good of the group over the good of the individual, and in Rousseau (chapter 7), who holds that it is the general will that is the true good, not individual preferences. We may call such group-centered theories "holism." On the other hand, we noted that Kant (chapter 8) put the emphasis on individual autonomy and that the existentialists (chapter 12) made individual choice absolute. The tension between the importance of the group and the individual goes to the core of who we are and what our moral duties are. Let us see if we can throw light on the subject, individualism versus holism.

How does individualism arise? How do we discover ourselves as separate from the group? Primitive humans, like other animals, worked in groups. Just as a group of hyenas will hunt and kill a much stronger lion by working in a cooperative manner, so humans can multiply their power by working together. They can win a battle against a foe with superior strength. They can push a heavy vehicle up a hill. They can run a ship, factory, or company for long hours over a long period of time by cooperative maneuvers.

The disagreement over the relationship of the individual to the group is analogous to that of the nature/nurture dispute. Our personalities are formed by both our genetic endowment and the environment in which we develop. An acorn, no matter how richly endowed, if planted in the Mojave Desert, will not grow into an oak tree. Just as nature and nurture cooperate to produce the unique individual, societies take newborn babies (with different potentials) and produce unique adults, hopefully autonomous individuals who live morally and think for themselves.

Yet, even for autonomous adults, certain environmental safeguards are necessary to promote full flourishing. Socrates (in Plato's *Crito*) says that without good institutions, life is not worth living, which led him to accept his fate when condemned to death by an Athenian court. Good laws, protecting human rights, are indispensable for human flourishing.

However, a good society is not enough. Once humans have their basic needs met, they must face the hard existential questions: What is the meaning of life? Does life have a purpose? How shall I live my life? Who am I? And even, pace Camus, Why not commit suicide? These are individual-type questions, though the group may affect their answer. The religious group will urge a God-centered answer (the purpose of life is to love and serve God and enjoy him forever). The communist group will urge a socialist answer (the purpose of life is to abolish property so that each individual can live a good life with equal dignity). The Stoic society will urge a Stoic answer (accept your fate and make the best of it). The hedonistic society will urge a hedonistic answer (eat, drink, and be merry, for tomorrow you die).

Louis Dumont argues that humans first saw themselves as parts of groups but gradually developed the concept of the individual.[14] He gives evidence that in both Asia and the West this development began with a religious, or "outworldly," orientation. First, the group endorses an idea of a relationship with God or some transcendent reality, with whom some individuals form special relationships. In forming such an outworldly relationship, they break, to some extent, with the "inworldly" dimension of their peers. Dumont shows that whereas Catholicism historically emphasized the inworldly dimension, obedience to the Church, the Protestant Reformation, emphasizing the idea of the priesthood of all believers, promoted widespread individualism. While the Catholic Church had an out-worldly dimension, it was reserved primarily for the hierarchy and priests, who were intermediaries between the transcendent and the laity. Protestantism, with its doctrines of the priesthood of the believer and the *sola scriptura* ("solely Scrip-ture"), democratized outworldiness. Protestantism said "You do not need a priest to show you the way to God. You can find it through reading the Bible." Luther was the first person to translate the Bible into German in order that the laity could read it themselves. He taught that each person should read the Bible for him or her self and become his own priest and interpreter of God's word. Trusting the individual to be his or her own priest opened the transcendent to each man and woman, giving rise to an individualism that, in the hands of John Calvin, spread into nonreligious areas of life: commerce and industry.

When we come to Hobbes and Rousseau (chapter 7), we see a revival of holism, with the state replacing the church as the locus of identity. For Hobbes, people do not become self-sufficient individuals in society any more than they were in the pitiable state of nature. The proper life of a human is that of dependence on the state, so closely tied to the state that one must identify oneself as part of the sovereign whole, becoming an artificial part of an artificial whole, the Great leviathan.

For Rousseau, we are first and foremost social beings who must identify with the mysterious general will, a sort of totalitarian democracy. Hence, when Robin-son Crusoe enters his lonely island apart from society, he is not bereft of society. Rather, he has brought society with him, having internalized its mores within his bosom.[15]

Kant represents the high watermark in the value of individualism (see chapter 8). The Lutheran doctrine of the priesthood of all believers lies behind Kant's thought, but Kant rationalizes the Protestant notion. Beginning with his Enlightenment notion *sapere aude* (think for yourself), he develops a radical notion of autonomy as it had never been dreamt of before. Each person has an obligation to use reason to discover his or her duty. If you can universalize the maxim of your proposed act, it is morally permissible. If you cannot do so, you must not do the deed.

With Søren Kierkegaard, Protestant–Kantian individualism is taken to a new extreme. However, it goes beyond reason, for reason is Janus-faced, willing to pay the highest bidder for a justification. For Kierkegaard, one must use reason to realize the limits of reason. Each person must see him- or herself as standing alone before God. Kierkegaard's theory of subjectivity as truth is the culmination of radical individualism. Each one of us must think for ourselves, be clear on our options, and make a leap of faith. Faith is like swimming over 70 fathoms of water, a precarious venture in which one may drown unless one is eternally vigilant.[16] Each person must make the leap for him- or herself, as a pure individual. Kierkegaard refers to himself as the "single individual."

Kierkegaard was an existentialist Christian, but the radical individualism he promoted was taken up by atheists like Frederich Nietzsche and Jean-Paul Sartre. Nietzsche calls on us "to become gods" to be worthy of the great crime of killing God[17] and proposes the ideal of the Superman (*Ubermensch*) as the fitting substitute for the Christian moralist. He substituted aesthetic choices for Kierkegaard's religious leap. Sartre goes even further than Kierkegaard or Nietzsche in that he even denies that we have an essential nature. We are condemned to freedom and must invent our nature through radical freedom.[18]

Radical Nietzschean individualism reaches its apex in the work of Ayn Rand's libertarian ethical egoism, set forth in her book fittingly entitled *The Virtue of Selfishness*. Rand holds that *altruism*, unselfish concern for others, is a vice. The only obligations we have are those we have voluntarily entered into.[19] One of her heroes declares,

> *I swear by my life and my love of it that I*
> *Will never live for the sake of another*
> *Man, nor ask another man to live for me.*[20]

In *Anthem*, her Promethean hero rebels against the collectivist mentality which forbids people from using the personal pronoun "I."

> *I am done with the creed of corruption.*
> *I am done with the monster of "We,"*
> *the word of serfdom, of plunder, of misery, falsehood and shame.*
> *And now I see the face of god,*
> *And I raise this god over the earth,*
> *This god whom men have sought since men came into being,*
> *This god who will grant them joy and peace and pride.*
> *This god, this one word: I*[21]

Robert Nozick takes this egoism to its logical conclusion, equating taxation with forced labor.[22]

Because it assumes a questionably atomistic view of human nature, libertarianism, such as that evinced in Rand's atomism and Nozick's contention that taxation is forced labor, seems implausible. The truth is, in the words of the poet John Donne, "No man is an island, entire of itself."[23] Animals live in groups, and this is especially true of human beings. We are social and political animals. We are nurtured by mothers, reared and socialized in families by parents, siblings, and other relatives. We are taught a language and a set of customs. We are educated into a culture, internalizing a tradition of myths, symbols, and history. We acquire social and academic skills which enable us to navigate through the labyrinthine maze of a complex, interpersonal world.

Think of all the things we daily use but take for granted that are the result of other people's inventions and contributions to our lives, such as the obvious inventions of the wheel, electricity, the incandescent lightbulb, the internal combustion engine, indoor plumbing, sanitation systems to filter sewage, and insulated buildings. Then there are the social institutions that help give our lives meaning and protect us from oppression, violence, and disease: the law, a just judicial system, the police, the army, codes of etiquette and moral conduct, hospitals and related medical knowledge, agricultural institutions and regulating agencies that enforce safety standards and morality itself. No one of us is sufficient in him- or herself for all the contingencies of life. We are interdependent. We are all in each other's debt.

In a thousand ways each day the "self-made man" is beholden to the composite and cooperative efforts of a myriad of predecessors who reach back into primitive times and thousands of contemporaries who add support to his life but whose non-cooperation could ruin it (think of how just 19 terrorists shook our world and disabused us of our illusions of invulnerability on September 11, 2001). We need each other. We are all part of a social nexus, an intricate, complex web of social and economic ties that bind us together. In such an interconnected web of relations, is it too much to ask each member to contribute a proportionate fraction of his or her income to help maintain the overall social system? The very liberty which enables us to enjoy a large measure of independence and affluence is predicated on social cooperation, and social cooperation in a society like ours, where there are wide gaps in wealth and income, seems to require tax contributions from its members in order to meet basic needs and provide fair equal opportunity. The Oxford philosopher of law H. L. A. Hart put it this way:

> Except for a few privileged and lucky persons, the ability to shape life for oneself and lead a meaningful life is something to be constructed by positive marshalling of social and economic resources. It is not something automatically guaranteed by a structure of negative rights.[24]

I would go further and argue that all of us are dependent on social support for our ability to develop our personalities to the point where we are able to live a worthwhile life. Some of us are given more support than others. Furthermore, given a moral principle of gratitude, those who benefit most from the underlying structures of our society should contribute most. A fair system of taxation is, ideally, both an expression of gratitude for the benefits of community and civilization and an acknowledgment that many people require aid through no fault of their own.

The truth about individualism versus holism lies somewhere in the middle. We are individuals who should be autonomous agents, responsible for our actions; but we are also social animals and, as such, owe our being and education to society, which nourished us and gave us the resources to become whatever we chose to become. We have the freedom to live as we wish, so long as we do not harm others; but we also have a responsibility to society, to heal its wounds, ameliorate its suffering, and make it a better place for those who come after us.

What Are Our Obligations to Others and How Far Do Our Ethical Obligations Extend?

Do our obligations extend only to our family and friends, to our class, to our country, or also to all humanity? Are all humans related to one another in a corporate solidarity? Recall John Donne's oration,

> No man is an island, entire of itself; every man is a piece of the continent, a part of the main. If a clod be washed away by the sea, Europe is the less, as well as if a promontory were, as well as if a manor of thy friend's or of thine own were. Any man's death diminishes me, because I am involved in Mankind; and therefore never send to know for whom the *bell* tolls; it tolls for *thee*.[25]

As we have seen, Christians hold all those of their religious persuasion in special regard. Augustine said they were all part of the City of God arrayed against the city of man. Marxists hold that the proletariats are connected by a common bond of solidarity, and feminists speak of a special sisterhood, while cosmopolitans extend moral rights to all human beings. As we saw in chapter 7, Hobbes, Burke, and other conservatives argue that we have special obligations toward our family and country (with whom we have a contractual relationship) and even our ancestors.[26] However, if Darwin is correct and we evolved from "lower animals," then we are related not only to other humans but to the entire animal kingdom (chapter 13). Something like Schopenhauer's will to live ideal and Schweitzer's reverence for life principle may be the proper extension of our moral consideration. Hinduism and Buddhism advocate *ahimsa*, total nonviolence, refraining from killing animals except when absolutely necessary. If Darwin is correct, we cannot easily give up our right to self-defense and adopt *ahimsa*, at least not until we build a world where there is universal brotherhood and sisterhood, a cosmopolitan world where freedom and justice apply to all people equally. If in their fight against highly armed criminals and terrorists, the police give up their weapons, who will be the only ones with them?

These are the kinds of questions and answers we have addressed in our study of theories of human nature. If, as Socrates said and I believe, "The unexamined life is not worth living," it is imperative that we come to a greater understanding of the available options for self-understanding. How you answer these questions is one of the most important things you can do in your life, for if Aristotle is correct and we are rational animals, then we must use the best reasons available to find answers to these questions.

In the future, some of these theories will wax or wane and new versions of old theories will no doubt develop. New theories will probably arise as psychology, science, and philosophy develop in new directions.

No one knows the future, but it offers plenty of challenges. Will genetic engineering create different beings, more intelligent and more prone to altruism, cooperation, and honesty (more or less autonomous)? Will new drugs create artificial states of consciousness? Will the nature of our families change as we live longer so that there is less room on Earth—and less need and desire—for children? If we are to survive as a civilization and species, we must find new and better theories or revise the old ones in a manner that leads to the Truth, for only the truth can set us free. The pursuit is worth the effort.

Theory	Diagnosis of the human condition	Metaphysical nature	Transcendent reality	Do humans have free will?	Destiny/telos
Christianity (Augustine), Judaism, Islam	Sinful	Spiritual being	God is the creator and redeemer	Yes	Salvation/heaven union with God
Hinduism	Suffering	Atman is Brahman/ spiritual being	True reality is divine	Yes	Moksa/nirvana/ reincarnation
Buddhism	Suffering in ignorance	An-atman, self is illusory	Nihilism	Yes	Enlightenment/ nirvana now
Plato	Ignorance	Dualism: spiritual (soul) being/ matter is illusory	World of forms	Yes	Enlightenment/ harmony of the soul
Aristotle	Self-interested, rational being	Soul is the form of the body	Unmoved mover	Yes	Reason liberates
Hobbes	Psychological egoist	A material being	Reality is material, only God has an incorporeal body	No	Reason shows us how to maximize expected utility
Rousseau	Good, noble savage	Acquisitive	A divine reality beyond us	Yes	Good education and socialization bring happiness

Theory	Diagnosis of the human condition	Metaphysical nature	Transcendent reality	Do humans have free will?	Destiny/telos
Kant	Self in a moral world	Rational	A personal God to act as moral judge	Yes	Acting on goodwill brings virtue and should be rewarded
Schopenhauer	Self in a world of suffering	Selfish but may become selfless	Secularism	No	Asceticism and altruism
Freud	Unstable, insecure	A sexual being	Secularism	No	Psychological wholeness, i.e. psychoanalysis
Marx	Blank slate	A material, economic being	Secularism	No	Communism will liberate
Existentialism	Self alienated	A free being	Religious and secular interpretations	Yes	There is no exit
Darwinism	Sociobiological basis of behavior	An animal with reason and language	Secularism	No	Socialization continuously evolving
Contemporary philosophers of mind	Sentient animal with a developing brain	Materialist monism: an animal with a complex neurology	Secularism	No	Psychological wholeness

Notes

1. "What is man that thou art mindful of him, and the son of man that thou dost care for him? Yet thou hast made him little less than God, and dost crown him with glory and honor" (Psalm 8).
2. Friedrich Nietzsche, *Joyful Wisdom* (Frederick Unger, 1968), p. 125.
3. Ludwig Wittgenstein, *Tractatus Logico Philosophicus* (Routledge, Kegan & Paul, 1932), section 6.2.
4. In his private notebooks, he puts it slightly differently: "The urge towards the mystical comes from the failure of science to satisfy our wishes. We feel that even if all possible scientific questions are answered, our problem still is not touched on. Admittedly, in this case, there remain no more questions; and this is the answer." (Notebooks, p. 51)
5. Dostoevsky was pessimistic about the future of society without religious faith. He wrote, "The first half of the history of man is the ascent from the gorilla to the man-god; the second half of the history of man is the descent from the man-god to the gorilla." (*The Possessed*, Penguin, 1954)

6. James Q. Wilson, *The Moral Sense* (Free Press, 1993), pp. 250–251.

7. Stuart Hampshire, *Innocence and Experience* (Harvard University Press, 1989), p. 90.

8. See Mary Wollstonecraft, *Vindication of the Rights of Women* (1792; Dover Publications, 1996, reprint); and John Stuart Mill, *On the Subjection of Women* (1869; Broadview Press, 2000, reprint).

9. See Denise Thompson, *Radical Feminism Today* (Sage Publications, 2001).

10. See Andrea Dworkin, *Intercourse* (Free Press, 1997), where she describes heterosexual intercourse as rape.

11. See Carol Gilligan, *In a Different Voice* (Harvard University Press, 1982).

12. Marianne Wiggins, *John Dollar* (Simon & Schuster, 1989). Note also the book Golding was responding to, *The Coral Island*, by R. M. Ballantyne (1858), which portrayed a group of virtuous boys who create a good society. Golding thought that Ballantyne had an all-too-rosy view of human nature, neglecting original sin. Might the same be said of those who generalize about the contrast between virtuous women and vicious males?

13. Glenn Gray, "The Enduring Appeals of Battle," in *Rethinking Masculinity: Philosophical Explorations in Light of Feminism* eds. Larry May and Robert Strikwerda (Rowman and Littlefield, 1992), p. 40. Sterling Harwood referred me to this quotation.

14. Louis Dumont, *Essays on Individualism: Modern Ideology in Anthropological Perspective* (University of Chicago Press, 1986), pp. 23–27.

15. Daniel Defoe, *Robinson Crusoe* (1719; Penguin Books, 1994, reprint).

16. Kierkegaard, *Concluding Unscientific Postscript*, trans. David F. Swenson (Princeton University Press, 1941), pp. 182–83.

17. Nietzsche, op. cit., p. 125.

18. Jean-Paul Sartre, *Existentialism* (Philosophical Library, 1948).

19. Ayn Rand, *The Virtue of Selfishness* (New American Library, 1964).

20. Ayn Rand, *Atlas Shrugged* (Dutton, 1957), p. 731.

21. Ayn Rand, *Anthem* (New American Library, 1938).

22. Robert Nozick, *Anarchy, State and Utopia* (Basic Books, 1974), p. 174.

23. John Donne, *Devotions upon Emergent Occasions*, no. 17. Originally published in 1624.

24. H. L. A. Hart, "Between Utility and Rights," in *The Idea of Freedom*, ed. Alan Ryan (Oxford University Press, 1979), p. 85.

25. John Donne, op. cit.

26. Recall Edmund Burke's statement "People will not look forward to posterity who never look back to their ancestors." *Reflections on the Revolution in France* (1790).

Glossary

Absolute—A principle that is universally binding and may never be overridden by another principle. Socrates seems to have held to absolute moral principles. Utilitarianism is a type of system that has only one absolute principle: "Do the action that maximizes utility." Kant's system has several absolutes, whereas other deontological systems may have only a few broad absolutes, such as "Never cause unnecessary harm."

Absolute freedom—A concept found in Jean-Paul Sartre's writings to indicate that we are always free to choose and are entirely responsible for our actions (see chapter 12).

Absolutism or **Ethical Absolutism**—The notion that there is only one correct answer to every moral problem. A completely absolutist ethic consists of absolute principles that provide an answer for every possible situation in life, regardless of culture. Diametrically opposed to ethical absolutism is ethical relativism, which says that the validity of ethical principles depends on social acceptance. In between these polar opposites is ethical objectivism. See **Objectivism, Relativism.**

Absurd—Irrational, paradoxical, or contradictory. Søren Kierkegaard uses the term in two ways: *(1)* to indicate the apparent contradictions in existence and *(2)* to signify the Christian doctrine of the Incarnation in which God becomes human in Jesus Christ. This is absurd, yet, for the passionate believer, the truth. Albert Camus, following Kierkegaard's first meaning, uses the concept to refer to "the confrontation of reasonable man and an indifferent universe" (see chapter 12).

Advaitanism—The version of Hinduism which holds that God is the only reality and that all else is illusion (see chapter 6). See **Maya.**

Agapeism—(from the Greek *agape*, "altruistic love") An ethical theory based on the principle of love. Sometimes this is based on the New Testament injunctions to love (Mt. 22:37–40, 1 Cor. 13, 1 Jn. 4:7–8). *Act-agapeism* holds that one ought always do whatever is the most loving thing to do; this has been called "situational ethics." *Rule-agapeism* holds that one ought to follow the most love-embodying set of rules. See the Bible and Augustine (see chapters 1 and 5).

Agent Causation—The thesis put forward by Libertarians that agents are sometimes underdetermined by antecedent causes, so that they can become the decisive cause of their actions (see chapter 15).

Altruism—Unselfish regard or concern for others; disinterested, other-regarding action. See **Egoism** (see chapter 4 and chapter 13).

An-atman—The not-self. A Buddhist concept denying the reality of a substantial self. Contrasts with the **atman** (see chapter 6).

a posteriori—Latin meaning "the later," knowledge that is obtained only from experience, such as sense perceptions or pain sensations (see chapter 8).

a priori—Latin meaning "preceding," knowledge that is not based on sense experience but is innate or known simply by the meaning of words or definitions. David Hume limited the term to "relations of ideas," referring to analytic truths and mathematics (see chapter 8).

Aretaic Ethics—(from the Greek *arête,* "virtue") The theory, first presented by Aristotle, that the basis of ethical assessment is character. Rather than seeing the heart of ethics in actions or duties, it focuses on the character and dispositions of the agent. Whereas deontological and teleological ethical systems emphasize doing, aretaic (or virtue) ethics emphasizes being—that is, being a certain type of person who will no doubt manifest his or her being in appropriate actions (see chapter 4).

Ataraxia—The Stoic word for tranquility, imperturbability. Socrates practiced it, as do Hindus and Buddhists (see chapter 6).

Atman—The Hindu idea of the self. "The atman is Brahma (God)" (see chapter 6).

Autonomy—(from the Greek for "self-rule") Self-directed freedom. The autonomous individual arrives at his or her moral judgments through reason rather than simple acceptance of authority. The autonomy thesis states that ethical truths can be known and justified on the basis of human reason without divine revelation (see chapters 5 and 7). See **Heteronomy.**

Avatar—A Hindu term, meaning a manifestation of God (see chapter 6).

Behaviorism—The view that no mental events exist or that they are unimportant for science. Statements about mental events are really about dispositions to behave. "She's angry with me" really means that she is disposed to do nasty things to me and say nasty things about me. The most important recent behaviorist was B. F. Skinner (see chapter 15).

Categorical Imperative—A command to perform actions that are necessary of themselves without reference to other ends. It contrasts with hypothetical imperatives, which command actions not for their own sake but for some other good. For Kant, moral duties command categorically; they represent the injunctions of reason, which endows them with universal validity and objective necessity (see chapter 8). See **Hypothetical Imperative.**

Causal Thesis—The thesis that every act and event in the universe is caused by antecedent events (see chapter 15).

Communism—The political–economic philosophy, developed in its most famous form by Karl Marx and Friedrich Engels in the nineteenth century, that holds to (1) economic determinism—the way a society produces its wealth determines all else—and (2) the notion of a class struggle in which the working class will eventually overthrow the bourgeoisie and establish a proletarian dictatorship (see chapter 10).

Compatibilism—The view that an act may be entirely determined and yet be free in the sense that it was done voluntarily and not under external coercion. It is sometimes referred to as "soft determinism." However, whereas soft determinism positively holds to determinism, the compatibilist may be agnostic on the truth of determinism, holding that if we are determined, only then could we still be said to act freely under some conditions (see chapter 15).

Contradictory—When one statement denies another, both of which cannot be true. For example, "God exists" and "God does not exist" (see chapter 2).

Deontic—(from the Greek *deon*, "duty" or "obligation") Refers to action-based ethical systems, such as deontological and teleological systems, and the type of judgment (i.e., evaluations of actions) that proceed from these systems, as opposed to judgments of motivation and character that proceed from aretaic systems (see chapter 8). See **Aretaic Ethics.**

Deontological Ethics—(from the Greek *deon*, "duty" or "obligation") Ethical system that considers certain features in the moral act itself to have intrinsic value. This contrasts with teleological ethics, which holds that the ultimate criterion of morality lies in some nonmoral value that results from actions. For example, for the deontologist, there is something right about truth telling, even when it may cause pain or harm, and there is something wrong about lying, even when it may produce good consequences (see p. 66 and chapter 8). See **Teleological Ethics.**

Determinism—The theory that every event and state of affairs in the world, including human action, is caused. There are two versions of determinism: hard determinism, which states that because every event is caused, no one is responsible for his or her actions, and soft determinism or compatibilism, which states that rational creatures can still be held accountable for their actions insofar as they acted voluntarily (see chapter 15). See **Compatibilism.**

Dialectical Materialism—Sometimes called "historical materialist determinism." Marx's theory that economics is driven by class struggle between capitalists and workers and will result in the overthrow of capitalism and the establishment of communism (see chapter 10). See **Historical Materialist Determinism.**

Ding an sich—German for "the thing in itself." A concept found first in Kant and then in Schopenhauer which refers to reality as opposed to appearance. We only experience appearances but infer a reality behind the appearances (see chapters 8 and 9).

Divine Command Theory—(DCT) The theory that holds that moral principles are defined in terms of God's commands or that moral duties are logically dependent on God's commands (see chapter 5).

Dualism or **Dualistic Interactionism**—The view that there are two types of substance or reality in conscious beings, mind and matter, and that these interact with each other, the body producing mental events and the mind leading to physical action (see chapter 14).

Egoism—*Psychological egoism* is a descriptive theory about human motivation, holding that people always act to satisfy their perceived best interests. *Ethical egoism* is a prescriptive, or normative, theory about how people ought to act; they ought to act according to their perceived best interests. Hobbes held this theory (see chapter 7).

Egotism—Selfishness. Ayn Rand seems to conflate selfishness with self-interest, but the latter can accommodate altruism, while the former cannot.

Eliminative Materialism—The view that folk psychology (commonsense language about mental states, including beliefs, emotions, desires, and intentions) will eventually be replaced by a neurologically accurate language reporting brain states. For example, instead of saying "I have a pain in my forehead," we might be led to say, "My C-fiber is firing at such and such a rate" (see chapter 14). See **Folk Psychology.**

Empirical Self—The idea that we have a sense of selfhood based on experience and memory. Buddhism asserts that this is an illusion (see chapter 6), and Kant denies that this is our true self, holding that we have a noumenal self which we can know only indirectly (see chapter 8).

Epiphenomenalism—The theory that the body (and its physical actions and reactions) causes mental events, but mental events do not cause anything at all. They are like the smoke from the car's exhaust pipe, a mere efflux or outflow. Marx and Freud seem to have this view (see chapters 10, 11, and 14).

Ethical Relativism—The theory that the validity of moral judgments depends on cultural acceptance. It is opposed to objectivism and absolutism. The Sophists held this position (see chapter 2). See **Objectivism, Absolutism.**

Ethical Situationalism—The theory that objective moral principles are to be applied differently in different contexts. It is sometimes confused with ethical relativism, but it differs in that it applies universal objective principles differently in different contexts, whereas ethical relativism denies universal ethical principles altogether. See **Ethical Relativism.**

Eudaimonia—Aristotle's word for "happiness" (see chapter 4).

Euthyphro's Dilemma—The puzzle set forth in Plato's dialogue *Euthyphro*, in which Socrates asks whether God loves the pious because it is pious or whether the pious is pious because God loves it. It is associated with divine command theory and the autonomy thesis (see chapter 2). See **Autonomy; Divine Command Theory.**

Folk Psychology—Our commonsense view about mental events (e.g., pains, beliefs, desires, emotions, and intentions) that sees them as of a different nature from physical events and substance (see chapter 14).

Functionalism—The theory that denies there need be a type–type relationship between mental events and mental states. Although mental events may be identical to certain processes in one brain, they may be identical to a different process in a different brain, and they may be eventually produced in robots without brains like ours (see chapter 14).

Great Chain of Being—The doctrine found in the Bible but developed by the Neoplatonists, Augustine, and others that holds that there is a hierarchical chain of being stretching from God to the lowest forms of nature and Satan. It offers a complete philosophical explanation of the universe and our place in it. Copernicus and Darwin set forth an attack on this chain (see chapters 5 and 13).

Hedon—(from the Greek *hedone*, "pleasure") Possessing a pleasurable or painful quality. Sometimes *hedon* stands for a quantity of pleasure.

Hedonism—*Psychological hedonism* is the theory that motivation must be explained exclusively through desire for pleasure and aversion of pain. *Ethical hedonism* is the theory that pleasure is the only intrinsic positive value and that pain or "unpleasant consciousness" is the only negative intrinsic value (or intrinsic disvalue). All other values derive from these two (see chapter 5).

Henotheism—The idea that although many gods exist, one commits oneself to one special God (see chapter 1).

Heteronomy—Kant's term for the determination of the will on nonrational grounds. It contrasts with autonomy of the will, in which the will is guided by reason (see chapter 8).

Historical Materialist Determinism—Marx's thesis that the laws of economics are fixed to bring about the victory of communism over capitalism (see chapter 10).

Hypothetical Imperative—A command that enjoins actions because they help attain some end that one desires. Ethicists who regard moral duties as dependent on consequences would view moral principles as hypothetical imperatives. They have the form "If you want X, do action A" (e. g., "If you want to live in peace, do all in your power to prevent violence"). This contrasts with the categorical imperative (see chapter 8). See **Categorical Imperative.**

Id—Freud's term for the powerful blind force within us which drives our conscious behavior (see chapter 11).

Intentionality—(from the Latin *intendo*, "to aim at" or "point at") Refers to the directness (or aboutness) of mental states. Consciousness is often directed at an object, its content—objects of desire, fear, belief, and appearances. Intentions are bidirectional: (1) from Mind to World and (2) from World to Mind. An example of (1) from Mind to World is our desire to change the world or an aspect in it, such as when I kick the soccer ball, aiming at scoring a goal, or when one invests money in stocks, hoping to improve one's financial situation. An example of (2) from World to Mind is an accurate belief that is formed about the makeup of this room when I open my eyes to perceive its content. When intentional acts are successful, they accomplish their task—fulfill a desire to obtain a true belief (see chapter 14).

Intrinsic Value/Worth—Good in itself. Something that has value in itself as opposed to instrumental value, having value because of its consequences.

Invisible Hand—Adam Smith in *The Wealth of Nations* claimed that in a free market system, while all entrepreneurs were working in their self-interest, an invisible hand turned their selfishness into general utility.

Karma—The Hindu–Buddhist doctrine that what we sow in one life we will reap in another. Connected to *reincarnation*, the passing of one soul into another body in a future life (see chapter 6).

Leibniz's Law—(identity of indiscernibles) Two things are numerically identical if and only if they have all the same properties in common (see chapter 14).

Libertarianism—The theory that humans have free will in the sense that, given the same antecedent conditions, one can do otherwise. That is, the self is underdetermined by causes and is itself the determining cause of action. This view is represented by William James. It is contrasted with compatibilism and determinism (see chapter 15). See **Compatibilism, Determinism.**

Materialism—The metaphysical view that only physical matter and its properties exist. What appears to be nonmaterial (e.g., consciousness) is really either physical or a property of what is physical (see chapters 3, 14, and 15).

Maya—The Hindu term for illusion. Advaitan Hinduism holds that everything except god is *maya* (see chapter 6).

Metaphysics—"Beyond physics." The study of ultimate reality, that which is not readily accessible through ordinary empirical experience. Metaphysics includes within its domain such topics as free will, causality, the nature of matter, immortality, and the existence of God.

Monism—The theory that reality is all of one substance, rather than two or more. Examples are *materialist monism*, which holds that matter is the single substance that makes up all there is, and *idealism*, which holds that all reality is spiritual or made up of ideas. Lucretius, Democritus, Bertrand Russell, and Richard Taylor all hold to materialistic monism. Baruch Spinoza, George Berkeley, and Hinduism are examples of proponents of idealism (see chapter 14).

Naturalism—The theory that rejects the idea of supernatural entities or intervention, such as providence and miracles in human existence. It denies the existence of spiritual forces, such as gods, ghosts, or souls (see chapter 14).

Natural Law—The theory that an eternal, absolute moral law can be discovered by reason. First set forth by the Stoics but developed by Thomas Aquinas in the 13th century (see p. 113 and chapter 3).

Nihilism—The view that there are no valid moral principles or values. Nothing matters (see chapter 12).

Norm—A rule of authoritative standard.

Normative—What ought to be the case, the rules that should govern our behavior.

Noumenal—Kant's idea of a transcendent self, our true self over and above our empirical everyday self (see chapter 8).

Occam's Razor—Named after William of Occam (ca. 1285–1349). Sometimes called the principle of parsimony, states that "entities are not to be multiplied beyond necessity." The razor metaphor connotes that useless or unnecessary material should be cut away from any explanation and the simplest hypothesis accepted (see chapter 14).

Panentheism—The thesis that God is in everything. Hinduism holds such a view (see chapter 6).

Panpsychism—The view that everything—that is, every object in the world (stones, blades of grass, molecules) as well as living beings—has a soul (see chapter 14).

Pantheism—The idea that everything is God. Some people believe Hinduism holds such a view (see chapter 6).

Paradox of Hedonism—The apparent contradiction that arises between two hedonistic theses: *(1)* pleasure is the only thing worth seeking and, whenever one seeks pleasure, it is not found; *(2)* pleasure normally accompanies the satisfaction of desire whenever one reaches a goal (see chapter 4).

Parallelism—The view first put forth by Gottfried Leibniz that there is no causal interaction between bodies and minds. Each proceeds on its own, parallel to but independent of the other (see chapter 14).

Perfect Duties—Kant's designation of duties which are absolute and specific, like not lying or breaking a promise. He contrasts these duties with imperfect duties (see chapter 8). See **Imperfect Duties.**

Predestination—The doctrine that God foreordained, before the creation of the world, who will be saved and damned. Augustine held this position (see chapter 5).

Prima Facie—(Latin for "at first glance") Signifies an initial status of an idea or principle. In ethics, beginning with W. D. Ross, it stands for a duty that has a presumption in its favor but may be overridden by another duty. Prima facie duties contrast with actual duties or all-things-considered duties (see chapters 2 and 8).

Principium Individuationis—The individuating principle. Schopenhauer uses this concept to refer to our notion of individualism, our separating ourselves from the world of appearances (see chapter 9).

Quantum Physics—The behavior of subatomic particles does not follow causal processes but instead yields only statistically predictable behavior. That is, we cannot predict the motions of individual particles, but we can successfully predict the percentage that will act in certain ways. A certain randomness seems to operate on this subatomic level. Hence, there is a case for indeterminacy (see chapter 15).

Reductionist Thesis—The thesis that all moral virtues can be reduced to principles (see chapter 8).

Reductive Materialism—The view that all mental states can be identified with states in the brain (see chapter 14).

Relativism—*Cultural relativism* is a descriptive thesis stating that moral beliefs vary enormously across cultures; it is neutral about whether this is the way things ought to be. *Ethical relativism,* on the other hand, is an evaluative thesis stating that the truth of a moral judgment depends on whether a culture recognizes the principle in question (see chapter 2). See **Ethical Relativism.**

Skepticism—The view that we can have no knowledge. *Universal skepticism* holds that we cannot know anything at all, whereas *local* or *particular skepticism* holds that we are ignorant in important realms (e.g., see Hume on metaphysics). *Moral skepticism* holds that we cannot know whether any moral truth exists. The Sophists were skeptics.

Subjective Truth—Kierkegaard's thesis that one must live passionately within his or her lights, internalizing one's ideals (see chapter 12).

Superego—Freud's term for the legislative branch of the personality, the center of morality and law (see chapter 11).

Supererogatory—(from the Latin *supererogatus,* "beyond the call of duty") An act that is not required by moral principles but contains enormous value; it is beyond the call of duty, such as risking one's life to save a stranger.

Teleological Ethics—This places the ultimate criterion of morality in some nonmoral value (e.g., happiness or welfare) that results from acts. Whereas deontological ethics ascribes intrinsic value to features of the acts themselves, teleological ethics sees only instrumental value in the acts but intrinsic value in their consequences. Both ethical egoism and utilitarianism are teleological theories (see chapter 4). See **Deontological Ethics, Utilitarianism.**

Telos—(from Greek, meaning goal or end) A teleological theory of nature holds that nature is purposive so that every being or species that exists, exists for a special purpose. Aristotle, Augustine, and most philosophers before Darwin held to this theory. Darwin's theory denies that this is the case.

Theonomous—Ruled by God, describes a life or community which is governed by religious principles, such as ancient Israel (see chapter 1).

Universalizability—This principle states that if some act is right (or wrong) for one person in a situation, then it is right (or wrong) for any relevantly similar person in that kind of situation. It is a principle of consistency that aims to eliminate irrelevant considerations from ethical assessment.

Utilitarianism—The moral theory held by J.S. Mill and Darwin that morality entails promoting the greatest possible happiness. It was opposed by Kant (see chapter 8).

Vaisnavism—The branch of Hinduism that worships Vishnu as the supreme being. Krishna is one of his avatars (see chapter 6). See **Avatar.**

Value—Worth, something good, desirable. The question of what kind of value human beings have is discussed in chapters 1, 3, 4, 5, and 13.

Virtue—(Greek *arête*) A good character trait, typically involving disposition to feel, think, and act in certain morally good ways. Aristotle made virtue the heart of his ethics (see chapter 4).

Index